Television:

The Lost Programs

2,077 Concepts That Never Became a Series, 1950-2020

Vincent Terrace

BearManor Media

Orlando, Florida

Television: The Lost Programs, 2,077 Concepts That Never Became a Series, 1950-2020
© 2021 Vincent Terrace. All Rights Reserved.

No portion of this publication may be reproduced, stored, and/or copied electronically (except for academic use as a source), nor transmitted in any form or by any means without the prior written permission of the publisher and/or author.

Published in the USA by
BearManor Media
1317 Edgewater Dr. #110
Orlando, FL 32804
www.BearManorMedia.com

Softcover Edition
ISBN: 978-1-62933-710-4

Printed in the United States of America

Table of Contents

Preface	vii
Chapter 1	1
Chapter 2	85
Chapter 3	199
Actors Index	211
Producers Index	221

Preface

In 1953, Frank Sinatra was signed to a potential television series called *Blues in the Night*. *The Blue Fox* (1962) was the title of the first proposed series about a disabled private detective. Ethel Merman, famous for her work on Broadway and in movies, was slated to host a TV variety series called *Carnival* (1958). Veteran movie stars Claudette Colbert (in 1954's *Author's Playhouse*) and Jane Wyman (in 1954's *Child Wanted*) were also signed to series projects. Even today's notables like Drew Barrymore (*Black Rose Anthology*, 2017) and Leonardo DiCaprio (*The Devil in the White City*, 2019) had assigned TV projects that were *never* produced.

Since the earliest days of American television, one aspect has remained the same: how a series is sold. It begins with an idea, which is then created as a script, and that script, in turn, made into a pilot film that could sell the idea for an actual series.

This book, *Television: The Lost Programs* covers—for the first time—that second step in the process: scripts that were written, assigned to producers, cast in many instances, but *never* made as either a pilot film or an actual TV series.

There are 2,077 programs presented in this volume covering the period from 1950 to 2020. *Chapter 1*: Spotlights the actors who were signed to a TV project; *Chapter 2:* Highlights well-known U.S. producers controlling a project; and *Chapter 3:* Presents 150 intriguing story lines that failed to convince any industry executive that they would make a great series.

Donna Reed, Hedy Lamarr, Eva Longoria, Connie Stevens, Angie Dickinson, Felicity Huffman, Basil Rathbone, Burt Reynolds, Richard Chamberlain (then billed as "Dick Chamberlain"), Debra Messing, Dennis Hopper, Joan Crawford, Alan Alda, Arnold Schwarzenegger, and Bill Cosby are among the many name performers whose previously unknown credits are being brought to light for the first time within the pages of this book.

This book not only presents the actors and producers involved in such unrealized TV projects, but the many unique story lines that never saw the light of day. For example, there was: *Suture Girl*, created in 2003, that told the story of a girl who, after killing her victims would tear them apart and then stitch them back together; *Black Stiletto* (2015) concerns a mysterious girl who battles evil while wearing her black stiletto shoes; *Chew* (2011) deals with a detective who acquires inspiration by eating foods that are a part of the crime scene; in *Sunshine Scouts* (2019) a group of teenage girls combat a mysterious force that has destroyed the Earth; life in contemporary America is explored in *Super Sad True Love Story* (2016); and the Jack Webb-created project, *Tokyo Police* (1958) utilized the "just the facts, ma'am" staccato format of his already successful *Dragnet* series but was set in Japan.

Television: The Lost Programs is just that—the first ever researched compilation of what could have been but never progressed past the script stage during the decades of American TV programming covered here. It is a fascinating journey into television's past that will reveal facts that, for the most part, cannot be found in any other source including the Internet. All information that is presented here has been researched and assembled from various printed matter (such as *TV Index* [a.k.a., The Ross Reports], *Variety*, *TV Guide,* and network press releases) and is as complete as possible based on what raw data still exists. During the process of research, much information was found but in such limited availability (such as only a title) that it could not even qualify for the skimpiest of entries for this book. Unfortunately, like U.S. series from TV's past that no longer exist, the same can be said of the scripts that were created for potential TV series but for unknown reasons were discarded rather than archived.

Whether you are seeking previously unknown credits for notable stars of the past and present; what TV executive produced what; or which concepts were considered for potential series, *Television: The Lost Programs* will provide you that first look at what could have been *but* never happened.

The author would like to thank James Robert Parish for his help in making this book possible.

CHAPTER 1: ACTORS

The A-Men (Drama, Syndication, 1952).
Producer: Ivan Tors, Curt Siodmak.
Cast: Richard Carlson (as Dr. Jeffrey Stewart).
Story: Agents (called A-Men) for The Office of Scientific Intelligence investigate cases of unusual magnetic activity in various communities across the U.S.

The Ace of Diamonds (Drama, ABC, 1957).
Producer: Bernard Luber.
Cast: Brian Donlevy.
Story: An agent for the diamond industry tackles cases involving precious gems smuggling. In 1961 Broderick Crawford starred in an aired version called *King of Diamonds*.

Action Scene (Comedy, Quibi, 2019).
Producer: Dave Becky, Kevin Hart. *Writer:* Dave Becky.
Cast: Kevin Hart.
Story: A struggling young actor's efforts to acquire a role that will propel him to instant fame.

The Adventures of Ali Baba (Adventure, NBC, 1960).
Producer: Mitchell Gertz.
Cast: Sabu.
Story: Adventures based on the Arabian tales of "Ali Baba and the Forty Thieves" wherein the thief, Ali Baba, risks his life to help people in trouble.

The Adventures of Archie Andrews (Comedy, Syndication, 1959).
Producer: Ted Lloyd.
Cast: Jimmy Boyd, Roberta Shore.
Story: Adaptation of the comic book about the teenage residents of Riverdale: Archie Andrews, Veronica Lodge, Betty Cooper, Jughead Jones and Reggie Mantle.

The Adventures of Roland, Knight of the Realm (Adventure, Syndication, 1956).
Producer: New World Productions.
Cast: Richard Todd.
Story: Period proposal about a Knight of King Arthur's Round Table as he battles injustice in medieval England.

The Adventures of Young Buffalo Bill, Jr. (Western, Syndication, 1955).
Producer: John Jay Franklin.
Cast: John Laurents (as Buffalo Bill, Jr.)
Story: Incidents in the life of Buffalo Bill, Jr., as a young man before he became an Old West legend. In 1955 the syndicated series *Buffalo Bill, Jr.* appeared with Dick Jones as the son of the frontiersman.

Aisha Tyler Untitled Project (Comedy, CBS, 2004).
Producer: Lisa Kudrow, Bill Martin.
Cast: Aisha Tyler.
Story: A young fashion designer attempts to cope with new responsibilities when she moves from a small design house to a large corporation.

Al Jennings of Oklahoma (Western, CBS, 1959).
Producer: Screen Gems.
Cast: Johnny Duncan (as Al Jennings).
Story: Fact mixed with fiction to recount events in the life of Al Jennings, a notorious bank robber of the Old West. Based on the 1951 Dan Duryea film of the same title.

Alec Baldwin Untitled 2015 Project (Drama, HBO, 2015).
Producer: Alec Baldwin, Cary Brokaw. *Creator-Writer:* Wells Tower.
Cast: Alec Baldwin (as Joseph Byrne).
Story: Real estate developer and philanthropist Joseph Byrne's experiences when he is drafted to become the mayor of New York City following a tragic accident that incapacities the incumbent mayor.

Alec Baldwin Untitled 2018 Project (Comedy, ABC, 2018).
Producer-Creator: Alec Baldwin, Julie Bean, Kenya Barris.
Cast: Alec Baldwin.
Story: An opinionated TV star's experiences when his series is cancelled and he moves in with his daughter, her girlfriend and the child they adopted and are raising together.

Ali Baba (Adventure, Syndication, 1957).
Producer: Eddie Danziger.
Cast: Sabu (as Ali Baba).
Story: A fantasy based on the legend of "Ali Baba and the 40 Thieves" wherein Ali Baba, the boy prince raised by thieves after his father was murdered, becomes a defender to the people of India.

All Fancy (Comedy, NBC, 2018).
Producer: America Ferrera, Anjelah Johnson.
Creator-Writer: Emilia Serrano.
Cast: Anjelah Johnson (as Veronica Jimenez).
Story: A Mexican-American woman's (Veronica Jimenez) experiences when she refuses to follow her cultural and social norms.

All Talk (Drama, HBO, 2012).
Producer: Scott Rudin, Ed Bush. *Creator-Writer:* Jonathan Safran.
Cast: Alan Alda, Ben Stiller.
Story: A "politically, religiously, culturally, intellectually and sexually irreverent" peek into the lives of a Jewish family living in Washington, D.C.

Allison Janney Untitled Project (Comedy, CBS, 2006).
Producer: Chuck Lorre, Kelly Kulchak. *Creator-Writer:* Lee Aronsohn.
Cast: Allison Janney.

Story: A woman's re-examination of her life when she hits the pinnacle of success but wonders if it was all worth it when she realizes what she denied herself to achieve it.

Almost Asian (Comedy, IFC, 2018).
Producer: Margaret Cho, Jessie Boemper, Sara Martin.
Creator-Writer: Katie Malia.
Cast: Katie Malia (as Katie).
Story: Katie, half Caucasian and half Asian, begins a journey to establish herself as a dancer in Los Angeles.

Alua (Drama, CBS, 1956).
Producer: Orville Hampton.
Cast: Gloria Talbott.
Story: The infatuation between an alluring Hawaiian woman (Alua) and the American pilot who becomes a part of her life. In 1957 the idea was recast with Pamela Duncan as Alua and Lyle Bettger as the pilot in a produced but never aired pilot film.

Alyssa Milano for Mayor (Comedy, Lifetime, 2017).
Producer: Alyssa Milano.
Cast: Alyssa Milano.
Story: Actress Alyssa Milano, known for the series *Who's the Boss?* and *Charmed*, finds herself giving up show business when a series of circumstances unexpectedly get her elected mayor of a small Los Angeles Community. Her experiences, totally unfamiliar with the political scene, were to be explored.

Alyx (Drama, ABC, 2003).
Producer: Madonna, Guy Oseary. *Producer-Writer-Creator:* Melissa Rosenberg.
Cast: Maria Sokoloff (as Alyx).
Story: Alyx, a 17-year-old recording personality, attempts to break away from her current situation (controlled by agents and music producers) to pursue her dream of becoming a real musician on her own.

Amber Tamblyn Untitled Project (Drama, Fox, 2011).
Producer: Amber Tamblyn, Katie Jacobs. *Creator-Writer:* Ed Burns.
Cast: Amber Tamblyn, Lin-Manuel Miranda.
Story: A young teacher's experiences when she becomes an instructor at a public school where students are anything but typical.

America's Finest (Anthology, Syndication, 1953).
Producer: Jennings Lang.
Cast: Joan Crawford and Ray Milland (signed as show guests).
Story: Dramas about people who have contributed to America's greatness from its founding to 1953.

American Monster (Comedy, ABC, 2013).
Producer: Chris Miller, Phil Lord. *Creator-Writer:* Rich Blomquist, Seth Cohen.
Cast: Kristen Schaal.
Story: How a young woman, considered a misfit in her town, becomes a celebrity when she is accused of a murder and her trial becomes the biggest news story of the year.

Americana (Comedy, NBC, 2011).
Producer: David Schwimmer, Jamie Tarses, Karey Burke.
Cast: Alyson Hannigan, Michael Landes.
Story: An alcoholic sister and her slacker brother attempt to form a relationship after years of separation.

Amy Poehler Untitled Project (Comedy, NBC, 2017).
Producer: Dave Becky, Amy Poehler. *Creator:* Kim Rosenstock.
Cast: Amy Poehler.
Story: A young mother's efforts to rebuild her life following a divorce that not only left her financially unstable but dependent on her overbearing family.

Amy Yasbeck Untitled Project (Cartoon, Fox, 2004).
Producer: Sarah Silverman.
Voice Cast: Amy Yasbeck, Sarah Silverman, Neil Flynn, Nat Faxon, Phil Hendrie.
Story: Life in a gated community as seen through a talk show host, his wife and their three children.

Andy Dick Untitled Project (Comedy, Comedy Central, 2004).
Cast: Andy Dick.
Story: A potpourri of skits, digital animation and man-in-the-street interviews to be overseen by comedian Andy Dick.

Andy Ritcher Untitled Project (Comedy, Comedy Central, 2008).
Producer: Kent Alterman, Tim Sarkes.
Cast: Andy Ritcher.
Story: Performances by improvisational actors that were to be hosted by comedian Andy Ritcher.

Angel City (Crime Drama, Fox, 1991).
Cast: Scott Plank, Julia Campbell, Dan Walker.
Story: Dissatisfied with life in Manhattan, a detective with the N.Y.P.D. moves to Los Angeles where, as a private detective, he hopes to find more meaning to life.

Angelica (Comedy, CBS, 1957).
Cast: Anna Magnani (as Angelica).
Story: Events in the life of a tempestuous actress (Angelica) struggling to cope with a strenuous private life. The program was to be filmed in Italy and presented in both English and Italian soundtracks.

Angie (Comedy, NBC, 1981)
Producer: Alan Katz.
Cast: Angie Dickinson (as Angie).
Story: Following her divorce, a glamorous woman (Angie) attempts to re-navigate both the work force and the dating scene.

The Animated Adventures of Bob & Doug MacKenzie (Cartoon, Fox, 2008).
Producer: Rick Moranis, Dave Thomas, Patricia Burns.
Voice Cast: Dave Thomas, Derek McGrath, Jayne Eastwood, Rick Moranis.
Story: An adaptation of the *Second City Television* characters created by Rick Moranis and Dave Thomas about two brothers plagued by life's everyday problems.

The Anna Neagle Theater (Anthology, Syndication, 1959).
Producer: Anna Neagle, Herbert Wilcox.
Cast: Anna Neagle (as Host).
Story: Actress Anna Neagle as the host of classic stories written by women (such as Jane Austen, the Bronte Sisters and Fanny Burney) reworked for television by women and starring prominent women in the leading roles. Had the project sold, the first two productions would have been *Jane Eyre* and *Pride and Prejudice*.

Annie (Comedy, ABC, 1971).
Producer: Joseph Cates.
Cast: Anne Meara (as Annie).
Story: A single woman's experiences after a financial setback forces her to move back in with her parents.

Anthony Edwards Untitled Project (Drama, Showtime, 2011).
Producer: Anthony Edwards, Mark Ruffalo.
Cast: Anthony Edwards.
Story: A behind-the-scene-look at a management consultant firm in Manhattan.

Applebaum (Crime Drama, CBS, 2011).
Producer: Jennifer Levin, Sherri Cooper, Jeff Rake. *Creator-Writer:* Chris Columbus.
Cast: Rachelle Lefevre (as Juliet Applebaum), Jay Mohr, Marlow Peyton.
Story: A former public defender (Juliet Applebaum) struggles to navigate a life wherein she is not only a mother but a private investigator as well.

April's Dream (Comedy-Drama, Syndication, 2016).
Producer: Bart Polin. *Creator-Writer:* Vincent Terrace.
Cast: April Brucker (as April).
Story: Present day sequences are coupled with flashbacks (to 1995) and flash forwards (to the year 2040) to relate incidents in the lives of three strangers (April, Lori and Bruce) who meet by chance at a bar and become life-long best friends.

Arabian Knights (Anthology, Syndication, 1956).
Producer: Douglas Fairbanks, Jr.
Cast: Gloria Talbott (as Scheherazade).
Story: Adaptations of ancient folklore as told by Scheherazade, the female story teller of the Middle Eastern collection of fables known as "One Thousand and One Nights."

Army Mess (Comedy, ABC, 1957).
Producer: Desi Arnaz.
Cast: Lou Costello.
Story: A military proposal based on Bud Abbott and Lou Costello's feature film *Buck Privates*. Lou Costello is the only cast member mentioned and it was to follow the mishaps of a private in the U.S. Army.

Around the World with Cugie and Abbe (Variety, Syndication, 1956).
Producer: Vittorio De Sica.
Cast: Xavier Cugat, Abbe Lane.
Story: Music with Xavier Cugat and His Orchestra and songs by Abbe Lane that was to focus on a specific locale and its music in each episode.

Ashley Tisdale Untitled Project (Comedy, CBS, 2012).
Producer: Louis C.K., Spike Feresten, Gil Berman, Lloyd Braun.
Cast: Ashley Tisdale.
Story: A young woman's experiences as she navigates the work force in difficult financial times.

Ask Uncle Charlie (Comedy, Syndication, 1954).
Producer: David Gerber, Lee R. Blevins.
Cast: Noah Beery, Jr.
Story: Quarter-hour program in which a newspaper advice columnist struggles to give advice that actually does some good.

Aspen Hill (Drama, CBS, 1961).
Producer: Robert Young.
Cast: Jane Wyatt.
Story: A female doctor's experiences in a rural community in the Sierra Nevada Mountains.

Atlanta's Most Wanted (Crime Drama, Fox, 2017).
Producer: Jerry Bruckheimer, Jonathan Littman.
Creator-Writer: Tip "T.I" Harris.

Cast: Tip "T.I." Harris (as Marcus Armstrong). *Story:* Marcus Armstrong, the son of a criminal father and a member of the Atlanta Police Department's Vice Squad, risks his life to apprehend the mobsters that are terrorizing Georgia.

Aunt Jill (Comedy, ABC, 2015).
Producer: Becky Jordan, Amy Poehler, Brooke Posch. *Creator-Writer:* Jordan Roter.
Cast: Mo Collins.
Story: The reflections of a 50-year-old woman who chose a career over marrying and having a family as she fills that void through her sibling's children.

Author's Playhouse (Anthology, Syndication, 1954).
Producer: United Television Programs.
Cast: Claudette Colbert (as Host).
Story: Adaptations of works by noted playwrights with actress Claudette Colbert to be a featured performer in each episode.

Awakening (Drama, CW, 2011).
Producer: Todd Cohen, Howard T. Owens.
Creator-Writer: Carolyn Bernstein, Bill Laurin.
Cast: Lucy Griffiths, Meredith Hagner.
Story: Two sisters, caught in the middle of a zombie uprising, join with other survivors in a quest to find a safe haven.

B Positive (Comedy, CBS, 2020).
Producer: Chuck Lorre. *Writer:* Marco Pennette.
Cast: Sara Rue (as Gina), Thomas Middleditch (as Drew), Annaleigh Ashford.
Story: When all hope seems lost to find a kidney donor, a divorced father (Drew) runs into Gina, a woman from his past who also happens to be a perfect donor match. She volunteers to donate a kidney and the bond that suddenly forms between the two is related.

The Baby (Comedy, NBC, 2016).
Producer: Dave Becky, Amy Poehler, Brooke Posch.
Cast: Seann William Scott.
Story: A profile of a female run organized crime family where the only male member of eight women (his mother and seven sisters) struggles to rise above his being treated like Cinderella and prove he too can be a ruthless gangster.

The Bachelor Game (Comedy, CBS, 1963).
Producer: Herb Meadow.
Cast: Joi Lansing (as Debutante).
Story: A beautiful Manhattan debutante's experiences as she begins a quest to find the man of her dreams.

Back on the Farm (Comedy, NBC, 2014).
Producer: Krysten Ritter, Lindsey Liberatore.
Creator-Writer: Maggie Bandur.
Cast: Krysten Ritter (as Melody Patterson).
Story: After suffering a mental breakdown during a film shoot, Melody Patterson finds her life changing when her therapist orders her to relax—by spending time on her family farm.

Bad Girl (Comedy, Fox, 2005).
Producer: Jonathan Prince.
Cast: Tara Reid.
Story: A black sheep member of a large family attempts to change her "wicked ways" and become a respectable member of society.

Band of Gold (Anthology, CBS, 1960).
Producer: Norman Lear. *Writer:* Katherine Eunson, Dale Eunson.
Cast: James Franciscus, Suzanne Pleshette.
Story: Incidents in the lives of married couples played by the same actors but in different roles each week.

The Bar (Comedy, ABC, 1971).
Producer: Alan King.
Cast: Fred Gwynne (as Bar owner).
Story: The situations encountered by a Manhattan bar owner who becomes involved in the personal issue of his patrons. Gabriel Dell would become the bar owner in the 1972 series *The Corner Bar*.

Barbary Coast (Drama, ABC, 1958).
Producer: Ben Schwab. *Writer:* David Victor, Herbert Little, Jr.
Cast: Larry Pennell, Peggy Webber.
Story: Life along San Francisco's notorious Barbary Coast of the 1880s as seen through the owner of a gambling casino.

BBF (Comedy, Fox, 2016).
Producer: Cedric the Entertainer, Eric Rhone. *Creator-Writer:* Sebastian Jones.
Cast: Kellee Stewart.
Story: A young woman, caught between two cultures (white and black) sets out on a path "to find her authentic self."

Beachwood (Comedy, ABC, 2003).
Producer: Bob Greenblatt. *Creator-Writer:* Chris Alberghini, Michael Chessler.
Cast: Chelsea Handler.
Story: Incidents in the lives of a group of friends living in a Los Angeles apartment complex.

Beesemeyer's Bungalows (Comedy, Syndication, 1955).
Producer: Sid Dorfman.
Cast: Zasu Pitts, Nancy Malone, Joe Flynn, Jack Kirkwood.
Story: The antics of a group of employees at a resort called Beesemeyer's Bungalows.

Behind the Scenes (Comedy, CBS, 1955).
Producer: Sidney Picker, Morton W. Scott.
Cast: Sally Fraser, Jill Jarmyn.
Story: Life in a theatrical rooming house as experienced by a group of hopeful actors.

Behind the Seams (Comedy, ABC, 2011).
Producer: Eva Longoria. *Creator:* Ernie Bustamante.
Cast: Eva Longoria.
Story: Two Latina sisters, one a fashion designer, the other a runway model, attempt to start a business as the owners of a bridal boutique when their careers begin to fall apart.

Bernie Mac Untitled Project (Comedy, Fox, 2005).
Producer: Bernie Mac, Steve Greener. *Creator-Writer:* Dean Young.
Cast: Bernie Mac.
Story: Newlyweds find their wedded bliss anything but blissful when they move next door to her meddling parents.

Beso: Waiting for Fame (Reality, VH-1, 2010).
Cast: Eva Longoria.
Story: Actress Eva Longoria is profiled as she ventures into a business called Beso, which attracts established celebrities and aspiring stars.

Betches (Cartoon, Freeform, 2020).
Producer: Emma Roberts, Aleen Kuperman, Jordana Abraham. *Creator-Writer:* Rachel Koller.
Cast: Emma Roberts.
Story: Three women and best friends working and living together in New York City navigate life's ups and downs.

The Big Fix (Comedy, Fox, 2002).
Producer: David Sacks.
Cast: French Stewart.
Story: A man is returned to earth after his passing to correct the mistakes he made as he conned his way to the top of the financial world.

Big Kids (Comedy, CBS, 2017).
Producer: Claudia Lonow, Ed Helms. *Creator:* Joe Wengert.
Cast: Claudia Lonow.
Story: The eldest sibling in a family, who believes he is a messiah, seeks to control and fix the lives of his sister and blue collar parents.

Big Loud Lisa (Comedy, ABC, 2005).
Producer: Lisa Lampanelli, J.P. Williams, Madeleine Smithberg. *Writer:* Steve Rudnick.
Cast: Lisa Lampanelli.
Story: After feeling unfulfilled, a young woman quits her corporate job, moves to a small town then struggles to adjust "to normal folks" as she seeks a more meaningful life.

Big Man, Little Lady (Comedy, ABC, 1971).
Producer: James Lee Barrett.
Cast: Claude Akins, Michelle Nichols.
Story: A rugged mountain man's adventures as he attempts to escort the teenage daughter of his late friend to relatives in California.

Big Roy (Comedy, Syndication, 1961).
Producer: Screen Gems.
Cast: Jack Carson, Elena Verdugo.
Story: The mishaps that befall a married couple living in a small rural town.

Big Time (Anthology, Syndication, 1957).
Producer: Irving Brecher.
Cast: Ray Bradbury (as Host).
Story: Adaptations of stories that appear in various magazines.

Bill Cosby Untitled Project (Comedy, NBC, 2014).
Producer: Bill Cosby, Mike Sikowitz, Tom Werner. *Creator-Writer:* Mike O'Malley.
Cast: Bill Cosby (as Jonathan Franklin).
Story: Jonathan Franklin, the patriarch of a multi-generational family, uses his experiences and wisdom to help guide his daughters, their husbands and grandchildren through life.

Bill Engvall Untitled Project (Crime Drama, TNT, 2012).
Producer: John Tinker, Bill Engvall, J.P. Williams.
Creator-Writer: John Tinker.
Cast: Bill Engvall.
Story: A small town Texas police officer faces new challenges when he transfers to the N.Y.P.D. to learn about big city crime fighting.

Billy Liar (Comedy, CBS, 1978).
Producer: John Rich.
Cast: Steve Guttenberg (as Billy Liar).
Story: William "Billy" Liar is a young man trapped in a miserable life: a boring job as an undertaker, parents who stifle him and a girlfriend who seems not to care for him. To escape what he faces, Billy becomes lost in a fantasy world where he was to be seen as a man in charge of his life.

Black Jack (Comedy, Comedy Central, 2011).
Producer: Danny McBride, David Gordon.
Creator-Writer: Michael Starrbury.
Cast: Ving Rhames (as Black Jack).
Story: A special operations agent, who has devoted most of his life to tackling dangerous, undercover missions for the government, struggles to adjust to a normal life after being discharged.

Black Rose Anthology (Anthology, CW, 2017).
Producer: Drew Barrymore, Anthony Masi, Chris Miller. *Creator:* Jill Biotevogel.
Cast: Drew Barrymore (as Host).
Story: Macabre stories that were to be written and directed by women and present events as seen from a woman's perspective.

Black Stiletto (Drama, ABC, 2015).
Producer: Mila Kunis, Cami Curtis. *Creator:* Raymond Benson.
Cast: Mila Kunis (as Judy Cooper).
Story: Judy Cooper, a young woman living in 1950s New York City, battles crime as the mysterious masked vigilante, Black Stiletto.

The Blade (Adventure, Syndication, 1957).
Producer: Official Films.
Cast: Edmund Purdom (as "The Florentine").
Story: A mysterious swordsman called "The Florentine" battles injustice in 18th century France.

The Blue Fox (Drama, CBS, 1962).
Producer: Blake Edwards.
Cast: Duncan McLain.
Story: One of the earliest proposals to feature a disabled character: here a blind detective whose base of operations is the Blue Fox, a famous San Francisco restaurant.

Blue Tilt (Drama, NBC, 2012).
Producer: Vincent D'Onofrio, Ethan Hawke.
Creator: Chris Brancato.
Cast: Ethan Hawke, Vincent D'Onofrio.
Story: Two homicide detectives, one married and one divorced, and how they combine family issues with solving crimes.

Blues in the Night (Drama, CBS, 1953).
Producer: Desi Arnaz.
Cast: Frank Sinatra (as Frank Simms).
Story: Frank Simms, a nightclub singer and amateur sleuth, helps the police solve crimes, especially when they involve friends from the music world.

Bob Newhart in Search of Comedy (Comedy, TBS, 2007).
Producer: Bob Newhart.
Cast: Bob Newhart (as Host).
Story: A proposed late night program of improvisational comedy sketches.

The Bob Saget Show (Talk, Syndication, 2002).
Host: Bob Saget.
Story: Daily talk show proposal with comedian Bob Saget as the host.

Bob Saget Untitled 2004 Project (Comedy, ABC, 2004).
Producer: Damon Wayans, Don Reo.
Cast: Bob Saget.
Story: A father's efforts to care for his children when he is granted custody of them following his divorce.

Bob Saget Untitled 2005 Project (Comedy, HBO, 2005).
Producer: Bob Saget, Tim Sarkes, Danny Sussman.
Cast: Bob Saget.
Story: A divorced father, working as a gynecologist and just granted custody of his 14-year-old son following his divorce, struggles to readjust his life while at the same time maintaining his social activities.

Bon Vivant (Drama, NBC, 1956).
Cast: Vincent Price (signed, first choice), Peter Lorre (second choice), Charles Laughton (third choice) to play Harry Fabian.
Story: An adaptation of the novel *Night and the City* by British author Gerald Kersh about Harry Fabian, a bon vivant (person with cultivated and refined tastes in food and drink) and amateur sleuth who helps the police solve crimes.

Boss of the House (Comedy, Syndication, 1955).
Producer: Bobby Ellis.
Cast: Don DeFore (as George), Peggy Webber (as Mary).
Story: Life as seen through the eyes of a baby as his parents, George and Mary, deal with the numerous issues that plague their daily lives.

Braco (Drama, Syndication, 1955).
Producer: Lou Morheim.
Cast: Allan Emery.
Story: An adaptation of the feature film about the adventures shared by a 13-year-old boy and his horse, Braco.

Brandy (Comedy, CW, 2006).
Producer: Mara Brock Akil, Neil Meron, Craig Zadan.
Cast: Brandy Norwood.
Story: A young woman attempts to begin a new life when she moves from Manhattan to Los Angeles to become an editor for an entertainment magazine.

Brett Butler Untitled 2003 Project (Crime Drama, USA, 2003).
Producer: Brett Butler, Daniel Petrie, Jr., Robert Lieberman.
Cast: Brett Butler.
Story: A single mother's efforts to provide a decent life for her daughter while working as a private investigator.

Brett Butler Untitled 2005 Project (Comedy, Comedy Central, 2005).
Producer: Chuck Sklar.
Cast: Brett Butler.
Story: Comedy mixes with reality as actress Brett Butler takes to the road to meet the eccentric residents of America's small towns.

The Brides (Drama, ABC, 2020).
Producer: Greg Berlanti, Sarah Schechter. *Writer:* Roberto Aguirre-Sacasa.
Cast: Gina Torres, Erin Richards, Sophia Tatum, Katherine Reis, Chris Mason.
Story: Gothic serial about a group of women, the immortal brides of the legendary Count Dracula, as they struggle to conceal their true identities while maintaining their prestige, wealth and legacy.

Brie Larson Untitled Project (Drama, Apple TV Plus, 2019).
Producer: Lynette Howell Taylor, Brie Larson, Samantha Housman. *Creator-Writer:* Megan Martin.
Cast: Brie Larson.
Story: A look at the CIA as seen through the eyes of a young woman's case assignments and the agents with whom she works.

Brief Case (Drama, CBS, 1956).
Producer: Worthington Miner.
Cast: Macdonald Carey.
Story: How cases are acquired by lawyers, the preparation required and how evidence is gathered for a trial.

Bringing Up Mother (Comedy, NBC, 1959).
Producer: Harry Ackerman.
Cast: Jan Sterling (Jan), Cheryl Holdridge (Holly), Evelyn Rudie (Madison), Sheila James (June).
Story: A recent widow (Jan) being "raised" by her three children (Holly, Madison and June) attempts to avoid their schemes as they seek to find her a new husband.

Buckley (Comedy, Syndication, 1955).
Producer: Mark Goodson, Bill Todman. *Creator-Writer:* Don Quinn.

Cast: Reginald Gardner (as Buckley). Dorothy Lamour is listed as "signed as lead opposite Reginald Gardner."
Story: Each week a Hollywood celebrity was to appear as a guest and have his or her problems resolved by Buckley, an English butler who remains with them only for the duration of the episode.

Burt Reynolds Untitled Project (Comedy, Fox, 2005).
Producer: Adam Sandler, Doug Robinson.
Creator-Writer: Fax Bahr, Adam Small.
Cast: Burt Reynolds (as Himself).
Story: Burt Reynolds, playing an exaggerated version of himself—a once popular movie and television star who must now deal with less notoriety and the prospect of finding any kind of work to support himself.

Bush Pilot (Drama, Syndication, 1957).
Producer: Bernard Van Marken.
Cast: Richard Denning.
Story: The work of a bush pilot who serves the remote regions of Australia.

Calling CQ (Drama, Syndication, 1960).
Producer: Lindsay Parsons.
Cast: Mark Damon, Richard Webb.
Story: Two government agents pose as Marines to perform undercover assignments for the government.

Cameo Kirby (Drama, Syndication, 1957).
Producer: Peter Hacker.
Cast: Claude Akins (as Cameo Kirby)
Story: Cameo Kirby, a 1800s Mississippi river boat captain, is followed as he deals with cargo and passengers.

Camryn Manheim Untitled Project (Comedy, ABC, 2004).
Producer: David E. Kelley, Dan O'Shannon.
Cast: Camryn Manheim (as Eleanor Frutt).
Story: A comical spin off from the dramatic series *The Practice* wherein attorney Eleanor Frutt would return to her home town to open a practice to be near her sister.

Can-Can (Comedy, ABC, 2020).
Producer: Sean Hayes, Todd Milliner.
Cast: Maysoon Zayid.
Story: Although billed as a comedy, it appears to be more of a drama as a Muslim woman, suffering from cerebral palsy, struggles to find love, a career and a life that is separate from her opinionated parents.

Candy (Comedy, CBS, 1957).
Producer: David Gerber, Josef Shaftel.
Cast: Connie Russell (as Candy).
Story: Musical comedy about a singer (Candy) and her involvement with a struggling jazz band. Press material indicates that each week a "disk (record) and music name" would appear as a guest.

Candy Cane (Comedy, NBC, 1960).
Cast: Arlene Howell (as Candy Cane).
Story: Simplistic tale of Candy Cane, a young backwoods girl raised by her grandfather as she interacts with the people of her small community.

Captain Charlie's Showboat (Variety, Syndication, 1956).
Producer: Irving Briskin.
Cast: Buddy Ebsen (as Host).
Story: Variety acts, including those from Vaudeville and Burlesque that were to be presented against the backdrop of a Mississippi River paddle showboat.

Captain Kidd (Adventure, Syndication, 1956).
Producer: Douglas Fairbanks, Jr. *Writer:* Jerry Juran.
Cast: Tony Dexter (as Captain Kidd).
Story: Tales of William Kidd, better known as Captain Kidd, a Scottish sailor of the 17th century.

Carla (Comedy, Fox, 2020).
Producer: Mayim Bialik, Jim Parsons, Angie Stephenson. *Creator-Writer:* Darlene Hunt.
Cast: Mayim Bialik (as Carla).
Story: An adaptation of the British series *Miranda* that relates incidents in the life of Carla (for America), a 39-year-old working woman struggling to cope with life's everyday problems while at the same time attempting to convince her spend thrift mother that buying everything she wants will not bring happiness.

Carmen Electra Untitled Project (Comedy, Fox, 2005).
Producer: Ashton Kutcher, Jason Goldberg, Pete Aronson.
Cast: Carmen Electra.
Story: Shortly after marrying, a woman learns that in order to inherit millions after her husband's untimely passing, she must abide by his last wish: keep his dysfunctional children as a family unit despite their desire to go their separate ways.

Carnival (Variety, Syndication, 1958).
Producer: Hal Roach, Jr.
Cast: Ethel Merman (as Host).
Story: Musical variety and comedy performances by top name celebrities.

Carol Leifer Untitled 2004 Project (Comedy, ABC, 2004).
Producer: Carol Leifer, J.J. Abrams, Thom Sherman.
Cast: Cheri Iteri, Carol Leifer.
Story: A young woman's experiences as she becomes an apprentice on a highly rated TV children's show.

Carol Leifer Untitled 2006 Project (Comedy, Fox, 2006).
Producer: Darryl Frank, Justin Falvey. *Creator-Writer:* Steven Spielberg. *Writer:* Carol Leifer.
Cast: Carol Leifer.
Story: The rather unusual friendship that develops between two divorced women, both members of New York's super elite.

Case History (Anthology, Syndication, 1952)
Producer: William F. Broidy.
Cast: Regis Toomey, Sara Hayden.
Story: Dramas based on the careers of leading doctors. In 1961 a pilot with Regis Toomey was produced but never aired.

Cassandra French's Finishing School for Boys (Drama, MTV, 2011).
Producer: Krysten Ritter. *Creator-Writer:* Eric Garcia.
Cast: Krysten Ritter (as Cassandra French).
Story: A 22-year-old woman, with her own idea as to what makes the perfect man, lures a guy to her home, imprisons him in her basement—then proceeds to train him to become the perfect gentleman.

Cedric the Entertainer Untitled 2007 Project (Comedy, ABC, 2007).
Producer: Larry Wilmore.
Cast: Cedric the Entertainer.
Story: A security chief at Los Angeles International Airport and the single father of a teenage girl struggles to divide his time between work and home.

Cedric the Entertainer Untitled 2010 Project (Comedy, ABC, 2010).
Producer: Eric Tannenbaum, Kim Tannenbaum, Mitch Hurwitz.
Cast: Cedric the Entertainer.
Story: A retired baseball player turned radio show host attempts to reevaluate his life when his estranged son and granddaughter re-enter his life.

Celebrity Garage Sale (Reality, A&E, 2007).
Producer: Illeana Douglas, David Franzke.
Cast: Illeana Douglas (as Host).
Story: Celebrities sell off their unwanted items in garage sales to benefit their favorite charities.

Chair on the Boulevard (Anthology, ABC, 1953).
Producer: Bing Crosby Enterprises.
Cast: Basil Rathbone (as Host).
Story: Dramatic productions based on the stories of writer Leonard Merrick.

The Charles Winninger Show (Variety, Syndication, 1960).
Producer: Harold Applebaum.
Cast: Charles Winninger (as Host).
Story: Variety acts hosted by actor Charles Winninger. Russell Arms and Virginia Gibson were slated to appear as singers while Gil Lamb was set to appear in comedy skits with the host.

Charlie Sheen's Bad Influence (Reality, WE, 2014).
Producer: Charlie Sheen, Bob Maron, Steve Tisch.
Cast: Charlie Sheen (as Host).
Story: Charlie Sheen, star of the TV series *Two and a Half Men*, in a proposal where newly engaged couples meet with Charlie, considered "America's favorite bad boy," to discuss their lives, especially how well they really know each other.

Charlotte Walsh Likes to Win (Drama, Amazon, 2020).
Producer: Julia Roberts, Marisa Gill, Laura Lewis. *Creator:* John Robin Baitz.
Cast: Julia Roberts (as Charlotte Walsh).
Story: Feeling that she needs to reconnect with her roots, Charlotte Walsh, a powerful Silicon Valley executive, quits her job and with her husband and three teenage daughters, attempts to restart life in a small Pennsylvania town.

Chelsea Handler Untitled Project (Comedy, NBC, 2012).
Producer: Chelsea Handler, Brad Wollack. *Creator-Writer:* Ingrid Haas.
Cast: Chelsea Handler (as Ingrid).
Story: When her parents separate, Ingrid, their daughter, finds her life changing when her father, Wayne, moves in with her and her roommate when he has no other place to live.

Child Wanted (Drama, NBC, 1954).
Producer: Ted Lloyd.
Cast: Jane Wyman.
Story: A look at the process of adoption as seen through a case worker for the New York City Child Adoption Services.

Chris Elliott Untitled Project (Comedy, Fox, 2005).
Producer: Chris Elliott. *Creator-Writer:* John Altschuler, Dave Krinsky.
Cast: Chris Elliott.
Story: A frustrated actor, father and real estate agent struggles to raise two teenage daughters, one of whom has aspirations to become a singer.

Christopher Titus Untitled Project (Comedy, Fox, 2010).
Producer-Creator-Writer: Christopher Titus, Michael Glouberman. *Producer:* Warren Littlefield.
Cast: Christopher Titus.
Story: A young man's efforts to deal with a down-to-earth girlfriend, his solid family, and a crazy ex-girlfriend when she comes back into his life.

C.I.D. (Drama, NBC, 1952).
Cast: Wendell Corey, Signe Hasso.
Story: Stories based on the Criminal Investigation Division (C.I.D.) of London's New Scotland Yard.

Cindy (Comedy, ABC, 1957).
Producer: Hal Roach, Jr.
Cast: Evelyn Rudie.
Story: A young girl's experiences when she comes to live with her bachelor uncle after the death of her parents in a car accident. The idea was reworked as the series *Bachelor Father*.

City of Dreams (Crime Drama, NBC, 2004).
Producer: Jerry Bruckheimer, David Mills.
Cast: Jimmy Smits.
Story: A Los Angeles-based private investigator with a knack for reading people helps troubled individuals for a substantial fee.

Clarice (Crime Drama, CBS, 2020).
Producer: Heather Kadin. *Writer:* Jenny Lumet, Alex Kurtzman.
Cast: Rebecca Breeds (as Clarice Starling), Kal Penn, Michael Cudlitz.
Story: A sequel of sorts set in 1993 after the events in the film *Silence of the Lambs* that focuses on Clarice Starling, a detective who probes cases involving sexual predators and serial murderers while navigating life in Washington, D.C.

Clarissa Explains It All (Comedy, Nickelodeon, 2018).
Producer: Melissa Joan Hart, Paula Hart. *Creator-Writer:* Mitchell Kriegman.
Cast: Melissa Joan Hart (as Clarissa Darling).
Story: Clarissa Darling was a 13-year-old girl who spoke directly to the viewing audience to relate her feelings about life (on the 1990s Nickelodeon series *Clarissa Explains It All*). Clarissa, now a young woman, was set to return to once again relate what happens as she experiences life as an adult.

Classic Stories of the Year (Anthology, Syndication, 1954).
Producer: Barney Ward.
Cast: Signe Hasso (as Host).
Story: Dramatizations of noteworthy stories that appeared in newspapers and magazines.

Claudia (Drama, Syndication, 1958).
Producer: William Meloney, Armand Deutsch.
Cast: Anne Francis (Claudia Brown), Doris Kenyon (Mrs. Brown, her mother).
Story: An adaptation of the radio series, *Claudia: The Story of a Marriage*, about a young newlywed couple and the wife's (Claudia) efforts to break the apron strings that tie her to her mother. In 1960 the idea was revised for CBS with George Burns as the producer and Patricia Michon as Claudia and Doris Kenyon as her mother.

The Code (Drama, NBC, 2005).
Producer: Donnie Wahlberg, Jon Avent. *Writer:* Jack Orman.
Cast: Donnie Wahlberg.
Story: An honest cop's experiences as he goes undercover to expose corrupt law enforcement officials.

Code J.D. (Drama, Syndication, 1956).
Producer: Theatrical Enterprises, Inc.
Cast: Rocky Graziano.
Story: The cases of a J.D. (Juvenile Delinquency) investigator in stories based on the files of state and federal juvenile agencies.

The Colonel's Lady (Comedy, ABC, 1961).
Producer: Stanley Roberts.
Cast: Eve Arden, Brooks West.
Story: Real life married couple Eve Arden and Brooks West in a proposal about a movie star who relinquishes her career to marry an army colonel. A similar project with Juliet Prowse as a movie star who married an Air Force sergeant aired on NBC in 1965 as *Mona McCluskey*.

Combat Correspondent (Drama, NBC, 1957).
Producer: Ray Singer, Dick Chevillat.
Cast: Lin McCarthy.
Story: World War II proposal about a newspaper reporter as he covers the activities of a group of U.S. Marines actively involved in the European Theater of the war.

Complicated (Comedy, ABC, 2012).
Producer: Ben Stiller, Debbie Liebling. *Creator-Writer:* Bonnie Hunt, Don Lake.
Cast: Bonnie Hunt.
Story: The incidents that befall an insecure woman whose life becomes complex due to her belief that what she will face will be far worse than what it actually is.

The Connie Stevens Show (Comedy, ABC, 1970).
Producer: Harry Ackerman.
Cast: Connie Stevens.
Story: The mishaps that befall a slightly off-center young woman who, with several female friends, runs an odd-job employment agency.

Corey Johnson (Comedy, Syndication, 1952).
Producer: John W. Loveton, Bernard L. Schubert.
Cast: Eddie Albert (as Corey Johnson).
Story: Corey Johnson, a hopeful actor, struggles to make a name for himself on Broadway.

Correspondent U.S.M.C. (Drama, Syndication, 1957).
Producer: Ray Singer, Dick Chevillat.
Cast: Lin McCarthy (as Sgt. Rick McKenna).
Story: Incidents in the lives of U.S. Marines as seen through the assignments of Sergeant Rick McKenna, a marine correspondent.

Cortes (Drama, HBO, 2014).
Producer: Martin Scorsese, Rick Yorn. *Creator-Writer:* Emma Tillinger.
Cast: Benicio Del Toro.
Story: Period drama about Hernan Cortes, the Spanish Conquisidor who, with the help of Malinche, a Mayan girl, seeks to capture Montezuma and destroy the Aztec empire.

Countdown (Anthology, ABC, 1959).
Producer: Charles S. Irving. *Writer:* Bernard Girard, Lee Hewitt.
Cast: Alex Nicol (as Host).
Story: Stories based on files of the Air Research and Development Command of the U.S. Air Force and the Department of Defense.

Counterthrust (Drama, ABC, 1959).
Producer: Ed Romero.
Cast: Tod Andrews, Diane Jergens.
Story: U.S. counter intelligence agents battle communism in the Far East.

Country Doctor (Drama, CBS, 1955).
Producer: William Spier. *Writer:* Sam Marx.
Cast: Charles Coburn, Arthur Franz, Cheerio Meredith.

Story: Turn-of-the-twentieth century story about a kind but elderly doctor in a small American town.

Courteney Cox Untitled 2004 Project (Comedy, WB, 2004).
Producer: Courteney Cox, David Arquette.
Creator-Writer: Patrick O'Neill, Steve Pink.
Cast: David Arquette.
Story: A hard-working young man attempts to change his miserable life around when he meets and falls in love with whom he believes is the girl of his dreams.

Courteney Cox Untitled 2005 Project (Comedy, ABC, 2005).
Producer: Courteney Cox, David Arquette.
Creator-Writer: Jeremy Stevens.
Cast: David Arquette.
Story: A laid back private detective attempts to deal with the situations that arise when his ex-wife and their ten-year-old son come back into his life.

Courteney Cox Untitled 2019 Project (Cartoon, Fox, 2019).
Producer: Courteney Cox, Timothy Stack.
Creator-Writer: Maz Jobrani.
Voice Cast: Maz Jobrani.
Story: Three generations of immigrants living in America try to adjust to a new lifestyle while their neighbors attempt to adjust to them.

The Coven (Drama, Lifetime, 2003).
Producer: Gale Anne Hurd, Wendy Grean.
Creator-Writer: Charles Craig.
Cast: Nia Peeples, Illeana Douglas, Paula Devicq.
Story: Three young women, descended from 17th century witches, use their powers to defeat the supernatural forces that threaten the modern-day world.

Crash Dummies (Drama, USA, 2009).
Producer: John Schneider, Jack Gill. *Creator-Writer:* Matt Pyken.
Cast: John Schneider.
Story: A veteran Hollywood stuntman teams with his son and a group of movie special effects artists to use their abilities to battle crime.

Crazylegs Hirsh (Drama, Syndication, 1955).
Producer: Hall Bartlett.
Cast: Elroy "Crazylegs" Hirsch (as Himself).
Story: Events in the life and career of football legend Elroy Hirsch, nicknamed "Crazylegs" for his unusual running style (his legs twisted as he ran). The proposal was to begin with his time as a half-back on the University of Wisconsin football team.

Crime Club (Anthology, Syndication, 1954).
Producer: Harry Alan Towers.
Cast: Ben Gazzara (as Host).
Story: Tales based on a global organization called the Crime Club where each week a member was to relate his latest adventure.

Criminal at Large (Crime Drama, Syndication, 1959).
Producer: Jerry Devine.
Cast: Stephen McNally.
Story: Relates police efforts to track down criminals still at large.

Criminal Behavior (Crime Drama, NBC, 2004).
Producer: John Davis. *Creator-Writer:* Shane Salerno.
Cast: Ray Liotta.
Story: The work of the Major Crimes Unit of the Los Angeles Police Department as they attempt to capture dangerous fugitives before they can strike again.

Crisis (Anthology, Syndication, 1952).
Producer: Basil Grillo.
Cast: Louis Bromfield (as Host).
Story: Various stories, ranging from comedy and drama to mystery and suspense that find people facing difficult situations.

Critical (Drama, NBC, 2014).
Producer: Eva Longoria, John Glenn. *Creator-Writer:* Katie Lovejoy.
Cast: Eva Longoria.
Story: A Latina doctor's efforts to help the people of her hometown when she leaves a big city hospital to be closer to her friends and family.

Crusoe's Island (Drama, Syndication, 1960).
Producer: Alvin Cooperman. *Writer:* Milt Rosen.
Cast: Dave King.
Story: Brief incidents in the lives of people who vacation at a privately owned tropical resort called Crusoe's Island as seen through the eyes of one of its workers.

The Crux (Drama, HBO, 2010).
Producer: Kevin Spacey, Dana Brunetti.
Cast: Kevin Spacey.
Story: Other than revolving around the activities of a charismatic cult leader, no other details have been released.

Cry Fraud (Drama, ABC, 1958).
Producer: Herb Meadow.
Cast: Forrest Tucker.
Story: An insurance investigator's assignments as he probes cases of possible insurance fraud during the latter 1870s.

Cry of the City (Anthology, Syndication, 1951).
Producer: Bing Crosby Productions.
Cast: John Newland (as Host).
Story: Dramatizations based on the lives of people who live in New York City.

Custard Pie Playhouse (Comedy, Syndication, 1959).
Producer: NTA (National Telefilm Associates).
Cast: Hans Conried (as Host).
Story: Theatrical shorts (called "Two Reelers") produced by Paramount Pictures in the 1930s and featuring Vaudeville performers were to be screened in a 15 minute program that allotted enough time for the short to run unedited. Mentioned film subjects were W.C. Fields, Jack Benny, Eddie Cantor, Lulu McConnell and Robert Benchley.

Daisy Hooper: CEO (Comedy, WB, 2004).
Producer: Kevin Kelly Brown, Lawrence Bender.
Creator-Writer: Jay Kogen.
Cast: Marissa Coughland (as Daisy Hooper).
Story: Daisy Hooper, a newly promoted big corporation CEO, struggles to navigate a world of big business she is not quite ready to tackle.

Dakota Diggs (Crime Drama, USA, 2003).
Producer: Sheldon Turner.
Cast: Vivica A. Fox (as Dakota Diggs).
Story: A beautiful African-American woman (Dakota Diggs) uses her own set of rules to battle crime as a detective with the Los Angeles Police Department.

Damascus (Drama, CBS, 2013).
Producer: America Ferrera, Teri Weinberg.
Creator-Writer: Nick Osborne.
Cast: America Ferrera.
Story: A Catholic nun, knowledgeable in the field of law, uses her ability to help people in trouble.

Damon Wayans Untitled 2008 Project (Comedy, ABC, 2008).
Producer: Damon Wayans, Don Reo.
Cast: Damon Wayans.

Story: A recent widower finds his life changing when he becomes the guardian of a 19-year-old step son he never knew he had (from his late wife's first marriage).

Damon Wayans Untitled 2011 Project (Comedy, ABC, 2011).
Producer: Damon Wayans, Don Reo.
Cast: Damon Wayans.
Story: An actor who plays the perfect father on a television series finds in real life, his family is anything but typical of his TV family.

The Dancers (Variety, NBC, 1955).
Producer: Jack Denove. *Writer:* George Bradshaw.
Cast: Bambi Linn, Rod Alexander.
Story: A weekly proposal that was to feature dancers performing to the music of various lands and cultures.

Danny DeVito Untitled Project (Comedy, Amazon, 2017).
Producer: Danny DeVito, Brian Grazer, Francie Calfo.
Cast: Danny DeVito (as Arlo), Jeff Goldblum (as Matt).
Story: Matt and Arlo, iconic music stars of the past who hate each other, must learn to get along with one another when they unite after a long absence to reignite their stagnant careers.

David Boreanaz Untitled Project (Drama, ABC, 2005).
Producer: Eric Tannenbaum, Kim Tannenbaum.
Cast: David Boreanaz (as Jack Ballantine).
Story: An undercover cop (Jack Ballantine) poses as a hit man to protect targets and uncover the reason why and who ordered the hit.

David Harum (Drama, CBS, 1959).
Producer: Screen Gems.
Cast: Chill Wills (as David Harum).
Story: Life in the small New England town of Homeville as seen through the eyes of David Harum, the town banker. Adapted from the radio series of the same title.

David Letterman Untitled Project (Comedy, Fox, 2013).
Producer: David Letterman, Ann Marie Wilkins, Harry Connick, Jr.
Cast: Harry Connick, Jr.
Story: A single father, working as an entertainer and estranged from his teenage daughter, attempts to reconnect with her and become the father he never was to her.

David Spade Untitled 2013 Project (Comedy, HBO, 2013).
Producer-Creator: David Spade, Dean Lorey.
Cast: David Spade (as Shane).
Story: Shane, a once famous band manager, struggles to regain his status by managing The Five Commandments, a Christian boy band.

David Spade Untitled 2018 Project (Comedy, HBO, 2018).
Producer: David Spade, Jason Reitman. *Creator:* Diablo Cody.
Cast: David Spade (as Calvin Wash).
Story: Calvin Wash, a former grunge musician whose career ended when he became addicted to drugs, attempts to relive his life through Bailey, a troubled but promising actress he takes under his wing.

The David Wayne Show (Comedy, ABC, 1960).
Producer-Writer: Arthur Marx.
Cast: David Wayne.
Story: A writer's efforts to work at home despite all the interruptions caused by his family.

Debra Messing Untitled Project (Comedy, NBC, 2009).
Producer: Howard Klein, Debra Messing.
Cast: Debra Messing.
Story: A laid off CEO plunges into a world she knows little about—full time mother while her husband sets out into a world he does not know—providing for his family.

Dennis Hopper Untitled Project (Comedy, NBC, 2004).
Producer: Matt LeBlanc. *Creator:* Michael Chessler, Chris Alberghini.
Cast: Dennis Hopper.
Story: A free-spirited but down-on-his-luck father must readjust to a new lifestyle when he moves in with his conservative daughter and her husband.

Deputy Seraph (Comedy, CBS, 1958).
Producer-Writer: Philip Rapp.
Cast: Groucho Marx, Harpo Marx, Chico Marx.
Story: A western-themed satire about a sheriff (Chico Marx) and his non-speaking deputy (Harpo Marx). Chico and Harpo were signed to star in 30 episodes with their brother, Groucho to guest star (as a conniving villain) in 13 episodes before the project was scrapped.

The Desilu Mystery Theater (Anthology, CBS, 1956).
Producer: William Spier.
Cast: Desi Arnaz (as Host).
Story: Mystery and suspense stories produced in association with Desilu Productions (the company run by Lucille Ball and Desi Arnaz). The idea was reworked as *The Desilu Playhouse* in 1957.

The Devil in the White City (Drama, Hulu, 2019).
Producer: Martin Scorsese, Emma Koskoff, Stacey Sher. *Creator-Writer:* Eric Larson.
Cast: Leonardo DiCaprio.
Story: An adaptation of the book by Erik Larson about an architect who seeks a serial killer at the time of the 1893 Chicago World's Fair.

Diamond Head (Crime Drama, CBS, 2002).
Producer: Jerry Bruckheimer.
Cast: Scott Glenn (as John Caine).
Story: An adaptation of the Charles Knief book series about John Caine, a retired Navy SEAL who opens a private detective agency in Hawaii.

Diane Farr Untitled 2003 Project (Comedy, ABC, 2003).
Producer: Deborah Oppenheimer, Diane Farr. *Creator:* Bruce Helford.
Cast: Diane Farr.
Story: A female buddy-buddy comedy about two 27-year-old friends living in Brooklyn, New York.

Diane Farr Untitled 2005 Project (Comedy, WB, 2005).
Producer-Creator: Diane Farr, Peter Tolan.
Cast: Diane Farr.
Story: The incidents that befall a group of women, each in their thirties, as they face life in Los Angeles.

Diarra Kilpatrick Untitled Project (Comedy, Showtime, 2019).
Producer: Eric Tannenbaum, Kim Tannenbaum, Scott Schwartz. *Creator:* Keenan Ivory Wayans, Diarra Kilpatrick.
Cast: Diarra Kilpatrick (as Maya).
Story: Maya, a young woman tied to a boyfriend with baggage (his dead beat friends) seeks her

idea of the perfect man—something she finds to be a most difficult task.

Discounted (Comedy, ABC, 2012).
Producer: Chelsea Handler, Brad Wollack.
Creator: Fortune Feimster, Jim Freeman.
Cast: Fortune Feimster.
Story: Two half-sisters who have nothing in common join forces to keep their family business (a furniture store) afloat after their father's passing.

D.L. Hughley Untitled Project (Comedy, FX, 2013).
Producer: Dave Becky, Michael Rothenberg.
Creator: D.L. Hughley, Michael Jamin.
Cast: D.L. Hughley (as Himself).
Story: A look at D.L. Hughley's life as a family man and radio talk show host before achieving fame as a stand-up comedian.

Dr. Broadway (Drama, Syndication, 1956).
Producer: Judson Cox.
Cast: David Brian.
Story: Dramas dealing with medical issues as seen through the cases of a doctor who practices from an office on Broadway in Manhattan.

Dr. Pygmalion (Anthology, Syndication, 1959).
Producer: Dennis Vance.
Cast: Paulette Goddard, Eric Portman (signed guests).
Story: Brief incidents in the lives of people who have elected to have plastic surgery in an effort to better their lives.

The Doctors Brennan (Drama, NBC, 1982).
Producer: David Victor.
Cast: Andy Griffith, Cassie Yates, Leslie Ackerman.
Story: Events in the life of a dedicated doctor with two daughters: one who shares his practice and one who is about to graduate from medical school and is undecided about whether to begin her own practice or join with her father and sister.

Dog Years (Comedy, NBC, 2000).
Cast: Anna Faris, Andy Ritcher.
Story: Incidents in the life of a young woman who lives with a most unusual dog—one who talks and guides her life.

A Dog's Life (Comedy, Syndication, 1954).
Producer: Andy Berger.
Cast: Gale Storm, Marcia Henderson, Carolyn Jones.
Story: People's foibles are explored through the experiences of three women who are just struggling to get by on what little they have.

Domestic Goddess (Talk, ABC Family, 2003).
Producer: R.J. Cutler.
Cast: Roseanne Barr (as Host).
Story: Cooking coupled with celebrity interviews.

Don Ameche Presents the Play of the Week (Anthology, Syndication, 1957).
Producer: TPA (Television Programs of America).
Cast: Don Ameche (as Host).
Story: Various presentations (comedy, drama, mystery) that were to be hosted by actor Don Ameche.

Don Johnson Untitled Project (Comedy, HBO, 2012).
Producer: Don Johnson, Jason Weinberg, W. Merritt Johnson.
Cast: Don Johnson.
Story: A suicidal television game show host with a dysfunctional family struggles to keep

his sanity as he deals with the problems that confront him.

Donny and Kathie Lee (Talk, Syndication, 2005).
Cast: Donny Osmond, Kathie Lee Gifford (as Hosts).
Story: A daily program of talk and celebrity interviews.

Doomsday (Cartoon, UPN, 2001).
Producer: Howard Stern. *Creator:* Tracy Torme.
Voice Cast: Howard Stern.
Story: Following an apocalypse that nearly destroys the world, two friends retreat to their basement where they begin a radio broadcast to keep what is left of the world entertained.

Door to Door (Variety, Syndication, 1954).
Producer: Jerry Gross, Norman Baer.
Cast: Morey Amsterdam (as Host).
Story: Comedy with comedian Morey Amsterdam and his guests coupled with audience participation contests for prizes.

Doorway to Fortune (Anthology, Syndication, 1955).
Producer: William Deering.
Cast: Melville Ruick (as Host).
Story: Adaptations of success stories that appear in *Fortune* magazine.

Doowinkle, D.A. (Comedy, NBC, 1960).
Producer: Henry Jaffe.
Cast: Eddie Bracken (as John Doowinkle).
Story: John Doowinkle, an attorney fascinated by astronomy, resorts to racketeering, bribery and the underworld to win cases for his clients.

Douchebag (Comedy, CBS, 2011).
Producer: Eric Tannenbaum, Kim Tannenbaum.
Creator: Matthew Carlson.
Cast: John Schneider.
Story: An aging but still popular rock star seeks a way to balance his work life style with that of raising a family.

Dream Wife (Comedy, CBS, 1965).
Producer: Stanley Chase.
Cast: Shirley Jones, Donald May.
Story: A housewife, possessed of psychic abilities, encounters numerous problems when she defies her husband's objections and sets out to help people in trouble.

Drew Barrymore Untitled Project (Talk, Syndication, 2019).
Producer: Drew Barrymore, Chris Miller, Ember Truesdell.
Cast: Drew Barrymore (as Host).
Story: Proposed daytime talk show featuring actress Drew Barrymore.

Driven (Comedy, USA, 2010).
Producer-Creator: Harry Thomason, Linda Bloodworth-Thomason (also the writer).
Cast: Ron White.
Story: An unemployed businessman's efforts to deal with his staff and customers when he opens a limousine service.

The Driver (Drama, Showtime, 2015).
Producer: Carl Beverly, Sarah Timberman, David Morrissey. *Writer:* Taylor Elmore.
Cast: David Morrissey.
Story: A family man struggles to turn his life around when, out of frustration to find a better job, he takes one as a driver, not realizing at first, it is for the mob.

The Drumbeater (Comedy, CBS, 1969).
Producer: Edward Montagne, Abner Greshler.
Creator: William Friedberg, Doc Simon.
Cast: Tony Randall (as Samuel Pitts).
Story: Tales of the Old West as depicted through Samuel Pitts, a reporter seeking stories for his newspaper but ill-equipped (no riding or shooting skills) to handle the situations he encounters.

The Eddie Albert Show (Comedy, CBS, 1957).
Producer: Harry Ackerman.
Cast: Eddie Albert.
Story: A newspaper reporter uses his ability to travel through time to seek people with interesting stories to tell.

Edison (Comedy, HBO, 2017).
Producer: Amy Poehler, Dave Becky. *Creator-Writer:* John Roberts.
Cast: John Roberts.
Story: Musical numbers mix with comedy to present the life of a 40-year-old real estate broker, stuck in a small New Jersey town, who dreams of a better life in Manhattan.

El Centro (Drama, FX, 2005).
Producer-Writer: Donal Logue. *Producer:* John Dahl, Rick Dahl.
Cast: Donal Logue.
Story: The peace-keeping efforts of a sheriff as he patrols the desert region along the California-Mexican border.

Elizabeth Street (Drama, ABC, 2000).
Cast: Patrick Dempsey, Patricia Manceri.
Story: Life of a beat cop living in New York's Little Italy.

Ellen Barkin Untitled Project (Comedy, HBO, 2009).
Producer: Jimmy Miller, Ellen Barkin, Ann Blanchard. *Creator-Writer:* Shauna Cross.
Cast: Ellen Barkin.
Story: A middle-aged woman ends her high profile marriage then returns to the dating scene only to find herself involved in a close relationship with the 24-year-old son of her ex-husband's first wife.

Emergency (Drama, Syndication, 1960).
Producer: Jack Wrather.
Cast: Arthur Hill.
Story: The work of a dedicated doctor attached to a Manhattan emergency hospital.

Emergency Sex (Drama, HBO, 2010).
Producer: Maria Bello, Russell Crowe, Keith Rodger. *Creator:* Andrew Thompson.
Cast: Maria Bello.
Story: A look at a group of workers at an organization where their sanities are tested by the atrocities, loneliness and primal desires they face.

Emma at Her Dad's (Comedy, Fox, 2017).
Producer: Sean Hayes, Todd Milliner. *Creator-Writer:* Claudia Lonow.
Cast: Claudia Lonow.
Story: A newly divorced mother with no place to go and seemingly lost without her husband by her side, moves in with her father then begins a mission to re-invent herself and become the woman she was meant to be.

The Equalizer (Crime Drama, CBS, 2020).
Producer: Queen Latifah, John Davis, John Fox.
Writer: Andrew Marlow, Terri Miller.
Cast: Queen Latifah, Lorraine Toussaint, Chris Noth.

Story: Remake of the 1980s CBS series about a man who uses his extraordinary skills to help people with nowhere to turn. Here the idea is re-imaged to star Queen Latifah as a woman who uses her skills to help people.

Eva Longoria Untitled 2014 ABC Project (Comedy, ABC, 2014).
Producer: Eva Longoria, Ben Spector. *Creator-Writer:* Emily Halpern.
Cast: Eva Longoria (as Eva).
Story: As a successful home renovator, Eva accomplishes a great deal, including solving the personal problems of her clients; however, when it comes to everyone else, including her eccentric family and a boyfriend who works as a deliveryman, she finds herself at a total loss as what to do.

Eva Longoria Untitled 2014 NBC Project (Comedy, NBC, 2014).
Producer: Eva Longoria, Ben Spector. *Creator-Writer:* Deborah Kaplan.
Cast: Eva Longoria.
Story: A female sex therapist capable of dealing with her patient's issues (from love to unusual fetishes) finds her own life in shambles attempting to deal with new relationships, an ex-husband, his new girlfriend and her overbearing mother.

Eva Longoria Untitled 2015 Project (Comedy, NBC, 2015).
Producer: Eva Longoria, Ben Spector. *Creator-Writer:* Peter Murrieta.
Cast: Erik Rivera (as Himself).
Story: A humorous look at the life of comedian Erik Rivera.

Eva Longoria Untitled 2016 Project (Comedy, NBC, 2016).
Producer: Eva Longoria, Ben Spector. *Creator-Writer:* Rob Sudduth.
Cast: Eva Longoria (as Catherine Cruz).
Story: A woman's efforts to adjust to a drastic life style change when she inadvertently catches a notorious serial killer and is recruited to become a Texas Ranger.

Eva Longoria Untitled 2017 Project (Drama, Lifetime, 2017).
Producer: Eva Longoria, Ben Spector. *Creator-Writer:* Holly Brix.
Cast: Eva Longoria.
Story: A select group of strangers, brought together by an unknown figure from their pasts, seek to find out who he is before his threat to reveal their hidden secrets can be accomplished.

Eva Longoria Untitled 2018 Project (Comedy, Fox, 2018).
Producer: Eva Longoria, Ben Spector.
Cast: Eva Longoria (as Amanda).
Story: Amanda, married to an Italian aristocrat and the co-host with him of a TV home shopping network program, finds her royal title in jeopardy when he decides to attend to official duties and leaves the show. Amanda's efforts to keep her princess title alive by enlisting the help of her estranged step-son to be her co-host was to be the focal point of the series.

Eve Untitled Project (Comedy, ABC, 2014).
Producer: Aaron Kaplan, Stacy Traub, Eve. *Creator-Writer:* Hunter Covington.
Cast: Eve (full name: Eve Jihan Jeffers Cooper).
Story: A successful business woman attempts to adjust to a new lifestyle when she falls in love with a less successful man with three children.

The Eve Arden Show (Comedy, CBS, 1965).
Producer: Lester Colodny.
Cast: Eve Arden.
Story: Eve Arden, star of the CBS series *Our Miss Brooks*, as a meaningful New York woman who attempts to help people she feels are in trouble.

The Evelyn Rudie Show (Variety, Syndication, 1958).
Cast: Evelyn Rudie.
Story: 1950s child star Evelyn Rudie (eight years old at the time) as the host to performances by and interviews with talented children.

Evil Genius (Comedy, Comedy Central, 2011).
Producer: Richard Allen Turner. *Creator-Writer:* David Martin, Paul F. Tompkins.
Cast: Paul F. Tompkins.
Story: A super villain named Tiberius Lynch hits on a plan to take over the world. After accomplishing his goal he realizes that ruling the world is not as simple as he thought.

The Exceptional (Comedy, NBC, 2018).
Producer: Seth Meyers, Mike Shoemaker. *Creator-Writer:* Josh Meyers, Steven Cragg.
Cast: Josh Meyers (as Justin).
Story: Justin, a resident of a Los Angeles condominium, finds his life changing for the worse when he agrees to join the HMO board and is suddenly elected its president and must deal with the numerous complaints that abound.

The Fabulous Oliver Chantry (Drama, CBS, 1957).
Producer: George Burns.
Cast: George Sanders (as Oliver Chantry).
Story: Events in the life of a newspaper columnist, critic, writer and lecturer.

Faizon Love Untitled Project (Comedy, Fox, 2005).
Producer: Brian Grazer, David Nevins.
Cast: Faizon Love.
Story: Incidents in the life of a Manhattan subway token booth collector as he struggles to adjust to his changing Harlem neighborhood.

Fame and Fortune (Variety, ABC, 1957).
Cast: Don DeFore (as Host).
Story: Talent competition wherein amateur singers vie for a chance to perform at a major night club.

Farrah Fawcett Untitled Project (Drama, ABC, 1982).
Producer: Aaron Spelling, E. Duke Vincent.
Cast: Farrah Fawcett.
Story: A dramatic reworking of Farrah Fawcett's 1971 comedy pilot *Inside O.U.T.* wherein she played an agent for the secret government organization O.U.T. (Office of Unusual Tactics). Farrah again plays an undercover agent, this time risking her life for a specialized U.S. government organization that tackles sensitive international affairs.

Father of the Bride (Comedy, CBS, 1959).
Producer: Al Lewis.
Cast: Jim Backus (as Stanley Banks), Patricia Blair (as Ellie Banks).
Story: An adaptation of the 1950 feature film about a father dealing with the emotional stress of losing his daughter to marriage. The idea was made into the 1961 TV series with Leon Ames and Ruth Warwick as Stanley and Ellie Banks.

Felicity Huffman Untitled Project (Drama, ABC, 2014).
Producer: Felicity Huffman, Julie Weitz, Rachel Winter. *Creator-Writer:* Carol Mendelsohn.

Cast: Felicity Huffman.
Story: The case assignments of agents assigned to the New York City Joint Terrorism Task Force.

The Fighting Marines (Anthology, NBC, 1960).
Producer: Jack Webb.
Cast: Jack Webb (as Host and Narrator).
Story: Dramatizations based on actual incidents in the lives of the men and women of the U.S. Marine Corps.

The Final Girls (Drama, ABC Family, 2013).
Producer: Jamie Lee Curtis, Steve Miner. *Creator-Writer:* Jeff Dixon.
Cast: Jamie Lee Curtis.
Story: Young women who have survived their own personal horror stories are brought together by a mysterious older woman to help others who are facing the same situations.

Finally Home (Drama, WB, 2000).
Cast: Melissa Gilbert, Jack Coleman.
Story: A loving couple attempt to start a new family following the death of their twin daughters by adopting a group of orphans.

Finding Love (Anthology, Lifetime, 2012).
Producer-Creator-Writer: Jennifer Love Hewitt, Matt Hastings.
Cast: Jennifer Love Hewitt (as Host).
Story: An adaptation of the book *The Day I Shot Cupid* by actress Jennifer Love Hewitt that was to present humorous stories of love based on Jennifer's personal dating experiences.

Fire Fighters (Drama, CBS, 1957).
Producer: Frank Telford, Ed Byron. *Writer:* George Belak.
Cast: Mark Miller.
Story: The work of the New York City Fire Department as seen through the eyes of a young firefighter.

First Nighter (Anthology, NBC, 1956).
Producer: Irving Briskin.
Cast: Les Tremayne (as Mr. First Nighter).
Story: An adaptation of the radio series about Mr. First Nighter, a patron of the theater who would invite listeners to join him in front row seats for "the evening's presentation" (an adaptation of a movie, book or Broadway play).

Fish Out of Water (Comedy, Amazon, 2020).
Producer: Brad Paisley, Bill Simmons, Will Arnett. *Creator-Writer:* A.D. Miles.
Cast: Brad Paisley.
Story: A country and western music star's experiences when, to be closer to his family, he gives up the hectic road life to become the host of a TV series about fishing.

Five Cornered Star (Anthology, ABC, 1958).
Producer: Louis Edelman, Walter Mirish.
Cast: Raymond Massey (as Host).
Story: Stories based on the files of the Secret Service.

Fix-It City (Comedy, CBS, 1979).
Producer: Bernard Rothman, Jack Wohl.
Cast: John Aprea (as Joey Bellino).
Story: Joey Bellino, the owner of a Fix-It City car repair shop, struggles to deal with customers and employees who are anything but normal.

Flying Fish (Drama, Syndication, 1957).
Producer: Louise Paget.
Cast: Donald May (as Donald Fish).
Story: Donald Fish, formally with New Scotland Yard, resigns to become the chief security officer for the British Overseas Airway Corporation.

For Men Only (Anthology, ABC, 1960).
Producer: Desi Arnaz.
Cast: Lee J. Cobb (as Host).
Story: Various stories involving the adventurous situations in which men involve themselves.

Foreign Legionnaire (Adventure, NBC, 1952).
Producer: Douglas Fairbanks, Jr.
Cast: Douglas Fairbanks, Jr. (as Captain).
Story: Incidents in the lives of the men of the French Foreign Legion. In 1955 Buster Crabbe would star in the series *Captain Gallant of the Foreign Legion.*

Forever... Eva (Anthology, Syndication, 1957).
Producer: Irving Briskin.
Cast: Eva Batrok.
Story: Actress Eva Bartok as the principal female performer in stories with a different male co-star each week.

Forever 31 (Comedy, ABC, 2014).
Producer: Mark Gordon, Andrea Shay, Kara Baker, Cindy Chupack.
Cast: Iliza Shlesinger.
Story: The situations that befall comedian Iliza Shlesinger (playing a fictionalized version of herself) as she and her group of thirty-something friends realize they are no longer "children" and must face life as adults in an ever-changing world.

Formula for Adventure (Anthology, ABC, 1959).
Producer: Leslie Stevens, Dominick Dunne, Stanley Colbert.
Cast: Vincent Price (as Host).
Story: Varying stories, from comedy to mystery that involve elements of science and superstition.

The Fortune Hunter (Drama, Syndication, 1956).
Producer: Roland Reed, J. Donald Wilson.
Writer: Charles Russell.
Cast: Roy Roberts, Nancy Hale, Britt Lomond.
Story: A team of specialized investigators seek to recover stolen property.

The Four of Us (Comedy, CBS, 1955).
Producer: Desi Arnaz.
Cast: Janis Paige (Janis), Evelyn Rudie (Julie).
Story: A nightclub singer struggles to raise her young daughter (Julie) while sharing a small Manhattan apartment with two non-show business girlfriends. The idea was revised and became the series *It's Always Jan* with Janis Paige as Jan and Jeri Lou James as her daughter, Josie.

Four Play (Comedy, CBS, 1999).
Producer: Jeffrey Klarik.
Cast: Lauren Holly, Jami Gertz.
Story: The situations that test the bond of friendship between best friends.

Foxy Brown (Crime Drama, Hulu, 2016).
Producer: Tony Krantz, DeVon Franklin, Jason Weinberg. *Creator-Writer:* Ben Watkins.
Cast: Megan Good (as Foxy Brown).
Story: An adaptation of the 1974 Pam Grier film of the same title, here as a voluptuous vigilante who helps people who are unable to turn to the police for help.

Free Spirit (Comedy, CBS, 1987).
Producer: Aaron Spelling.
Cast: Lisa Eilbacher, Robin Thomas.
Story: A widow remarries only to encounter the ghost of her first husband when he returns from the beyond to offer her spiritual guidance.

Freelancers (Comedy, Fox, 2013).
Producer: Zooey Deschanel, Rivka Sophia Rossi.
Creator-Writer: Mickey Rapkin.
Cast: Zooey Deschanel.
Story: A woman, recently divorced, just turning 30 and fired from her job with a prestigious law firm, faces new challenges when she attempts to restart her life.

The French Detective (Crime Drama, ABC, 2017).
Producer: James Patterson. *Creator-Writer:* Adam Cooper, Bill Collage, Jonathan Collier.
Cast: Jean Dujardin (as Luc Moncrief).
Story: An adaptation of James Patterson's book series about Luc Moncrief, a French detective who attempts to begin a new career as a detective with the N.Y.P.D.

French Provincial (Comedy, CBS, 1957).
Producer: Andrew Solt, Gina Kaus.
Cast: Barbara Bel Geddes.
Story: A woman's adventures as she embarks on a vacation in Europe.

Fresh Meat (Comedy, WB, 2000).
Cast: Natalia Cigliuti, Steffianna DeLa Cruz.
Story: A group of young hopefuls are followed as they attempt to make their mark in Hollywood.

The Freshman (Comedy, CBS, 1954).
Cast: Edward Everett Horton.
Story: A retired man's experiences when he enrolls in college to get the education he was denied when he was younger.

Front Office (Drama, CBS, 1958).
Producer: Fred Coe.
Cast: William Windom, Joan Taylor, Cara Williams.
Story: Incidents in the life of a top executive at a large corporation.

Frontier Correspondent (Western, Syndication, 1959).
Producer: Jack Wrather.
Cast: Burt Douglas, Karl Swenson.
Story: An Eastern newspaper reporter's experiences when he is assigned to report stories of life on the Western Frontier.

The Frontiersman (Western, Syndication, 1960)
Producer: Joel McCrea, Walter Mirisch. *Writer:* Robert Schaefer, Eric Friewald.
Cast: Gene Evans (as Jason Montgomery).
Story: Jason Montgomery, a school teacher in an Old West town, attempts to battle injustice through words rather than guns.

Fun (Comedy, CBS, 2020).
Producer: Becki Newton, Michael Urie. *Writer:* Michael Patrick King, Tracy Poust.
Cast: Becki Newton, Michael Urie.
Story: The incidents that befall a brother and sister who always encouraged each other to have fun in everything they do. When each suffers a career setback they reunite to help each other out (and still have fun).

Galaxy (Anthology, NBC, 1960).
Producer: Jerry Stagg.
Cast: Nelson Case (as Host).
Story: An adaptation of the radio series *X Minus One* that used adaptations of stories from *Galaxy* magazine to explore what could occur in the world beyond tomorrow—from the advances in technology to visitors from other planets.

The Gene Burns Show (Children, Syndication, 1954).
Producer: Jules Weill. *Creator-Writer:* Gene Burns.
Cast: Gene Burns.
Story: Gene Burns, creator of the comic strip

Reg'lar Fellas in a program that features animated stories and art instruction.

The Gentle Years (Drama, Syndication, 1952).
Producer: Hal Roach, Jr.
Cast: Walter Brennan.
Story: Life in a small American town at the turn of the 20th century as seen through the eyes of the owner of the local general store.

The Gentleman (Drama, FX, 2004).
Producer-Creator-Writer: Sheldon Turner.
Cast: Scott Foley.
Story: Events in the life of a man who appears to be a friendly medical supplies salesman but is actually evil and struggling to control his rage to kill.

George Clooney Untitled Project (Comedy, HBO, 2005).
Producer: Mark Waters, Jessica Tuchinsky.
Creator-Writer: Annie Hendy.
Cast: George Clooney.
Story: A look at a fictional NBA expansion team as seen through the eyes of four people: a rookie, a cheerleader, a seasoned player, and the coach.

George Jessel's Music Hall (Variety, Syndication, 1957).
Producer: George Jessel.
Cast: George Jessel (as Host).
Story: The idea was to screen short subjects filmed by Paramount Pictures for theaters during the 1930s and 1940s and have as a guest the star of that particular variety short. New footage was to have been added to conform to the particular subject of a show.

Germany (Cartoon, Comedy Central, 2016).
Producer: Channing Tatum, Peter Kiernan, Reid Carolin. *Creator-Writer:* Aaron Karo.
Voice Cast: Channing Tatum.
Story: Life with a group of germs that exist in a Petri dish in a lab at the University of Berlin in Germany.

Ghost Angeles (Drama, NBC, 2011).
Producer: Stephanie Savage, Leonard Goldstein.
Creator-Writer: Josh Schwartz, Henry Alonso Myers.
Cast: Rachel Bilson.
Story: A take off on CBS's *Ghost Whisperer* about a young woman living in Los Angeles who has the ability to talk to dead people—but also has a knack for becoming involved in their problems when she tries to help them.

Ghosts (Comedy, CBS, 2020).
Producer: Matthew Baynton, Jim Howick, Debra Hayward. *Writer:* Joe Port, Joe Wiseman.
Cast: Rose McIver, Brandon Scott Jones.
Story: A young couple's efforts to deal with the supernatural when they inherit a country home and not only find it in need of extensive repairs, but inhabited by the spirits of its previous owners.

Gideon's Knight (Crime Drama, Syndication, 1958).
Producer: Michael Killanin.
Cast: Patrick O'Neal (as George Gideon).
Story: An adaptation of the crime novels by J.J. Marric about George Gideon, a chief inspector with London's New Scotland Yard. The idea was made into the 1959 feature film *Gideon of Scotland Yard* with Jack Hawkins as George Gideon and the 1964 TV series *Gideon's Way* (a.k.a., *Gideon, C.I.D.*) with John Gregson as George Gideon.

Girl 10 (Drama, HBO, 2016).
Producer: Jessica Alba. *Creator-Writer:* Ken Woodruff.
Cast: Jessica Alba (as Elle).
Story: Elle, designated Girl 10, is one of ten synthetic humans that have been created in a lab. She is identical to a human girl in every aspect and she, herself, believes she is human. When Elle learns that a rogue scientist involved in her creation has begun a process to change the programming of synthetic humans to become weapons of destruction, she begins a quest to bring him down and stop his plan to take over the world with an army of deadly synthetics.

Girl Waits with Gun (Drama, Amazon, 2018).
Producer: Jennifer Crittenden, Max Handelman, Elizabeth Banks. *Creator-Writer:* Gabrielle Allan.
Cast: Elizabeth Banks (as Constance Kopp).
Story: An adaptation of the book by Amy Stewart that chronicles the life of Constance Kopp, a woman who became the first female to hold the job of a United States sheriff in the year 1914.

Girls on Girls (Talk, Spike TV, 2004).
Producer: Kelsey Grammer.
Cast: Camille Grammer (as Host).
Story: A daily program of discussions with a panel of female guests.

The Glorious Fourth (Drama, NBC, 1960).
Producer: Richard Alan Simmons, William Sackheim.
Cast: Dick York.
Story: Incidents in the lives of the men of the Fourth Regiment of the Confederate Army during the Civil War.

Goody's (Comedy, NBC, 2005).
Producer: Dick Wolf. *Creator-Writer:* David Flebotte.
Cast: Vincent Pastore, Michael Weaver.
Story: An old school Italian family's effort to run a Boston diner.

The Goop Lab with Gwyneth Paltrow (Reality, Netflix, 2019).
Producer: Gwyneth Paltrow, Elise Loehnen.
Cast: Gwyneth Paltrow.
Story: A lifestyle proposal, based on Gwyneth Paltrow's Internet site that explores health and wellness issues.

The Governor (Comedy, ABC, 2000).
Producer: Dan McDermott. *Creator-Writer:* Maria Bello.
Cast: Maria Bello.
Story: The incidents that befall an ordinary woman when, after a series of events place her in a governor's race, she becomes the head of her state.

The Great Dane (Comedy, NBC, 1960).
Producer: Alex Gottlieb.
Cast: Lauritz Melchoir.
Story: A world famous opera star finds a new life to contend with when he impulsively decides to retire to spend more time with his family. The 1952 series *Bonino* used the same concept.

Great Loves (Anthology, Syndication, 1953).
Producer: Victor Pahlin.
Cast: Hedy Lamarr (as Host).
Story: Dramatizations based on famous lovers throughout history.

The Greatest Game (Drama, CBS, 1966).
Cast: Britt Eklund, Nehemiah Persoff, George Coulouris.

Story: The planning and execution operations of a group of international jewel thieves who seek only the world's most valuable treasures.

The Green Hornet (Crime Drama, NBC, 1951).
Producer: George W. Trendle.
Cast: Robert Lowry (as Britt Reid).
Story: An adaptation of the radio series and comic book stories about Britt Reid, a newspaper publisher who is secretly the Green Hornet, a mysterious figure who dispenses justice with the aid of his chauffeur, Kato.

Green Peacock (Comedy, CBS, 1957).
Producer: Ida Lupino, Howard Duff. *Creator-Writer:* David Friedkin, Morton Fine.
Cast: Cara Williams, John Drew Barrymore.
Story: The incidents that befall an American couple living in Latin America.

Gregory Hines Untitled Project (Comedy, NBC, 2002).
Producer: Gregory Hines, Bob Delegali.
Cast: Gregory Hines.
Story: A former actor and dancer attempts to run an instructional dance studio.

Grocery Boy (Comedy, Syndication, 1954).
Producer: Jerry Warner. *Writer:* Dane Lussier.
Cast: Jack Carson.
Story: The mishaps that befall an easily aggravated manager of a small town grocery store.

Groober Hill (Comedy, NBC, 1966).
Cast: Kaye Stevens (as Kaye), Stubby Kaye (as Stubby).
Story: Kaye, an aspiring singer and actress begins the first step in her career as a performer on a small town TV station run by a former vaudeville performer (Stubby).

Growing Ivy (Comedy, NBC, 2013).
Producer: Susan Sarandon, Rashida Jones.
Creator-Writer: Will McCormack, Eva Amurri Martino.
Cast: Susan Sarandon (Frankie), Eva Amurri Martino (Ivy).
Story: Ivy Davis, a young woman who grew up in a rather unstable environment, attempts to reconnect with her negligent, eccentric mother (Frankie) and create a relationship they never had before.

Gunfighter (Western, CBS, 1959).
Producer: Martin Manulis.
Cast: Peter Breck (Jimmy Ringo).
Story: An adaptation of the feature film about Jimmy Ringo, an ex-gunfighter seeking to go straight but always using his former reputation to help people in trouble. Don Durant played the same type of role in the 1959 series *Johnny Ringo*.

The Guys (Comedy, ABC, 2012).
Producer: Tony Danza, Peter Billingsley, Vince Vaughn. *Creator-Writer:* Ian Gurvitz, David Richardson.
Cast: Tony Danza.
Story: The incidents that befall three friends who become roommates in the same neighborhood where their children and grandchildren reside.

Halfway House (Comedy, CBS, 1963).
Producer: Mark Goodson, Bill Todman. *Writer:* Elaine May, Bud Austin.
Cast: Verna Felton, Ellen Corby.
Story: Two spinsters and the situations that arise when they open a boarding house that harbors ex-convicts.

Halfway There (Comedy, CBS, 2018).
Producer: David Martin, Kara Baker. *Creator-Writer:* Ellen Plummer-Kreamer, Iliza Shlesinger, Sherry Bilsing-Graham.
Cast: Iliza Shlesinger.
Story: A stand-up comedienne's efforts to readjust her hectic lifestyle when her half-sister decides to move in with her.

Halle Berry Untitled Project (Drama, CBS, 2014).
Producer: Halle Berry, Kate Jacobs, Elaine Goldsmith-Thomas. *Creator-Writer:* Larry Kaplow.
Cast: Halle Berry.
Story: A doctor's experiences operating a state-of-the-art private hospital on the grounds of a prison.

Hand and Seal (Anthology, Syndication, 1952).
Producer: Leslie Roush.
Cast: Basil Rathbone (as Host).
Story: Dramatic stories based on authentic historical documents (the initial script presents an Abraham Lincoln document and a letter from Rachel Walker-Revere to her husband, silversmith Paul Revere).

The Hanging Judge (Western, CBS, 1960).
Producer: Joel McCrae, Walter Mirisch.
Cast: Frank Lovejoy (as Isaac Parker).
Story: Incidents in the life of Isaac Parker, a judge in the Oklahoma territory who was feared for his swift and sure justice (by hanging).

The Happy Time (Drama, ABC, 1960).
Producer: Charles Irving. *Writer:* Samuel Taylor.
Cast: Claude Dauphin, Mischa Auer.
Story: A French-Canadian family's experiences at the turn of the 20th century.

Harbor Inn (Anthology, ABC, 1956).
Producer: Ben Fox.
Cast: William Schallert [billed as "Bill Schallert"] as the inn owner).
Story: Incidents in the lives of guests who stay at Harbor Inn, a waterfront hotel that caters to people associated with the sea.

Hard Cases (Crime Drama, CBS, 1960).
Producer: Four Star Television.
Cast: Dean Jones (as Dean Smith), Nita Talbot (as Jane Foster).
Story: A modern day ranch foreman (Dean Smith) doubles as a private detective to solve cases that involve his ranch and the citizens in the nearby town; he is assisted by Jane Foster, his girlfriend, who believes she has the ability to solve crimes.

The Harry Belafonte Show (Variety, Syndication, 1955).
Producer-Writer: Jay Richard Kennedy.
Cast: Harry Belafonte (as Host).
Story: Singer Harry Belafonte was to host off-beat guest personalities, sing folk tunes, demonstrate the dance steps of various countries and recite translated versions of poetry.

Harry's Business (Comedy, ABC, 1960).
Producer: Alvin Cooperman. *Writer:* Henry Sharp, Barbara Hammer.
Cast: Ray Walston, Elena Verdugo.
Story: The situations that befall a small town druggist, his girlfriend and the people of the community he serves.

Haunted (Drama, CBS, 1965).
Producer: Joseph Stefano.
Cast: Martin Landau, Nellie Burke.
Story: A restoration expert with psychic abilities battles the ghosts he encounters during renovations of Victorian homes.

Havana (Drama, Starz, 2015).
Producer: Tom Fontana, Antonio Banderas, Julia Sereny, Jennifer Kawaja. *Creator-Writer:* Eduardo Machado.
Cast: Antonio Banderas (as Mario Conde).
Story: An adaptation of the *Havana* books by Eduardo Machado about Mario Conde, an alcohol-addicted police detective whose ambition is to become a writer but, for the time being, risks his life solving crimes for the Havana, Cuba, Police Department.

Hef's Super Bunnies (Cartoon, MTV, 2005).
Producer: Stan Lee, Hugh Hefner.
Voice Cast: Hugh Hefner (as Hef).
Story: An extraordinary group of Playboy Bunnies—scantily clad, buxom girls who, on behalf of their leader, Hugh "Hef" Hefner (the publisher of *Playboy* magazine) battle evil wherever it exists.

Heidi and Friends (Drama, CBS, 1957).
Producer: Four Star Television. *Writer:* David Dortort, Eugene Vale.
Cast: Evelyn Rudie (as Heidi), Beverly Washburn (Lydia).
Story: A young orphan girl attempts to adjust to a new life when she is sent to live with her grandfather, a lonely man in the Swiss Alps. It is here that she befriends a group of children, especially Lydia, and her adventures were to be depicted in an adaptation of the novel by Johanna Spyri.

Heidi Perlman Untitled Project (Comedy, UPN, 2004).
Producer: Kerry McCluggage. *Creator-Writer:* Heidi Perlman.
Cast: Heidi Perlman.
Story: A behind-the-scenes look at the pre-airing process of a late-night talk show whose staff are anything but competent.

Hell Marines (Drama, NBC, 1959).
Producer: Richard Tregaskis.
Cast: Ron Ely.
Story: Incidents in the lives of a group of U.S. Marines stationed in Europe during World War II.

The Henchman (Comedy, Fox, 2016).
Producer-Creator-Writer: Damon Wayans, Jr., Jake Johnson.
Cast: Damon Wayans, Jr.
Concept: A young man, plagued by a dysfunctional family, attempts to also cope with his job—henchman for an idiotic super villain.

Henry D. (Drama, ABC, 1960).
Producer: Norman Lear. *Writer:* James Hanlon.
Cast: Tex Ritter, Charles Aidman.
Story: Billed only as "A small town lawyer is the central character in this drama."

Her Majesty, the Queen (Comedy, NBC, 1957).
Producer: Carol Irwin.
Cast: Myrna Loy.
Story: A widowed mother of four children struggles to keep her family together in trying times.

Here Comes Calvin (Comedy, NBC, 1956).
Cast: Jack Carson (as Calvin), Allen Jenkins (as Manager).
Story: A manager's efforts to find work for his client, Calvin, a not-so-successful ex-Vaudeville performer.

Hey, Taxi! (Anthology, Syndication, 1955).
Producer: Robert Erlik.
Cast: Claude Akins (as Host).
Story: Ambitious idea that was to relate incidents in the lives of a different taxi cab driver each week. It was to be produced with the

cooperation of the Teamsters' Union and each selected participant (an actual cab driver) was to be paid between $50 and $100 for the rights to use his experience.

Hick Spanic (Comedy, Showtime, 2007).
Producer: Jeffrey Kramer, Scott Montoya.
Creator-Writer: Michael Glouberman.
Cast: Alex Reymundo.
Story: A Mexican-American, married to a gorgeous blonde, blue-eyed backwoods girl and living in her small Kentucky town face numerous problems from their in-laws—who can't figure out why he married her and vice versa.

High Time Inn (Comedy, Syndication, 1960).
Producer: Seymour Burns, Cecil Burke.
Cast: Keefe Brasselle (as Singer), Stubby Kaye (as Comedian).
Story: The mishaps that befall the trouble prone social directors of a mountain resort—one who can sing, the other a comedian.

Hilary Duff Untitled 2003 Project (Comedy, CBS, 2003).
Producer: Susan Duff, Nina Wass, Gene Stein.
Cast: Hilary Duff.
Story: A woman faces life on her own for the first time after she leaves the family nest to find her place in the world.

Hilary Duff Untitled 2004 Project (Reality, MTV, 2004).
Producer: Susan Duff, Hilary Duff.
Cast: Hilary Duff.
Story: A profile of Hilary Duff, star of the TV series *Lizzie McGuire* (and its feature film version *The Lizzie McGuire Movie*) as she navigates life in Hollywood.

The Hoaxers (Anthology, Syndication, 1957).
Producer: Arthur S. Katz. *Writer:* Shelly Lowenkopf.
Cast: Reed Hadley (as Host).
Story: Dramatizations that depict the art of the con, what to watch out for and what to do if you are caught in one. Similar to the series *Racket Squad* which starred Reed Hadley.

Holiday for Hire (Drama, NBC, 1964).
Producer: Gerald Mohr.
Cast: Gerald Mohr (as Matt Holiday).
Story: Matt Holiday, a travel service company owner, is followed as he not only arranges vacations, but solves the problems of his clients.

Hollywood at Work (Anthology, Syndication, 1953).
Producer: Robert Gurney.
Cast: George Jessel (as Host).
Story: Dramatizations based on true incidents in the lives of Hollywood celebrities.

Hollywood Yesterday (Anthology, NBC, 1964).
Producer: George Jessel.
Cast: George Jessel (as the Host).
Story: Select Hollywood celebrities are honored by tracing their film careers through clips and recollections from friends and family.

Holy! (Comedy, ABC, 2016).
Producer: Mila Kunis, Cami Curtis. *Creator-Writer:* Susan Curtin, Kevin Parker Flynn.
Cast: Nick Thune (as Minister).
Story: A minister, newly assigned to a struggling church, seeks ways to revive its congregation while at the same time adapting modern theological theories to a community somewhat accustomed to old world religion.

Home Economics (Comedy, ABC, 2020).
Producer: Topher Grace, Eric Tannenbaum, Kim Tannenbaum. *Writer:* Michael Colton, John Aboud.
Cast: Topher Grace.
Story: The incidents that befall three adult brothers: one who is struggling to keep his head above water; one who is middle class; and one who is wealthy and believes he is above everyone else.

The Home Team (Comedy, ABC, 1960).
Producer: Alvin Cooperman.
Cast: Don DeFore (as George), Evelyn Rudie (as Nina), Beverly Washburn (as Peggy), Candy Moore (as Delores), Gina Gillespie (as Wendy).
Story: A widower's mishaps as he struggles to raise four lively and mischievous daughters.

Homecoming Queen (Comedy, ABC, 1999).
Producer: Don Reo, Gene Stein, Nina Wass. *Creator-Writer:* Don Reo.
Cast: Brett Butler.
Story: A former high school homecoming queen turned business woman with two children struggles to rebuild her life following a divorce that leaves her at rock bottom.

Hong Kong Deadline (Drama, Syndication, 1956).
Producer: Raymond Freedgen.
Cast: Jim Davis.
Story: The assignments of a wire service reporter stationed in Hong Kong.

Hoodlum Empire (Anthology, Syn, 1956).
Producer: Hollywood Television Service.
Cast: Broderick Crawford (as Host).
Story: Weekly dramas that present a different cast and story each week and drawn from "tales of gangland."

House of Moore (Drama, ABC, 2016).
Producer: Felicity Huffman, Aaron Kaplan, Elizabeth Craft, Sarah Fein. *Creator:* Daniel Barnz.
Cast: Felicity Huffman (as Constance Moore).
Story: A look at the fashion industry as seen through the eyes of Constance Moore, head of the iconic Moore fashion family and concealing many dark secrets.

Howell and Hummell (Comedy, Syndication, 1957).
Producer: Diana Green, Eddie Joy, Monty Shaff.
Cast: Menasha Skulnik (as Menasha Hummell), Dennis King (as Dennis Howell).
Story: Two famed but mismatched lawyers, Menasha Hummell and Dennis Howell use their differing ways to defend clients in the late 19th century.

A Hundred Girls and a Chef (Comedy, CBS, 1955).
Producer: Desilu Productions.
Cast: Lauritz Melchior (as Chef), Joi Lansing (as Daughter).
Story: A middle-aged chef attempts to run a restaurant staffed by a bevy of beautiful servers but also deal with his daughter, a gorgeous, flirtatious blonde who serves as his assistant but has little genius at preparing meals.

Hunted (Drama, Freeform, 2016).
Producer: Mila Kunis, Susan Curtis, Cami Curtis. *Creator-Writer:* Hugh Sterbakov.
Cast: Mila Kunis.
Story: A young woman's flight from justice as she attempts to prove that she is innocent of the murder of her husband.

The Hunters (Drama, NBC, 1961).
Producer: Robert Blees.
Cast: Brett Halsey, Guy Stockwell.
Story: Two American big game hunters retreat to Africa to begin a safari tourist service.

Hurricane Kelly (Drama, Syndication, 1955).
Producer: Don Sharpe.
Cast: Frank Lovejoy.
Story: The cases of a tough ex-cop turned two-fisted private detective operating out of New York City.

Hyena (Comedy, HBO, 2015).
Producer: Mark Wahlberg, Stephen Levinson.
Creator-Writer: Ally Musika, Jude Angelini.
Cast: Jude Angelini (as Himself).
Story: Humorous look at the not-so-normal life of Jude Angelini, a real hip hop radio show host as he leaves his home in Detroit and ventures forth to find fame and fortune (and all the downfalls that go along with it).

I Am a Lawyer (Drama, CBS, 1959).
Cast: Cameron Mitchell.
Story: A lawyer's defense of people by going beyond what is common or traditional to help his clients.

I Am Storm Carlson (Drama, CBS, 1955).
Producer: Screen Gems.
Cast: John Hodiak (signed, first choice), Barry Nelson (signed, second choice).
Story: The adventures of a newspaper sportswriter who always seems to find more than he is looking for when covering stories.

I Don't Care About Your Band (Comedy, HBO, 2011).
Producer: Will Ferrell, Adam McKay, Jessica Elbaum, Lizzy Caplan. *Creator-Writer:* Julie Klausner.
Cast: Lizzy Caplan (as Julie Klausner).
Story: Humorous incidents based on the life of Julie Klausner, writer, podcaster and comedian—from pre-adolescence "to the unsavory details of sleeping with a gallery of losers" over the years.

I Like You Just the Way I Am (Comedy, ABC, 2014).
Producer: Jamie Tarses, Karen Kehela-Sherwood.
Creator-Writer: Jenny Mollen.
Cast: Jenny Mollen.
Story: An adaptation of the book by Jenny Mollen which chronicles her "impulsive and outrageous life" with her friends and husband, actor Jason Biggs.

I Love a Mystery (Mystery, Syndication, 1956).
Producer: ZIV-TV. *Creator:* Carlton E. Morse.
Cast: Paul Kelly (as Jack Bannon), Aria Riva (as Jerri Booker).
Story: A partial adaptation of the radio series (1939-1944) that focuses on Jack Bannon, head of the A-1 Detective Agency, and his secretary, Jerri Booker, as they tackle any case, anywhere. In the original series Jack was teamed with fellow detectives Doc Long and Reggie York.

I Love You Like a Brother (Comedy, CBS, 2012).
Producer: Eric Tannenbaum, Kim Tannenbaum, Rob Long. *Creator-Writer:* Tad Safran.
Cast: Kevin Connolly.
Story: The youngest of three brothers attempts to not only resolve their differences but those of his non-communicating parents and create a typical American family.

I'm with Stupid (Comedy, ABC, 2010).
Producer: Richard Lewis, Steven Pearl. *Creator-Writer:* Elaine Szewczyk.
Cast: Judy Greer (as Cassidy).
Story: While on a safari in Africa, a young New York socialite (Cassidy) has an affair with a dim-witted park ranger. Shortly after returning home, Cassidy finds her life complicated by the park ranger—who fell head-over-heels in love with her and somehow managed to track her down. Cassidy's effort to contend with her unwanted, intellectually challenged lover was to be the series focal point.

I'm with the Band (Comedy, HBO, 2010).
Producer: Jill Soloway, Sarah Jackson. *Creator-Writer:* Pamela Des Barres.
Cast: Zooey Deschanel (as Pamela Des Barres).
Story: It is the 1960s and Pamela Des Barres is a young woman obsessed with the various rock bands that are appearing on the scene. The proposal was to follow Pamela as she attaches herself to members of various rock bands.

ICE (2003) (Crime Drama, CBS, 2003).
Producer: Nancy Miller.
Cast: Melina Kanakaredes.
Story: Cases handled by the Bureau of Immigration and Customs Enforcement, a segment of Homeland Security that was formally known as The Immigration and Naturalization Service.

Icon (Drama, NBC, 2015).
Producer: Cindy Crawford, Anne Heche, James Tupper. *Creator-Writer:* Robin Bissell.
Cast: Anne Heche.
Story: Serial-like proposal based on the real life 1980s modeling wars rivalry between the Ford Modeling Agency and Elite Model Management.

Impulse (1952) (Anthology, CBS, 1952).
Producer: Don Sharpe, Larry Marcus.
Cast: John Newland (as Host).
Story: Psychological based dramas that were to feature a different cast each week.

Impulse (1960) (Anthology, NBC, 1960).
Cast: Maria Palmer (Host-Narrator).
Story: Stories, approved by the American Psychiatric Association, about people who commit crimes without thinking first.

Indictment (Anthology, CBS, 1958).
Producer: Everett Rosenthal.
Cast: Richard Kiley (as Host).
Story: Dramas based on the files of the New York City District Attorney's office.

The Inside Dope (Comedy, NBC, 1955).
Producer: Martin Rapf.
Cast: Cliff Arquette, Bill Goodwin.
Story: The mishaps that befall two newspaper reporters as they struggle to get "the inside dope" on the stories they are covering.

Intelligence (Comedy, HBO, 2007).
Producer: Patton Oswalt, Bradley Cooper. *Creator-Writer:* Michael Patrick Jann.
Cast: Patton Oswalt, Bradley Cooper.
Story: The assignments of a group of counter-intelligence agents whose cover is that of disgruntled civil servants.

Intercepted (Drama, Starz, 2019).
Producer: La La Anthony, Curtis "50 Cent" Jackson. *Creator-Writer:* Alexa Martin.
Cast: La La Anthony (as Marlee Harper).
Story: After Marlee Harper, a young woman dating a quarterback for the Denver Mustangs (Chris Alexander) catches him cheating on her, she leaves him vowing to never again date

football players. Conflict enters her life when Gavin Pope, hired to replace a poorly performing player, sets his sights on her.

The International (Drama, CBS, 2020).
Producer: Dolph Lundgren, Sylvester Stallone, Braden Aftergood, Tony Krantz. *Creator-Writer:* Ken Sanzel.
Cast: Dolph Lundgren (as Anders Soto).
Story: Anders Soto, an international spy and negotiator attempts to solve delicate and complex international issues as an agent for the United Nations.

The International Show (Variety, Syndication, 1957).
Producer: Telecast Pictures.
Cast: Hildegard Halliday (as Host).
Story: Each episode was to be filmed in a different international city and present the local talent (singers, dancers and comedians).

The Interventionist (Comedy, Paramount Network, 2017).
Producer: Tom Arnold, Dana Honor, Aaron Kaplan. *Creator-Writer:* Tom Arnold.
Cast: Tom Arnold (as Himself).
Story: Humorous look at one aspect of actor Tom Arnold's life—that of an interventionist for substance abusers after overcoming his own addiction.

It Happened in Sun Valley (Comedy, Syndication, 1959).
Producer: Bernard Girard. *Writer:* Douglas Morrow.
Cast: Richard Denning.
Story: A middle-aged writer's observations on the people who live in and visit the Sun Valley neighborhood in the San Fernando region of California, which is known for its youthful population.

It's a Great Country (Anthology, ABC, 1955).
Producer: Robert Sisk.
Cast: Peggy Webber (as Host).
Story: Stories based on incidents in the lives of ordinary American people.

It's About This Guy (Comedy, CBS, 2000).
Cast: Jeremy Piven.
Story: A playwright's efforts to rethink his oath to remain a bachelor when the unexpected happens: the girl of his high school dreams re-enters his life.

It's Always a Pleasure (Comedy, CBS, 1957).
Producer: Emily Kimbrough.
Cast: Eve Arden.
Story: The mishaps that befall a department store sales clerk who often becomes involved in the personal problems of her customers.

Jamie Foxx Untitled Project (Cartoon, Comedy Central, 2009).
Producer: Jamie Foxx, Marcus King, Lana Crouther.
Voice Cast: Jamie Foxx.
Story: Comedian Jamie Foxx in a fictionalized version of himself wherein he and a group of friends meet at a bar called the Foxxhole to discuss various aspects of life.

Jason Alexander Untitled Project (Drama, CBS, 2008).
Producer: Jason Alexander, Simon Barry.
Cast: Jason Alexander.
Story: When his TV series about a brilliant detective is cancelled, the star uses the knowledge he acquired from his role to become "a real life" detective and joins his ex-wife's private investigative firm to solve actual crimes.

Jason Miles (Drama, CBS, 1979).
Producer: Bud Austin, Burt Sugarman. *Writer:* A.C. Ward, Earl Lyon.
Cast: LeVar Burton (as Jason Miles).
Story: A young African-American school teacher's experiences in a New Orleans public high school.

Jeff Foxworthy Untitled Project (Cartoon, Fox, 2008).
Producer: Jeff Foxworthy, John Lehr, J.P. Williams.
Voice Cast: Jeff Foxworthy.
Story: A father who believes he is normal attempts to cope with his dysfunctional family.

Jen (Comedy, FX, 2013).
Producer: Chelsea Handler, Brad Wollack, Tom Brunelle, Jen Kirkman.
Cast: Jen Kirkman.
Story: After a devastating divorce, a woman (Jen) sets her goals to begin a new life where her needs come first, not those of a husband.

Jennifer Lopez Untitled 2008 Project (Reality, TLC, 2008).
Producer: Gay Rosenthal, Jennifer Lopez, Marc Anthony, Simon Fields.
Cast: Jennifer Lopez.
Story: A glimpse into the world of Jennifer Lopez as she navigates the music, fashion and film scene.

Jennifer Love Hewitt Untitled 2010 Project (Comedy, Fox, 2010).
Producer: Jennifer Love Hewitt, Walt Becker, Dana DuBois. *Creator-Writer:* Tiffany Paulson.
Cast: Jennifer Love Hewitt.
Story: A career-driven woman's attempts to distance herself from work and lead a normal social life, including finding the man of her dreams.

Jennifer Love Hewitt Untitled 2011 Project (Comedy, Fox, 2011).
Producer: Jennifer Love Hewitt, Tiffany Paulson, Walt Becker.
Cast: Jennifer Love Hewitt.
Story: A female version of CBS's *The Big Bang Theory* about a nerdy but gorgeous physicist and her group of brainy girlfriends.

Jericho (Adventure, Syndication, 1960).
Producer: Helen Ainsworth. *Writer:* Herb Meadow.
Cast: Guy Madison.
Story: A gentleman gunfighter's assignments as an unofficial Secret Service agent for the President of the U.S. during the late 19th century.

Jerry O'Connell Untitled Project (Comedy, CBS, 2012).
Producer: Michael Rothenberg, Richard Abate.
Cast: Jerry O'Connell.
Story: A struggling writer must prove that what he wrote is actually possible when his fabricated book on child rearing becomes a best seller.

Jessica Simpson Untitled Project (Comedy, NBC, 2013).
Producer: Ben Silverman, Jessica Simpson, Joe Simpson. *Creator-Writer:* Nick Bakay, Robin Bakay.
Cast: Jessica Simpson.
Story: Humorous incidents based on the life of singer Jessica Simpson.

Jigger (Drama, Syndication, 1955).
Producer: Alan Handley.
Cast: Dan Dailey.
Story: A foreign café owner's involvement with the people who find his establishment a place of refuge.

The Joan Crawford Show (Drama, CBS, 1957).
Producer: Screen Gems.
Cast: Joan Crawford.
Story: The cases of a shrewd female attorney. In 1952, then again in 1959, Joan Crawford appeared as the host of an anthology series proposal (*The Joan Crawford Show*) that resulted in two unaired pilot films.

The Joan Cusack Show (Comedy, Syndication, 2002).
Cast: Joan Cusack (as Host).
Story: Chatter coupled with celebrity interviews.

Joan Cusack Untitled 2008 Project (Comedy, NBC, 2008).
Producer: Julie Yen. *Creator-Producer-Writer:* Joan Cusack, John Markus.
Cast: Joan Cusack.
Story: A humorous look at the world of psychiatry as seen through a woman who can help her patients but has a rather difficult time coping with the situations she encounters.

Joan Cusack Untitled 2019 Project (Drama, HBO Max, 2019).
Producer: Kimberly Carver, Chris Keyser. *Creator-Writer:* Daniel Goldfarb.
Cast: Joan Cusack (as Julia Child).
Story: Incidents in the life of Julia Child, a famous chef and TV personality from 1962 through 1976 (at which time she hosted her own PBS-TV cooking series).

JoAnna Garcia Untitled Project (Comedy, ABC, 2012).
Producer-Creator: Shana Goldberg-Meehan.
Cast: JoAnna Garcia.
Story: The incidents that befall a young wife when she and her husband are forced to move in with her in-laws.

Jody and Me (Comedy, Syndication, 1955).
Producer: Don Sharpe.
Cast: George Brent (as Grandfather), Lydia Reed (as Jody).
Story: The relationship between Jody, a young girl, and her grandfather as seen through his eyes after he moves in with her family after his wife's passing.

The Joe DiMaggio Show (Anthology, Syndication, 1958).
Producer: Hal Roach, Jr.
Cast: Joe DiMaggio (as Narrator).
Story: True stories based on various sports figures.

Joe Dirt (Cartoon, TBS, 2009).
Producer: Fred Wolf. *Creator-Writer:* David Spade, Doug Robinson.
Voice Cast: David Spade.
Story: Mishaps in the life of Joe Dirt, a loser with a heart of gold who loves muscle cars and sports a mullet.

Joe Domino (Drama, CBS, 1960).
Producer: Al Simon. *Writer:* Leonard Heideman.
Cast: Brett Halsey (as Joe Domino).
Story: Joe Domino, a man with a unique perspective on life, takes on the cases of people who need something done but is not easily accomplished.

John Doe (Anthology, CBS, 1956).
Producer: Don Fedderson.
Cast: Hugh Beaumont (as Host).
Story: Dramatic stories billed as an "Anthology series with a hook; dramas dealing with what happens as a result of some slight incident in a person's life."

John Leguizamo Untitled Project (Comedy, AMC, 2014).
Producer: Jeff Goldenberg, John Leguizamo.
Cast: John Leguizamo.
Story: A look at the lives of three friends tackling careers, relationships and family responsibilities.

Johnny and the Gaucho (Comedy, NBC, 1955).
Producer: Al Simon. *Writer:* Senor Wences.
Cast: Senor Wences.
Story: Wenceslao Moreno, better known as the ventriloquist Senor Wences (and best known for his puppet Pedro, the talking head in a box) as an entertainer who draws inspiration (and snide remarks) from Johnny, his hand puppet (in his later appearances on *The Ed Sullivan Show*, Johnny would be seen as a face he drew on his hand and with whom he would converse).

Johnny Wildlife (Adventure, Syndication, 1956).
Producer: Jack DeWitt.
Cast: John Agar (as Johnny), Gloria Talbott (as Jean), Cheryl Holdridge (as Annette).
Story: A naturalist's (Johnny) experiences living in the wilderness with his wife (Jean) and daughter (Annette).

Jon Lovitz Untitled Project (Comedy, CBS, 2005).
Producer: David Franzke, Wayne Allan Rice.
Cast: Jon Lovitz.
Story: Hidden camera proposal wherein comedian Jon Lovitz oversees a program wherein unsuspecting people are caught in outrageous situations.

Judy Greer Untitled Project (Comedy, ABC, 2012).
Producer: Deborah Kaplan, Judy Greer, Paul Young.
Cast: Judy Greer.
Story: A couple's efforts to adjust to a new life style when they leave Los Angeles to raise their children in a small suburban town.

Just off Broadway (Comedy, CBS, 1955).
Producer: Desi Arnaz.
Cast: Rose Marie.
Story: Musical comedy about an aspiring singer and dancer hoping for her big break on Broadway. The idea was revised in 1956 with Peggy Ryan as the lead.

Justice of the Peace (Drama, ABC, 1960).
Producer: Vincent Fennelly. *Creator-Writer:* John Robinson.
Cast: Mark Stevens.
Story: A young man, a Justice of the Peace in a small Northern California town, finds himself not only trying cases but becoming the only law there is.

Juvenile Court Judge (Drama, Syndication, 1953).
Producer: Bailey Campbell. *Writer:* Ben Kerner.
Cast: Jan Sterling (as Camille Kelley).
Story: Incidents based on the career of Camille Kelley, a judge who served 31 years on the bench of the Memphis Juvenile Court and won national recognition for her work with teenagers.

Kandid Kids (Children, Syndication, 1951).
Producer: Bring Crosby Enterprises. *Creator-Writer:* Hal Goodman, Ruth Stevens.
Cast: Hy Averback (as Host).
Story: A panel of five children discusses new inventions and toys with the host.

Kate on Later (Comedy, NBC, 2014).
Producer: Ellen DeGeneres, Jeff Kleeman.
Creator-Writer: Lauren Graham, Liz Tuccillo.

Cast: Lauren Graham (as Kate).
Story: Based on NBC's rather skimpy press release, it appears to focus on an actress (Kate) as she conducts a late night talk show in front of a live studio audience.

Katie Holmes Untitled Project (Drama, Cinemax, 2015).
Producer: Katie Holmes. *Creator-Writer:* Mike Daniels.
Cast: Katie Holmes.
Story: A young woman, an advocate for equal rights, becomes a mysterious figure for justice when she is attacked by a stalker and takes to the streets seeking revenge.

Kathy Griffin Untitled Project (Reality, NBC, 2003).
Producer: Kathy Griffin, Stuart Krasnow.
Cast: Kathy Griffin.
Story: A slightly warped view of life as seen through the eyes of comedienne Kathy Griffin as she interacts with people from all walks of life.

Keeping It Real (Comedy, Showtime, 2016).
Producer: Sarah Timberman, Carl Beverly, Nat Faxon. *Creator-Writer:* Charles Randolph.
Cast: Walton Goggins (as Walter Griffith).
Story: Walter Griffith, a movie star who believes he is the solution to every problem, sets out to do so but ultimately causes more problems for the people he chooses to help.

Kellie Pickler Untitled Project (Comedy, Fox, 2007).
Producer: Simon Fuller, Brad Johnson. *Creator-Writer:* Chris Peterson, Malcolm Young.
Cast: Kellie Pickler.
Story: Kellie Pickler, an *American Idol* winner in a satire about a pretty but naïve small town girl whose life becomes complex when she learns that her biological father is the state's well-respected governor.

Kelly Ripa Untitled 2006 Project (Comedy, Comedy Central, 2006).
Producer: Kelly Ripa, Jeff Hodes.
Cast: Kelly Ripa, Mark Consuelos.
Story: A behind-the-scenes look at the making of a TV soap opera as seen through a married couple who are also the stars.

Kelly Ripa Untitled 2012 Project (Comedy, ABC, 2012).
Producer: Kelly Ripa, Mark Consuelos, Aaron Kaplan. *Creator-Writer:* Peter Murrieta.
Cast: Mark Consuelos.
Story: A blue collar Queens (New York) handyman and his son move to Manhattan's Upper West Side to become a part of a non-traditional family unit.

Kevin Kline Untitled Project (Drama, HBO, 2010).
Producer: Gavin Polone, Judy Hofflund, Kevin Kline. *Creator-Writer:* David Auburn.
Cast: Kevin Kline.
Story: After serving a 15 year prison sentence for killing his mistress, a once prominent doctor attempts to restart his life.

The Keys (Drama, ABC Family, 2011).
Producer: Ashley Tisdale, Jessica Rhoades, Tom Forman. *Creator-Writer:* Zach Hyatt.
Cast: Ashley Tisdale.
Story: A young woman's experiences when she begins investigating the mysterious happenings at a Florida resort.

Kill the Orange Face Bear (Comedy, Comedy Central, 2017).
Producer: Alex Karpovsky, Jake Szymanski, Steve

Fisher. *Creator-Writer:* Chris Romano.
Cast: Alex Karpovsky.
Story: A plot that could only happen on Comedy Central: A young man's comical efforts to track down and kill the bear that ate his girlfriend in front of his eyes.

Kipling's Jungle Book (Adventure, Syndication, 1956).
Producer: Frank Ferrin.
Cast: Sabu.
Story: An adaptation of Rudyard Kipling's *The Jungle Book* about Indian lore "including tiger hunts, elephant stampedes and other jungle backgrounds."

Kirstie (Talk, Syndication, 2008).
Producer: Oprah Winfrey.
Cast: Kirstie Alley (as Host).
Story: A daily program of talk and celebrity interviews.

Kirstie Alley Untitled Project (Comedy. CBS, 2004).
Producer: Rob Long, Dan Staley.
Cast: Kirstie Alley (as Mother), Ricki Lake (as Daughter).
Story: The situations that occur when a cop's widow moves in with her mother and together they attempt to run a bar that caters to police officers.

Kiss Me, Guido (Comedy, CBS, 2000).
Cast: Jason Bateman, Danny Nucci.
Story: An adaptation of the feature film about Frankie, a gay actor, and Warren, a straight guy who lives with him (thinking that when seeing an ad for a roommate with "GWA" it meant "Guy with Money," not "Gay White Male").

Kitty Hawk (Drama, Syndication, 1959).
Producer: Bernard Girard. *Writer:* Douglas Morrow.
Cast: Herbert Marshall (as Orville Wright), Tom Duggan (as Wilbur Wright), Kathleen Crowley (as Mary).
Story: Period proposal that was to chronicle the events leading up to Wilbur and Orville Wright's historic flight at Kitty Hawk, North Carolina in December of 1903.

Kristen Schaal Untitled Project (Comedy, ABC, 2018).
Producer: Kristen Schaal. *Creator-Writer:* Simon Rich.
Cast: Kristen Schaal.
Story: The incidents that befall a seemingly normal family as seen through the eyes of its youngest member, a child who still believes there are monsters under his bed.

Kristin Davis Untitled Project (Comedy, HBO, 2004).
Producer-Creator-Writer: Stacy Traub.
Cast: Kristin Davis.
Story: A single woman's efforts to support herself as a high stakes Las Vegas poker player.

Kristy Kottis (Drama, ABC, 2017).
Producer: Felicity Huffman, Liza Chasin, Andrew Stearn. *Creator-Writer:* Tim Bevan.
Cast: Felicity Huffman (as Kristy Kottis).
Story: A former New York City public school teacher (Kristy Kottis) turned FBI agent tackles cases where her academic knowledge plays a major role in her solving crimes.

Krysten Ritter Untitled Project (Comedy, NBC, 2013).
Producer: Aaron Kaplan, Krysten Ritter. *Creator-Producer:* Liz Vassey.

Cast: Krysten Ritter.
Story: Six friends and members of a bowling team gather once a week at a bowling alley to catch up on each other's lives and what happened during the prior week.

Kung Fu (Drama, CW, 2020).
Producer: Olivia Liang, Greg Berlanti, Sara Schechter. *Writer:* Christina M. Kim.
Cast: Olivia Liang, Jon Prasida, Shannon Dang, Tzi Ma, Kheng Hua Ta, Gwendoline Yeo.
Story: A re-imaging of the 1970s ABC series *Kung Fu* (with David Carradine). Here a young Chinese-American woman, overcome by a quarter-life crisis, drops out of college to embark on a life-changing journey to an isolated monastery in China (where she learns from the monks of the Shaolin Temple, the art of Kung Fu). Her time at the temple saw an unknown assassin kill her mentor and he is now targeting her. But on her return to her hometown she sees that her community has become overrun with crime and corruption. With her newly acquired skills, the girl becomes a figure for justice and constantly on the watch for her mentor's unknown assassin.

Kyra Sedgwick Untitled Project (Comedy, HBO, 2014).
Producer-Creator: Kari Lizer.
Cast: Kyra Sedgwick (as Kate).
Story: Kate, a nun in the order of the Sisters of Mercy, attempts to begin a new life when she feels she can no longer serve God in her present capacity.

L.A. Sheriff's Homicide (Crime Drama, NBC, 2000).
Cast: Miguel Ferrer.
Story: The work of the homicide detectives attached to the L.A. Sheriff's Office.

Ladder 54 (Comedy, CBS, 2017).
Producer: Aaron Kaplan, Cedric the Entertainer, Dana Honor. *Creator-Writer:* Mike Schiff.
Cast: Cedric the Entertainer.
Story: Incidents in the lives of a group of firefighters mostly during their time when regulated to a large Los Angeles fire department.

The Lady and the Senator (Comedy, CBS, 1955).
Producer: Mark Goodson, Bill Todman. *Writer:* Sidney Sheldon.
Cast: Donna Reed.
Story: The romantic adventures of a senator when he meets and falls in love with a girl who opposes his politic issues.

Lanny Budd (Drama, ABC, 1954).
Producer: Mort Briskin.
Cast: John Barrymore, Jr. (as Lanny Budd).
Story: An adaptation of the *Lanny Budd* novels by Upton Sinclair that charts the life of Lanning "Lanny" Budd, beginning with his glamorous life in 1913 on the French Riviera.

Lara Flynn Boyle Untitled Project (Reality, E!, 2011).
Producer: Lara Flynn Boyle.
Cast: Lara Flynn Boyle.
Story: A profile of actress Lara Flynn Boyle as she balances her career in Hollywood with her marriage to real estate broker Donald Ray Thomas in Texas.

Las Vegas Gentleman (Drama, Syndication, 1955).
Producer: Joel McCrea.
Cast: Peter Graves.
Story: A former police officer uses his talents as a troubleshooter for the Las Vegas Hotel Owners Association.

Leah (Talk, Syndication, 2008).
Cast: Leah Remini (as Host).
Story: A daily program of talk and celebrity interviews.

The Learning Curve (Drama, WB, 2000).
Cast: Debbi Morgan, Eric Mabius.
Story: Life in high school as seen from the point of view of a group of teachers.

Leave It to Arthur (Comedy, Syndication, 1952).
Producer: Jack Jason.
Cast: Rita Colton, Andrew Duggan (credited as "Andy Duggan").
Story: The mishaps that befall a young man as he goes about doing what he thinks is best to help those he believes are in trouble.

Leave It to Liz (Comedy, NBC, 1954).
Cast: Claudette Colbert (as Liz).
Story: A newspaper advice columnist's mishaps when she begins taking the letters she receives too personally and goes about finding the sender to resolve the problem.

Leave Me Alone (Comedy, NBC, 2002).
Producer: Adam Sandler, Doug Robinson.
Cast: Jon Lovitz, Norm MacDonald.
Story: Two men with opposing personalities attempt to share an apartment without killing each other in the process.

Legal Ease (Drama, CBS, 2015).
Producer: Halle Berry, Elaine Goldsmith-Thomas. *Creator-Writer:* Steven Lichtman.
Cast: Halle Berry.
Story: A brash female African-American attorney and a by-the-books Caucasian male lawyer attempt to defend clients despite their vastly differing beliefs.

The Legend of Billy the Kid (Western, ABC, 1960).
Producer: Jerry Schafer.
Cast: Wayne Rogers (as Billy the Kid).
Story: Partly fictionalized accounts in the life of William Boney, alias the outlaw Billy the Kid.

The Legend of Hemp Brown (Western, NBC, 1954).
Producer: Bernard Girard.
Cast: Noah Beery, Jr. (as Hemp Brown).
Story: Tales of the Old West as seen through the travels of Hemp Brown, a defender of range justice.

The Legend of Tom Horn (Western, Syndication, 1960).
Producer: Joel McCrae, Walter Mirisch. *Writer:* Paul Savage.
Cast: Patrick O'Neal (as Tom Horn).
Story: Dramatizations based on the life of Tom Horn, Indian scout, cowboy, soldier and Pinkerton detective during the late 19th century.

The Legionnaire (Anthology, CBS, 1956).
Producer: Tony Bartley. *Writer:* Paul Monash.
Cast: Errol Flynn (as Host), Yvonne DeCarlo, Merle Oberon (signed guests).
Story: Dramatizations based on the experiences of the men of the French Foreign Legion in Morocco. The idea was later revised in 1956 as *Tales of the Foreign Legion* with Errol Flynn singed to host the first episode; guest hosts were to appear on future installments. At this same time, Buster Crabbe starred in the 1955 series *Captain Gallant of the Foreign Legion*.

Lenny Clarke Untitled Project (Comedy, ABC, 2006).
Producer-Creator-Writer: Don Reo.
Cast: Lenny Clarke.

Story: A Boston patrol cop must not only enforce the law but deal with a beat that covers an area riddled with dysfunctional characters.

Let's Stay Together (Comedy, ABC, 2019).
Producer-Creator-Writer: Don Reo, Damon Wayans.
Cast: Damon Wayans.
Story: A single father finds his life complicated when his son and his family move in with him.

Letter of Credit (Anthology, Syndication, 1957).
Producer: Don Sharpe, Warren Lewis. *Writer:* Jerome Weldman.
Cast: Jerome Weldman (as Host).
Story: Adaptations of short stories written by Jerome Weldman.

Lies I Tell My Daughter (Comedy, NBC, 2013).
Producer: Zooey Deschanel, Molly McAleer.
Creator-Writer: Deb Schoeneman.
Cast: Zooey Deschanel.
Story: A mother's efforts to deal with her unpredictable family by stretching the truth to a point where she allows them to think they have gotten the best of her.

Life and Deaf (Comedy, Disney Plus, 2020).
Producer: Marlee Matlin, Patricia Heaton, David Hunt. *Creator-Writer:* Lizzy Weiss.
Cast: Marlee Matlin (as the Mother).
Story: Humorous incidents in the life of a child growing up in the 1970s with deaf parents.

Life Can Be Beautiful (Drama, CBS, 1955).
Producer: John L. Clark.
Cast: Rusty Lane, Wendy Drew, Beverly Washburn.
Story: An adaptation of the 1938-1954 NBC radio series of the same title that was billed as "an inspiring message of faith drawn from life" and tells the story of "Papa" David Solomon, the kindly owner of the Slightly Read Book Shop.

Life Size (Anthology, Syndication, 1957).
Producer: Mark Stevens.
Cast: Mark Stevens (as Narrator).
Story: Adaptations of stories written by Turnley Walker for *Pageant* magazine that relate incidents in the lives of "colorful personalities in many pursuits."

Life with Valerie (Comedy, CBS, 2000).
Cast: Valerie Harper.
Story: A former movie and TV child star faces the challenges of life after having been raised in a show business atmosphere.

The Lincoln Lawyer (Drama, CBS, 2020).
Producer: Ted Humphrey, Ross Fineman. *Writer:* David E. Kelley.
Cast: Logan Marshall-Green (as Mickey Haller), Kiele Sanchez, Jazz Raycole.
Story: An adaptation of the feature film about Mickey Haller, a lawyer who operates from his Lincoln Town car to help people in need wherever they may be.

Lindsay Lohan Untitled Project (Reality, MTV, 2009).
Producer: Lindsay Lohan, Steller Stolper, Michael Hirschorn.
Cast: Lindsay Lohan.
Story: Actress Lindsay Lohan reflects on her career as she overcame numerous obstacles since starring in the film *The Parent Trap*.

Lisa Kudrow Untitled 2005 Project (Comedy, CBS, 2005).
Producer: Lisa Kudrow, Dan Bucatinsky. *Creator-Writer:* Ilene Rosenzweig.

Cast: Lisa Kudrow.
Story: Incidents in the lives of a carefree married couple who are also romance novelists.

Lisa Kudrow Untitled 2006 Project (Comedy, Bravo, 2006).
Producer: Lisa Kudrow, Dan Bucatinsky.
Cast: Lisa Kudrow (as Host).
Story: Improvisational comedy sketches that were to be hosted by Lisa Kudrow.

Lisa Kudrow Untitled 2007 Project (Drama, CW, 2007).
Producer: Lisa Kudrow, Dan Bucatinsky.
Cast: Lisa Kudrow.
Story: A woman working at a Manhattan auction house suddenly finds her life changing when she is mistaken for someone else and becomes immersed in high society.

Lisa Kudrow Untitled 2015 Project (Comedy, ABC, 2015).
Producer: Nina Wass, Lisa Kudrow, Ryan Seacrest. *Creator-Writer:* Ken Kirkman, Dan Bucatinsky.
Cast: Lisa Kudrow.
Story: Four female friends now in their forties decide to reshape their lives by embarking on a mission to enjoy what they can while they can.

Lisa Lampanelli Untitled Project (Comedy, HBO, 2008).
Producer: Jim Carrey, Lisa Lampanelli. *Creator-Writer:* Kario Salem.
Cast: Lisa Lampanelli (as Lisa).
Story: When she unexpectedly inherits a Los Angeles comedy club, a young woman (Lisa) finds her life changing when she not only has to run the club but become the den mother to a group of resident comics who are anything but normal.

Logan (Drama, ABC, 1960).
Producer: Hubbell Robinson.
Cast: Richard Chamberlain (billed as "Bill Chamberlain").
Story: The activities of a young attorney working for a large law firm in New York City.

Long Island Sound (Comedy, ABC, 2005).
Producer: Eric Tannenbaum, Kim Tannenbaum, Emilio Estevez. *Writer:* Danny Jacobson.
Cast: Emilio Estevez.
Story: A Long Island (New York) family man tries to rebuild his life as a small business owner after he loses his engineering job with a big company.

The Long Walk (Drama, Fox, 2017).
Producer: Carol Mendelsohn, Julie Weitz, Morris Chestnut. *Creator-Writer:* Thomas Perry.
Cast: Morris Chestnut (as Dick Stahl).
Story: Dick Stahl, a retired bomb technician now working as a security guard, finds a renewed calling in life when he is recruited by the Los Angeles Bomb Squad for assistance, initially to trap a killer threatening to blow up the city.

Lost and Found (Comedy, ABC, 2000).
Cast: Geena Davis.
Story: The situations that befall a single woman living in New York City when she meets the man of her dreams, marries him and becomes a step-mother to his children.

The Louella Parsons Show (Talk, Syndication, 1951).
Cast: Louella Parsons (as Host).
Story: Hollywood gossip with newspaper columnist Louella Parsons.

Love Scenes (Anthology, Syndication, 1953).
Producer: United Producers Studios.

Cast: Paul Garrison (as Narrator).
Story: Dramatizations based on romantic stories adapted from various literary works.

Lyle and Caroline (Cartoon, Fox, 2018).
Producer: Lisa Kudrow, David Miner. *Creator-Writer:* Eric Stangel.
Cast: Lisa Kudrow (as Caroline).
Story: The relationship between a loving grandmother (Caroline) and her grandson (Lyle).

Lynda Lopez Untitled Project (Talk, Syndication, 2004).
Producer: Jennifer Lopez, Julia Caro.
Cast: Lynda Lopez.
Story: Lynda Lopez, the sister of singer Jessica Lopez, as host of a program of celebrity interviews, pop culture discussions, and beauty and fashion advice.

The Mae Williams Show (Anthology, Syndication, 1955).
Producer: Arthur B. Weber, Martyn E. Schiff.
Cast: Mae Williams (as Host).
Story: Biological sketches and success stories of show business personalities. Charles King was signed to provide the music.

Magic Lantern Time (Children, Syndication, 1957).
Producer-Writer: Mac Lee.
Cast: Mac Lee (as Host).
Story: The rabbit puppet Hoppy Bright first introduces children to animation fantasies then with his human co-host, Mac Lee, relates tales of hunting expeditions to various foreign lands.

The Magnificent Orlando (Drama, Syndication, 1958).
Producer: Herb Meadow.

Cast: Edward Andrews (billed as "Ed Andrews").
Story: An 1890s stage magician uses his ability to not only entertain but solve crimes.

Male Secretary (Comedy, NBC, 1954).
Producer: Mickey Rooney.
Cast: Keefe Brasselle, Janis Paige.
Story: A male secretary's mishaps as he takes a position with a beautiful but strict business woman.

Mama's Boarding House (Comedy, CBS, 1956).
Producer: Edward Feldman.
Cast: Paul Douglas (as Jeff Hefferan), Alexis Smith (as Emily Hefferan).
Story: A resourceful housewife recalls twenty years of her husband's financial mistakes while she runs a boarding house to support her family (the program was to be set in 1910).

Man/Child (Comedy, Fox, 2013).
Producer: Damon Wayans, Jr., Christie Smith.
Creator-Writer: Reed Agnew.
Cast: Damon Wayans, Jr.
Story: The situations that befall two single fathers when they move in together to save on expenses then discover they know little about raising children without a woman's touch.

The Man from Cooks (Comedy, Syndication, 1957).
Producer: Sid Ellis, Gene Gutowski.
Cast: Eddie Albert.
Story: Follows a troubleshooter for the Thomas Cook Travel Agency whose antics cause more problems than solutions.

The Man from Nogales (Western, CBS, 1968).
Producer: Andrew J. Fenady.
Cast: Lloyd Bridges.
Story: An adaptation of the Zane Grey story

about a wandering cowboy who fights for right on the lawless frontier.

The Man in the Streets of Europe (Drama, Syndication, 1961).
Producer: Paul Vario.
Cast: Cesar Romero.
Story: A suave and sophisticated troubleshooter's experience in various European cities as he comes to the aide of people in trouble. Had the project sold it would have been filmed in various capital cities throughout the world.

Mandrake the Magician (Drama, Syndication, 1966).
Producer: Al Brodax. *Writer:* Harry W. Junkin.
Cast: Vic Morrow (as Mandrake).
Story: An adaptation of the comic strip created by Lee Flak about a magician who uses his abilities to battle evil. In 1954 NBC produced a pilot called *Mandrake the Magician* that starred Woody Strode as Mandrake.

Mayday (Drama, Syndication, 1958).
Producer: Harold Gast.
Cast: Rick Jason.
Story: Incidents in the lives of the men in service to the Air Transport Command.

Maria Bello Untitled Project (Crime Drama, HBO, 2009).
Producer: Gavin Polone, Maria Bello, John Carrabino. *Creator-Writer:* Gary Lennon.
Cast: Maria Bello.
Story: After the murder of her husband, a woman turns to a life of crime to support herself and her children.

Marissa (Comedy, ABC, 2004).
Producer: Marissa Jaret Winokur, Michael Valeo. *Creator-Writer:* Dana Klein.
Cast: Marissa Jaret Winokur (as Marissa).
Story: The situations that befall a working class girl and her husband when they win money in a lottery and move into an exclusive gated community.

Mark Trail (Adventure, Syndication, 1955).
Producer: Drex Hines.
Cast: John Larkin (as Mark Trail).
Story: An adaptation of the 1950-1952 radio series about Mark Trail, an adventurer, called "The Guardian of the Forests, Protector of Wildlife, and Champion of Man and Nature" as he battles to keep forests and wildlife safe.

Marley (Comedy, WB, 2005).
Producer: Deborah Oppenheimer. *Creator-Writer:* Bruce Helford.
Cast: Marley Shelton.
Story: A hard-working woman raised in a modest middle-class environment, ventures forth to seek the life of luxury she has read about and seen in movies and on TV.

Marvel's Ghost Rider (Adventure, Hulu, 2019).
Producer: Jeph Loeb. *Creator-Writer:* Ingrid Escajeda.
Cast: Gabriel Luna (as Robbie Reyes).
Story: An adaptation of the Marvel comic book about Robbie Reyes, a resident of a Texas-Mexico border town who is secretly Ghost Rider, an avenger consumed by hellfire and supernaturally bound to a demon, who fights evil wherever he finds it.

McCloud (Crime Drama, CBS, 2014).
Producer: Brett Butler, Daniel Petrie, Jr., Robert Lieberman.
Cast: Brett Butler (as Samantha McCloud).
Story: A remake of the 1970-1977 NBC series of the same title (about Sam McCloud, a deputy

marshal from New Mexico who joins the N.Y.P.D. to learn about big city crime solving) but here in the form of his daughter, Samantha McCloud.

Meet the Mate (Interview, NBC, 1953).
Cast: Arlene Francis (as Host).
Story: Proposed weekly program wherein married couples are interviewed on a topic first with the wife then with the husband.

Meg Ryan Untitled Project (Comedy, NBC, 2013).
Producer: Meg Ryan, Jane Berliner. *Creator-Writer:* Marc Lawrence.
Cast: Meg Ryan (as Megan).
Story: Megan, a non-confrontational single mother who works as an editor at a publishing house, faces new challenges when a neurotic, anxiety ridden woman who is everything she is not becomes her boss.

Melissa Etheridge Untitled Project (Comedy, ABC, 2004).
Producer: Brad Grey, Peter Traugott. *Creator-Writer:* Linda Wallem.
Cast: Melissa Etheridge (as Melissa).
Story: A lesbian music teacher (Melissa) finds herself becoming a substitute mother when her straight male roommate invites his teenage daughter to move in with them.

The Member Guest (Comedy, HBO, 2011).
Producer: Aaron Kaplan, Tom Mangan. *Creator-Writer:* Neil LaBute.
Cast: Kevin Bacon.
Story: A once famous golf pro, now working as a golf instructor at a country club, seeks to regain his former status while attending to the needs of the club members.

Men of Destiny (Anthology, Syndication, 1960).
Producer: Barnet Glassman.
Cast: Bob Considine (as Host-Narrator).
Story: Events in the lives of prominent people are traced through Pathe theatrical news footage (that dates back to the days of Teddy Roosevelt).

Men of Justice (Anthology, Syndication, 1953).
Producer: Roland Reed.
Cast: Broderick Crawford (as Host).
Story: Various dramas that detail the work of law enforcement officers across the United States.

Merrill's Marauders (Adventure, NBC, 1958).
Producer: Sam Gallu.
Cast: John Agar (as Frank Merrill).
Story: Stories based on the real life Merrill's Marauders, a unit of the United States Army Long Range Penetration Special Operations formed by Frank Merrill and officially named the 5307th Composite Unit that fought in the South East Asian Theater during World War II.

Michelle Trachtenberg Untitled Project (Drama, CW, 2010).
Producer: Stephanie Savage, Josh Schwartz, Len Goldstein. *Creator-Writer:* Stuart Zicherman.
Cast: Michelle Trachtenberg.
Story: A young criminology student with a gift for profiling uses her abilities to help the police solve baffling crimes.

Miracle Man (Drama, NBC, 2015).
Producer: Kevin Sorbo, Sam Raimi. *Creator-Writer:* Robert Eisele.
Cast: Kevin Sorbo (as Jason Greene).
Story: After returning from military duty in Afghanistan, Army Ranger Jason Greene discovers he has the ability to make miracles happen. Unsure as to why (although he believes it has something to do with his almost being

killed in combat) Jason begins a quest to not only change people's lives but find out how he came to possess the power.

Miss Most Likely (Comedy, ABC, 2012).
Producer: Mandy Moore, Shawn Levy, Becky Clements. *Creator-Writer:* Rich Appel.
Cast: Mandy Moore (as Mandy).
Story: A young woman (Mandy) seeking to begin a life of her own away from her intrusive family, takes the first step and "runs away" only to find that her family has also run away to join her.

Mr. and Mrs. Wiley (Drama, ABC, 1970).
Producer: Arnold Margolin, James Parker.
Cast: Gary Collins, Penny Fuller.
Story: A private detective and his slightly scatterbrained wife team to solve crimes.

Mr. Blandings (Comedy, NBC, 1957).
Producer: Warren Lewis.
Cast: Macdonald Carey (as Jim Blandings), Phyllis Thaxter (as Muriel Blandings).
Story: An adaptation of the feature film *Mr. Blandings Builds His Dream House* that follows a couple's mishaps as they deal with the after effects of a Connecticut home that they had built to their specifications but turned out to be anything but a dream house.

Mr. Digby (Comedy, Syndication, 1956).
Producer: Television Programs of America (TPA).
Cast: William Demarest (as Mr. Digby).
Story: An adaptation of the *Saturday Evening Post* stories by Douglas Welch about a free-lance photographer whose assignments are anything but normal.

Mister Doc (Comedy-Drama, CBS, 1961).
Producer: Ralph Nelson.
Cast: Dean Jagger.
Story: The life of a doctor in a small town in the early 1900s.

Mr. Harkender and Mr. Sweeney (Comedy, CBS, 1959).
Producer: Stanley Roberts.
Cast: Gale Gordon (as George Harkender), William Frawley (as Bill Sweeney).
Story: Two friends with opposite opinions on everything attempt to get along while running a business together.

Mr. Mosby, Private Citizen (Comedy, NBC, 1953).
Producer: Robert Welch. *Writer:* Robert Riley Crutcher.
Cast: Dennis O'Keefe (as Mr. Mosby).
Story: A middle-aged man, just released from the armed services, returns to his home town where his efforts to find a life of peace and quiet appear not to be in the books for him.

Mo Mandell Untitled Project (Comedy, NBC, 2011).
Producer-Creator-Writer: Mo Mandell.
Cast: Mo Mandell.
Story: Events in the lives of a group of young people five years before the earth is destroyed by a meteor.

Mo's House (Comedy, ABC, 2005).
Producer: Courtney B. Conte, Serrie McGhee.
Cast: Mo'Nique.
Story: A mother's efforts to make ends meet by working as a clerk in a grocery store.

Molly Ringwald Untitled Project (Drama, Lifetime, 2012).
Producer-Creator: Molly Ringwald.
Cast: Molly Ringwald.

Story: After years of being away, a woman, now the mother of two children, returns to her hometown where her experiences as she confronts the social issues of her past as well as the Queen B's of her high school years, were to be depicted.

Molly Shannon Untitled 2010 Project (Comedy, HBO, 2010).
Producer: Molly Shannon, Steven Levy. *Creator-Writer:* Tim Long.
Cast: Molly Shannon.
Story: A nun's spiritual awakening when she decides to leave the convent and experience life in the outside world.

Molly Shannon Untitled 2013 Project (Comedy, Fox, 2013).
Producer: David Miner, Greg Walter. *Creator-Writer:* Bruce McCulloch.
Cast: Molly Shannon (as Fiona).
Story: The clash between a woman at the height of her professional career (Fiona) and her daughter, who is pregnant, refuses to take responsibility for what happened and unwilling to find a job.

Mommy (Comedy, Fox, 2005).
Producer-Creator-Writer: Susan Dickes.
Cast: Margaret Cho.
Story: The experiences of a mother as imagined by comedienne Margaret Cho (based on her stand-up comedy routine).

Moon Cruise (Comedy, TBS, 2016).
Producer: Jonathan Stern, David Wain, Michael Showalter. *Creator-Writer:* Michael Ian Black.
Cast: Michael Ian Black.
Story: The ABC series *The Love Boat* taken a giant step forward: Incidents in the lives of the passengers who book flights on a space shuttle.

Morena Baccarin Untitled Project (Drama, NBC, 2016).
Producer: Tony Krantz, Morena Baccarin.
Creator-Writer: Ken Sanzel.
Cast: Morena Baccarin (as Morena).
Story: Morena, a former police detective turned attorney for a prestigious New York City law firm, uses her police training as a means to defend clients who have been falsely convicted of a crime.

Motel (Anthology, Syndication, 1958).
Producer-Writer: Walt Canter.
Cast: Glenda Farrell.
Story: Incidents in the lives of the guests who check into a modest motel overseen by a middle-aged woman.

Mother of All Something (Comedy, CBS, 2010).
Producer: Jessica Alba, Jhoni Marchinko. *Creator-Writer:* Kelly Oxford.
Cast: Jessica Alba.
Story: A mother of three, accustomed to working in an office, struggles to adjust to a new situation when she becomes a stay-at-home mother.

Mother's the Governor of Texas! (Comedy, Syndication, 1959).
Producer: Bernard Girard. *Writer:* Douglas Morrow.
Cast: Barbara Britton (as Barbara), Sheila James (as Cindy), Candy Moore (as Julie).
Story: The incidents that befall a family when the mother (Barbara) is elected the Governor of Texas.

Mouthpiece (Comedy, Showtime, 2009).
Producer-Writer: Carol Leifer.
Cast: Marlee Matlin (as Susan).
Story: The cases acquired by a prestigious law

firm with a particular focus on Susan, a hearing impaired attorney who is also the most successful member of the group.

Mrs. G's Bigger Love (Drama, Lifetime, 2012).
Producer: Jennifer Love Hewitt, Jeanie Bradley.
Creator-Writer: Julie Golden.
Cast: Jennifer Love Hewitt.
Story: In an attempt to relieve the boredom she faces, a housewife creates an Internet blog wherein she pretends to be a polygamist. Unexpectedly, the blog goes viral and, to continue doing what she loves, she struggles to keep her real life (with one husband) a secret.

Mrs. Mike (Drama, Syndication, 1955).
Producer: Screen Gems. *Writer:* Nancy Freeman, Benedict Freeman.
Cast: Barbara Britton (as Linda), Glenn Langan (as Mike).
Story: Life with a Canadian Northwest Mounted Policeman (Mike) as seen through the eyes of his wife, Linda, as she relocates to the Canadian wilderness.

Murder Town (Crime Drama, ABC, 2015).
Producer: Jada Pinkett Smith, Miguel Melendez.
Creator-Writer: Rob Fresco, Barry Schindel.
Cast: Jada Pinkett Smith.
Story: The cases prosecuted by a woman who becomes Wilmington, Delaware's first African-American District Attorney.

My Favorite Love Story (Anthology, CBS, 1961).
Producer: Richard Collins.
Cast: June Allyson (as Premiere Host).
Story: Adaptations of romantic stories selected by a guest celebrity (who would also host and star in that particular episode).

My Inappropriate Life (Comedy, Fox, 2012).
Producer: Chelsea Handler, Tom Werner.
Creator-Writer: Dava Savel, Heather McDonald.
Cast: Heather McDonald.
Story: A working mother's efforts to adjust to the life that surrounds her: a stay-at-home husband, her parents who live next door, a sister desperate to have a child but unable (and constantly begging her for one of her eggs) and neighbors who have stopped talking to her.

My Sister and I (Drama, Syndication, 1954).
Producer: Eddie Connie.
Cast: Adele Mara (as Peggy), June Kenney (as Lois), Robert Hutton (as Michael).
Story: Daily soap opera proposal about incidents in the lives of two close-knit sisters, Peggy and Lois.

My Village (Comedy, ABC, 2020).
Producer: Kyra Sedgwick. *Writer:* Kari Lizer.
Cast: Kyra Sedgwick, Rachel Sennott, Emma Caymares, Joey Bradd, Austin Crute.
Story: After her children move out of the house, a mother (Kyra) begins to feel the empty nest syndrome and decides to do something about it: she relocates and reinserts herself into her children's lives, believing they still need her guidance.

The Mysterious Traveler (Anthology, Syndication, 1956).
Producer: Mark Stevens.
Cast: Vincent Price (as The Mysterious Traveler).
Story: An adaptation of the radio series wherein a man who traveled by train would introduce stories ranging from the supernatural to murder and mayhem. Like the radio series, the TV version was also set to use the original opening. A man seated on a train as it journeys to a destination that only he knows, would speak

directly to the audience: "This is the Mysterious Traveler, inviting you to join me on another journey into the strange and terrifying. I hope you will enjoy the trip that it will thrill you a little and chill you a little. So settle back, get a good grip on your nerves and be comfortable—if you can!"

Natasha Lyonne Untitled Project (Comedy, Fox, 2012).
Producer: Dave Becky, Natasha Lyonne, Jonathan Berry.
Cast: Natasha Lyonne (as Stella).
Story: Natasha Lyonne (from the film *The Slums of Beverly Hills*) as Stella, a woman just released from rehab and hoping to lead a sober life, who finds new challenges when she moves in with her conservative brother, his wife and their children.

The Naturals (Crime Drama, NBC, 1983).
Producer: William Blinn, Larry Thor.
Cast: Stephen Parr, Michael Brandon.
Story: Two detectives with the Houston Police Department tackle crime with methods that are often just above what the law prescribes.

The Neighbors (Comedy, ABC, 1971).
Producer: Gene Reynolds. *Creator-Writer:* Jay Dyer.
Cast: Cindy Williams, Darrel Larsen.
Story: Romeo and Juliet-like project about the daughter of a conservative family who falls in love with the son of a liberal family.

The New Adventures of Tom and Huck (Comedy, Syndicated, 1955).
Producer: Revue Productions.
Cast: Bobby Clark (as Tom Sawyer), Donald MacDonald (as Huck Finn), Tina Thompson (as Becky Thatcher).
Story: Tom Sawyer, Huck Finn and Becky Thatcher, the characters created by Mark Twain in new adventures as children living along the Mississippi River during the 1800s.

Nicky (Comedy, CBS, 2013).
Producer: Channing Tatum, Andrew Reich.
Creator-Writer: Nick Zano, Ted Cohen.
Cast: Nick Zano.
Story: A 30-year-old man attempts to raise his 13-year-old sister following the death of their parents in a car accident.

Nicole Richie Untitled Project (Comedy, ABC, 2010).
Producer: Jamie Tarses. *Creator-Writer:* Daisy Gardner, Jeff Rake.
Cast: Nicole Richie.
Story: A professional woman's journey through life as she struggles to cope with the situations that surround her, feeling she is stuck in a rut while other members of her family move on.

Night People (Comedy, ABC, 1959).
Producer: Harry Ackerman.
Cast: Cyd Charisse, Tony Martin.
Story: Dancer Cyd Charisse and singer Tony Martin, married in real life, portray a comical version of themselves as they perform song and dance numbers in various nightclubs.

Night Watch (Reality, Syndication, 1955).
Producer: Jim Hadlock, Hal Roach, Jr.
Cast: Don Reed (as "The Police Recorder"), Det. Sgt. Ron Perkins (as Himself).
Story: An adaptation of the radio series wherein a radio sound crew rode with a police patrol car to record what happens as it makes its rounds (if the project had sold it would have used a camera crew and follow Squad Car 56).

No Dinner, No Desert (Comedy, ABC, 2000).
Cast: Hank Azaria.
Story: A view of family life in the 21st century as seen through the eyes of an irreverent diner cook.

No Place Like Home (Comedy, ABC, 1960).
Producer-Writer-Creator: Ed James.
Cast: Gordon MacRae, Sheila MacRae.
Story: The home and working lives of a TV producer and his wife.

Noble Quest (Drama, ABC, 1991).
Producer: David L. Wolper.
Cast: Keith Cooke (as Ty Nuygen).
Story: Ty Nuygen was born in Vietnam during the war. Twenty years later, Ty makes a pledge to his dying mother to find his American father. The project was to relate Ty's travels across the U.S. as he searches for the father he has never known.

Nobody Trusts Maz (Comedy, CBS, 2012).
Producer: Eric Tannenbaum, Kim Tannenbaum.
Creator-Writer: Phoef Sutton.
Cast: Maz Jobrani (as Maz).
Story: An Irish-American girl (Jenny) and a Persian-American man (Maz) marry, set up housekeeping in the suburbs then find their lives complicated by her intrusive father (who is distrustful of Maz) and his equally concerned mother.

Northern Exposure (Drama, CBS, 2018).
Producer: Rob Morrow, Ben Silverman. *Creator-Writer:* Joshua Brand.
Cast: Rob Morrow (as Joel Fleischman).
Story: A revival of the CBS series of the same title (about a New York doctor who moves to Cicely, Alaska, to take up practice) that re-introduces the doctor, Joel Fleischman as he returns to Cicely, initially to attend the funeral of an old friend, but elects to remain and once again re-establish his medical practice.

Nosey and the Kid (Comedy, CBS, 1979).
Producer: Quinn Martin, Al Rogers.
Cast: Cindy Baines (as Cindy), John Byner (as Nosey's voice).
Story: A pretty but shy young girl (Cindy) finds companionship from a talking dolphin (Nosey) she finds and befriends at the beach.

Occult (Anthology, Syndication, 1956).
Producer: Harry Alan Towers, Paul Douglas, Peter Rathvon.
Cast: Paul Douglas (as Host).
Story: Dramas based on the files of the London Physical Research Society which deals with aspects of the occult including mediums and clairvoyance.

Occult Crimes Task Force (Drama, A&E, 2012).
Producer: Rosario Dawson, Gale Anne Hurd.
Cast: Rosario Dawson (as Sophia Ortiz).
Story: Sophia Ortiz, head of the N.Y.P.D.'s Occult Crimes Task Force, battles the supernatural elements that plague the city.

Occupation Female (Comedy, CBS, 1961).
Producer-Writer: Luther Davis.
Cast: Polly Bergen.
Story: The mishaps that befall a female newspaper reporter during the early 1930s as she tries to beat her male colleagues to the headline-making stories.

Odd Jobs (Drama, NBC, 2011).
Producer: J.J. Abrams, Bryan Burk. *Creator-Writer:* Josh Applebaum, Andre Nemec.
Cast: Terry O'Quinn, Michael Emerson.

Story: Two former agents with Special Operations begin new careers as the operators of Odd Jobs, a company that tackles dangerous assignments.

Odd Man In (Comedy, ABC, 2005).
Producer: Tom Arnold, Brad Gray. *Creator-Writer:* Joshua Sternin, Peter Traugott.
Cast: Tom Arnold.
Story: An unmarried man, living next door to a single mother with children, finds his life changing when he becomes a surrogate-like father caring for her children while she works.

Oh, Johnny! (Comedy, CBS, 1961).
Producer: Harry Ackerman.
Cast: Johnny Carson (as Johnny).
Story: Follows a manager (Johnny) as he and his all-girl orchestra begin a European tour. The idea was later seen (1963) as the series *Harry's Girl's* with Larry Blyden as the manager of an all-girl singing and dancing group.

Old City Blues (Drama, Hulu, 2019).
Producer: Kerry Washington, Chris Black.
Creator-Writer: Allison Davis.
Cast: Kerry Washington.
Story: A look at life in the year 2048 in New Athens, once called Greece, and now controlled by the criminal elements of society, including smugglers, drug dealers and high tech mobsters.

On Ice (Comedy, CBS, 1979).
Producer: Eugenie Ross-Leming, Brad Bruckner.
Cast: Julie Cobb.
Story: A woman's efforts to run the Wild Walrus, a bar she inherited from her late father—despite its location in Alaska and a group of off-the-wall patrons.

One Eyed Jacks Are Wild (Drama, ABC, 1966).
Producer: Herbert Brodkin.
Cast: George Grizzard, Diana Dors.
Story: An American's experiences when he takes a most unusual job: replacing the Prince of a European Kingdom until such time as those seeking to assassinate him can be uncovered and brought to justice.

One Hit Wendy (Comedy, Fox, 2017).
Producer: Diane Warren, Julianne Hough. *Creator-Writer:* Lesley Wake Webster.
Cast: Julianne Hough (as Wendy).
Story: Wendy, a young singer who achieved only one hit song during her music career, begins a new quest to guide her talented niece (Jordan) on a path of musical stardom.

One Police Plaza (Crime Drama, ABC, 2010).
Producer: Mark Gordon, Deborah Spera. *Creator-Writer:* Linda Fairstein.
Cast: Angela Bassett.
Story: The activities that surround the first female commissioner of the N.Y.P.D.

Open All Year (Comedy, ABC, 1960).
Producer: Phil Silvers.
Cast: Alan King.
Story: Events in the life of a night club comedian who retires to a New Hampshire hotel to find a life of peace and quit.

Original Arabian Nights (Anthology, Syndication, 1958).
Producer: Lee Garmes. *Writer:* Michael Sayers.
Cast: John Derek (as Host).
Story: Stories based on tales of the Arabian Nights (a collection of Indian, Persian and Arabian folk tales that has its origins in Scheherazade, who told her husband, the sultan, a different story each night for 1,001 days; hence they are also

known as "The Thousand and One Nights"). Had the project sold it would have been the first India-American telefilm deal.

Other People's Business (Comedy, WB, 2003).
Producer: Danny DeVito.
Cast: Judy Greer, Timm Sharp, Cory Gums, Dave Annable.
Story: The experiences of four friends who enroll in college in anticipation of becoming private investigators.

Other People's Houses (Drama, Fox, 2020).
Producer: Sarah Michelle Geller, Neil Meron.
Creator-Writer: Mark Nicholson.
Cast: Sarah Michelle Geller.
Story: Larchmont Village in Los Angeles provides the setting for a look at a group of people as they navigate life through social media.

Our Town (Drama, Syndication, 1958).
Producer: Jerry Stagg. *Writer:* Joseph Schrank.
Cast: Burgess Meredith (as the Stage Manager).
Story: An adaptation of the Thornton Wilder play about life in the fictional town of Grover's Corners as told through the Stage Manager, who appears as various characters as well as the narrator.

Out in the Burbs (Comedy, Logo, 2012).
Producer: Carol Leifer, Pam Post, Troy Miller, Christopher Willey.
Cast: Carol Leifer.
Story: Carol and Patrice, a lesbian couple living in a suburban neighborhood, struggle to fit into a community that sees their marriage as strange.

Out of the Door (Comedy-Drama, CBS, 2020).
Producer: Jerry Bruckheimer, Jonathan Littman, Kristie Anne Reed. *Writer:* Evan Katz.
Story: An L.A.P.D. detective, looking forward to his retirement so he can enjoy life, finds his plans changing when he is told he will have to wait several years. To make sure he retires when he is supposed to, he begins a campaign to do everything possible to get fired; unfortunately for him, everything he does leads to him solving crimes and showing his worth.

Outpost (Western, ABC, 1956).
Producer: Pine-Thomas Productions.
Cast: Lex Baxter.
Story: Events in the lives of the men of the U.S. Cavalry during the 1860s.

Outrider (Western, Amazon, 2018).
Producer: Arnold Schwarzenegger, Mace Neufeld. *Creator-Writer:* Mark Montgomery, Trey Calloway.
Cast: Arnold Schwarzenegger.
Story: An honest deputy sheriff, teamed with a ruthless bounty hunter by a "notoriously brutal judge," patrol Oklahoma's Indian Territory of the 1880s to see that justice is properly served.

Pair of Aces (Drama, ABC, 2015).
Producer: Eva Longoria, Ben Spector, Dawn Ostroff.
Cast: Eva Longoria (as Maria Reyes).
Story: An ambitious mother (Maria Reyes) attempts to manipulate her sons, Chris and Alex Reyes, to further her own goals by grooming them for political office in Texas.

Pancho Villa (Drama, Syndication, 1959).
Producer: Harry Mandrell, Irving Levin, Maurice Duke.
Cast: Pedro Armendariz (as Pancho Villa), Harry Carey, Jr.
Story: Stories based on the real life of Pancho Villa, hailed as both a Mexican Revolutionary War hero (a general) and a cutthroat bandit.

Pandora (Drama, Amazon, 2015).
Producer: Charlize Theron, Laverne McKinnon.
Creator-Writer: Josh Pate, Jonas Pate.
Cast: Charlize Theron (as Pandora).
Story: A former C.I.A. agent (Pandora) teams with a group of rogue agents to stop an awakened sleeper cell from unleashing a great evil on the world.

Paradise (Drama, NBC, 1961).
Producer: Paul Monash.
Cast: Richard Chamberlain (as Mark Paradise).
Story: Following the death of his father, Mark Paradise, a student at Harvard University in Boston, leaves school to run Paradise, the family ranch in Hawaii.

The Paradise Kid (Western, NBC, 1960).
Producer: George Shupert.
Cast: Richard Chamberlain.
Story: A wandering cowboy's adventures as he helps people facing injustice on the Western Frontier of the 1860s.

Parker Kane (Crime Drama, Fox, 1990).
Producer: Joel Silver.
Cast: Jeff Fahey (as Parker Kane).
Story: A former cop with the Long Beach, California Police Department, battles injustice in a new capacity as a private detective.

Pastor Jazz (Drama, TNT, 2009).
Producer: Charles S. Dutton, Robin Green, Mitchell Burgess.
Cast: Charles S. Dutton (as Pastor Jazz).
Story: A minister, nicknamed Pastor Jazz for his love of music, seeks to help the people of his parish—from the wealthy to the most poor.

Patachou (Variety, Syndication, 1955).
Producer: Ray Ventura, Nat Hiken.
Cast: Henriette Ragon.
Story: Henriette Ragon, a French singer known as Patachou, performs and hosts a proposed program of entertainment acts to be filmed in Paris.

Patience (Drama, Fox, 1999).
Producer: Gavin Polone, Maya Forbes.
Cast: Mary McCormick (as Patience Moore).
Story: A 30-year-old therapist (Patience Moore) who is capable of resolving her patient's problems struggles to solve the problems she faces outside the office. In 2001 Fox produced a comedy pilot (unaired) based on the above story with Jennifer Esposito as Patience Moore. Robert Zemeckis was the producer.

Paul Pine (Crime Drama, ABC, 1967).
Producer: Quinn Martin.
Cast: David Janssen (as Paul Pine).
Story: The cases of Paul Pine, a tough private detective based in Chicago.

Paul Rodriguez Untitled Project (Comedy, WB, 2006).
Producer: Joe Roth, David Goetrich.
Cast: Paul Rodriquez.
Story: A father's attempts to readjust his life after he is reunited with his son after years of separation.

Paula Abdul Untitled Project (Reality, MTV, 2003).
Cast: Paula Abdul.
Story: Singer Paula Abdul, an ex-Lakers Girl Cheerleader, as the host and principal judge of a competition wherein college cheerleaders face various challenges seeking to become a top cheerleader.

Paula Marshall Untitled Project (Comedy, NBC, 2002).
Producer: Jill Franklin, Maria Pennette.
Cast: Paula Marshall.
Story: A Caucasian woman and an African-American woman attempt to share an apartment but also live with each other's quirks.

The Peggy Lee Show (Comedy, NBC, 1960).
Producer: Harry Ackerman.
Cast: Peggy Lee.
Story: Singer Peggy Lee as a kind-hearted music teacher who often goes beyond the call of the classroom to help her students.

Peggy Lee Untitled Project (Drama, Syndication, 1954).
Producer: Rod Amateau.
Cast: Peggy Lee.
Story: A drama with songs that was to feature singer Peggy Lee as a nightclub owner in Palm Springs. The idea was again proposed in 1958 with Gene Corman as the producer.

Penn and Teller (Comedy, ABC, 2009).
Producer: Penn & Teller, Peter Golden. *Creator-Writer:* Leonard Dick.
Cast: Penn & Teller.
Story: Stage magicians Penn and Teller as performers at night and detectives by day who use their wizardry to solve crimes.

Penny Dreadful (Anthology, Syndication, 1959).
Producer: Harry Redmond. *Writer:* George Van Marter.
Cast: Dan O'Herlihy (as the Host).
Story: Dramas based on 19th century English literature dubbed "Penny Dreadful" (inexpensive crime magazines that featured stories about detectives, criminals or supernatural entities).

Pepe La Moko (Adventure, Syndication, 1955).
Producer: Lou Morheim.
Cast: Anthony Quinn (as Pepe La Moko).
Story: A refugee, assuming the identity of a dead thief, becomes a symbol for justice when he fights for the rights of others.

Personal and Confidential (Anthology, Syndication, 1988).
Producer: Donald Kushner, Peter Locke.
Cast: Cyndy Garvey (as Host).
Story: Dramatizations based on advice column letters written by people seeking help with their problems.

Personal Service (Comedy, CBS, 1957).
Producer: Zsa Zsa Gabor (under her company, World Television Services).
Cast: Zsa Zsa Gabor (credited as "Ssa Ssa Gabor").
Story: A gorgeous Hungarian woman, the head of a travel agency in Europe, seeks to help tourists in trouble. Had the idea sold it would have been filmed in Paris.

Peter V (Comedy, CBS, 1959).
Producer: Lasslo Vadnay.
Cast: Don DeFore.
Story: An abdicated king seeks to reinvent himself as a salesman to survive.

The Pet Set (Comedy, NBC, 1966).
Producer: Harry Ackerman.
Cast: Barbara Rush, Ann Jillian.
Story: A veterinarian's attempts to mix family responsibilities with work when she begins a practice from her home.

The Phantom Knight (Adventure, Syndication, 1954).
Producer: James V. Kern. *Writer:* Frederick

Hazlitt Brennan.
Cast: Forrest Tucker (as The Phantom Knight).
Story: The project, to be filmed in England and in color, tells of a mysterious knight of King Arthur's Roundtable who secretly battles injustice as The Phantom Knight.

Pistol Point (Drama, Syndication, 1957).
Producer: Official Films.
Cast: Louis Hayward (as Highwayman).
Story: Seventeenth century England provides the backdrop for a look at a Highwayman, a mysterious thief who robs from the rich (and here to give to the needy).

Point of View (Variety, ABC, 1961).
Producer: Michael Ross, Samuel Lax.
Cast: Nipsey Russell (as the Host).
Story: A late night proposal that was to feature guest stars, jazz music and interviews with people from all walks of life.

Popular Science (Anthology, Syndication, 1951).
Producer: Jerry Fairbanks.
Cast: Dr. Frank Baxter (as Host).
Story: Dramatizations based on articles appearing in *Popular Science* magazine.

Port Love (Comedy, ABC, 2011).
Producer: Kelly Ripa. Aaron Kaplan, Mark Consuelos.
Cast: Kelly Ripa, Mark Consuelos.
Story: A behind-the-scenes look at the cast and crew of *Port Love*, a TV program where there is more going on behind the cameras than in front of them.

Portland Mason Untitled Project (Anthology, Syndication, 1954).
Producer: James Mason, Pamela Mason.
Cast: Portland Mason.
Story: Biblical or historical events as seen through the eyes of six-year-old Portland Mason (daughter of actors James and Pamela Mason).

Poseurs (Comedy, CW, 2011).
Producer: Alan David, Sara Rue. *Creator-Writer-Producer:* Sara Rue.
Cast: Sara Rue.
Story: Two girlfriends, finding the perfect apartment, create a web of deception when they pretend to be a lesbian couple then actually wed to stay in the married couples only residence.

The President of Love (Comedy, NBC, 1983).
Producer: Chris Thompson.
Cast: Van Johnson, Robert Pierce.
Story: An eccentric billionaire and his assistant help deserving people solve their romantic problems through an unusual gift—a million dollars.

Pretty (Comedy, CBS, 2019).
Producer: Kaley Cuoco, Danielle Stokdyk. *Creator-Writer:* Lindsey Kraft, Michelle Nader.
Cast: Lindsey Kraft, Santina Muha.
Story: A young woman, feeling she has the passion and talent to become the country's next Oprah Winfrey, leaves her home in New Jersey and travels to California where her mishaps as she attempts to become a talk show host are anything but successful.

The Princess and the Beggar (Drama, Syndication, 1955).
Producer: Conne-Stephens Productions.
Cast: Maria English (as Weeping Princess).
Story: The love between a young maiden, known as the Weeping Princess, and a poor beggar named Pabo Ondal.

The Private Eyeful (Crime Drama, Syndication, 1957).
Producer: Henry Kane, Eddie Buzzell. *Writer:* Eddie Buzzell.
Cast: Marilyn Maxwell (as Maria Trent), Ron Randall, Jolene Brand, Frederick Ford.
Story: An adaptation of the novel by Henry Kane about Maria Trent, "a sensational blonde with a shapely figure" who has a doctorate in abnormal psychology and, after inheriting money from her inventor father, resigns from her job at a public relations firm to establish her own detective agency, Maria Trent Enterprises (her nickname, "The Private Eyeful," comes from her prior job co-workers).

The Professor (Comedy, ABC, 1956).
Producer: Mark Stevens. *Writer:* Frank Gill, Jr.
Cast: Alan Young.
Story: The incidents that befall a married college professor at an all-girl college.

Promenade Home (Drama, Syndication, 1958).
Producer: Sam Katzman.
Cast: Helen Traubel.
Story: Incidents in the lives of the people who book rooms at Promenade Home, a residence run by woman with a mysterious past.

The Protectors (Anthology, Syndication, 1960).
Producer: William D. Coates. *Writer:* Calvin J. McKinney.
Cast: George Raft (as Host).
Story: Stories based on the files of various police departments across the U.S.

Proud Earth (Drama, CBS, 1960).
Producer: William Sackheim. *Writer:* Sam Rolfe.
Cast: John Larch, Vivi Janiss.
Story: A family's struggles as they leave their home in the East to seek what they believe will be a better life in the west of the 1880s.

Psychic Investigator (Anthology, Syndication, 1955).
Cast: Truman Bradley (as Host).
Story: True stories based on people who have experienced ghostly happenings with psychic investigators (played by guest stars) stepping in to investigate the occurrence.

Punching the Clown (Comedy, Showtime, 2012).
Producer: Sarah Silverman, Chuck Martin.
Cast: Henry Phillips.
Story: A singer-songwriter attempts to revitalize his career after dumb luck brought him overnight fame that lasted only as quickly as he achieved it.

Quality of Life (Comedy, CBS, 2017).
Producer: Jamie Lee Curtis, Eric Tannenbaum, Kim Tannenbaum. *Creator-Writer:* Janis Hirsch.
Cast: Jamie Lee Curtis.
Story: A look at a family, headed by a somewhat offbeat mother, and their perspectives on life having grown up as part of a family-run funeral parlor.

Queen of Everything (Cartoon, Fox, 2014).
Producer: Zooey Deschanel, Sophia Rossi. *Creator-Writer:* Ali Waller.
Voice Cast: Zooey Deschanel (as the Queen).
Story: An evil queen, living in a modern fairytale land, struggles to run her "Queendom" despite the fact that she is hated by everyone and has no skill as how to be a ruler.

The Quiet Man (Western, Syndication, 1959).
Producer: Frank Gruber.
Cast: Jack Lord.
Story: A recent Harvard Law School graduate,

returning to his home town to set up a practice, abandons his dream when he begins a quest to find the killer of his fiancée and father.

Rabbit Hole (Comedy, IFC, 2011).
Producer: Chelsea Handler, Brad Wollack, Tom Brunelle. *Creator-Writer:* Kerri Kenney-Silver, Jamie Denbo.
Cast: Kerri Kenney-Silver (as Dame Delilah).
Story: While the proposal sounds a bit risqué, it is actually a humorous look at the activities at a Nevada brothel overseen by the captivating Dame Delilah.

Rachet (Comedy, CBS, 2018).
Producer: Michael Rotenberg, Jon Liebman. *Creator-Writer:* Natasha Leggero, Moran Murphy.
Cast: Natasha Leggero (as Jessica Rachet).
Story: Jessica Rachet is a woman who had it all—beauty, riches and a fiancé who catered to her every whim. Her life changes when her fiancé dies suddenly, she is left penniless and she must now fend for herself to survive.

The Rackets (Drama, ABC, 2003).
Producer: Sydney Pollack, Scott Vila. *Creator-Writer:* James Manos, Jr.
Cast: William Baldwin.
Story: An adaptation of the book by Thomas Kelly about the inner workings of the New York City political system.

Rafferty's Angels (Drama, CBS, 1958).
Producer: Herb Meadow, Frank Cooper.
Cast: Jim Davis, Forrest Tucker.
Story: Incidents in the lives of the men of a unit of the U.S. Cavalry during the 1860s.

Raised by Wolves (Comedy, CBS, 2020).
Producer: Julie Bowen. *Writer:* Max Mutcnick, David Kohan.
Cast: Julie Bowen (as Frankie Wolfe).
Story: The uneasy relationship between two sisters, Frankie and Tommie Wolfe, and how they bond over caring for Quincy, an inner-city child in need of foster parents.

The Ralph Show (Comedy, Fox, 2004).
Producer: Todd Holland, Ralph Macchio. *Creator-Writer:* Matt Ember.
Cast: Ralph Macchio.
Story: 1970s and 1980s actor Ralph Macchio in a fictionalized version of himself—a 40-year-old family man living on Long Island in New York and the star of a fledging television sitcom.

Rapture (Comedy, Showtime, 2009).
Producer: Lisa Kudrow, Paul Miller, Kimber Rickabaugh. *Creator-Writer:* Craig Chester.
Cast: Lisa Kudrow.
Story: The world of a 9-year-old boy whose life is surrounded by confusion—from dealing with his sexual orientation to living with a mother who believes she has visions of God and a father who is obsessed with rock and roll music.

Rated "P" for Parenthood (Comedy, ABC Family, 2014).
Producer: Kelly Ripa, Mark Consuelos. *Creator-Writer:* Jamie Denbo
Cast: Kelly Ripa.
Story: A look at modern-day parenting as seen through a group of parents who are raising children but still feel like they are kids themselves.

The Raven (Drama, NBC, 1959).
Producer: Screen Gems.
Cast: Cliff Robertson (as Dan Raven).
Story: Billed as "A police lieutenant's probe of crime in the entertainment district of a major city." In 1960 the series *Dan Raven* appeared with Skip Homeier as Dan Raven, a police

lieutenant working the Sunset Strip section of Hollywood.

Rawhide Riley (Anthology, NBC, 1959).
Cast: Richard Arlen (as Rawhide Riley).
Story: Tales of the Old West as hosted and narrated by Rawhide Riley, an old timer who runs a barber shop.

Ray Romano Untitled Project (Comedy, HBO, 2006).
Producer: Ray Romano, Joel Surnow, Howard Gordon. *Creator-Writer:* Dennis Klein.
Cast: Ray Romano.
Story: A forty-year-old billionaire must decide what to do with his money after he learns he has only six months to live.

Real Deal (Drama, CBS, 2013).
Producer: Eva Longoria, Ben Spector. *Creator-Writer:* Craig O'Neill.
Cast: Eva Longoria.
Story: Two polar opposite women, one an overly ambitious FBI agent, the other an out-of-control undercover confidential informant, team to solve heinous crimes in Los Angeles.

The Real Fairy Godmother (Comedy, ABC, 2017).
Producer: Craig Zadan, Cathy Yuspa, Kristin Chenoweth. *Creator-Writer:* Alan Zachary.
Cast: Kristin Chenoweth.
Story: Following her discovery that she is a descendant of The Secret Order of Fairy Godmothers, a housewife must now use her magical abilities to people in trouble.

Reese Witherspoon Untitled Project (Drama, ABC, 2015).
Producer: Reese Witherspoon, Rick Porras.
Creator-Writer: Rob Long.
Cast: Reese Witherspoon.
Story: A billionaire acquitted of a false murder charge teams with the female detective who gathered the evidence against him to help people unjustly convicted of crimes.

Rehab (Drama, HBO, 2005).
Producer: Courteney Cox, David Arquette.
Writer: Nick Cassavetes.
Cast: Courteney Cox (as Taylor Kennedy).
Story: Portrait of Taylor Kennedy, a glamorous but alcoholic actress struggling to overcome her addiction.

Relief (Drama, NBC, 2017).
Producer-Creator: Maria Bello, Jessica Goldberg.
Cast: Maria Bello.
Story: A successful female doctor working in a Los Angeles hospital relinquishes her position to join her estranged brother, a doctor on a remote island when an earthquake ravages the country.

The Replacement (Reality, TBS, 2005).
Producer: Ben Silverman.
Cast: Tom Arnold (as Host).
Story: The host steps into the shoes of ordinary people for a day to experience how the other half lives and works.

The Republic of Sarah (Drama, CW, 2020).
Producer: Marc Webb, Mark Martin, Jeff Grosvenor, Leo Pearlman. *Writer:* Jeffrey Paul King.
Cast: Stella Baker (as Sarah Cooper), Landry Bender, Luke Mitchell, Izabella Alvarez, Hope Lauren.
Story: As a greedy mining company begins to take over her town and she sees it as her town's eventual destruction, high school student Sarah Cooper uncovers an obscure cartographical loophole that allows her to declare her town an

independent. Her problem is depicted: with her friends she must to establish her country from scratch.

Rescue 3 (Drama, Syndication, 2012).
Producer-Creator: Gregory J. Bonan, Tai Collins.
Cast: Dolph Lundgren (as John Matthews).
Story: The work of John Matthews, head of Southern California's Elite Multi Task Force, as firefighters, the coast guard and lifeguards work together to ensure the safety of the public.

Rest (Drama, NBC, 2011).
Producer: Craig Zadan, Marc Silvestri. *Creator-Writer:* Philip Levins.
Cast: Milo Ventimiglia (as John Bennett).
Story: John Bennett appears to be a typical white collar worker. He lives in Manhattan and has prestige, but he is also into narcotics. One drug in particular, however, has an unusual side effect: it prevents John from requiring sleep. The proposal follows John as he seeks a cure for what has now become a life where sleep doesn't matter.

The Revengers (Drama, CW, 2013).
Producer: Rashida Jones, Will McCormack.
Cast: Rashida Jones.
Story: After two women discover they have been dating the same man, they extract their revenge on him then form The Revengers, a payback business wherein they get even with strangers for their clients.

Riddle and Rhyme (Game, ABC, 1954).
Producer: Herbert Rudley.
Cast: Ogden Nash (as Host), Abner Dean, Ilka Chase, Faye Emerson, Howard Dietz (as the Panel).
Story: A panel situated in a living room setting ask specific question of the host who answers in rhyme.

Riders of the Pony Express (Western, Syndication, 1956).
Producer: Dave Savage.
Cast: Tony Arden, Judy Tyler.
Story: Tales of riders for the 1860 to 1861 Pony Express mail service focusing in particular on a young rider and his wife.

The Right Mistake (Drama, HBO, 2013).
Producer: Laurence Fishburne, Diane Houstin, Helen Sugland. *Creator-Writer:* Walter Mosley.
Cast: Laurence Fishburne (as Socrates Fortlow).
Story: After serving 27 years in prison, Socrates Fortlow, the literary character created by Walter Mosely, begins a quest to find redemption despite the fact that his inner demons compel him to return to his criminal past.

The Ripples (Comedy, NBC, 2003).
Producer: Peter Mehlman, Jon Hayman.
Cast: Adam Arkin, Diane Farr (as the Parents).
Story: Life with a very old couple—married for 4,000 years (but look to be in their 40s) and their 3,985-year-old son, who appears to be just 15.

Rising (Drama, Freeform, 2016).
Producer: Aaron Kaplan, Selena Gomez, Mandy Teefey.
Cast: Selena Gomez.
Story: The incidents that befall a group of people in a low income housing development as they struggle to better their lives.

River Dogs (Comedy, Comedy Central, 2013).
Producer: Will Ferrell, Adam McKay. *Creator-Writer:* Andrea Savage.
Cast: Andrea Savage.
Story: A group of young people, experts at playing poker, seek to broaden their abilities and prove to the world they are also great athletes (but their poker prowess doesn't seem to apply to athletics).

Road Warriors (Comedy, Syndication, 1992).
Producer: Judd Apatow, Pete Segal.
Cast: Colin Quinn (as Colin), Mario Joyner (as Mario).
Story: Believing they need to broaden their act, standup comedians Colin and Mario take to the road to seek fresh material.

Rob Lowe Untitled 2013 Project (Comedy, NBC, 2013).
Producer: Rob Lowe, Marc Gurvitz. *Creator-Writer:* Alex Gregory, Peter Huyck.
Cast: Rob Lowe.
Story: A negligent father decides to become the devoted parent he never was even though his children are now teenagers.

Robbers (Drama, TNT, 2015).
Producer: Carl Beverly, Sarah Timberman. *Creator-Writer:* Michael Dinner.
Cast: Tim McGraw.
Story: Two friends, wanted for a string of robberies in Texas, flee the law and now as fugitives seek to remain free despite the persistent efforts of a police detective to bring them to justice.

Robert Duvall Untitled Project (Western, AMC, 2008).
Producer: Robert Duvall, Robert Carliner, Richard Donner. *Creator-Writer:* Erik Jendressen.
Cast: Robert Duvall.
Story: A new look at a short-lived part of American history: The Pony Express, the mail service that operated in dangerous Indian and outlaw territory from 1860 to 1861.

Rocky Times (Comedy, NBC, 2000).
Cast: Breckin Meyer, John Corbett.
Story: The problems that befall a young man when he leaves Chicago to follow his true love to Colorado.

Roma Downey Untitled Project (Drama, CBS, 2009).
Producer: Mark Burnett, Roma Downey. *Creator-Writer:* Craig Wright.
Cast: Roma Downey (as Ghost).
Story: Shortly after recovering from a near-fatal car crash, a lawyer finds his life changing when the ghost of his ex-wife appears to provide the guidance he needs to successfully defend clients.

Roommates (Comedy, NBC, 1956).
Producer: Ralph Freed.
Cast: Maureen O'Sullivan (Headmistress), Sue George (June), Diane DuBois (Monique).
Story: Life in a co-educational college as seen through an American girl (June) and her roommate, a French foreign exchange student (Monique).

Rosario Beach (Drama, CBS, 2017).
Producer: Benny Medina, Jennifer Lopez, Matt Lopez, Elaine Goldsmith-Thomas. *Creator-Writer:* Nick Weiss.
Cast: Jennifer Lopez.
Story: Two attorneys, one a loose cannon female, the other a tightly wound male, team to establish a practice in San Diego to take on cases that occur along the U.S.-Mexican border.

The Ruling Class (Comedy, Fox, 2001).
Producer: Ron Howard, Brian Grazer, Tony Krantz. *Creator-Writer:* Bill Oakley, Josh Weinstein.
Cast: Simon Helberg.
Story: The situations that befall a group of teenagers, friends since they were eight years old, as they tackle life in high school.

The Russians Are Coming (Comedy, NBC, 2015).
Producer: Mila Kunis, Cami Curtis, Susan Curtis, Lisa Sterbakov. *Creator-Writer:* Sam Wolfson.
Cast: Mila Kunis.
Story: A recently married husband, feeling that he now has the perfect life, finds anything but when his wife's Russian in-laws rent the apartment above theirs.

Safari (Anthology, CBS, 1959).
Producer: Four Star Television.
Cast: Stewart Granger (as Host).
Story: Dramatizations of both fictional and actual safaris in Africa and India.

St. George's Island (Drama, NBC, 2002).
Producer: Tommy Lynch.
Cast: Mel Harris, Ed Quinn.
Story: A family's adventures as they begin new lives in Africa.

Salomy Jane (Western, Syndication, 1957).
Producer: Lou Edelman.
Cast: Joi Lansing (as Salomy Jane), Edgar Buchannon (as Madison Clay).
Story: An adaptation of the comical western story by Brett Harte that follows a flirtatious young woman (Salomy Jane) who travels west from Kentucky with her father, Madison Clay, to begin a new life in the lawless Hangtown.

Sam Houston (Drama, ABC, 1955).
Producer: Lou Edelman.
Cast: Jack Lord (as Sam Houston).
Story: Dramas based on incidents in the life of Sam Houston, an American politician and soldier who served as the first and third president of the Republic of Texas.

Sammy Kaye Untitled Project (Variety, ABC, 1955).
Cast: Sammy Kaye (as Host).
Story: A clip proposal that was to feature filmed highlights from orchestra leader Sammy Kaye's prior TV series, *So You Want to Lead a Band*.

The Sanchez Way (Comedy, ABC, 2018).
Producer: Kelly Ripa, Mark Consuelos. *Creator-Writer:* Isaac Gonzalez.
Cast: Mark Consuelos.
Story: Events in the lives of a Mexican-American family as they struggle to maintain strict adherence to their heritage despite all the temptations that threaten to change their way of thinking.

Sands of the South Seas (Adventure, Syndication, 1955).
Producer: Jon Hall, George Bilson.
Cast: Jon Hall (as John Sands).
Story: An American adventurer's escapades in the South Seas are chronicled.

Sandy Savage—Bush Pilot (Adventure, Syndication, 1957).
Producer: Jack Bordley.
Cast: John Russell (as Sandy Savage).
Story: The adventures of a Canadian bush pilot for hire. The series was to be filmed on location in Canada had the project sold.

Sarah Chalke Untitled Project (Drama, ABC, 2019).
Producer: Bill Lawrence, Jeff Ingold. *Creator-Writer:* Emily Fox.
Cast: Sarah Chalke.
Story: Two sisters, each with a differing personality, struggle to work together when they take over the adoption agency previously run by their parents.

Savage Is the Name (Drama, CBS, 1959).
Producer: Aaron Spelling.
Cast: Pat O'Brien (as Jack Savage), Barry Sullivan (as Mike McCoy).
Story: The methods of operation employed by Jack Savage and Mike McCoy, detectives who work for a major airline.

Say Uncle (Comedy, NBC, 1977).
Producer: Don Kirshner.
Cast: Richard B. Shull (as Jack Wacker), Dennis Cooley (as Bill Wacker).
Story: A young singer (Billy) must not only contend with the pressure of show business but those presented to him by his Uncle Jack, his outspoken and flamboyant manager.

Scattergood Baines (Comedy, Syndication, 1954).
Producer: John W. Loveton, Bernard L. Schubert.
Cast: Will Rogers (as Scattergood Baines), Margaret Field, William Fawcett.
Story: A newspaper editor's mishaps in the small American town of Cold River. Based on the novel by Clarence Buddington Kelland where Scattergood was the owner of the local hardware store.

Scott Baio Untitled Project (Comedy, NBC, 2006).
Producer: Kelly Kulchak, Blake McCormack, Jace Richdale.
Cast: Scott Baio.
Story: After achieving success as the star of the TV series *Charles in Charge*, Scott Baio finds himself mostly lacking any acting assignments. Now, as a 40-year-old, Scott finds his life turned upside down when he becomes roommates with a guy half his age.

The Searchers (Drama, Syndication, 1959).
Producer-Writer: Bernard Girard.
Cast: Neville Brand.
Story: A government narcotics agent risks his life to stop the illegal flow of drugs.

Secret Files of the American Police (Crime Drama, Syndication, 1958).
Producer-Writer: Clarence Eurist.
Cast: Pedro Armandariz, Carlos Musquiz.
Story: Dramatizations based on the actual case files of the Mexico City Police Department.

Section 13 (Drama, CBS, 2013).
Producer: Tom Welling. *Creator-Writer:* Carla Kettner.
Cast: Tom Welling.
Story: A former CIA black ops agent's experiences when he joins a covert organization that tackles extremely dangerous assignments for the U.S. government.

See It Again Theater (Films, Syndication, 1953).
Producer: Crater-Oak Tree Tele-Pictures.
Cast: Allen Prescott (as Narrator).
Story: First time television airings of silent motion pictures but edited ("cut down versions" as the press material indicates) to fit into a 15 minute time slot. The initial presentation was to be western star William S. Hart in *The Wickedest Town in the West*.

Sela Ward Untitled Project (Comedy, ABC, 2006).
Producer: Sela Ward, Linda DeKoven. *Creator-Writer:* Donald Todd.
Cast: Sela Ward.
Story: Life in a small Southern town as seen through the eyes of four women who are best friends.

Selena Gomez Untitled Project (Drama, Lifetime, 2016).
Producer: Selena Gomez, Dana Brunett, Kevin Spacey, Mandy Teefey. *Creator-Writer:* Selena Gomez.
Cast: Selena Gomez.
Story: Actress Selena Gomez's real life experiences as she navigates a career in Hollywood (achieving her big break as the star of the Disney Channel series *The Wizards of Waverly Place*).

Sendera (Drama, ABC, 2011).
Producer: Eva Longoria, Kathryn Morris, Josh Gold, Alan Barnette. *Creator-Writer:* Sally Robinson.
Cast: Eva Longoria, Kathryn Morris.
Story: The rivalry between two wealthy families—one from Texas, the other from Mexico as they struggle for power.

Sensitive Skin (Comedy, HBO, 2008).
Producer: Kim Cattrall, Robin Green, Mitchell Burgess.
Cast: Kim Cattrall (as Davinia Jackson).
Story: An adaptation of the British series about an affluent couple (Al and Davinia Jackson) living in New York City and the mishaps that occur when Davinia, the head of an art gallery, realizes she has reached middle age and begins to question the choices she has made in life.

Settle the Score (Talk, Syndication, 2004).
Producer: Joan Rivers, Philip Gurin.
Cast: Melissa Rivers (as Host).
Story: Daily talk program that combines celebrity interviews with current issues discussions.

Seven Cannery Row (Drama, ABC, 1961).
Producer: Sam Gallu.
Cast: Robert Knapp (as Mitch Carstairs).
Story: Cannery Row, a depressed section of Monterey, California, known for its mostly abandoned cannery plants, is home to Mitch Carstairs (living at Number 7 Cannery Row), a troubleshooter who risks his life to protect the area from criminals.

Shakespeare Loves Rembrandt (Comedy, Syndication, 1974).
Producer: Chris Hayward.
Cast: Bert Convy (as Writer), Jo Ann Pflug (as Painter).
Story: When they feel they are meant for something better, a writer and a painter combine their talents to begin a greeting card company. The proposal was to relate their mishaps as they struggle to make their business a success.

Sherri Shepherd Untitled Project (Comedy, TV Land, 2012).
Producer: Nina Wass, Sherri Shepherd. *Creator-Writer:* Christine Zander.
Cast: Sherri Shepherd.
Story: Two high school friends find misadventure when they reunite years after graduating to open a weight-loss center together.

Sherwood (Drama, Syfy, 2011).
Producer: Amanda Tapping, Martin Wood. *Creator-Writer:* Damian Kindler.
Cast: Amanda Tapping.
Story: Greatly updated version of the Robin Hood legend that is set in the 23rd century and follows a man of wealth who teams with a misfit space ship crew (of the *Sherwood*) to right wrongs.

Ship's Doctor (Drama, Syndication, 1958).
Producer: George Stern. *Writer:* Herb Meadow, Curt Siodmak.
Cast: Bruce Bennett (as Doctor).
Story: Incidents in the lives of passengers aboard

a cruise ship. The idea was made into a pilot (unaired) in 1961 with Victor Jury as the doctor.

Side By Side (Comedy, CBS, 1978).
Producer: Don Nicoll, Bernie West, Michael Ross.
Cast: Steve Anderson (as Jeff), Ginger Flick (as Kim), Malcom McCalman and Barbara Perry (as Parents).
Story: Steve, a young department store manager traumatized by his parents' recent divorce, meets and falls in love with Kim, a publishing house editor. Talk of marriage enters their lives as they date but Steve, afraid to make a commitment, convinces Kim to move in with him. Kim's parents object to their daughter living with a man and their effort to make their relationship work was to be the focus of the series.

Sidekicks (Drama, Fox, 2017).
Producer: Eva Longoria, Ben Spector, Evan Katz.
Creator-Writer: Tracy McMillan.
Cast: Eva Longoria (as Shay Kendricks).
Story: Shay Kendricks, a homicide detective with the Detroit Police Department, finds her life changing when she is teamed with her father, a just released criminal informant, to solve crimes.

Silent Witness (Drama, NBC, 1999).
Cast: Regina Taylor, Paige Tuerco.
Story: A young African-American medical examiner's experiences as she goes beyond the confines of the coroner's office to solve cases.

The Silver Eagle (Adventure, Syndication, 1954).
Producer: Jewell Radio and TV Productions.
Cast: Buddy Baer (as Jim West).
Story: An adaptation of the 1951 ABC radio series about Jim West, a sergeant with the Royal Canadian Mounted Police who uses a bow with silver eagle feather arrows (thus nicknamed "The Silver Eagle") to uphold law and order.

Simon Said What? (Comedy, Nickelodeon, 1997).
Cast: Mila Kunis.
Story: A pretty 14-year-old girl's adventures as she hacks into government files to use the information she gathers to help people in trouble.

Sinbad (Adventure, Syndication, 1960).
Producer: Sidney Cole.
Cast: Steve Reeves (as Sinbad).
Story: A live-action proposal that was to follow Sinbad, the fictional sailor, as he defends the helpless. See also *Sinbad the Sailor* below.

Sinbad the Sailor (Children, Syndication, 1957).
Producer-Creator-Writer: Bil and Cora Baird.
Puppets-Voices: Bil and Cora Baird.
Story: Puppets were to be used to tell tales of the legendary fictional sailor, Sinbad, as he roams the Middle East during the 8th and 9th centuries. See also *Sinbad* above.

Single at 40 (Comedy, Fox, 2011).
Producer: Patton Oswalt, Scott Armstrong.
Creator-Writer: Scott Ackerman.
Cast: Patton Oswalt.
Story: After his marriage of 20 years ends, a man finds himself facing something he is not prepared to tackle—single and forced to re-enter the dating scene.

Sister Veronica (Drama, Syndication, 1954).
Cast: Irene Dunne (as Sister Veronica).
Story: A nun's efforts to help the people of her poor parish.

610 Park Avenue (Crime Drama, CBS, 1960).
Producer: Arthur Lewis, Herbert Brodkin.

Writer: Ernest Kinoy.
Cast: Chester Morris, Robert Sterling.
Story: An older private detective set in his ways, teams with a younger, progressive investigator to solve crimes.

Snoop Dogg Untitled Project (Cartoon, Comedy Central, 2008).
Producer: Snoop Dogg, Tom Lynch.
Voice Cast: Snoop Dogg.
Story: Rap singer Snoop Dogg as a 15-year-old growing up in the 1980s and coping with the pressures of friends, family and life in the Hood.

Social Creatures (Drama, ABC Family, 2015).
Producer: America Ferrera, Teri Weinberg.
Creator-Writer: Ryan Piers Williams.
Cast: America Ferrera.
Story: Four friends, working and living in Manhattan, were to be followed as they navigate the complex world of dating in the digital age.

Solitaire (Drama, Syndication, 1961).
Producer-Writer: Robert Blees.
Cast: Ray Danton, John van Dreelen.
Story: A troubleshooter based in Europe uses his charm and wits to resolve cases for his clients. Had the project sold, it would have been filmed on location.

Solvang (Comedy, NBC, 2003).
Producer: D.L. Hughley, Donick Cary.
Cast: D.L. Hughley.
Story: The owner of a less-than-prestigious winery attempts to cope with the numerous problems he encounters while trying to keep his business afloat.

Sonja Henie Presents (Variety, NBC, 1958).
Producer: Alan Neuman.
Cast: Sonja Henie (as the Host).
Story: Olympic ice skating star Sonja Henie oversees a program that was to be filmed at famous European landmarks where she would perform as well as introduce name European performers.

The Spade Cooley Show (Variety, Syndication, 1955).
Cast: Spade Cooley (as Host).
Story: Music with big band leader Donnell Clyde Cooley, better known as the American swing musician Spade Cooley.

The Spencer Tapes (Comedy, NBC, 2014).
Producer: Will McCormack, Rashida Jones.
Creator-Writer: Andrew Dawson, Tim Inman.
Cast: Will McCormack (as George Spencer).
Story: After finding a box of his old homemade VHS tapes, college professor George Spencer sees that what he predicted for his future self has not happened. With those tapes as his guide, George sets out to redirect his life.

Spirited (Drama, ABC, 2017).
Producer: Elizabeth Banks, Max Handelman.
Creator-Writer: Heather Mitchell.
Cast: Laverne Cox (as Psychic).
Story: A young woman, working as a private detective and possessed with the ability to communicate with the dead, acquires the assist of spirits to help her solve crimes.

Stakeout (Drama, CBS, 1958).
Producer: Sam Katzman.
Cast: Eli Wallach.
Story: A look at police stakeouts and how they affect the officers that are assigned to oversee them.

Stanley Against the System (Comedy, CBS, 1968).
Producer: Bob Sweeney.
Cast: Larry Hovis (as Stanley), Penny Gatson (as His Wife).
Story: A married man's struggles to cope with the pressures of everyday life.

Stanley Tucci Untitled Project (Drama, HBO, 2010).
Producer: Stanley Tucci, Steve Buscemi, Wren Arthur.
Cast: Stanley Tucci.
Story: A once powerful politician struggles to rebuild his career after he is brought down by a scandal.

Stephen Colbert Untitled Project (Comedy, NBC, 2003).
Producer: Jon Stewart, Stephen Colbert.
Cast: Stephen Colbert.
Story: Humorous incidents in the life of comedian Stephen Colbert as a young man growing up in South Carolina.

Steubenville (Comedy, CBS, 1977).
Producer: John Rich.
Cast: Jack Grimes (as Widower), Rick Hurst (as Worker), Charles Murphy (as Slacker).
Story: An adaptation of the British series *Likely Lads*, transposed here to follow a widower who works in a Steubenville, Pennsylvania steel plant with his sons: a hard worker and a slacker.

Stitch 'n' Bitch (Comedy, HBO, 2010).
Producer-Creator-Writer: Alia Shawkat, Sean Tillman, Ellen Page.
Cast: Alia Shawkat, Ellen Page.
Story: Two local "hipster girls" decide to reinvent themselves by moving from Brooklyn, New York, to Los Angeles to become "artists of any kind."

Stone Walls Do Not (Comedy, CBS, 1965).
Producer: Harry Ackerman.
Cast: Don Rickles (as Don Wilcox).
Story: Follows Don Wilcox, a prisoner and ringleader who enjoys his confinement (manipulating the system) but fears his life of luxury may soon come to an end if he is released.

The Story Teller (Anthology, NBC, 1955).
Producer: Hal Roach, Jr.
Cast: John Nesbitt (as Narrator).
Story: A projected weekly program of stories ranging from fantasies to comedies.

Sullivan (Drama, ABC, 1984).
Producer: Robert Conrad.
Cast: Robert Conrad.
Story: The work of a former narcotics officer assigned to the juvenile division of the Fort Lauderdale, Florida, Police Department.

Sullivan Street (Drama, WB, 2000).
Cast: Rob Estes, Sam Trammell.
Story: A team of young lawyers, based in a firm on Sullivan Street in Manhattan, tackle various non high profile cases as they learn the ins and outs of the legal system.

Super City (Comedy, ABC, 2012).
Producer: Aaron Kaplan, Carthew Neal. *Creator-Writer:* Madeleine Sami.
Cast: Madeleine Sami.
Story: The situations that befall five different characters but all played by the same actress.

Surprise with Jenny McCarthy (Reality, NBC, 2013).
Producer: Arthur Smith, Paul Buccieri.
Cast: Jenny McCarthy (as Host).
Story: While billed as a reality series, it is actually more of a variety outing wherein actress Jenny McCarthy presents unique entertainment acts.

Suspense (Anthology, NBC, 2003).
Producer: Gavin Polone.
Cast: Dennis Hopper (as Host-Narrator).
Story: Dramatizations of people trapped in unusual situations and their desperate struggle to free themselves. While not stated it is most likely based on the 1940s radio series of the same title.

Sweet Potato Queens (Comedy, WB, 2001).
Producer: Pamela Eells. *Creator-Writer:* Jill Conner Brown.
Cast: Delta Burke, Ronnie Claire Edwards, Allison Munn.
Story: Events in the lives of three middle-aged women who refuse to accept the fact that they are growing older and continue living the fun life they had when younger.

Tails (Comedy, Fox, 2018).
Producer: Amy Poehler, Dave Becky. *Creator-Writer:* Riki Lindhome.
Cast: Riki Lindhome (as Erika).
Story: A middle-aged woman's escapades as she continues to live a carefree life with no plans on settling down or even changing the way she is.

The Talent Agency (Reality, Syndication, 2003).
Producer: Eva Longoria.
Cast: Eva Longoria, Alex Thomas (as Hosts).
Story: A weekly competition wherein singers, dancers, models and standup comedians vie for a chance at possible discovery.

Tales from the Hoff (Reality, E!, 2007).
Producer: Ryan Seacrest. *Creator:* Dan O'Keefe.
Cast: David Hasselhoff.
Story: A fictional slant on the life of actor David Hasselhoff (*Knight Rider, Baywatch*) as he attempts to rebuild his life after his divorce.

Tales of Alan Pinkerton (Drama, ABC, 1955).
Producer: Desilu Productions.
Cast: Alan Hale, Jr. (as Alan Pinkerton).
Story: Alan Pinkerton, son of the founder of the Pinkerton Detective Agency, goes to where the need be to investigate crimes.

Tales of Hellinger (Anthology, Syndication, 1957).
Producer: Charles Weintraub, Art Leonard.
Cast: Julie London (as Host).
Story: Adaptations of stories written by newspaper columnist Mark Hellinger.

Taming of the Shrew (Comedy, ABC, 2012).
Producer: Julia Roberts, Elaine Goldsmith-Thomas. *Creator-Writer:* Marc Hyman.
Cast: Julia Roberts.
Story: Variation on Shakespeare's *Taming of the Shrew* that focuses on a heartless, tyrannical company CEO whose staff constantly devises ways to change her.

Taygar of the Jungle (Comedy, CBS, 1967).
Producer: Dee Caruso. *Writer:* Gerald Gardner, Dee Caruso.
Cast: Mike Henry (as Taygar), George Kirby (as Native chief).
Story: A white jungle savior (Taygar) teams with a native chief to protect Africa from evil.

Teen Court (Reality, MTV, 1999).
Producer: Leeza Gibbons, Alan Sawyer.
Cast: Shawn Chapman (as the Judge).
Story: A variation on TV court programs that features actual small claims court cases but geared to a teenage audience.

The Tender Years (Comedy, NBC, 1959).
Producer: Harry Ackerman.
Cast: Michael Landon, Olive Sturgess.

Story: The struggles faced by a young lawyer and his wife as they begin their lives together as newlyweds.

Test Pilot (Drama, Syndication, 1955).
Producer: Roland Reed.
Cast: Preston Foster, K.T. Stevens, Pat Conway, Bobby Clark.
Story: Incidents in the lives of Air Force test pilots and their families.

Thicker Than Water (Comedy, Lifetime, 2004).
Producer-Writer: Carol Leifer.
Cast: Carol Leifer.
Story: A comedy writer's struggles to cope with her dysfunctional family: her two sex obsessed sisters, a dentist brother and a mother who works as a TV sex therapist.

The Thing About Family (Comedy, NBC, 2000).
Cast: Essence Atkins, David Ramsey.
Story: Humorous incidents in the lives of four generations of an African-American family.

The 33rd (Crime Drama, CBS, 1958).
Producer: Screen Gems. *Writer:* Jack Patrick.
Cast: Charles Bickford, Ruth Storey, Ken Lynch, Tammy Windsor.
Story: The cases of detectives with the 33rd precinct of an unidentified city.

This American Housewife (Drama, Lifetime, 2012).
Cast: Melanie Griffith (as the Housewife).
Story: The situations that befall a housewife who is prone to hearing voices and having conversations with herself.

This Is Happening (Comedy, NBC, 2016).
Producer: Will Ferrell, Claudia Lonow, Owen Burke, Adam McKay. *Creator-Writer:* Amy Rhodes.
Cast: Claudia Lonow.
Story: An uptight single woman in her mid-thirties attempts to adjust to a new lifestyle when she acquires a position with a website and begins "hanging out" with co-workers who are ten years her junior.

This Life (Drama, NBC, 1999).
Cast: Samantha Mathis, Sydney Tamila Poitier.
Story: The cases of a group of young San Francisco lawyers who just beginning their legal careers.

Thoroughbreds (Drama, ABC, 1959).
Cast: Linda Darnell (as Mother), Lynn Loring (as Daughter).
Story: Following the death of her husband, a mother attempts to raise their daughter while at the same time operating the family's legacy—a horse breeding ranch.

Those Landers Girls (Reality, E!, 2010).
Producer: Judy Landers.
Cast: Judy Landers, Lindsay Landers, Kristy Landers.
Story: Judy Landers, one of the sexiest women on TV during the 1980s (co-starring in the series as *B.J. and the Bear* and *Madame's Place*) has since retired from show business and is the mother of Lindsay and Kristy. The proposal was to profile Lindsay and Kristy as they seek careers as singers.

Those Were the Days (Drama, Syndication, 1953).
Producer: Bing Crosby Productions.
Cast: Charles Winninger (as Grandfather),

Carolyn Jones (as Louise), Beverly Washburn (as Natalie), Cheryl Holdridge (as Dorothy).
Story: Life in a small American town during the early 1920s as seen through the eyes of a grandfather, his widowed daughter (Louise) and her children (Natalie and Dorothy).

Those Who Can (Drama, NBC, 2000).
Cast: Lori Loughlin, Jim Breuer.
Story: Tale of an independent bachelor who becomes the mentor to a young orphan boy.

A Thousand and One Nights (Musical Drama, Syndication, 1954).
Producer: Jean-Paul Blondeau.
Cast: Yvonne DeCarlo (as Singer), Alfred Drake (as Club owner).
Story: Proposal about a nightclub owner and a singer who become involved in the troubles of their clients. Had the series sold it would have been filmed in French Morocco.

The Three Stooges (Comedy, Syndication, 1960).
Producer: Norman Maurer Productions, Comedy Three Productions.
Cast: Moe Howard, Joe DeRita, Larry Fine (mistakenly credited as "Barry Fine").
Story: A half-hour project that was to combine a Three Stooges cartoon with a live action segment featuring The Three Stooges in a skit that was to be tailored to children and less violent than their theatrical comedy shorts of the 1940s and 1950s (where Curly Howard then Shemp Howard appeared with Moe Howard and Larry Fine). While the overall project never sold, the cartoon segments were produced and syndicated in 1965 as *The New Three Stooges*.

Three Way Love (Comedy, CBS, 1978).
Producer: Gail Parent.
Cast: Anne Wedgeworth, Marcia Rodd, Alix Elias.
Story: It is not explained how but two women (called "femmes" here) marry the same man then struggle to live a life as normal as possible until they can resolve the situation.

Three Wishes (Comedy, ABC, 1960).
Producer: Don Sharpe, Warren Lewis. *Creator-Writer:* Douglas Fairbanks, Jr., Robert Riley Crutcher.
Cast: Rustavio Rajo (as Genie), Evelyn Rudie (as Girl).
Story: A young girl's adventures when she finds a magic lamp and releases a genie that can grant her any wish.

Tia Mowry Untitled Project (Comedy, Nickelodeon, 2013).
Producer: Tia Mowry, Aaron Kaplan. *Creator-Writer:* Dan Kopelman.
Cast: Tia Mowry.
Story: A mother's efforts to curtail the antics of her 12-year-old daughter who lives with her, a drill sergeant, on an army base. A similar pilot film titled *Little Leatherneck* aired on ABC in 1966.

Tijuana Beach (Cartoon, Comedy Central, 2016).
Producer: Eva Longoria. *Creator-Writer:* Al Madrigal, Greg Bratman, Tommy Dewey.
Voice Cast: Eva Longoria.
Story: A Mexican-American family's efforts to operate an inherited rundown resort in Mexico.

Timeless (Science Fiction, NBC, 2013).
Producer-Creator-Writer: Deborah Pratt.
Cast: Deborah Pratt (as Alexandra King).

Story: A woman's (Alexandra King) experiences when she acquires the ability to time travel and what happens when she is caught between the love of two men—one in her current time and one in a past time.

Times Square Varieties (Variety, NBC, 1958).
Producer: Carl Eastman, Al White, Jr., Ernest Chappelle.
Cast: Peter Donald (as Host).
Story: A mixed bag of performances from top name entertainers to Vaudeville-like novelty acts of the 1920s.

Tiny Beautiful Things (Drama, HBO, 2015).
Producer: Reese Witherspoon, Laura Dern, Jayme Lemons. *Creator-Writer:* Cheryl Strayed.
Cast: Reese Witherspoon.
Story: An adaptation of the book by Cheryl Strayed about a Portland, Oregon family who live by a code that telling the truth will never kill you.

Titans (Drama, NBC, 2000).
Producer: Aaron Spelling.
Cast: Yasmine Bleeth, Victoria Principal.
Story: Follows the lives of a group of young people living in Beverly Hills.

Today Will Be Different (Drama, HBO, 2017).
Producer: Julia Roberts, Megan Ellison, Sue Naegle. *Creator-Writer:* Maria Semple.
Cast: Julia Roberts (as Eleanor Flood).
Story: Eleanor Flood, a middle-age woman unhappy with who she is, attempts to make herself better but as she faces each day "life happens" and she finds herself in the same rut as before.

Todd Barth Can Help You (Comedy, IFC, 2016).
Producer: Bryan Cranston, Steven Weber.
Creator-Writer: Clay Graham.
Cast: Steven Weber (as Todd Barth).
Story: Todd Barth, a conservative insurance company adjuster, believes he has what it takes to become a new age, self-help guru and begins a quest to do just that—by attempting to help people with no experience to back him up.

Tokyo Dispatch (Drama, Syndication, 1958).
Producer: George P. Breakstone.
Cast: Peter Dynely.
Story: The experiences of an American wire service reporter stationed in Japan.

Toni Braxton Untitled Project (Comedy, WB, 2004).
Producer: Suzanne Daniels, Sheila Duckworth.
Creator-Writer: Saladin K. Patterson.
Cast: Toni Braxton.
Story: Singer Toni Braxton in a fictionalized version of herself as she attempts to balance her career and family.

The Tony Orlando Show (Talk, Syndication, 1987).
Producer: Ernie DiMassa, Alan Frank, Bill Walker.
Cast: Tony Orlando (as Host).
Story: Celebrity interviews and entertainment acts hosted by singer Tony Orlando.

Tony Take the Wheel (Comedy, CBS, 2016).
Producer: Eric Tannenbaum, Kim Tannenbaum, John Stephens. *Creator-Writer-Producer:* Cedric the Entertainer.
Cast: Cedric the Entertainer.
Story: The situations that befall two very different brothers struggling to preserve their family auto business when, after a dispute, one of them

hires his slacker teenage nephew to work at his custom car shop.

Tori Spelling Untitled Project (Comedy, NBC, 2003).
Producer: Gavin Polone Tori Spelling. *Creator-Writer:* Lawrence Broch.
Cast: Tori Spelling (as Victoria).
Story: Victoria, a woman eager to rise in position at her Manhattan publicist company, finds her chances continually hampered by the assignments she acquires: the company's low level, practically meaningless accounts.

Tortilla Soup (Comedy, CBS, 2002).
Producer: Andrew D. Weyman, Howard J. Morris.
Cast: Hector Elizondo.
Story: A retired Mexican-American chef's efforts to raise three beautiful, single daughters in Los Angeles.

Trader Horn (Drama, Syndication, 1956).
Producer: Michael Jarike.
Cast: Jon Hall (as Trader Horn).
Story: Aloysius Horn, called "Trader Horn," a white merchandise trader in darkest Africa, risks his life to help people in trouble.

The Trail Maker (Western, CBS, 1955).
Producer: Harry Ackerman, John Dunkel.
Cast: Fess Parker (as John C. Fremont).
Story: Dramas based on the adventures of John C. Fremont, an early trailblazer of the Old West.

The Trailsman (Western, Syndication, 1959).
Producer: Four Star Television.
Cast: Cameron Mitchell (as Steve Landry).
Story: U.S. Marshal Steve Landry's undercover assignments, posing as the outlaw Durango to bring criminals to justice in the Old West.

Trauma (Anthology, Syndication, 1952).
Producer: Bernard Girard.
Cast: John Newland (as Host-Narrator).
Story: Proposal for a series of weekly "psychological suspense dramas."

Trending (Drama, CW, 2011).
Producer: Katherine Heigl, Nancy Heigl. *Creator:* Cynthia Langston. *Writer:* Gren Wells.
Cast: Katherine Heigl.
Story: Serial-like proposal about a woman's efforts to stay ahead of her competitors by incorporating the newest trends into her business.

Triage (Drama, ABC, 2020).
Producer: Steven Marrs, Courtney Hazlett, Caitlin Foito. *Writer:* Erica Messer, David Cornue.
Story: Pioneering surgeon Dr. Finley Briar is followed over three decades at the same hospital as she deals with the advances in medicine in the time frames covered.

Turning Point (Drama, NBC, 1964).
Producer: Russell Rouse, Clarence Green.
Cast: Mike Connors (as Teacher), Charles Bickford (as Principal).
Story: Incidents in the lives of teachers and students at a Los Angeles high school.

Twenty-Five to Life (Drama, CBS, 2006).
Producer: Eriq La Salle, Terri Lubaroff.
Cast: Eriq La Salle (as Gabriel Santana).
Story: F.B.I. agents team with convicted felons released in a special program to solve crimes.

27 Joy Street (Comedy, CBS, 1977).
Producer: Alan King, Rupert Hertzog.
Cast: Jack Weston (as Landlord).
Story: An adaptation of the British series *Rising Damp* here to focus on the landlord of a

Cambridge, Massachusetts boarding house who involves himself in the problems of his tenants.

Two Black Cadillac's (Drama, Fox, 2014).
Producer: Jerry Bruckheimer, Jonathan Littman, Carrie Underwood.
Cast: Carrie Underwood.
Story: Serial-like proposal that is set in the South and explores a murderous love triangle (that was to be played out over a season).

Two Families (Comedy, CBS, 2001).
Producer: Chuck Lorre, Pamela Fryman.
Cast: Anne Meara, Brian Dennehy, Laurie Metcalf.
Story: Blended family proposal wherein two friends, a widow and widower, decide to reunite their extended families and live together in the same house.

Two Idiots (Comedy, IFC, 2013).
Producer: Megan Mullally. *Creator-Writer:* Tina Kapousis.
Cast: Megan Mullally.
Story: Two sisters, raised in a sheltered environment in a Beverly Hills hotel, face new challenges when they encounter the actual world for the first time as adults.

Two Young Men and a Girl in the Meat Grinder (Mystery, NBC, 1967).
Producer: Norman Felton.
Cast: Joanie Sommers, Bernie Kopell, Clarence Williams III.
Story: Three young attorneys (a girl and two men, one African-American) join forces to not only defend clients but solve the mysteries that appear as they investigate cases.

Two's Company (Comedy, ABC, 1964).
Producer: Peter Tewksbury.
Cast: Paul Lynde and Mary LaRoche (as Married Couple).
Story: A newlywed couple—a trial attorney and a fashion model struggle to survive the difficult first year of marriage. The idea was made into a pilot (unaired) the following year with Marlo Thomas and Ron Husmann as the couple.

Uncle Willie (Comedy, Syndication, 1960).
Producer: Jerry Layton. *Creator-Writer:* Robert J. Corrocran.
Cast: Charles Ruggles (as Uncle Willie).
Story: A 76-year-old ex-Vaudeville entertainer's attempts to adjust to a life he feels has passed him by.

Under Construction (Comedy, ABC, 2011).
Producer: Ashley Tisdale, Jessica Rhoades, David Holden.
Cast: Ashley Tisdale.
Story: A young woman who thought she was independent encounters just the opposite when she buys a home, discovers it needs numerous repairs and finds herself moving in with her father while renovations are made.

Underground U.S.A. (Drama, ABC, 1960).
Producer: Lew Landers. *Creator-Writer:* Alyce Canfield.
Cast: Colleen Gray (as Marion Miller).
Story: Incidents based on the real life exploits of Marion Miller, an undercover government agent and one of the most decorated women in the country at the time.

Underwater Counterspy (Drama, Syndication, 1961).
Cast: Brett Halsey.
Story: The cases of an ex-Navy frogman as he performs hazardous underwater assignments for the government. With two similar series on the

air—*Sea Hunt* and *Assignment Underwater*, the project was most likely passed over.

The Unknown (Anthology, Syndication, 1950).
Producer: Warren Wade.
Cast: Vincent Price (as Host).
Story: A proposed fifteen minute program of mystery and suspense dramas.

Unspeakable (Comedy, Hulu, 2018).
Producer: Chelsea Handler, Andrew Stearn.
Creator-Writer: Cynthia Mort.
Cast: Mary McCormack.
Story: Follows a 45-year-old woman as she deals with life in her own unique style—raw humor and radical honesty.

The U.S. Secret Service (Anthology, ABC, 1959).
Producer: Don Fairchild, Peter Martin.
Cast: Peter Graves (as Host).
Story: Dramas based on the actual files of the U.S. government's battle against crime at the turn of the 20th century.

Valentine (Comedy, HBO, 2011).
Producer: Kevin Bacon, Laurie MacDonald.
Creator-Writer: Bryan Sipe.
Cast: Kevin Bacon (as Johnny Valentine).
Story: The incidents that befall Johnny Valentine, a middle-aged, married three times man who is over burdened by back alimony and trying to make ends meet by working as a radio talk show host.

Valley Trash (Comedy, ABC, 2020).
Producer: Jennifer Carreras, Nahnatchka Khan.
Writer: Niki Schwartz-Wright.
Cast: Lulu Wilson (as Abby Harman), Jason Lee.
Story: The Harmans are a family "living in the deep Valley" whose lives change when their 14-year-old daughter, Abby, is accepted into a prestigious Los Angeles private school and she finds the students and their parents want nothing to do with her, her family or anyone else in their 818 area code.

Vanessa L. Williams Untitled Project (Comedy, NBC, 2003).
Producer: Vanessa L. Williams, Richard Schenkman, Adam Belanoff.
Cast: Vanessa L. Williams.
Story: A former Broadway star's experiences when she relinquishes her career to become a teacher in her small home town.

Vanishing Point (Drama, NBC, 2012).
Producer: Angela Bassett, Deborah Spera, Maria Grasso. *Creator-Writer:* Ben Ripley.
Cast: Angela Bassett.
Story: A brilliant female attorney, working for a prestigious New York law firm finds her life changing forever when she is diagnosed with a serious health issue and must find a way to balance her career and personal life and not let each interfere with the other.

Vega vs. Vega (Drama, NBC, 2013).
Producer: Ben Spector, Eva Longoria. *Creator-Writer:* Laurie Silverstein.
Cast: Eva Longoria.
Story: A young lawyer, successful in her own right, joins with her mother, a pioneering attorney to not only defend clients but bond after years of living a love-hate relationship.

The Venturers (Adventure, CBS, 1960).
Producer: Burt Leonard. *Writer:* Sterling Silliphant.
Cast: Jim Brown, Johnny Seven, Keir Dullea.
Story: Three war veterans pool their resources

and purchase a miniature submarine to start an underwater salvage business in the Mediterranean.

The Vidal Sisters Untitled Project (Comedy, ABC, 2006).
Producer: George Lopez, Ana Serrano. *Creator-Writer:* Laura Knightlinger.
Cast: Christina Vidal, Lisa Vidal, Tanya Vidal.
Story: Incidents in the lives of three sisters who are part of multi-generational, interracial family.

Viola Davis Untitled Project (Comedy, HBO, 2011).
Producer: Viola Davis, John Lesher. *Creator-Writer:* Margaret Nagle.
Cast: Viola Davis.
Story: Incidents in the life of a woman who has been appointed the headmaster of an exclusive prep school.

Visit (Variety, CBS, 1952).
Producer: Russell Crouse, Dorothy Stickney, Howard Lindsay.
Cast: Arlene Francis (as Host).
Story: Visits to celebrities in their homes "taking the interview off the couch and bringing it to life in the subject's home." Inspired the Edward R. Murrow series *Person to Person* (CBS, 1953-1961).

Vivian Lives (Comedy, CW, 2005).
Producer-Writer: Carol Leifer. *Creator-Writer:* Sherrie Krantz.
Cast: Carol Leifer (as Vivian).
Story: Although intended for the broadcast channel the CW, the project relates the adventures of a 26-year-old small town woman who acquires a job as a publicist for the cable channel VH-1.

Walker Dick and His All-American Boys (Children, Syndication, 1955).
Producer: Walker Dick, Jim Hetzer. *Writer:* Walker Dick.
Cast: Walker Dick (as Himself).
Story: Real life trampoline artist Walker Dick as the head of "The All-American Boys," a group of athletic children who were to experience a different adventure each week.

Wanted (Crime Drama, CBS, 2003).
Producer: Sarah Timberman, Carl Beverly.
Cast: Louise Lombard, Yancey Arian, Scott Glenn.
Story: The Fugitive Retrieval Division of the Los Angeles Police Department is depicted as its agents set out to recapture escaped felons.

The Warden (Drama, Syndication, 1963).
Producer: Walter Rapf.
Cast: Robert Webber (as Sam Morrison).
Story: Sam Morrison, a prison warden with liberal ideas, was to be profiled as he attempts to introduce modern techniques to the antiquated prison system.

Wayne Brady Untitled Project (Comedy, WB, 2005).
Producer: Bernie Brillstein, Brad Grey, Peter Traugott.
Cast: Wayne Brady.
Story: A personal injury lawyer's unusual acceptance of cases: investigating first to discover if his client is telling the truth or lying.

Wayneheads (Cartoon, Fox, 1991).
Producer: Damon Wayans, Eric Gold.
Voice Cast: Nell Carter, David Allen Grier, Kim Wayans.
Story: Clay animation proposal about the Wayneheads, a family with oversized heads.

We, the People (Comedy, NBC, 2016).
Producer: Ed Helms, Mike Falbo. *Creator-Writer:* Charlie Sanders.
Cast: Anjelah Johnson (as Mallory Ruiz).
Story: A Los Angeles case worker's experiences as she (Mallory Ruiz) helps aliens gain their citizenship papers.

We're in the Band (Comedy, Comedy Central, 2004).
Producer: Tom Hanks, Alanis Morisette, Johanna Stern, Jeff Rosenthal.
Cast: Alanis Morisette.
Story: Alanis Morisette is an improvisational actress who has just acquired her own road crew. The proposal (with improvisational actors playing all the roles) was to follow Alanis as she begins a road tour across America.

The Weaker Sex (Anthology, Syndication, 1957).
Producer: Kurt Keumann.
Cast: Gloria Talbott (as Host).
Story: Dramas based on famous women throughout history.

Western Editor (Western, Syndication, 1956).
Producer: Andrew White.
Cast: Tom Black.
Story: A newspaper editor based in a ruthless town of the Old West fights injustice through the power of the press.

Western Musketeers (Comedy, Syndication, 1956).
Producer: Albert C. Gannaway.
Cast: Carl Smith, Webb Pierce, Marty Robbins.
Story: A trio of "hillbilly singers" band together to not only entertain but bring criminals to justice.

What Are Friends For? (Comedy, CBS, 1978).
Producer: Ted Bergman.
Cast: Paul Sand, Anne Schedeen (as Married Couple), Ted Shackelford (as Friend).
Story: An adaptation of the British series *Cuckoo Waltz* about a penny pinching married couple who, to save money, share a home with their spend-thrift bachelor friend.

Whatever You Do, Don't Panic (Comedy, CBS, 1962).
Producer-Writer: Hubbell Robinson.
Cast: Dana Wynter (as Dana).
Story: Dana, a Manhattan-based fashion model possesses beauty, charm, sophistication and one other trait—panic. What happens when she is given an assignment and panics was to be the focal point of the series.

When the Ball Drops (Comedy, ABC, 2013).
Producer: Brad Garrett, Keghan Lyvers. *Creator-Writer-Producer:* Chuck Tatham.
Cast: Brad Garrett.
Story: A look at life through the eyes of a middle-aged man as he struggles with work, raising a family and realizing that he is growing older.

Where There's Life, There's Hope (Drama, Syndication, 1956).
Producer: Ken Rich, Jack Welch.
Cast: Hope Howard.
Story: Proposal for a 15 minute daily serial that was to explore the life of a woman as she struggles to overcome a devastating divorce and get her life back on tract.

White Dave (Comedy, ABC, 2017).
Producer: Gabrielle Union, LeBron James, Maverick Carter. *Creator-Writer:* David E. Talbert.
Cast: Gabrielle Union.

Story: Dave, an African-American teenager raised in an all-white suburban community, finds his life changing when his mother remarries, moves to an all-black neighborhood and he must adjust to a life he has never known before.

The Whole Shebang (Drama, Fox, 2013).
Producer: Jennifer Garner. *Creator-Writer:* Jason Micallef.
Cast: Jennifer Garner.
Story: A single mother's efforts to adjust to a new life when she inherits a decrepit male strip club and becomes a den mother to the somewhat dysfunctional staff.

Whoopi Goldberg Untitled Project (Drama, Bravo, 2016).
Producer: Whoopi Goldberg, Tom Leonardi, Stephanie Drackovitch.
Cast: Whoopi Goldberg (as Crime Boss).
Story: The tensions that arise when a Harlem (New York) crime boss learns her estranged son, whom she thought was dead, re-enters her life and she discovers he is running for mayor and poses a threat to her organization.

Wife Nanny (Comedy, Fox, 2013).
Producer: Jason Bateman, Spike Feresten, Peter Morgan. *Creator-Writer:* Spike Feresten.
Cast: Jason Bateman.
Story: The situations that develop when a sports executive hires his gay best friend to assist his wife as a nanny to their children.

Wildcatters (Drama, ABC, 1959).
Producer: John Wayne.
Cast: Claude Akins, Patrick Wayne.
Story: The adventures of two wildcatters as they solve problems related to oil fields.

Will Sasso Untitled Project (Comedy, ABC, 2005).
Producer: Gene Stein, Nina Wass. *Creator-Writer-Producer:* Chuck Tatham.
Cast: Will Sasso.
Story: A country club bartender's effort to raise his younger sister and brother.

William Baldwin Untitled Project (Drama, CBS, 2002).
Producer: Tom Fontana, Barry Levinson, Michael Dinner.
Cast: William Baldwin.
Story: A look at both sides of the law as seen through the eyes of two brothers: one involved in politics and the other involved with organized crime.

Willie (Comedy, ABC, 1959).
Producer-Writer: Paul Bogart.
Cast: Robert Morse (as Willie).
Story: The experiences of a Brooklyn shipping clerk who aspires to become a great actor.

The Willies (Comedy, NBC, 1965).
Producer: Frank Price.
Cast: George Gobel.
Story: After inheriting a haunted house and the friendly spirits that inhabit it, a man struggles to curtail their antics when they decide to go outdoors and haunt their neighbors.

Wing Mom (Comedy, NBC, 2014).
Producer-Creator-Writer: Kari Lizer.
Cast: Kari Lizer.
Story: A woman's efforts to re-enter the dating scene following her divorce and her children leaving the nest.

The Witch's Tale (Anthology, Syndication, 1961).
Producer: Mitch Hamilburg, Leon Fromkess.
Creator: Alonzo Deen Cole.
Cast: Jeanette Nolan (as Old Nancy).
Story: An adaptation of the radio series that features tales of suspense and horror as told by Old Nancy, a witch who has experienced what few others have.

Witchcraft (Anthology, Syndication, 1954).
Producer: Charles Norton.
Cast: Franchot Tone (as Host).
Story: Dramas based on recorded and mythical tales of witchcraft.

A Woman of Steel (Drama, ABC, 2011).
Producer: Eva Longoria, Tariq Jalil. *Creator-Writer:* Jorge Zamacona.
Cast: Eva Longoria.
Story: A wealthy Texas heiress, left penniless when she squanders her fortune, attempts to rebuild her life by moving back home and assuming duties on her family ranch.

A Woman's Diary (Drama, Syndication, 1955).
Producer: Richard Lewis.
Cast: Virginia Bruce (as Beth).
Story: Incidents in the lives of the guests at a metropolitan woman's hotel as observed by its owner, a woman named Beth.

A Woman's World (Talk, Syndication, 1970).
Producer: Marty Pasetta.
Cast: Betty White (as Host), Nancy Ames (as Segment Host).
Story: Information geared to housewives with Betty White's segments to be filmed at her Brentwood home; and remote segments, conducted by Nancy Ames, to be presented from various locations across the country.

Women's Studies (Comedy, HBO, 2009).
Producer-Creator: Ben Karlin, Theresa Rebeck, Julie White.
Cast: Julie White (as Julie).
Story: Julie is a young woman who, after the glory of her novel about feminism falters and she finds herself being just an ordinary girl again, decides to return to her job as a teacher. The adult-in-nature proposal was to follow Julie as she begins her job at a liberal arts college.

The Wonderful World of Little Julius (Comedy, Syndication, 1960).
Producer-Writer: Norman Jewison.
Cast: Eddie Hodges, Gregory Rostoff, Sam Levine.
Story: A peek into the imagination of a young boy where the adventures he experiences were to be shared by viewers.

A Word from Our Sponsor (Game, Syndication, 1955).
Producer: Harry S. Goodman.
Cast: Quentin Reynolds (as National Host).
Story: Questions based on feature films were to be asked by a national host then the program turned over to a host in each local market that carried the program. Here the host would place a phone call to a home viewer for the correct answer. After five minutes, the national host appeared again to give the correct answer and relate another question.

Work Wife (2018) (Comedy, ABC, 2018).
Producer: Kelly Ripa, Mark Consuelos, Nina Wass, Ryan Seacrest. *Creator-Writer-Producer:* Michael Ian Black.
Cast: Kelly Ripa, Mark Consuelos.
Story: A look at how married couples cope with two different life styles—at work where their

relationships with co-workers are explored and at home where they interact with each other.

Work Wife (2020) (Comedy, ABC, 2020).
Producer: Kelly Ripa, Ryan Seacrest, Mark Consuelos. *Writer:* David Windsor, Casey Johnson.
Cast: Angelique Cabral (as Dani) Tone Bell (as Scott), Christopher Gorham, Maile Flanagan, Kelly Ripa.
Story: Dani and Scott are a couple who share everything but in a platonic relationship. Tired of working for someone else, they decide to take their real estate experience and start their own company. Their effort to apply the fundamentals of their private lives to their work lives is depicted.

Working Class Hero (Cartoon, Fox, 2012).
Producer: Patton Oswalt. *Creator-Writer:* Brent Woods, Mike Barker, Jordan Blum.
Voice Cast: Patton Oswalt, Paget Brewster.
Story: It is a time when super heroes are paid minimum wage and work for the U.S. government. One such hero is followed, a family man with no spectacular abilities, dysfunctional co-workers and a misfit son with amazing powers and no idea how to use them for the greater good.

Working Girls (Comedy, CBS, 1961).
Producer: Desi Arnaz.
Cast: Tuesday Weld (as Angela), Joi Lansing (as Rosemary), Mamie Van Doren (as Julie).
Story: A reworking of both the feature film and TV series *How to Marry a Millionaire* that follows three working girls who share a Manhattan apartment and attempt to help each other find their perfect mate (but not wealthy here).

The World of Barbara (Comedy, Syndication, 1955).
Producer: Frank Wisbar.
Cast: Barbara Nichols (as Barbara), Cheryl Holdridge (as Janey), Beverly Washburn (as Lindsey).
Story: A young widow (Barbara) attempts to maintain the family ranch and raise two children (Janey and Lindsey) following her husband's passing.

The World of White (Drama, ABC, 1959).
Cast: Darryl Hickman, Dick York, Robert Keith.
Story: Proposed medical drama about incidents in the working lives of three young doctors.

Yoga Man (Comedy, Showtime, 2006).
Producer-Creator: David Duchovny, Scott Burns, Bart Feundlich.
Cast: David Duchovny.
Story: A look at the staff and clientele of a yoga studio where the owner is a lustful ladies' man.

You and Me and He (Comedy, CBS, 2010).
Producer-Writer-Creator: Carol Leifer.
Cast: Carol Leifer.
Story: A recently divorced woman, feeling she is more comfortable with women, begins a lesbian relationship then discovers she is pregnant by her ex-husband. She opts to stay with her girlfriend and together they will raise the baby—with a little help from her ex.

You Are Only Young Once (Comedy, CBS, 1954).
Producer: Frank Wisbar.
Cast: Joan Bennett (as Bettina), Melinda Markey (as Alison), Richard Carlson.
Story: Actress Joan Bennett appears with her 18-year-old daughter, Melinda in a project that explores the life of a mother and daughter.

You Won't Know I'm Here (Comedy, ABC, 2011).
Producer-Creator-Writer: Diane English.
Cast: Jim Belushi.
Story: The situations that arise when a working father gains primary custody of his teenage daughter following his divorce.

Young Man with a Badge (Crime Drama, NBC, 1960).
Producer: John Florea. *Writer:* Bob Hammer.
Cast: Peter Breck.
Story: Details a police detective's battle against juvenile delinquency.

Youngmania (Comedy, CBS, 1953).
Producer: King Productions. *Creator-Writer:* Henny Youngman.
Cast: Henny Youngman.
Story: 15 minute proposal that highlights the comedy of Henny Youngman.

You're Not Doing It Right (Comedy, ABC, 2012).
Producer: Ben Stiller, Ted Schachter. *Creator-Writer-Producer:* Michael Ian Black.
Cast: Michael Ian Black.
Story: A look at marriage and parenting as seen through a happily married couple who suddenly realize they are not actually living their lives but living their lives for their children.

Zapata, Texas (Crime Drama, TNT, 2009).
Producer-Creator-Writer: Kevin Bacon, Kyra Sedgwick.
Cast: Kyra Sedgwick.
Story: A small town Texas sheriff and her efforts to deal with the sudden increase in crime due to the rising drug smuggling operations from Mexico.

Zero Motivation (Drama, BBC America, 2016).
Producer: Amy Poehler, Natasha Lyonne, Brooke Posch.
Cast: Natasha Lyonne, Amy Poehler.
Story: Comedy blends with drama to follow a group of young women with the Israeli army who are assigned to clerical duties at a human resources office located in the middle of the Negev desert.

CHAPTER 2
Programs listing both actors as producers and producer only programs.

Abandon (Mystery, USA, 2014).
Producer: Darryl Frank, Justin Falvey. *Creator-Writer:* Blake Crouch.
Story: Two explorers investigate Abandon, a Colorado mining town whose entire population disappeared under mysterious circumstances. Modern-day sequences were to be interspersed with flashbacks to the 19th century.

Absolutely American (Drama, ABC, 2004).
Producer: James D. Parriott, Marc E. Platt. *Writer:* David Lipsky.
Story: The lives of West Point cadets were to be chronicled from enrollment through graduation.

Accidentes (Comedy, ABC, 2015).
Producer: Eric Tannenbaum, Kim Tannebaum. *Creator-Writer:* Mark Perez.
Story: A Latino attorney, fired from his Wall Street firm due to improprieties, returns to his home in Little Havana to work at his family-run law firm.

Acquired (Drama, ABC, 2018).
Producer: Jennifer Gwartz. *Creator-Writer:* Robby Hull, Jon Harmon Feldman.
Story: A young man, acquiring genius intellect following a near fatal accident, uses his abilities to help the police solve baffling crimes.

Acquittal (Drama, CBS, 2014).
Producer: Jerry Bruckheimer, Jonathan Littman. *Creator-Writer:* Rick Eid.
Story: A trial consultant incorporates his training as a psychologist to resolve matters for the court system.

Adult Children (Comedy, CBS, 2015).
Producer: Aaron Kaplan, Wendi Trilling. *Creator-Writer:* Gabrielle Allan, Jennifer Crittenden.
Story: After settling into a life she feels comfortable with, a woman finds her serenity destroyed when her father, a forgotten 1970s rock star, moves in with her.

Adultish (Comedy, Fox, 2012).
Producer: Brian Grazer, Francie Calfo. *Creator-Writer:* Dan Gregor, Douglas Mand.
Story: An immature thirty-something couple attempt to become responsible adults.

The Adventures of Jack London (Anthology, CBS, 1968).
Producer: Andrew J. Fenady.
Story: Stories based on incidents in the life of writer Jack London.

The Adventures of Robin Hood (Adventure, Syndication, 1951).
Producer: Robert L. Lippert.
Story: The first television adaptation of the legendary thief who stole from the rich to give to the poor. In 1955, the series *The Adventures of Robin Hood* appeared with Richard Green in the title role.

The Advocate (Drama, CBS, 2013).
Producer: Carol Mendelsohn, Judy Smith, Julie Weitz. *Creator-Writer:* Avelet Waldman.
Story: Dissatisfied with the way hospitals treat patients, a doctor resigns her staff position to become an advocate for patients and their families.

Affirmative Action (Drama, Fox, 2015).
Producer: Jennifer Klein, Sheldon Turner. *Creator-Writer:* Kevin Costello.
Story: Addison Cain, the female head of a Federal Task Force based in Houston, Texas, investigates crimes with a team comprised of various minorities.

The After Hours Club (Comedy, Comedy Central, 2000).
Producer: Paul Miller, Kimber Rickabaugh.
Story: Improvisation is coupled with music as skits explore the rise to fame of a New York cabaret band called Lust Pollution.

After Thought (Drama, NBC, 2011).
Producer: Melissa Rosenberg.
Story: A specialized team of FBI agents attempt to solve murders through a unique process: entering the minds of victims within six hours after clinical death to get the evidence they need before time runs out with cellular death.

AKA Jessica Jones (Drama, ABC, 2011).
Producer: Howard Klein, Melissa Rosenberg.
Story: When Jessica Jones, a super hero in the Marvel Cinematic Universe, develops post traumatic stress syndrome and is unable to perform as she once did, she uses her abilities as a private detective to battle crime. The series *Jessica Jones* appeared on Netflix in 2015 with Krysten Ritter as Jessica.

Alex + Amy (Comedy, ABC, 2012).
Producer: Darryl Frank, Justin Falvey. *Creator-Writer:* Diablo Cody.
Story: The problems that befall two people in love—Alex, an ambitious 22-year-old Millennial, and Amy, a Generation X woman who is ten years his senior.

Alice (Comedy, Fox, 2018).
Producer-Creator: Liz Astrof, Diablo Cody.
Story: A remake of the CBS 1975-1985 series created by Robert Getchell about Alice Hyatt, a Long Island waitress seeking to begin a new life as a singer who becomes stranded in Arizona and, for the time being, takes a job as a waitress at Mel's Diner.

Alicia Keys Untitled Project (Drama, CW, 2006).
Producer: Alicia Keys, Jeff Robinson. *Creator-*

Writer: Felicia D. Henderson.
Story: Incidents inspired by singer Alicia Keys real-life experiences about a music prodigy born into a bi-racial family and living in the Hell's Kitchen section of Manhattan.

All Grown Up (Comedy, Fox 2012).
Producer: Aaron Kaplan. *Creator-Writer:* Chris Hayward, Nat Saunders.
Story: A down-on-his-luck young man, fired from his job and forced to move back in with his family, finds a new meaning to life when his childhood toys come to life and become his guiding light.

All In (Comedy, CBS, 2014).
Producer: Will Gluck, Lucas Carter.
Story: A young woman, pregnant by an unknown man after a series of one night stands, finds that after the birth of her child, three men have come forward each claiming to be the father. Not sure who is the father, the men come to an agreement: become the fathers to help raise the child.

All of Me (Comedy, NBC, 2015).
Producer: Todd Garner, Jeremy Stein. *Creator-Writer:* Betsy Thomas.
Story: Edwina Cutwater, an eccentric dying millionaire, hires attorney Roger Cobb to rewrite her will, making a beautiful young woman the sole beneficiary. Unknown to Cobb, Edwina arranges for a mystic to transfer her soul into the young woman's body, hence giving her a second life. As the mystic attempts to make the transfer, something goes wrong and Edwina's soul becomes part of Cobb's body. Cobb must now live a life with Edwina as a part of him until he can find a way to reverse the spell.

All the Light We Cannot See (Drama, Netflix, 2019).
Producer: Shawn Levy, Josh Barry, Dan Levine.
Writer: Anthony Doerr.
Story: World War II love story about Marie-Laure, a blind French teenager, and Werner, a German soldier, who meet in occupied France and seek a way to survive the devastation that surrounds them.

All the Pretty Faces (Drama, Bravo, 2014).
Producer: Jennifer Garner. *Creator-Writer:* J. Mills Goodloe.
Story: Two rival families, living in the beach town community of Half Moon Bay, California, seek to uncover the mystery of their pasts when it is discovered they are Immortals.

Almost (Drama, A&E, 2008).
Producer: Will Smith, Jada Pinkett Smith. *Creator-Writer:* Peter Mattei.
Story: Deceased souls regulated to a mysterious roadside motel are given one last chance at redemption or finding closure by rejoining the land of the living for one day.

Alphaville (Drama, Showtime, 2009).
Producer: Robert DeNiro, Spike Lee, Jane Rosenthal.
Story: A look at New York City's East Village when corruption was rampant and the underworld ruled.

Alter Road (Drama, NBC, 2003).
Producer: David Schwimmer. *Writer:* Lowell Cauffield.
Story: Events in the lives of the people of Grosse Pointe, a Detroit suburb whose population is separated by race and class status.

Alternative Family (Comedy, NBC, 2011). *Producer-Writer:* Jamie Tarses. *Story:* A straight single woman's experiences when her two gay friends offer to help her raise her son.

The Ambassador (Drama, ABC, 2019). *Producer:* Eva Longoria, Ben Spector. *Creator-Writer:* Ilene Chaiken. *Story:* When her husband, Bill, the U.S. Ambassador to France is killed in a boating accident, his wife, Nicole, becomes his replacement and with no real experience, attempts to fill his shoes.

America Ferrera Untitled Project (Drama, NBC, 2017). *Producer:* Teri Weinberg, America Ferrera, Drew Brown. *Creator-Writer:* Sunil Nayar. *Story:* Follows Amrita Kaur, a student at a student-run law firm that tackles cases involving colleges and institutions.

America's Son (Drama, Fox, 2012). *Producer:* Justin Falvey, Darryl Frank. *Creator-Writer:* Paul Redford. *Story:* Following the mysterious death of his father, a presidential candidate, a young man begins a quest to uncover the reason why his father was killed and extract revenge on those responsible.

The American (Drama, UPN, 2004). *Producer:* Aaron Spelling, E. Duke Vincent. *Writer:* James Carlos Coto. *Story:* A Guatemalan immigrant, granted American citizenship after fighting in the Iraq War, becomes a private detective to help people who are unable to help themselves.

American Alien (Comedy, NBC, 2017). *Producer:* America Ferrera, Sierra Teller. *Producer-Creator-Writer:* Teri Weinberg. *Story:* A brother and sister, living and working in Tucson, Arizona, are secretly the protectors of a group of extraterrestrials who have landed on Earth and require their help to assimilate into society (press information does not state why they came to Earth).

American Crime (Crime Drama, A&E, 2010). *Producer:* Mark Gordon, Deborah Spera. *Creator-Writer:* Tanya Wexler. *Story:* A team of FBI agents (one male, one female) assist local law enforcement officers who require federal help in solving difficult crimes.

American Dream (Drama, NBC, 2011). *Producer:* Mariska Hargitay, Andrew Lazar. *Creator-Writer:* Paul Kolsby. *Story:* A behind-the-scenes look at the process of casting reality shows—from the people chosen to their interactions with network officials.

American Exile (Drama, NBC, 2011). *Producer:* McG, Peter Johnson. *Writer:* Michael Oates Palmer. *Story:* An American ambassador's experiences when he is transferred to a corrupt European country.

American Gigolo (Drama, Showtime, 2016). *Producer:* Jerry Bruckheimer, Kristie Anne Reed. *Creator-Writer:* Neil LaBute. *Story:* An adaptation of the 1980 Richard Gere film about the life of a male escort in Los Angeles.

American Tabloid (Drama, HBO, 2009). *Producer:* Tom Hanks, Gary Goetzman. *Writer:* James Ellroy.

Story: An alternative history proposal set in the early 1960s that follows three men and their shifting alliances with the Kennedy family, the CIA and the Mafia.

Americanized (Comedy, ABC, 2018).
Producer: Reese Witherspoon. *Creator-Writer:* Sara Saedi.
Story: The situations that befall an off-beat Iranian family struggling to work, remain unnoticed and keep a secret: they are undocumented immigrants living the U.S.

Amerikhans (Comedy, CBS, 2018).
Producer: Brian Grazer, Brian Volk-Weiss.
Story: A young unmarried Pakistani couple faces new challenges when his estranged cousins and grandfather move in with them and take over their lives.

Among the Spirits (Drama, Syfy, 2011).
Producer: Steve Valentine, Daniel Frey. *Creator-Writer:* Paul Chart.
Story: It is the early 1900s and magician Harry Houdini, novelist Sir Arthur Conan Doyle and Valerie Van Helsing (daughter of a vampire slayer) team to solve bizarre murders that appear to be linked to the supernatural.

Amy After Dark (Drama, Fox, 2006).
Producer: Todd Holland. *Creator-Writer:* John Scott Shepherd.
Story: A young woman, bitten by a vampire and cursed to a life without daylight, uses her abilities to help the people who dwell in the shadows of the night.

Amy Devlin Mysteries (Crime Drama, E!, 2012).
Producer: Andy Bourne, Eric Gitter. *Creator-Producer:* Daniel Barnz.

Story: Amy Devlin, a homicide detective with the Cold Case Division of the Baltimore Police Department, is followed as she investigates unsolved crimes through her unique POV (Point of View) perspective.

Amy Poehler Untitled Project (Comedy, NBC, 2014).
Producer: Amy Poehler, Dave Becky. *Creator-Writer:* Aisha Muharrar.
Story: After inheriting a church from her father, a pastor, a young woman who has shunned religion attempts to continue where he left off with a congregation of eccentric parishioners.

An American Couple (Comedy-Drama, TBS, 2011).
Producer: Conan O'Brien, David Kissinger. *Producer-Creator-Writer:* Mike O'Malley.
Story: An engaged couple living in Illinois and destined to be married are followed from their first meeting through their courtship and eventual marriage.

Angel Time (Drama, CBS, 2013).
Producer: Carl Beverly, Sarah Timberman. *Creator-Writer:* Liz W. Garcia, Joshua Harto.
Story: An adaptation of the book, *Songs of the Seraphim* by Anne Rice about Toby O'Dare, a ruthless assassin-for-hire known as "Lucky the Fox," who receives a visit from an angel (Seraphim) and must redeem himself or forever be cursed to hell.

Angelina Jolie Untitled Project (Drama, HBO, 2007).
Producer: Angelina Jolie, Brad Pitt. *Creator-Writer:* Scott Burns.
Story: A look at humanitarian workers and the dangerous situations they encounter to help people in need.

Angie's Body (Drama, Showtime, 2012).
Producer: Jodie Foster, Rob Fresco. *Creator-Writer:* Russ Krasnoff.
Story: Depiction of a family crime syndicate overseen by a sexy, ruthless woman who will do what it takes to remain in power.

Angry Little Girls (Cartoon, Oxygen, 2006).
Producer: Jennifer Love Hewitt. *Creator-Writer:* Alex Borstein.
Story: An adaptation of the book by Lela Lee about a group of frustrated elementary school girls who voice their objections on the issues that troubles them. The project was presented to Fox (but rejected) in 2009 with Brian Grazer and David Nevins as the producers.

Animal Kingdom (Comedy, NBC, 2012).
Producer: Anthony Russo, Scott Armstrong, Alessandro Tanaka.
Story: The situations that befall a city veterinarian who bases his procedures on the laws of the jungle.

Animals (Cartoon, Fox, 2006).
Producer: Adam Sandler, Doug Robinson, Robert Smigel. *Creator:* Greg Cohen.
Story: Life in suburbia as seen through the eyes of humans who resemble animals.

Anne of Hollywood (Drama, ABC, 2011).
Producer: John Wells. *Creator-Writer:* Carol Wolper.
Story: England's Anne Boleyn and her husband, Henry VIII are placed in modern-day Los Angeles with the loves, intrigues, infidelity and treachery of their time re-imagined for the 21st century.

Anonymous (Drama, TNT, 2014).
Producer: Peter Billingsley, Victoria Vaughn,

Vince Vaughn. *Creator:* Chris Collins.
Story: A former Special Operations agent, forced to go off the grid when he uncovers a global conspiracy, finds a new purpose to life when he begins helping people with no where else to turn.

The Apartment (Drama, Bravo, 2012).
Producer: Karey Burke, Todd Holland. *Creator:* Jessica Queller.
Story: Brief incidents in the lives of people who frequent an Upper West Side Manhattan apartment for only one purpose: extra marital affairs.

Apex (Drama, CBS, 2018).
Producer: John Davis, John Fox. *Creator:* Terry Matalas.
Story: A former FBI agent living a life of seclusion after her father was revealed to be a notorious serial killer, returns to her job determined to make up for her father's evil deeds by tracking down murderous felons.

Apocalipstick (Comedy, NBC, 2011).
Producer: Gil Berman, Gene Stein. *Creator-Writer:* Julie Klausner.
Story: A young woman's attempts to deal with her middle-aged father who is dating her twenty-something high school nemesis.

Apparition (Drama, Fox, 2015).
Producer: Tom Lassally. *Creator-Writer:* Albert Torres.
Story: A young female doctor, possessed with the ability to communicate with the dead, teams with a reality TV series ghost hunter to help troubled souls find peace by seeing the light and moving on.

April Woo (Drama, CBS, 2011).
Producer: Denis Leary, Jim Serpico. *Creator:*

Amy Bloom.
Story: An adaptation of the novel by Leslie Glass about April Woo, a young Chinese-American who becomes the first female head of detectives for the N.Y.P.D. on Coney Island (in Brooklyn).

Arc (Drama, FX, 2010).
Producer: Ridley Scott, Tony Scott.
Story: A highly skilled CIA agent attempts to lead a normal life after performing numerous mind-numbing experiments.

The Archived (Drama, CW, 2020).
Producer: Joanna Klein, Jennie Snyder Urman. *Creator-Producer:* Liz Sczudlo.
Story: Two sisters, one possessed with the ability to see ghosts and called "The Chosen One," and the other, a normal girl with a keen interest in hunting ghosts, join forces to battle elements of the supernatural.

Are You Being Served? (Comedy, CBS, 1978).
Producer: Garry Marshall, Tony Marshall, Bill Idelson, Sheldon Bull, Jeremy Lloyd, David Croft.
Story: An adaptation of the British series about the staff of a retail floor of a major department store (Grace Bros. in the original version).

The Ark (Drama, NBC, 2017).
Producer: Robert Zemeckis, Robyn Meisinger. *Creator:* Daniel Kunka.
Story: A modern retelling of the Biblical story of Noah's Ark wherein an engineer who, after the death of his wife, receives a vision to construct a ship capable of carrying people into space at the same time the world is predicted to come to an end.

Ashton Kutcher Untitled 2005 Project (Drama, ABC, 2005).
Producer: Ashton Kutcher, Karey Burke, Jason Goldberg. *Creator:* Mark Lord.
Story: Fantasy proposal about a mysterious community where single parents and children are sent to live after a divorce is finalized.

Ashton Kutcher Untitled 2006 Project (Comedy, Fox, 2006).
Producer: Ashton Kutcher, Karey Burke, Jason Goldberg. *Writer:* Trent Jones.
Story: A man, who grew up in a family with seven siblings, finds his life becoming even more complex when he marries a woman with an even larger family.

Assisted Loving (Comedy, NBC, 2014).
Producer: Aaron Kaplan, Tracy Katsky. *Creator-Producer-Writer:* Claudia Lonow.
Story: The problems encountered by two half siblings as they attempt to care for their cantankerous elderly father after their mother's passing.

At Ease (Comedy, NBC, 2012).
Producer: Jerry Bruckheimer, Jonathan Littman. *Creator-Writer:* Kristie Anne Reed, Jonathan Fener.
Story: A group of young people attempt to live and work at an active military base that is located in a desert in the middle of nowhere.

Athena (Drama, Fox, 2012).
Producer: Peter Chernin, Katherine Pope. *Creator-Writer:* Lisa Joy.
Story: A young woman's efforts to adjust to a new life when, on her twenty-third birthday, she discovers she is the reincarnation of Athena, the Greek goddess of wisdom and war.

Athens (Drama, Fox, 2004).
Producer: McG, Stephanie Savage, Robert DeLaurentis. *Writer:* Josh Schwartz.
Story: Incidents in the lives of the people who reside in Athens, a small but prestigious community in New England.

Atlantis (Adventure, Fox, 2013).
Producer: Jennifer Klein. *Creator-Writer-Producer:* Ken Nolan, Sheldon Turner.
Story: A quest undertaken by two brothers as they follow a series of clues they believe will lead them to uncover the fabled lost kingdom of Atlantis.

The Avalon (Drama, ABC, 2011).
Producer: Ben Silverman, Chris James. *Creator:* Martha Kauffman, Nelia Molato-Sustrino.
Story: Incidents in the lives of the staff and the patrons of The Avalon, a Los Angeles cabaret-restaurant.

Avery House (Drama, Syfy, 2007).
Producer: Mark Burnett, Ron West. *Creator-Writer:* Dava Savel.
Story: A family, relocating from Los Angeles to the small New England town of Brighton, encounters the unknown when they move into a long-vacated Victorian estate reputed to be haunted.

Ayuda (Comedy, Showtime, 2007).
Producer: Jennifer Lopez, Alexa Judge, Simon Fields.
Story: Incidents in the lives of four Latina women who live and work in Los Angeles.

The B Side (Comedy, NBC, 2012).
Producer: Jerry Bruckheimer, Jonathan Littman. *Creator-Writer:* Sheri Elwood.
Story: A woman's efforts to overcome the traumas of a bitter divorce by turning to the only people she believes can help her—her best friends from high school.

The B Team (Comedy, Fox, 2012).
Producer: Francie Calfo, Brian Grazer. *Creator-Writer:* Jake Johnson, Max Winkler.
Story: Lacking any super powers but tired of being taken advantage of, five friends form "The B Team," avengers who uses their intelligence to battle injustice.

Baby Dolls (Comedy, MTV, 2008).
Producer: Bryan Moore, Chris Peterson, Danny Villa.
Story: The situations that befall a young, naïve woman who works as the assistant to the woman she idolizes—a famous actress who sees her nothing more than an assistant.

Babylon (Drama, NBC, 2013).
Producer: Ben Silverman. *Creator-Writer:* Daniel Knauf.
Story: Supernatural-themed project about six governesses in the Hancock Park Women's Club who are actually the power that controls Los Angeles.

Bad Dog (Comedy, NBC, 2011).
Producer: Vivian Cannon, Neal H. Moritz. *Creator-Writer:* Darlene Hunt.
Story: A young man, believing his "wild and crazy" dog is responsible for all the mishaps he encounters finds his life turned upside down when the dog is found to be normal and he is the problem.

Bad Fairy (Comedy, Nickelodeon, 2012).
Producer-Creator: Eric Seaton, Scott Thomas.
Story: The friendship between a nerdy 14-year-old girl and a rebellious teen fairy who agree to

help each other overcome the stumbling blocks that are hindering their lives.

Bad Mommy (Comedy, ABC, 2007). *Producer:* Justin Falvey, Daryl Frank. *Creator-Writer:* Clay Graham.
Story: Jennie Williams, a young woman accustomed to a carefree lifestyle, finds her life changing when she marries and becomes a housewife and a mother to her new-born baby and her two stepdaughters.

Bad Mothers (Comedy, NBC, 2007). *Producer:* Justin Falvey, Darryl Frank. *Creator-Writer:* Cheryl Holliday.
Story: Child rearing as seen through a group of mothers who believe the old world custom of parenting is the way their children should be raised.

Bad News (Comedy, ABC, 2015). *Producer:* Aaron Kaplan. *Creator-Writer:* Dana Klein.
Story: A once prestigious television news anchor, fired from his job in Manhattan, attempts to adjust to his new position as a human interest reporter on a low rated Nebraska station.

Bad Seeds (Drama, Fox, 2012). *Producer:* Jimmy Fallon, David Hudgins, Amy Ozols. *Creator-Writer:* Robert Olsen.
Story: A group of teenagers secretly form a gang to bring justice to those who are corrupting their high school.

Bad Sugar (Comedy, Fox, 2016). *Producer:* Dana Honor, Aaron Kaplan. *Creator-Writer:* Sam Bain.
Story: A fight over an inheritance as seen through the activities of the heirs to a mining operation as each scheme to become head of the empire.

Bad Taste in Men (Comedy, ABC, 2011). *Producer:* Jennifer Love Hewitt, Danielle Thomas. *Creator-Writer:* Austin Weinberg.
Story: A woman's search to find the ideal mate—a goal made more difficult by the fact that she has a tendency to fall for men with bad attributes.

Bagel Nation (Comedy, ABC, 2013). *Producer:* Jerry Bruckheimer, Jonathan Littman. *Creator-Writer:* Sheri Elwood.
Story: The situations encountered by a Lebanese family when they purchase and attempt to run a Jewish delicatessen.

The Bait (Crime Drama, Fox, 2006). *Producer:* Jerry Bruckheimer, Jonathan Littman. *Creator:* Jake Wade Wall.
Story: Ordinary people who possess certain traits are recruited by the U.S. government to act as the bait to trap criminals.

Bait & Tackle (Comedy, CBS, 2018). *Producer:* Holly Brown, Johnny Galecki, Brian Kelly. *Creator:* Linda Figueiredo.
Story: Three adult siblings attempt to run the family business, a bait-and-tackle shop after their father's passing.

Ball & Chain (Drama, Syfy, 2010). *Producer:* J.J. Jamieson. *Creator-Writer:* Andrew Miller.
Story: After nearly being killed by a meteorite, ex-lovers Edgar and Mallory acquire extraordinary powers which they use to battle crime.

Bang Bang (Drama, USA, 2012). *Producer:* Pierce Brosnan, Beau St. Clair. *Creator:* Tim Schlattman.
Story: Two hit men, Danny, a veteran, and Marco, a novice, team to carry out the contracts of the people who hire them.

Bar Scene (Drama, NBC, 2012). *Producer:* Stephanie Davis, Seth Gordon, Jamie Tarses. *Creator-Writer:* Mike Chessler. *Story:* When they are unable to acquire jobs with legitimate law firms, several foul-up attorneys begin their own firm and find their quirky abilities are their best tools in defending clients.

Basketball Wives (Drama, Fox, 2005). *Producer:* Darren Star. *Writer:* Ayanna Floyd. *Story:* Incidents in the lives of women married to professional basketball players.

The Bass Player, His Neighbors, Their Landlord & Their Lovers (Comedy, NBC, 2013). *Producer:* Jerry Bruckheimer, Jonathan Littman. *Creator-Writer:* Pam Veasey. *Story:* Had the idea sold it would have been the TV series with the longest title but a rather simplistic plot: The experiences of three men and two women living in the Foggy Bottom neighborhood of a small town.

Bastards (Drama, ABC, 2012). *Producer:* Mark Gordon, Salma Hayek. *Creator-Writer:* Silvio Horta. *Story:* An influential Cuban-American family's efforts to deal with the situations that arise when it is revealed that the family patriarch had an affair with the family maid that resulted in a child.

Bazirkus (Drama, ABC, 2011). *Producer:* Kim Moses, Ian Sander. *Creator-Producer:* Mitchell Kapner. *Story:* The story of a girl, brought up with performers in a legendary circus troupe, who becomes the first female circus owner.

Beantown (Drama, ABC, 2003). *Producer:* Francie Calfo, Stu Bloomberg. *Creator:* Stuart Beattle. *Story:* A Boston mayor attempts to do his job despite the fact that people believe he is corrupt and manipulating the political system for his own gain.

The Beautiful Bureaucrat (Drama, CW, 2015). *Producer:* Neal Baer. *Creator-Producer:* Alexandra McNally. *Story:* A young woman's experiences working at a corporation where the information contained in its data bases has the ability to affect fate.

Beautiful Gangsters (Drama, ABC, 2012). *Producer:* Bob Cooper, J.J. Jamieson, Anthony LaPaglia. *Creator:* Ryan Tavlin. *Story:* Three Mafia wives, given new identities after testifying against their husbands, attempt to begin new lives as part of the FBI's Witness Protection Program.

Beautiful Strangers (Drama, CW 2012). *Producer:* Jennifer Gwartz, Rob Thomas, Vin DiBona. *Creator-Writer:* Dan Thompsen. *Story:* Two incarcerated thieves are given a chance for redemption by using their unique skills as agents for the FBI.

Behind the Blue (Crime Drama, ABC, 2010). *Producer:* Taye Diggs. *Creator-Writer:* Scott Veach. *Story:* Events in the lives of a family of police officers—a female police chief and her four children, each of whom is involved in a different aspect of law enforcement.

Bell Heights (Comedy, Fox, 2016). *Producer:* Eva Longoria, Greg Walter. *Creator-Writer:* Bobby Bowman.

Story: A look at life in a family of six (parents and four children) living in the Bell Heights section of Los Angeles.

Bells and Whistles (Comedy, Fox, 2015).
Producer: Jack Black, Spencer Berman, Dwight Yoakam. *Creator:* Alex McAulay.
Story: When he loses his job in the Silicon Valley, a father moves his family to Nashville, Tennessee, where he hopes to fulfill a dream and become a musician.

Ben Affleck Untitled Project (Comedy, Fox, 2014).
Producer: Ben Affleck, Jennifer Todd, Matt Damon. *Creator-Writer:* Colleen McGuinness.
Story: The situations that befall a 25-year-old woman, working as a server in a frozen yogurt shop when she discovers she has telekinetic abilities.

Beneath (Drama, ABC, 2012).
Producer: Rachel Kaplan. *Creator-Writer:* Jay Beattie, Peter Traugott.
Story: An energy company drilling for natural gas in a small town must battle an unknown force it unleashes and now poses a threat to the workers and the townspeople.

Bergdorf Blondes (Drama, WB 2005).
Producer: Karey Burke, Jamie Tarses. *Creator-Writer:* Josh Safran.
Story: The escapades of a young heiress (Julie Bergdorf) and her circle of rich and spoiled twenty-something girl friends.

Best Wishes (Drama, ABC, 2019).
Producer: Jennifer Gwartz, Jon Feldman. *Creator-Writer:* Geoff Moore.
Story: Nick Day, a man who believes wishes are just a waste of time, finds his life changing when he is approached by a mysterious woman with remarkable powers to help her grant the wishes people make.

Beta (Drama, ABC, 2013).
Producer: Larry Gelbart, Marty Bowen, Paul Weitz. *Creator-Writer:* Lindsay Devlin.
Story: Futuristic drama where human cloning has been accomplished but where such clones have become the enslaved work force for the rich and powerful.

Between Smith and Jones (Drama, Lifetime, 2009).
Producer: Carl Beverly, Sarah Timberman. *Creator-Writer:* Mimi Schmir.
Story: Events in the lives of three Santa Monica families as seen through the eyes of the nanny they share.

Between Two Kings (Comedy, ABC, 2012).
Producer: Ben Stiller, Debbie Liebling. *Creator-Writer:* Stuart Comfeld.
Story: A divorced father with custody of his 11-year-old son, moves in with his father and soon finds himself at the beck and call of both his self-centered father and his demanding son.

Bewitched (Comedy, ABC, 2019).
Producer: John Davis, Lucy Fisher, John Fox. *Creator:* Kenya Barris, Marc Lawrence.
Story: A reboot of the 1964-1972 ABC series of the same title that keeps the plot but changes the characters. Samantha is a hardworking African-American single mother who is also a witch while Darren, the white mortal she marries, is depicted as somewhat of a slacker (in the original series, both characters are white with Samantha, the witch, becoming a housewife and Darren, an ad agency executive).

Bicoastal (Drama, Showtime, 2008).
Producer: Sean Hayes, Todd Milliner. *Creator-Writer:* Mike Kelley, Doug Stockstill.
Story: A successful businessman struggles to lead two completely different lives: one in Los Angeles with his wife and children and one in New York with his male lover.

Big Dreams (2006) (Drama, Showtime, 2006).
Producer: Billy Joel, Andrew Harrison Leeds, Todd Milliner. *Creator-Writer:* Howard Klein.
Story: Dramatic incidents in the life of music icon Billy Idol that begins in the mid-1970s with his marriage to his business manager Elizabeth Weber.

Big Dreams (2010) (Comedy, CBS, 2010).
Producer: Howard Klein. *Creator-Writer:* Andy Breckman.
Story: A family man's efforts to cope with life—first seen as a fantasy sequence of the situation he must face then as the actual situation, which is rarely the same as he imagined.

The Big Easy (Drama, CBS, 2012).
Producer: Carl Beverly, Sarah Timberman. *Creator:* Liz Garcia.
Story: Jack Lyons, a New Orleans jazz musician (playing trumpet) possessed by supernatural forces, helps people threatened by the unknown.

Big Ed (Comedy, NBC, 2007).
Producer: Darryl Frank, Justin Falvey. *Creator:* Jeff Martin.
Story: An American car dealership owner attempts to adjust to new situations when a Japanese automotive corporation becomes his new landlord.

The Big Empty (Drama, Spike, 2006).
Producer: Denis Leary, Jim Serpico. *Writer:* Ken Sanzel.
Story: Billed as "A look at the reality of ordinary P.I.'s [private investigators] in the middle of an unsavory world."

The Big Girls (Drama, HBO, 2011).
Producer: Ben Silverman, Adam Mazer. *Creator:* Susanna Moore.
Story: A prison psychiatrist's interactions with the women who are found to be criminally insane.

The Big House (Comedy, ABC, 2014).
Producer: Dana Honor, Aaron Kaplan. *Creator-Writer:* Liz Astrof.
Story: The situations that develop when a newly engaged woman, her son, and her fiancé move into a new home and find themselves with a roommate—her first husband, an ex-con released from jail on good behavior but with no place to live.

Big of Me (Comedy, NBC, 2016).
Producer: Eva Longoria, Ben Spector. *Writer:* Lauren Iungerich.
Story: The friendship between two women from completely different walks of life who are brought together when their mutual husband dies.

Big Shot (Comedy, TBS, 2007).
Producer: Jamie Foxx, Marcus King, Adrian Lopez. *Creator:* Lamont Farrell.
Story: A look at the life of a teenage "big shot"—a promising NBA rookie who still lives at home under the iron rule of his parents.

Bill Cosby Untitled Project (Comedy, Fox, 2004).
Producer: Suzanne Daniels, Sheila Duckworth. *Creator-Writer:* Bill Cosby, Chris Case.
Story: A recent college graduate uncertain about

his future moves back in with his parents only to find his father seeking ways to coax him out of the house.

Billy Stiles (Drama, Fox, 2009).
Producer: Denzel Washington, Todd Black.
Creator-Producer: Virgil Williams.
Story: A former gang member turned undercover police detective uses his knowledge of the underworld to bring criminals to justice.

The Bishop (Drama, Syfy, 2006).
Producer-Writer: Freddie Prinze, Jr., Conrad Jackson.
Story: A young slacker, suddenly endowed with supernatural powers, must choose how to use those powers—for good or evil.

Bishop to Pawn (Crime Drama, TNT, 2012).
Producer: Jerry Bruckheimer, Jonathan Littman.
Creator: Greg Plageman.
Story: The cases of a private detective who operates a pawn business on the side.

Bitches (Comedy, Hulu, 2016).
Producer: Ben Stiller, Fernanda Torturra. *Creator-Writer:* G.L. Lambert.
Story: The "dirty secrets" women are hiding are explored when, at a hair salon, they reveal what they know to their stylists.

Bitches in Britches (Drama, CW, 2010).
Producer-Creator-Writer: Mel Harris, Bob Brush.
Story: The incidents that befall a family who operate a horse riding stable in Millbrook, New York.

Black Don't Crack (Comedy, ABC, 2017).
Producer: Viola Davis, Julius Tennon, Larry Wilmore, Regina Hicks.
Story: Three former sorority sisters, there for each other during college, reunite after a long absence to again help each other overcome the complexities of life.

Black Girl Magic (Comedy, NBC, 2020).
Producer: Gabrielle Union, Bryan Brucks.
Creator-Writer: Crystal Boyd.
Story: Three sisters, each possessing magical abilities, join forces to protect the people of New Orleans from the supernatural.

Black Oak (Drama, CBS, 2013).
Producer: Greg Berlanti, Melissa Kellner Berman. *Creator-Writer:* Julia Hart.
Story: A young woman's experiences as the owner of Black Oak, a family hotel she inherited that not only has a curse, but a link with demons and ghosts.

Blackout (2011) (Comedy, Showtime, 2011).
Producer: Marta Kauffman. *Creator-Writer:* John Gordillo, Reginald Hunter.
Story: A somewhat strange view of race relations as seen through the eyes of a repressed middle class white woman and her alter ego, a free thinking black man.

Blackout (2013) (Drama, Lifetime, 2013).
Producer: Eva Longoria, Ben Spector. *Creator-Producer:* Elle Triedman.
Story: After failing in the business world, a woman returns to her small home town to begin a new life.

Blackwood (Drama, MTV, 2012)
Producer: Kelsey Grammer, Brian Sher. *Creator:* Gwenda Bond.
Story: While visiting the mysterious Roanoke Island (where centuries earlier a colony of people mysteriously disappeared) a modern-day 19-year-old girl (Miranda Blackwood)

experiences a similar incident when 114 people, including her father, vanish without a trace. Miranda's effort to uncover the island's mystery was to be explored as she seeks her missing father.

Bless Her Heart (Comedy, ABC, 2019).
Producer: Jim Parsons, Todd Spiewak. *Creator-Writer:* Chuck Tatham.
Story: After suffering serious financial setbacks, two powerful but very different Texas matriarchs move into together to salvage what remains.

Bling High (Drama, UPN, 2002).
Producer: Ron Howard, Brian Grazer. *Creator-Writer:* Mike Elliot.
Story: The activities that surround a group of highly gifted children attending a Philadelphia performing arts school.

Blink (Drama, Syfy, 2006).
Producer: Eric McCormack, Michael Fairman. *Writer:* Irving Belateche.
Story: Celestial agents for After Life, a heavenly investigative service, seek people who are about to make the wrong decisions and, in the blink of an eye, give them the opportunity to return to the past to change what could be sealed in fate forever.

Blood Defense (Drama, NBC, 2016).
Producer: David Hoberman, Todd Lieberman. *Creator-Writer:* Marcia Clark, Sara Fain.
Story: A profile of Samantha Brinkman, a Los Angeles attorney whose cases involve her defense of high profile criminals.

Bloom (Drama, Netflix, 2020).
Producer: Barack Obama. *Creator-Writer:* Michelle Obama, Callie Khouri, Clement Virgo.
Story: The issues faced by women and people of color in a post World War II New York City with a particular focus on the fashion industry.

Blur (Drama, UPN, 2003).
Producer: Danny DeVito, John Landgraf, Michael Shamberg. *Creator:* Robert Franke.
Story: An ex-con and his street-wise brother team to help the police infiltrate the Las Vegas criminal underworld.

Boarding Party (Comedy, CBS, 1978).
Producer: Ted Bergman. *Writer:* Alan Jay Leavitt.
Story: An adaptation of the British series *The Cuckoo Waltz* about struggling newlyweds who rent a room in their apartment to a young man to help ease their financial burdens.

Bob's New Heart Show (Comedy, Fox, 2013).
Producer: Conan O'Brien, David Kissinger, Jeff Ross. *Creator-Writer:* Ben Wexler.
Story: Although the title sounds like it refers to comedian Bob Newhart, it is far from that as it focuses on a doctor, who after receiving a heart transplant, leaves his big city job to take over his small family practice in a working class neighborhood.

Bone House (Drama, CW, 2014).
Producer: Jerry Bruckheimer, Jonathan Littman. *Creator-Writer:* Sheri Elwood.
Story: Rather unsettling proposal about siblings who own a private autopsy company and take it upon themselves to solve crimes when autopsy results suggest foul play.

Bonita & Mechelle (Comedy, NBC, 2015).
Producer: Eva Longoria, Ben Spector. *Creator-Writer:* Kriss Turner Towner.
Story: Life as experienced by two single women, one African-American and one Hispanic, as they move into together when faced with financial short comings.

Book Club (2012) (Comedy, CW, 2012).
Producer: Jennifer Gwartz. *Creator-Writer:* Nina Colman.
Story: The incidents that befall a young woman when she starts a book club with three friends but also allows her mother and grandmother to participate.

Book Club (2014) (Comedy, ABC, 2014).
Producer: Eva Longoria, Ben Spector. *Creator-Writer:* Patti Carr, Lara Olsen.
Story: Four women attempt to escape the pressures and responsibilities of the adult world by pretending to be in a book club.

Boost Unit (Crime Drama, Fox, 2016).
Producer: Dwayne Johnson, Tim Kring. *Creator-Writer:* Zach Hyatt.
Story: The L.A.P.D.'s Auto Theft Task Force is profiled with a look at the cases they handle as seen through the experiences of Joseph Vitale, a reformed criminal getaway driver with a mysterious past.

Boring, Oregon (Comedy, ABC, 2017).
Producer: Jack Black, Eric Appel. *Creator-Writer:* Stephen Soroka.
Story: Jonna Miles is the sheriff of the small town of Boring, Oregon. She is dedicated to stopping crime but the citizens appear not to be concerned, even as an elusive serial killer is stalking the town. Jonna's efforts to uphold the law in a town that doesn't seem to care what happens was to be depicted.

Borne to Be Wilde (Comedy, TBS, 2013).
Producer: Courteney Cox, David Arquette. *Creator-Writer:* Billy Eddy, Matt Eddy.
Story: Three bickering siblings attempt to operate their parents' auto repair shop on the outskirts of Phoenix, Arizona.

The Bounty (Drama, ABC, 2013).
Producer: Anthony E. Zuiker, David McIlvain, Margaret Riley. *Creator:* Matt Cirulnick.
Story: A woman's search to find those who killed her family—aided by an Internet account where people have contributed money to make it the largest bounty ever offered as a reward—with anyone also able to claim it.

The Box (Crime Drama, A&E, 2012).
Producer: Tom Fontana, Barry Levinson. *Creator:* Tom Fontana.
Story: The interrogation aspect of police work as seen through the detectives who question key suspects or witnesses in criminal cases.

The Brady Bunch (Comedy, CBS, 2012).
Producer: Peter Billingsley, Lloyd Schwartz. *Creator-Writer:* Mike Mariano.
Story: A revival of the ABC 1969-1974 series that updates the original format (a man with three sons and a woman with three daughters marry to create a blended family). Here Bobby Brady, a widower with three children, marries a divorced woman with three children to create a new blended Brady bunch.

The Brain (Comedy, CBS, 2014).
Producer: Aaron Kaplan. *Creator-Writer:* Michelle Morgan.
Story: The events that befall a young, dim-witted and far less intelligent young man, when he develops superior intelligence after suffering a traumatic head injury.

Brand (Drama, USA, 2014).
Producer: Jodie Foster, J.J. Jamieson. *Creator-Writer:* Bill Wheeler.
Story: After a life of criminal activity and alcohol addiction, a man returns to his home town to become a minister in his brother's small church.

Complications ensue when a "mega church" moves into the community, threatens his ministry and he must use his unethical ways to save it.

Brethren (Drama, Fox, 2006).
Producer: Jennifer Lopez, Barbara Cox. *Creator:* Alfonso Moreno.
Story: A former gangster turned attorney uses his knowledge of the underworld to defend his clients.

The Brew Crew (Comedy, Fox, 2012).
Producer: Francie Calfo, David Nevins. *Creator-Writer:* Kevin Biggins, Travis Bowe.
Story: Two brothers with differing personalities attempt to work together to operate Oregon's second largest brewery.

The Brides (Drama, NBC, 2015).
Producer: Greg Berlanti, Sarah Schechter. *Creator:* Roberto Aquirre-Sacasa.
Story: Three women, secretly vampires and members of a powerful family, are followed as they do what is necessary to maintain their wealth and prestige.

The Bridge (Drama, Syfy, 2006).
Producer: Sean Hayes, Todd Milliner. *Creator:* Julia Dahl.
Story: Flawed souls regulated to Purgatory but returned to earth for redemption, must help people facing a decision make the right choice.

Bright Young Things (Drama, ABC, 2013).
Producer: Leslie Morganstein, John Wells. *Creator-Writer:* Sheila Callaghan.
Story: Two young women leave their small Midwestern town to pursue their dreams in New York City in 1939—one as a singer and the other involved in crime when she discovers her estranged father is the head of a crime ring.

Broad City (Comedy, FX, 2012).
Producer: Amy Poehler, Dave Becky, Ilana Glazer, Abbi Jacobson.
Story: The incidents that befall four female friends (called "broads") living and working in New York City.

Broken (Drama, FX, 2010).
Producer: Jennifer Klein. *Creator-Producer:* Sheldon Turner.
Story: An investigative reporter for the New Orleans *Gazette* turns vigilante to skirt the law and bring criminals to justice.

Brother Voodoo (Drama, Syfy, 2003).
Producer: Ben Silverman.
Story: An adaptation of the DC comic book about a voodoo priest (Jericho Grumm) and a psychologist who team to investigate bizarre occurrences.

Brotherhood (Comedy, CBS, 2016).
Producer: LL Cool J, Kenton Allen. *Creator-Writer:* Michael Borkow.
Story: Two brothers living completely different lives join forces to care for their 10-year-old brother after their parents are killed in a car accident.

Brotherly Love (Comedy, CBS, 2016).
Producer: LeBron James, Kourtney Kang. *Creator-Writer:* Michael Levin, Patrick Kang.
Story: Events in the lives of siblings in a multi-ethnic family.

The Brothers Brink (Comedy, NBC, 2018).
Producer: David Hoberman, Laurie Zaks. *Creator-Writer:* Scott Prendergast.
Story: After years of arguing and disagreeing with each other, two brothers attempt to keep a pledge: make up and begin a friendship.

Brothers from Another Mother (Comedy, Comedy Central, 2011).
Producer: Eric Tannenbaum, Kim Tannenbaum.
Creator: Nat Bernstein.
Story: Following their father's passing, three brothers' ban together to run the family's barbecue restaurant.

BS (Boarding School) (Comedy, Fox, 2002).
Producer: Ron Howard, Brian Grazer. *Creator-Writer:* Aaron Peters, Ross McCall.
Story: Incidents in the lives of the students and teachers at a Vermont boarding school.

Buddies (Comedy, ABC, 2007).
Producer: Kim Tannenbaum, Eric Tannenbaum. *Creator:* Jonah Lobis.
Story: The home and working lives of two patrol car officers with the N.Y.P.D. during the 1980s.

The Buddy System (Comedy, CBS, 2010).
Producer: Jamie Tarses, Brian Volk-Weiss, Barry Katz. *Creator-Writer:* Matt Lawron.
Story: The relationship between four men as they navigate life as fathers.

Bunker (Crime Drama, FX, 2011).
Producer: Katherine Pope, Peter Chernin. *Creator-Writer:* Dennis Lehane.
Story: Jessica Bowman, a private detective with a degree in criminal psychology, works with the Boston Police Department to help bring criminals to justice.

The Bureau (Crime Drama, CBS, 2012).
Producer: Jerry Bruckheimer, Jonathan Littman. *Creator:* Aron Eli Colette.
Story: Cases handled by agents of the New York City FBI Field Office.

The Business (Crime Drama, NBC, 2006).
Producer: Jerry Bruckheimer, Jonathan Littman.
Writer: Sheldon Turner.
Story: A former CIA agent turned private detective joins with his son, a lawyer, to help people with the odds stacked up against them.

But I Played One on TV (Reality, Bravo, 2003).
Producer: Adam Sandler, Fax Bahr, Doug Robinson.
Story: Real actors who played a fictional character on a TV series attempt to perform that character's job in real life.

By the Book (Comedy, NBC, 2015).
Producer: Dava Savel, Craig Zadan, Neil Meron, Tasha Brown. *Creator-Writer:* Tim Sullivan.
Story: A father struggling to raise two children with no idea as to how after his wife's passing, receives the guidance he needs in an instruction manual he finds in his wife's effects.

California (Drama, NBC, 2015).
Producer: Jennifer Lopez, Benny Medina. *Creator-Writer:* Barbara Martinez-Jitner.
Story: Incidents in the lives of a Latino family that spans over 200 years from their time in Mexico to establishing themselves in California.

The Call (Drama, CW, 2008).
Producer: Neal H. Moritz, Jeff Eastin, Vivian Cannoni.
Story: People with seemingly ordinary skills are recruited by the government to perform highly dangerous missions.

Call Me Marty (Comedy, Fox, 2006).
Producer: Justin Falvey, Darryl Frank. *Creator-Writer:* Danny Jacobson.
Story: A blue collar butcher living in Yonkers, New York, finds his life changing when a

customer asks him and his family to join a snobbish Westchester Country Club.

Capital (Drama, NBC, 2020).
Producer: Carol Mendelsohn, Julie Weitz, Julie Anne Robinson.
Story: Joanna Ward, head of a special team of FBI agents, tackles cases that involve the country's most dangerous criminals and their quest for money (hence the title).

Caroline's (Comedy, ABC, 2006).
Producer: Denis Leary, Caroline Hirsh, Jim Serpico. *Creator-Writer:* Chuck Martin.
Story: A young woman's efforts to run a Manhattan comedy club called Caroline's and deal with her staff, clientele and the improvisational comics that frequent her establishment.

Carry Me (Comedy-Drama, Showtime, 2009).
Producer: Carl Beverly, Sarah Timberman. *Creator-Writer:* Dan Bucatinsky.
Story: In an attempt to earn money, a woman "rents her womb" to people seeking a child but who are unable to have one on their own. While not made clear, it appears that each season would focus on the couple to whom the woman becomes a surrogate.

Cartel Trilogy Series (Drama, FX, 2020).
Producer: Ridley Scott, Don Winslow. *Creator-Writer:* Shane Salerno.
Story: An adaptation of Don Wilson's three book series about Art Keller, a DEA agent and his battle against the drug cartel over a 45 year period.

Cartoon Marriage (Comedy, ABC, 2012).
Producer: Jennifer Garner. *Creator-Writer:* Terri Minski.
Story: A view of married life as seen through the eyes of two cartoon artists for the *New Yorker* magazine.

The Cartoon Show (Cartoon, IFC, 2011).
Producer: Jonathan Stern. *Creator-Writer:* Chris Burns.
Story: Iconic cartoon characters, from Popeye and Olive Oyl to Fred and Wilma Flintstone "come to life" to produce their own daily variety series.

Casa (Drama, CW, 2016).
Producer: Greg Berlanti, *Creator-Writer:* Ed Gonzalez.
Story: Six Hispanic siblings struggle to make it on their own after their parents are "unjustly deported."

Casino (Drama, NBC, 2016).
Producer: Eva Longoria, Ben Spector. *Creator-Writer:* Carlos Portugal.
Story: Following the mysterious death of her husband, a man with links to organized crime, his wife and her illegitimate son join forces to save her husband's legacy, a famed casino from those who are threatening to take it away from her.

Celebra-Date (Cartoon, TBS, 2005).
Producer: Denis Leary, Jim Serpico.
Story: An imagined look at what happens when mismatched celebrities marry and attempt to begin new lives together.

Celebrity (Comedy, HBO, 2003).
Producer: Steve Martin, Marcy Carsey, Arleen Sorkin, Tom Werner, Caryn Mandabach.
Story: Celebrity portraits with a look at both the glamorous and not so sensational moments in their lives.

Celebrity Game Night (Reality, NBC, 2011).
Producer: Sean Hayes, Todd Milliner.
Story: Comedy mixes with reality as celebrities enter the homes of ordinary people to join them in their weekly game night.

Centralia (Drama, NBC, 2015).
Producer: Darryl Frank, Justin Falvey. *Creator-Writer:* Meredith Averill.
Story: In 1962, an underground explosion in the real Pennsylvania town of Centralia in Columbia County killed a number of miners and started a fire that in 2020 is still burning. Only a handful of the 1,000 original residents remain and their experiences were to be explored as they protect what remains from the restless spirits that have turned Centralia into a ghost town.

The Chairman of Chatsworth (Comedy, Fox, 2009).
Producer: Brian Grazer, Daniel Palladino, David Nevins. *Creator-Writer:* Brian Grazer.
Story: A somewhat exaggerated look at the life of producer Brian Grazer's father, Tom, an attorney with his own ideas as to how the law should be dispensed.

Chameleon (2010) (Drama, Fox, 2010).
Producer: Tom Fontana, Barry Levinson. *Creator-Writer:* Tom Fontana.
Story: Unusual police drama that revolves around a detective who, after mysteriously disappearing for several weeks, returns as a changed and delusional man with a different perception on investigating crimes.

Chameleon (2011) (Crime Drama, ABC, 2011).
Producer: Anthony Zuiker, JoAnn Alfano, Margaret Riley. *Creator-Writer:* Andrea Berloff.
Story: A female undercover agent achieves her goals by incorporating her mastery of disguises to collar criminals.

Champion: The Jeff Beekman Story (Comedy, Fox, 2015).
Producer: Mila Kunis, Cami Curtis, Susan Curtis. *Creator-Writer:* Lisa Sterbakov.
Story: The daily experiences of a good-natured but hyper-competitive father and family man but seen as a sports documentary with commentary and analysis.

Change of Plans (Comedy, ABC, 2011).
Producer: Todd Lieberman, David Hoberman, Marsh McCall. *Creator-Writer:* Ryan Raddatz.
Story: The mishaps that befall a family when they decide to operate a business from their home.

Chasers (Drama, CBS, 2017).
Producer: Jerry Bruckheimer, Jonathan Littman, Kristie Anne Reed. *Creator-Writer:* Shane Brennan.
Story: A group of cops, considered "Broken Badges" (relieved of active duty for various reasons) team to battle crime in New York City.

Cher Untitled Project (Drama, Logo, 2013).
Producer-Creator: Cher, Ron Zimmerman.
Story: Billed only as "A period drama set in Hollywood during the 1960s." Being it was designed for Logo, a gay network, it would most likely have aspects of gay and lesbian characters.

Chi-Town (Drama, CBS, 2003).
Producer: Mel Gibson, Bruce Davey, Nancy DeLos Santos.
Story: Incidents in the lives of two sisters who are also politicians in Chicago.

Chill-O-Rama (Anthology, MTV, 2000).
Producer: Gene Simmons.
Story: The horror films of the 1940s and 1950s provide the inspiration for a weekly series of "monster movies" produced especially for television.

Chloe (Drama, CW, 2011).
Producer: Marti Noxon, Dawn Parouse. *Creator-Writer:* Jason Fuchs.
Story: A young female con artist (Chloe), killed during a botched scheme, is reincarnated as an angelic covert operator to perform seemingly impossible missions for the U.S. government.

Chloe Gamble (Drama, CW, 2009).
Producer: Ashton Kutcher, Karey Burke. *Creator-Writer:* John Strauss.
Story: A Texas beauty pageant queen (Chloe Gamble) attempts to begin a new life by moving to Hollywood to seek her fame and fortune.

The Church (Drama, NBC, 2012).
Producer: Dick Wolf, Danielle Gelber. *Creator-Writer:* Howard Franklin.
Story: The activities that abound in a cult that disguises itself as a religious organization.

The Church of Reggie (Comedy, Fox, 2008).
Producer-Writer: Ron Howard, Chuck Tatum. *Producer:* Brian Grazer.
Story: A man with an optimistic outlook on life but accomplishing nothing begins his own religion to preach what he believes is the right thing.

The Church of Steve (Comedy, Fox, 2006).
Producer: Will Ferrell, Adam McKay. *Creator-Writer:* Will Ferrell.
Story: A New Jersey blue collar man, told he is descended from Jesus Christ by a biblical scholar, begins a crusade to become the savior of mankind.

CIPHA (Cartoon, BET, 2007).
Producer: Will Smith, Jada Pinkett Smith, James Lassiter.
Story: Music-themed proposal set in the futuristic world of CIPHA where America's youth unite to keep the ideals of the past alive when hip hop music is outlawed.

The Circle (Drama, ABC, 2011).
Producer: Shonda Rhimes, Betsy Beers. *Creator-Writer:* Richard Robbins.
Story: Ten young adults, adopted and raised by a reclusive billionaire since they were infants, begin a quest to discover who they are following the mysterious death of one of their own.

The Cisco Kid (Drama, CBS, 2013).
Producer: Salma Hayek, Jack Leslie, Lauren Shuler Donner.
Story: An update of the Old West character created by O. Henry. Cisco is now an Afghanistan war veteran who teams with a fellow Marine and his best friend, Sam, to battle injustice.

Citizen Houlihan (Comedy, Fox, 2012).
Producer: Mike O'Malley, Andrew Stearn, John Wells. *Creator-Writer:* Mike O'Malley.
Story: An ordinary citizen, dismayed by the situations that surround him in everyday life, believes it is his civic duty to do something about it and begins a crusade to change the world for the better.

City Hall (Drama, Fox, 2020).
Producer: Gail Berman, Brian Volk-Weiss. *Creator-Writer:* Gail Berman.
Story: A profile of three powerful Los Angeles political figures: Ben Bautista, the Mayor; Maya Phillips, his Chief of Staff; and Jack Cavanaugh, the Deputy Mayor.

City of Gold (Drama, WB, 2005).
Producer: Joe Davola, Brian Robbins, Michael Tollin, Shelley Zimmerman. *Writer:* Harley Peyton.

Story: A father and son team of archeologists begin a quest to find the supposed hidden gold of the Amazon.

The Clan (Drama, ABC, 2012).
Producer: Charlize Theron. *Creator-Writer:* Terry George.
Story: Period drama set in the Scottish Highlands that depicts the conflicts in the various clans as they battle Viking invaders.

Clash of the Music Videos (Reality, VH-1, 2007).
Producer: Drew Barrymore, Chris Miller, Jill Holmes.
Story: Contestants must recreate classic 1980s music videos with the original artists of the videos serving as the judges.

Class Action (2006) (Drama, NBC, 2006).
Producer: Erin Brockovich, Gina Matthews. *Writer:* Mark Gibson, Philip Halprin.
Story: A group of high profile lawyers are followed as they pursue class action lawsuits.

Class Action (2009) (Drama, TNT, 2009).
Producer-Creator-Writer: Steven Bochco, Stephen Godchaux.
Story: An attorney disenchanted with the prestigious law firm for which he works quits to help people who are unable to afford legal assistance.

Class 11 (Drama, ABC, 2006).
Producer: Gina Matthews, Grant Scharbo. *Creator-Writer:* T.J. Waters.
Story: A look at the students who become part of the CIA's first spy class following the September 11th terrorist attacks.

Clive Barker's Hotel (Drama, ABC, 2010).
Producer: McG, Clive Barker, Marcus Dunston.
Story: Guests encounter strange happenings at a haunted hotel (the title is named for the producer).

Clive Barker's Lord of Illusion (Drama, Showtime, 2003).
Producer-Creator: Clive Barker.
Story: A detective with a link to the supernatural solves crimes with the help of spirits of deceased souls seeking justice.

Clive Barker's The Evil One (Drama, Syfy, 2003).
Producer-Creator: Clive Barker.
Story: Anthology-like project wherein an evil demon relates tales where both the forces of good and evil battle for a soul

Cloak (Drama, ABC, 2003).
Producer: Kelsey Grammer, Steve Stark. *Creator-Writer:* John Ward.
Story: The cases of a physicist turned spy for the U.S. Bureau of Diplomatic Security.

Cloak and Dagger (Drama, ABC Family, 2011).
Producer: Jeph Loeb.
Story: An adaptation of the Marvel comic about Tandy Bowen and Tyrone Johnson, teenage runaways who, after taking an experimental drug, battle evil with their newly acquired super powers: Tandy to emit light daggers; and Tyrone to engulf his enemies in darkness.

Close to Heaven (Comedy, NBC, 2017).
Producer: Aaron Kaplan, Dana Honor. *Creator-Writer:* Brad Copeland.
Story: Events in the life of a pastor who, after serving many years as a missionary in Africa, struggles to adjust to life in America as head of a small town church.

Clothing Optional (Comedy, Fox, 2013).
Producer: Mark Gordon. *Creator-Writer:* Scott King.
Story: Events in the lives of the guests who check into an exclusive resort where clothing is optional.

The Club (Comedy, CBS, 2012).
Producer: Eric Tannenbaum, Kim Tannenbaum. *Creator-Writer:* Chris Chase.
Story: A down-on-his-luck golf pro seeks to find a new meaning to his life when he accepts a job at an exclusive country club.

The Code (Drama, Fox, 2015).
Producer: Michael Dinner. *Creator-Writer:* Fred Golan, Graham Yost.
Story: The activities of two brothers, each with a different calling—one who is a journalist; the other, a computer hacker.

Cold Blood (Drama, ABC, 2014).
Producer: Aaron Kaplan. *Creator-Writer:* Janine Sherman Battois.
Story: The mysteries that surround New York Memorial Hospital as seen through the activities of Dr. Cara West, an African-American surgeon who joins the staff after the strange disappearance of one of its doctors.

Cold Feet (Drama, TNT, 2012).
Producer: Robert Zemeckis, Jackie Levine. *Creator-Writer:* Dave Ryan.
Story: A young woman feeling that the whole world is against her, wishes that she was never born. Unknown powers grant her wish and she is no longer recognized by anyone she once knew. Now possessed of knowledge as to what happened to her, she decides to change her past to affect her future.

Cole Tracer, P.I. (Crime Drama, ABC, 2005).
Producer: Anthony Russo, Sean Bailey. *Writer:* Joe Russo.
Story: After his detective TV series is cancelled, its star becomes a "real life" investigator by incorporating the knowledge he learned on television to help people in trouble.

Collision (Drama, NBC, 2015).
Producer: Anthony Horowitz, Julie Weitz. *Creator-Writer:* Carol Mendelsohn.
Story: Incidents in the past (through flashbacks) and present-day lives of a group of strangers who are brought together during a major traffic accident.

Committed (Anthology, ABC, 2019).
Producer: David Hoberman, Todd Lieberman. *Creator-Writer:* Jerome Schwartz.
Story: Varying dramas and casts that were to explore contemporary marriage in America.

The Company (Drama, ABC, 2005).
Producer: Carl Beverly, Sarah Timberman. *Writer:* Richard Dresser.
Story: The intrigues and deceptions associated with the pharmaceutical industry.

The Compass (Drama, NBC, 2007).
Producer: Daryl Frank, Justin Falvey. *Creator-Writer:* Wesley Strick.
Story: A reworking of *The Mod Squad* series about youthful-looking FBI agents who infiltrate organizations that poses a threat to the national safety.

Complications (Drama, ABC, 2007).
Producer: Jerry Bruckheimer, Jonathan Littman. *Creator-Writer:* Amy Holden Jones.
Story: Life in a metropolitan hospital as seen through the eyes of both the doctor and the patient.

Conan (Adventure, Amazon, 2018).
Producer: Mark Wheeler, Fredrik Malmberg, Warren Littlefield. *Creator-Writer:* Ryan Condal.
Story: Robert E. Howard's literary hero, Conan the Barbarian is again brought to life on television (the first time in the 1998 series *Conan*) where he wanders across a treacherous land helping people in need but searching for his true purpose in life.

Confessions of a Backup Dancer (Drama, CW, 2011).
Producer: Bob Levy, Leslie Morgenstein.
Creator-Writer: Ilene Chaiken.
Story: Serial-like project that follows the life of a young woman who becomes a backup dancer to a popular recording star.

Connect (Crime Drama, Fox, 2018).
Producer: McG, Howard Gordon, Joe Wiggins.
Creator-Writer: Rashad Raisani.
Story: Two brothers join forces to battle crime: one a police detective, the other a civilian with a gift to figure out the criminal mind.

Conquest (Drama, Showtime, 2013).
Producer: Ron Howard, Francie Calfo, David Nevins. *Creator-Writer:* Ron Howard.
Story: Period drama about Hernan Cortes, the Spanish Conquistador and his battle against Montezuma II, the ruler of the Aztec Empire.

Consulting Adults (Drama, NBC, 2011).
Producer: Katherine Pope, Peter Chernin.
Creator-Writer: Victoria Strouse.
Story: A team of corporate consultants attempt to help people not only fix their businesses but their dysfunctional lives as well.

The Continental (Drama, Starz, 2019).
Producer: Keanu Reeves, David Leitch, Derek Kolstad.
Story: A look at an exclusive hotel called The Continental, which serves as a refuge for assassins and underworld figures seeking to escape the law.

Control (Drama, CBS, 2020).
Producer: Josh Berman, Chris King. *Creator-Writer:* Jonathan Collier.
Story: Incidents in the lives of members of the C.D.C.'s (Center for Disease Control) Rapid Response Team who risk their lives to investigate cases involving diseases.

Control, Alt., Delete (Comedy, Showtime, 2014).
Producer: Katherine Pope, Peter Chernin.
Creator-Writer: Simeon Goulden.
Story: Strange proposal about a group of young attorneys, working for a less-than-prestigious law firm, who are struggling for advancement despite the fact that any one of them could become the next victim of "the office serial killer."

The Conversation (Drama, AMC, 2008).
Producer: Francis Ford Coppola, Heather McQuarrie, Tony Krantz. *Creator-Writer:* Christopher McQuarrie, Erik Jendersen.
Story: Adaptation of the 1974 feature film about the work of Harry Caul, an electronics surveillance expert.

Conway (Crime Drama, TNT, 2014).
Producer: Vin Diesel, Shana C. Waterman.
Creator: Jonny Umansky.
Story: A St. Louis police detective (Cal Conway) shot while investigating a case awakens from a coma with enhanced cognitive abilities that enables him to solve complex crimes.

The Cool Girl Hate Club (Reality, Style, 2009).
Producer: Finola Hughes.
Story: Documentary-like project that follows a group of Indiana University graduates as they begin their careers in New York City.

Cooler Kings (Crime Drama, A&E, 2009).
Producer: Jerry Bruckheimer, Jonathan Littman. *Creator-Writer:* Tristan Patterson.
Story: A group of detectives called "The Cooler Kings" battle crime and corruption in Hawaii.

The Correspondents (Drama, ABC, 2006).
Producer: Mark Gordon, Peter Horton, Betsy Beers, Julie Lynn. *Producer-Creator-Writer:* Shonda Rhimes.
Story: A team of female journalists representing TV, radio and the press ban together to acquire stories.

Couch Detective (Crime Drama, ABC, 2014).
Producer: Jerry Bruckheimer, Jonathan Littman. *Creator-Writer:* Lauren Iungerich.
Story: A young woman, equipped with knowledge of crime solving based on her viewing television crime series and movies, puts her abilities to the test by helping the police solve real life crimes.

Couple Time (Comedy, Fox, 2016).
Producer: Ellen DeGeneres. *Creator-Writer:* Allyn Rachel, Patrick Carlyle.
Story: A young couple, having grown up together but never really maturing, face new challenges when they graduate from college and realize they must confront life as adults.

Courteney Cox Untitled Project (Comedy, Fox, 2013).
Producer: Courteney Cox, David Arquette. *Creator-Writer:* Vijal Patel.
Story: A married couple attempt to raise smart, confident children who they know will grow up to become smart confident teenagers and make their life miserable.

Courtroom 302 (Drama, ABC, 2011).
Producer: Mark Gordon, Noah Hawley. *Creator-Writer:* Steven Maeda.
Story: A look at the criminal proceedings of the Cook County (Chicago) Criminal Courthouse as seen through the experiences of the men and women who work there.

The Courtship of Eddie's Father (Comedy, Fox, 2014).
Producer: Conan O'Brien, David Kissinger, Willie Garson. *Creator-Writer:* Jennifer Flackett, Mark Levin
Story: A remake of the ABC 1969-1972 series about Tom Corbett, a widowed magazine publisher whose son, Eddie, believes he should marry and proceeds to introduce him to women he feels will also make the perfect mother.

The Cove (Drama, CW, 2018).
Producer: Robert Zemeckis. *Creator-Writer:* Chad Fiveash, James Stoteraux.
Story: Following the death of their father, two estranged sisters are brought together when they inherit his Caribbean island hotel and the numerous mysteries that surround it, including a supposed hidden treasure.

Cracker (Drama, TNT, 2008).
Producer: Robert Duvall, Robert Carliner. *Creator-Writer:* Jason Horwitch.
Story: An adaptation of the British series about a criminal psychologist with his own problem—severe drug addiction.

Craig Ferguson Untitled 2012 Project (Comedy, CBS, 2012).
Producer: Craig Ferguson, Rebecca Tucker. *Creator-Writer:* Aaron Shure.
Story: A young man, re-married and the stepfather to his new wife's two children, finds his life complicated by his ex-wife—who lives next door to him.

Craig Ferguson Untitled 2013 Project (Comedy, CBS, 2013).
Producer: Craig Ferguson, Rebecca Tucker. *Creator-Writer:* Adam Chase.
Story: A group of male friends in their thirties make a pledge to remain single as long as possible despite the temptation that surrounds them: everyone they know is getting married and starting families.

Crescent Heights (Comedy, Fox, 2014).
Producer: Aaron Kaplan, Tracy Katsky. *Creator-Writer:* Allyn Rachel, Patrick Carlyle.
Story: A young couple's experiences when they move into the Crescent Heights apartment complex and discover they are the only normal ones amid residents with dark, hidden secrets.

Crimes of the Century (Reality, TNT, 2008).
Producer: Ridley Scott, Tony Scott, Skip Chaisson.
Story: Recreations of notorious crimes committed over the past one hundred years.

Criminal (Drama, ABC, 2016).
Producer: Greg Berlanti, Sarah Schechter. *Creator-Writer:* Brendan Gail.
Story: After being caught in a CIA sting operation, a brilliant con artist is recruited to perform missions that involve the recovery of virtually unknown relics that could change the course of the world if they fall into the wrong hands.

Criminal Magic (Crime Drama, CW, 2016).
Producer: Rob Thomas, Danielle Stokdyk, Graham Norris.
Story: A young woman, possessed of incredible magical powers, uses her abilities to help authorities capture criminals.

Criminology (Crime Drama, A&E, 2010).
Producer: David W. Zuiker, Ridley Scott, Tony Scott. *Creator-Writer:* W. Blake Herron.
Story: Sarah O'Rourke, a psychology professor who can reveal a person's true motives by setting simple verbal traps or false pretexts, teams with police detective John Acer to solve crimes through Sarah's seemingly simple study of human nature.

C.R.I.S.P.R. (Science Fiction, NBC, 2016).
Producer: Jennifer Lopez, Benny Medina. *Creator-Writer:* Anthony Cipriano.
Story: A scientist with the CDC teams with an FBI agent to bring down a twisted scientist who has created a devise by which she can control humanity.

Cross Roads (2008) (Crime Drama, FX, 2008).
Producer: McG. *Creator:* Laurence Malkin, Chad Thumann.
Story: "A high action cop show" about a group of law enforcers who adapt Old West–like tactics to keep the peace.

Cross Roads (2011) (Drama, CBS, 2011).
Producer: Denis Leary, Elle Johnson. *Creator-Writer:* Jim Serpico.
Story: The work of three doctors, graduates of the same medical school, as they begin their residency in the same university hospital.

Crown in Shield (Crime Drama, NBC, 2012).
Producer: David W. Zucker, Ridley Scott.
Creator-Writer: William Monahan.
Story: A brilliant private investigator teams with a slick, compulsive thief to combine their abilities to solve crimes.

The Cru (Drama, CBS. 2008).
Producer: James Patterson. *Creator-Writer:* Josh Berman, Katherine Ramsland.
Story: A homicide detective's experiences as the head of the Catastrophic Response Unit, a police division that deals exclusively with hostage situations.

The Crusaders (Drama, Spike TV, 2014).
Producer: Pierce Brosnan, Beau St. Clair. *Creator:* Pierce Brosnan, David Franzoni.
Story: Billed as "An event series" that explores the Third Holy Crusades after the fall of Jerusalem to Saladin's armies.

Crushers Club (Drama, NBC, 2017).
Producer: Vin Diesel, Shana C. Waterman.
Creator-Writer: Virgil Williams.
Story: A financially strained boxing gym, which serves as a second home for kids in Chicago's toughest neighborhoods, provides the backdrop for a look at Sonia, a single mother whose life changes when she finds a purpose at the club.

The Cut (2003) (Drama, ABC, 2003).
Producer: Debrah Farentino, Gregory Hoblit.
Creator-Writer: Jason Cahill.
Story: The trying times of a group of first year medical students at a Boston hospital.

The Cut (2016) (Drama, Fox, 2016).
Producer: McG, Mary Viola. *Creator-Writer:* Lili Fuller, Joe Sofranko.
Story: Students at the Manhattan School of Dance in New York City are profiled as they seek their fame and fortune in the world of dance.

The Cut-Up Kids (Comedy, Syndication, 1954).
Producer: Al Joyce. *Writer:* Al Martin.
Story: The project was to use talented children to spoof then current-day television series through sketches (examples given were *The $64,000 Jelly Bean* [spoof of *The $64,000 Question*] and *I Love Everybody* [spoof of *I Love Lucy*]).

Cutter (Drama, CBS, 2006).
Producer: Ridley Scott, Stephen Dorff. *Creator-Writer:* Jim Kouf.
Story: The work of the crew of a Coast Guard cutter as they patrol and protect U.S. coast lines.

Cyber Crimes (Crime Drama, CBS, 2010).
Producer-Creator-Writer: Anthony Zuiker.
Story: Specialized U.S. government agents battle Internet and technology-based crimes.

Dad, Stop Embarrassing Me (Comedy, TBS, 2013).
Producer: Jamie Foxx, Jamie King. *Creator-Writer:* Jamie King, Marsh McCall.
Story: The relationship between a father and his 18-year-old daughter is explored as he tries to become more a part of his daughter's life but more often than not embarrasses her in front of her friends.

Dad vs. Father (Comedy, CBS, 2018).
Producer: Cedric the Entertainer, Eric Rhone.
Creator-Writer: Kurt Braunohler.
Story: When a financial situation forces a young couple with an infant daughter to move in with his deadbeat father, his younger wife and their two teenage daughters, a competition begins with father and son out to prove who the better father is.

Daisy Dooley Does Divorce (Comedy, ABC, 2006).
Producer: Ashton Kutcher, Karey Burke. *Writer:* Ben Wexler, Anna Pasternack.
Story: Divorce and its consequences as seen through the eyes of a group of newly divorced young people who are also friends.

Daisy Jones and the Six (Drama, Amazon, 2020).
Producer: Reese Witherspoon, Brad Mendelsohn, Taylor Jenkins. *Creator-Writer:* Reese Witherspoon, Scott Neustadter.
Story: The struggles of a 1970s fictional rock band as they navigate the Los Angeles music scene.

Damage Control (Comedy, ABC, 2015).
Producer: Jeph Loeb, David Miner. *Creator-Writer:* Ben Karlin.
Story: While super heroes battle criminals and save people, they also leave behind a mess that needs to be cleaned up. Such is the Marvel Universe Super Hero Cleanup Crew who must deal with the aftermath of such conflicts.

Damn! (Drama, Fox, 2014).
Producer-Creator-Writer: Glenn Gordon Caron.
Story: A disreputable con artist receives a chance at redemption when he is killed during a scam and made an angel to use his skills to help people in trouble.

Damnation (Comedy, Fox, 2007).
Producer: Anthony LaPaglia, J.J. Jameson. *Creator-Writer:* Morris Panych.
Story: To avoid being sent to Hell, a recently deceased man who believes he did all the right things in life must convince celestial forces they made a mistake by helping deserving people on earth.

Danger Girls (Drama, UPN, 2003).
Producer: Charles Gordon, Adrian Askarieh, Ana Lisa LaBianco. *Creator-Writer:* J. Scott Campbell.
Story: An adaptation of the comic book about a group of female secret agents known as the Danger Girls: Abbey Chase, an expert sharpshooter and world history scholar; Sydney Savage, the Australian member of the team, who is anything but orthodox and uses her beauty to achieve results; Silicon Valerie, a brilliant teenager who is a Danger Girl in training; and Deuce, a former British Secret Service agent who heads the female espionage network.

The Danger List (Drama, Fox, 2011).
Producer: Vin Di Bona, Bruce Gersh, Susan Levison. *Creator-Writer:* Stephen Gallagher.
Story: A doctor with knowledge in many areas of medicine turns detective to investigate cases of medical abuse, conspiracies and crimes.

Darcy's Town (Drama, Lifetime, 2012).
Producer: Jennifer Love Hewitt, Jeanie Bradley. *Creator:* Sheryl Anderson.
Story: A modern retelling of the Jane Austen classic, *Pride and Prejudice* that explores life and love in a small Virginia town.

Dark Heart (Drama, A&E, 2012).
Producer: Aaron Kaplan. *Creator:* Craig Van Sickle, Steven Long Mitchell.
Story: After receiving a heart transplant, a dedicated police officer begins to act differently when he discovers he was given the heart of a psychopath and must now live a life where evil is attempting to control his actions.

Darkness Falls (Drama, CBS, 2012).
Producer: Mark Gordon, Nicholas Pepper. *Creator-Writer:* Erica Messer.

Story: An FBI psychologist and a homicide detective team to solve the unusual crimes that plague small communities across America.

Darknet (Drama, USA, 2012).
Producer: Aaron Kaplan. *Creator-Writer:* Rene Balcer.
Story: The conspiracy theories uncovered by a team of cyber crime investigators as they probe the Internet for suspicious activity.

Darkside (Science Fiction, Fox, 2004).
Producer: Gina Matthews, Grant Scharbo. *Creator:* Brandon Beckner, Scott Sampila.
Story: A group of astronauts, lured to the dark side of the moon while tracking an S.O.S. signal, find themselves facing a mysterious enemy when they stumble upon a compound that indicates some form of life.

Deadline (Drama, NBC, 2017).
Producer: Josh Berman, Jess Cagle, Chris King.
Story: A former FBI agent turned investigative journalist seeks to help the victims of crimes by reporting their stories in his magazine.

Dear Girls Above Me (Comedy, CBS, 2010).
Producer: Ashton Kutcher, Jason Goldberg. *Creator:* Justin Lader.
Story: A look at how the female mind works as seen through a man who gathers information by eavesdropping on the unsuspecting women who live in the apartment above him.

Dear God (Drama, TNT, 2010).
Producer: Roma Downey, Mark Burnett, Mark Gordon, Deborah Spera. *Creator:* Joel Fields.
Story: A team of humanitarians attempt to help people on the verge of losing their faith by answering their letters to God (which are placed in the Dead Letters Bureau Department of the U.S. Postal Service).

Death Becomes Her (Drama, Bravo, 2012).
Producer: Robert Zemeckis, Jack Rapke, Jackie Levine.
Story: An adaptation of the 1992 feature film (with Meryl Streep and Goldie Hawn) about two women and their quest for eternal youth.

Debbie Allen Untitled Project (Drama, CW, 2013).
Producer: Debbie Allen, Sam Haskell.
Story: Incidents in the lives of the teachers and students at a prestigious Los Angeles performing arts high school.

Déjà vu (Drama, ABC, 2015).
Producer: David Hoberman, Laurie Zaks, Todd Lieberman. *Creator:* Eric Charmelo.
Story: After losing her husband 22 years ago, a woman meets a man and is enjoying a second chance at love but faces a dilemma when she meets a man who is the exact double of her former husband. The press release, however, is somewhat confusing as it states the same thing but in a weird manner: The man who is her husband's reincarnation is the man her daughter is dating (it is not made clear why the daughter would date a man who is her father's exact double or if it is only the mother who can see the resemblance).

Delivery (Drama, NBC, 2017).
Producer: Reese Witherspoon, Lauren Levy Neustader. *Creator-Writer:* Rob Wright.
Story: The experiences of a group of doctors as they navigate their personal and professional lives as part of a gerontology unit.

Denis Leary Untitled Project (Comedy, Fox, 2006).
Producer: Denis Leary, Jim Serpico. *Creator:* Don Reo.

Story: The situations encountered by a larcenous 15-year-old boy when he moves in with his grandfather, a once notorious thief.

Designing Women (Comedy, NBC, 2017).
Producer: Harry Thomason, Linda Bloodworth Thomason (also the creator).
Story: An update of the CBS series *Designing Women* (1986-1993) that would have focused on the children of Julia and Suzanne Sugarbaker as they take over the designing firm (Sugarbaker & Associates) run by their mothers.

Desperado (Crime Drama, CBS, 2011).
Producer: Anthony Zuiker, Matthew Weinberg. *Creator-Writer:* Kyle Ward.
Story: A group of lawmen use Old West tactics to apprehend criminals in modern-day San Antonio, Texas.

Detail (Drama, CBS, 2010).
Producer: Anthony Zuiker, Matthew Weinberg. *Creator-Writer:* Sarah Thorp.
Story: The work of a female private security expert whose cases involve safeguarding celebrities.

Devil Docs (Drama, ABC, 2003).
Producer: Carl Beverly, Sarah Timberman. *Creator-Writer:* Gary Tieche.
Story: A modern day update of the series M*A*S*H that explores the lives of doctors assigned to war zones.

Devil's Advocate (Drama, Syfy, 2006).
Producer: Mark Burnett, Justin Falvey, Darryl Frank. *Creator-Writer:* Jonas McCord.
Story: A group of researchers, called Devil's Advocates, investigate cases of unusual circumstances to determine whether they can be explained naturally or are linked to the supernatural.

Dial 116 (Anthology, Syndication, 1958).
Producer: Herbert B. Leonard.
Story: Dramas based on the files of the Rescue Squad Division of the Los County Fire Department (116 is its telephone number).

Diane Keaton Untitled Project (Comedy, HBO, 2009).
Producer: Diane Keaton, Dawn Parouse. *Creator-Producer:* Marti Noxon.
Story: A woman, inspired by 1970s activist Gloria Steinem, attempts to reignite her cause by starting a *Playboy*-like magazine devoted to feminine issues.

Diary of a Manhattan Call Girl (Comedy, HBO, 2008).
Producer: Darren Star, Elaine Goldsmith-Thomas. *Creator:* Tracy Quan.
Story: A satire on the escort business as seen through a group of high-priced Manhattan escorts as they navigate their jobs, clients and relationships.

The Dicicco Brothers (Comedy, USA, 2011).
Producer: Kelsey Grammer, Brian Sher, Stella Stolper.
Story: An Internet entrepreneur finds his life complicated by the antics of his uncouth family.

Difficult Women (Drama, CBS, 2012).
Producer: Ridley Scott, David Zucker. *Creator:* Barbara Hall.
Story: Incidents in the lives of three empowered women who live together in the same house: a grandmother, her daughter and granddaughter.

Digital Fortress (Drama, ABC, 2014).
Producer: Brian Grazer, Francie Calfo. *Creator-Writer:* Josh Golden.
Story: An elite team of cyber detectives, lead by a

female cryptographer, tackle cases where hackers threaten to expose government secrets.

Dime (Crime Drama, Fox, 2007).
Producer: Neal H. Moritz, Vivian Cannon. *Creator:* Toni Graphia.
Story: A young woman, recently released from jail for a series of robberies, uses her street smarts as an investigator for the district attorney.

The Dinner Party (Drama, Fox, 2004).
Producer: Lisa Kudrow, Sandy Isaac. *Creator-Writer:* Dan Bucatinsky.
Story: A dinner party is established. Over the course of one season, flashbacks were to be used to explore the lives of the guests attending the affair.

Dirty (Comedy, HBO, 2012).
Producer: Caryn Mandebach, Andrea Arnold. *Creator:* Danny Brocklehurst.
Story: A spoof of police officers as seen through the experiences of Danny Vogel, a Chicago detective who manages to squeeze in illicit affairs on and off the job.

Dirty Birds (Comedy, ABC, 2007).
Producer: Neil H. Moritz, Susan McMartin. *Creator:* Vivian Cannon.
Story: Three women, whose biological clocks are ticking, begin a quest to seek the perfect mates.

Dirty Deeds (Drama, Fox, 2014).
Producer: Sheldon Turner, Jennifer Klein. *Creator:* Sheldon Turner, Thomas Schlamme.
Story: Tommy Deeds, an ATF (Alcohol, Tobacco and Firearms) agent is followed as he takes on a second job as an undercover hit man for the government.

Dirty Girls (Comedy, ABC, 2012).
Producer: Mark Gordon, Andrea Shay. *Creator-Writer:* Moe Jelline.
Story: The secret lives women lead is revealed through the discussions of a group of female friends who delight in uncovering the dirt on people.

Dish (Comedy, ABC, 2014).
Producer: Karey Burke, Todd Holland. *Creator-Writer:* Cindy Chupack.
Story: Each week three female friends meet at a diner called Dish to discuss what occurred in their lives over the past seven days.

The Disrupters (Drama, ABC, 2016).
Producer: Sheldon Turner, Kim Moses, Jennifer Klein. *Creator-Writer:* Carla Kettnner.
Story: An idealistic physician teams with a former Hollywood studio executive to manipulate the system to ensure that his patients receive the best treatment possible.

Documenting Love (Comedy, ABC, 2016).
Producer-Creator: Mara Brock Akil, Salim Akil.
Story: Events in the lives of a modern-day African-American power couple.

Dona Flor and Her Two Husbands (Comedy, Showtime, 2003).
Producer: Jason Alexander, Christopher May.
Story: After the death of her charming but roguish husband, a woman seeks to recapture the life she had with him but encounters only men who are nothing like him.

Don't Panic (Comedy, ABC, 2011).
Producer-Creator: Jennifer Crittenden, Gabrielle Allan.
Story: Three women navigate the ups and downs of life living in Manhattan.

Dorothy (Drama, CBS, 2013).
Producer: Carl Beverly, Sarah Timberman. *Creator-Writer:* Emily Fox.
Story: A young doctor (Dorothy) beginning her internship at a metropolitan hospital encounters patients and themes attributed to the L. Frank Baum children's classic, *The Wizard of Oz*.

The Double Life of Emily Reed (Drama, ABC, 2013).
Producer: Larry Gelbert, Marty Bowen. *Creator:* David Diamond, David Weissman.
Story: Through circumstances that are not revealed in ABC's press release, a 35-year-old divorcee is seen living each day twice—once as a successful New York City business woman, the other as a mother with two children in New Jersey.

Doubting Thomas (Drama, Showtime, 2008).
Producer: George Clooney, Grant Heslov. *Writer:* Tom C. Smith, Peter Spears.
Story: A black sheep family member returns to the flock after his father suffers a heart attack to continue the family business as television evangelists.

The Down Beat (Drama, CBS, 2015).
Producer: Ryan Seacrest, Nina Wass, Chris "Ludacris" Bridges.
Story: A business tycoon's efforts to curtail the gang violence in Atlanta by recruiting teenagers and offering them refuge as part of a high school band.

Down Lo (Drama, HBO, 2013).
Producer: John Legend, Tony Krantz. *Creator:* Seth Zvi Rosenfeld.
Story: Life on Miami's South Beach is explored through the activities of the people who are part of the town's music, sports and fashion scenes.

Dream House (Comedy, Fox, 2011).
Producer: Tom Lassally, Jonathan Berry. *Creator:* Dottie Zicklin, Eric Zicklin.
Story: A young woman's efforts to keep her sanity and her dysfunctional family together when her father moves out and into the backyard; her mother remains with her; and her two siblings move into an unfurnished model home across the street.

Dry (Comedy, Showtime, 2009).
Producer: Ashton Kutcher, Karey Burke, Jason Goldberg. *Creator-Writer:* Augustren Burroughs.
Story: The incidents that befall an advertising executive once addicted to alcohol, as he attempts to overcome the situations that test his ability to remain sober.

Dumb Guy (Comedy, ABC, 2012).
Producer: Vin Di Bona, Susan Levison, Bruce Gersh. *Creator:* Hank Nelken.
Story: An average man married to a brilliant woman faces new challenges in life when they move in with her intelligent but emotionally deprived family.

The Dunnings (Drama, NBC, 2017).
Producer: Mary Page Keller. *Creator-Writer:* Sean Hayes, Todd Milliner.
Story: A young woman's efforts to save her family's dancing school after her father, who ran it for 40 years, dies, leaving the company on the brink of bankruptcy.

Echelon (Drama, NBC, 2011).
Producer: Brian Grazer, Francie Calfo. *Creator-Writer:* Michael Gordon.
Story: A team of paranormal investigators attempt to discover if, what is caught on surveillance cameras, is true or a hoax.

Echo Park (Comedy, FX, 2006).
Producer: Jennifer Lopez, Simon Fields. *Creator-Writer:* Ian Edelman.
Story: The Echo Park neighborhood of Los Angeles provides the backdrop for a humorous look at the Latino, hipster and yuppie cultures that thrive there.

Eden (Adventure, NBC, 2004).
Producer: Mark Burnett. *Creator-Writer:* Douglas Day Stewart.
Story: A group of young people struggle for survival after their cruise ship is destroyed by a storm at sea and they are marooned on a deserted tropical island.

The Edge (Drama, Fox, 2016).
Producer: Kenny Ortega, Jennifer Beals. *Creator-Writer:* Annie Burgstede.
Story: The world of dance is explored through the students who attend a Los Angeles dance academy where unscrupulous men and women will do what it takes to make it to the top.

Eight Count (Drama, Fox, 2018).
Producer: Mary J. Blige, Gail Berman, Laurieann Gibson. *Creator-Writer:* Erika L. Johnson.
Story: Following a scandal that destroys her career as a choreographer, a young woman seeks to regain her reputation by grooming her younger sister to become a top recording artist.

The 808 (Drama, Fox, 2016).
Producer: Sheldon Turner, Jennifer Klein.
Story: Serial-like proposal that is set within the Maui surf culture and focuses on a feud that exists between two of its most powerful families.

86 Ocean Avenue (Comedy, ABC, 2006).
Producer: Todd Lieberman, David Hoberman. *Creator-Writer:* Rachel Sweet.
Story: Humorous incidents in the lives of a group of people who reside in an apartment building at 86 Ocean Avenue.

The 87th Precinct (Crime Drama, NBC, 2011).
Producer: Stanley Tucci, Amy Bloom, Steve Buscemi.
Story: An adaptation of the novel *Lightning* by Ed McBain that details the work of Steve Carella, a detective with the 87th Precinct in Manhattan.

Einstein (Drama, CBS, 2019).
Producer: Andy Breckman, Carol Mendelsohn, Howard Klein. *Creator-Writer:* Andy Breckman.
Story: The great grandson of scientist Albert Einstein, working as a college professor, joins with a police detective to solve puzzling crimes.

Electropolis (Drama, CW, 2012).
Producer: J.J. Abrams, Ken Olin, Bryan Burk. *Creator-Writer:* Ken Olin.
Story: A profile of the people of Los Angeles who come to life at night while most of the city sleeps.

Elements (Science Fiction, USA, 2016).
Producer: Darryl Frank, Justin Falvey. *Creator-Writer:* James Frey.
Story: A look at what might happen if the environment were to suddenly change—from snow in Miami and Los Angeles to rain and winter in deserts.

Eligible (Drama, ABC, 2017).
Producer: Jennifer Levin, Marlene King. *Creator-Writer:* Sherri Cooper Landsman.
Story: A modern-day version of *Pride and Prejudice* that explores the lives of the five Bennett sisters as they journey through life.

Ellen DeGeneres Untitled 2012 Project (Comedy, NBC, 2012).
Producer: Ellen DeGeneres. *Creator-Writer:* Lauren Pomerantz.
Story: A successful woman's efforts to reconstruct her life when she buys a home and notices she is listed as a 32-year-old single woman on the contract.

Ellen DeGeneres Untitled 2013 Project (Comedy, Fox, 2013).
Producer: Ellen DeGeneres, Judge Greg Mathis. *Creator-Writer:* Todd Jones, Earl Richey Jones.
Story: A former hoodlum turned judge finds he is able to control his courtroom but cannot deal with raising his four rambunctious children.

Ellen's Home Design Challenge (Reality, HBO, 2020).
Producer: Ellen DeGeneres, Jeff Kleeman.
Story: Home design experts compete in challenges that explore their abilities to create homes that go beyond what is traditional.

Embrace (Drama, CW, 2012).
Producer: Darryl Frank, Justin Falvey. *Creator-Writer:* Glenn Davis, William Laurin.
Story: A young woman (Violet Eden) faces a new challenge in life when she discovers she is half angel and becomes involved in a mission to redeem fallen angels.

Emerald City (Comedy, NBC, 2010).
Producer: Karey Burke, Marti Noxon, Todd Holland. *Creator-Writer:* Sarah Haskins.
Story: A modern re-telling of *The Wizard of Oz* that follows a young woman and her friends (who have personalities reminiscent of the Lion, Scarecrow and Tin Man) as they navigate life in New York City.

Emmis (Drama, Amazon, 2016).
Producer: Marta Kauffman, Robbie Tollin. *Creator-Writer:* Ethan Cohen.
Story: An American adaptation of the Israeli series *Shtisel* that looks at the incidents that befall an ultra-orthodox family.

Empowered (Drama, NBC, 2013).
Producer: Shaun Cassidy. *Creator-Writer:* Lawrence Trilling.
Story: A look at Omni Health, a large pharmaceutical company with its hands in everything legal (as well as illegal) as seen through the eyes of Charlotte Davis, the company's public relations girl.

Encore (Comedy, CBS, 2016).
Producer: Eric Tannenbaum, Kim Tannenbaum, Donnie Wahlberg. *Creator-Writer:* Doug Ellin.
Story: The incidents that befall a long forgotten boy band who reunite after 20 years to recapture their past glory in a world that has passed them by.

The End (Comedy, Fox, 2017).
Producer: Michael Jacobs, Milo Ventimiglia. *Creator-Writer:* Michael Jacobs.
Story: A mismatched young couple with children as equally flawed attempt to adjust to a life that becomes even more complicated when the wife's divorced parents move in with them.

End of the World (Comedy, ABC, 2012).
Producer: Anthony Russo, Joe Russo. *Creator-Writer:* Steve Hely.
Story: After discovering that the world is coming to an end, three scientists decide to give up their careers and enjoy life before the earth is destroyed.

Enemy of the State (Drama, ABC, 2016).
Producer: Jerry Bruckheimer, Jonathan Littman, Kristie Anne Reed.
Story: An idealistic female attorney teams with an FBI agent to bring down a NSA spy who is threatening to expose national secrets.

Enigma (Anthology, TNT, 2011).
Producer: Anthony Zuiker. *Creator-Writer:* Ed Whitmore, Matt Weinberg.
Story: Based on the rather vague press release, it appears to be a proposed mystery series wherein a different sleuth will attempt to solve a complex crime each week.

Eraser (Drama, Fox, 2006).
Producer: Gina Matthews, Grant Scharbo. *Creator-Writer:* J. Israel, M.A. Fortin.
Story: People facing danger are helped by "The Eraser," a mysterious man who arranges for them to vanish from their daily lives and live as someone else in a safe zone.

The Erotic Silence of the American Housewife (Drama, ABC, 2014).
Producer: Tony Krantz. *Creator-Writer:* Sally Robinson.
Story: Adult-themed proposal that looks at a group of women and the illicit affairs they struggle to keep secret from their mates.

Esmeralda (Drama, ABC, 2013).
Producer: David Hoberman, Todd Lieberman, Laurie Zaks. *Creator-Writer:* Evan Daugherty.
Story: The Victor Hugo book, *The Hunchback of Notre Dame* retold with events seen through the eyes of Esmeralda, the gypsy who becomes the fascination of Quasimodo, the hunchback bell ringer at Notre Dame Cathedral.

Eva Longoria Untitled 2006 Project (Anthology, HBO, 2006).
Producer: Eva Longoria, Ben Spector. *Creator-Writer:* Andrea Newman.
Story: Stories based on Hispanic folklore and myth. Each selected legend was to be set in the Southwest and detailed over a full season.

Eva Longoria Untitled 2013 Project (Drama, CW, 2013).
Producer: Eva Longoria, Ben Spector. *Creator-Writer:* Albert Kim.
Story: A woman, imprisoned for a murder she did not commit, uses her time to become a lawyer. After evidence is uncovered that proves her innocence, she acquires a position with a prestigious law firm where, while defending clients, she seeks to discover who framed her and why.

Eva Longoria Untitled 2016 Project (Comedy, ABC, 2016).
Producer: Eva Longoria, Ben Spector. *Creator-Writer:* Bobby Bowman.
Story: A meticulous Latino chef and his unpredictable partner, his wife's Caucasian husband, also a chef, attempt to run a restaurant together.

Eva Longoria Untitled 2017 Project (Drama, Fox, 2017).
Producer: Eva Longoria, Ben Spector. *Creator-Writer:* Emily Fox.
Story: The incidents that befall four close friends with diverse careers: June (an actress), Reza (lawyer), Indie (entrepreneur) and Amelia (writer-producer).

Every Other Saturday (Comedy, ABC, 2013).
Producer: Darryl Frank, Justin Falvey, Jon Pollack. *Creator-Writer:* Neil Forsyth.

Story: A recently divorced father's efforts to gain more custody of his son while, at present, being restricted to visits every other Saturday.

Everybody Hurts (Drama, HBO, 2009).
Producer: Norman Lear, Lara Bergthole. *Creator-Writer:* Aaron Blitzstein.
Story: A look at the world of professional wrestling during the 1970s as seen through the activities of the wrestlers and their fans.

Everything Is Wrong with Me (Comedy, NBC, 2007).
Producer: Darryl Frank, Justin Falvey. *Creator-Writer:* Jason Mulgrew.
Story: A man in his twenties decides to retire and enjoy life while he is still young.

Everything You Know Is (Ping) Pong (Comedy, NBC, 2012).
Producer: Vin Di Bona, Bruce Gersh, Susan Levison. *Writer:* Michael Colton.
Story: A young man who is a champion at table tennis but who lives in a sheltered world must learn to face life and function in the real world.

Everything's Under Control (Comedy, ABC, 2018).
Producer: Jamie Tarses. *Creator-Writer:* Megan Gailey, Aaron Burdette.
Story: A middle class family living in the Midwest finds that in addition to keeping their lives under control they must now deal with another issue when their grandmother is diagnosed with Alzheimer's disease.

Evidence Room (Crime Drama, NBC, 2016).
Producer: John Glenn, Danielle Woodrow. *Creator-Writer:* John Glenn.
Story: Dramas based on items used as weapons that are stored in the Evidence Room of a police station.

Evil (Drama, CW, 2006).
Producer: Eric McCormack, Michael Foreman. *Creator-Writer:* Michael Reisz.
Story: Horror film spoof that details what happens as a mysterious figure terrorizes the members of a summer camp reunion.

Ex-Best (Comedy, Freeform, 2018).
Producer: Jennifer Gwartz, Jon Harmon Feldman. *Creator-Writer:* Diana Gettinger, Monica Hewes.
Story: Two women, breaking up after a long friendship, find themselves unable to function until they realize they can remain friends consciously but not physically.

The Ex-Factor (Comedy, Fox, 2003).
Producer: Kelsey Grammer, Steve Stark.
Story: A man in his mid-twenties with no place to live moves in with his two ex-girlfriends in a slight reworking of the series *Three's Company*.

The Ex-Man (Comedy, UPN, 2004).
Producer: Kelsey Grammer, Steve Stark. *Creator-Writer:* Mort Nathan.
Story: The incidents that befall three friends—an ex husband, an ex-millionaire and an ex-TV comedy star.

Ex-Stepmom (Comedy, NBC, 2017).
Producer: Aaron Kaplan, Dana Honor. *Creator-Writer:* Danielle Schneider, Dannah Phirman.
Story: A young woman, recently acquiring her Master's degree but broke and unable to find a job, moves in with her ex-stepmother, a woman who is her total opposite.

The Exchange (Crime Drama, ABC, 2016).
Producer: David Hoberman, Todd Lieberman, Laurie Zaks. *Creator-Writer:* Nicholas Osborne.
Story: Criminal investigations as seen through

a female detective with the New Orleans Police Department and her partner, a male detective with England's New Scotland Yard who has been assigned to study American police procedures.

The Exes-in-Law (Comedy, NBC, 2019).
Producer: Sean Hayes, Todd Milliner. *Creator-Writer:* Niki Schwartz-Wright.
Story: A couple, breaking up after a bitter non marital relationship, pretend to be a happy couple when they learn their younger siblings have been dating and plan to marry.

Exhibit A (Drama, ABC, 2016).
Producer: Ben Silverman, Daniel Dae Kim.
Story: An adaptation of the South Korean series *My Lawyer, Mr. Cho*, about Andrew Cho, a lawyer seeking to take down the corrupt power brokers who are destroying his city.

Expectations (Drama, CW, 2012).
Producer: Reese Witherspoon, Evelyn O'Neill. *Creator-Writer:* J. Mills Goodloe.
Story: Modern-day adaptation of Charles Dickens' *Great Expectations* about a small town girl whose hope of achieving success in San Francisco are shattered when she discovers the harsh realities of big city life.

The Expendables (Drama, Fox, 2015).
Producer: Sylvester Stallone, Avi Lerner, Kevin King. *Creator:* Kirk Ward, Shane Brennan.
Story: An adaptation of the feature film about a group of highly skilled operatives tasked to stopping terrorists.

The Expert (Crime Drama, USA, 2006).
Producer: Darryl Frank, Justin Flavey. *Creator-Writer:* Chris Murphey.
Story: Alana Castro, a librarian with Synesthesia, a condition that allows her to combine her five senses, joins with the police to solve puzzling crimes.

Extended Family (Comedy, Fox, 2009).
Producer: Denis Leary, Jim Serpico. *Creator-Writer:* Ron Hart, John Beck.
Story: A young mother's experiences when she volunteers to care for a group of foster children.

The Eye and I (Comedy, NBC, 1960).
Producer: John Florea, Dick Donovan.
Story: A somewhat mishap prone private detective finds even more complications when his wife, who believes she is an amateur sleuth, joins him on cases.

Eye for an Eye (Drama, FX, 2012).
Producer: Ice Cube, Josh Barry, Matt Alvarez.
Story: A paramedic dissatisfied with just treating victims of violent crimes begins a quest to seek out and kill those responsible for what has happened.

Everyday Insanity (Drama, Fox, 2020).
Producer: Ken Olin, Danielle Reardon, Laura Bensick.
Story: Three families, each having loved ones diagnosed with mental illness, form a bond to support each other through the trying times that lie ahead.

Fade to Black (Drama, Showtime, 2009).
Producer: Sarah Timberman. *Creator-Writer:* Carl Beverly, Amy Lippman, Chris Keyser.
Story: The Hollywood blacklisting of actors, writers and directors during the early 1950s is dramatized as it looks at how such people were affected and how it altered their lives.

Fairy Tale Theater (Comedy, FX, 2012). *Producer:* Billy Crystal. *Creator-Writer:* J. Michael Feldman.
Story: Puppets perform adult versions of classic fairy tales that are nothing like the originals (as they center on relationships, sex and real life issues).

Faith (Comedy, NBC, 2012). *Producer:* Karey Burke, Todd Holland. *Creator-Writer:* Jamie Rhondeimer.
Story: A young couple's efforts to deal with an unlikely situation—a frustrated football fan who has camped out on the roof of their home and has made himself an unwanted part of their marriage.

The Fall of Bob (Comedy, Showtime, 2008). *Producer:* George Clooney, Grant Heslov. *Creator-Writer:* Danny Zuiker.
Story: Flashbacks are used to relate the good and bad times of a man as he stands on the ledge of a building and contemplating suicide.

Fallen (Drama, Fox, 2010). *Producer:* Peter Chernin, Katherine Pope. *Creator-Writer:* John Glenn.
Story: Angels who have fallen from grace are depicted as vigilantes seeking their own personal revenge.

Fame Whore (Comedy, Showtime, 2012). *Producer:* Eric Tannenbaum, Kim Tannenbaum, John Legend. *Creator-Writer:* John Scott Shepherd.
Story: A young backup singer already blessed with beauty and talent feels that she needs more and sets out on quest to become recognized and adored wherever she goes.

Family Affair (Drama, NBC, 2012). *Producer:* Greg Berlanti, Melissa Kellner. *Creator-Writer:* Sara Goodman.
Story: The incidents that befall a reluctant blended family when the mother of one family and the father of another family, both having a secret affair, are killed in a traffic accident and their survivors decide to live together.

Family Business (Comedy, CBS, 2016). *Producer:* Aaron Kaplan, Dana Honor, Liz Feldman. *Creator-Writer:* Wendi Trilling.
Story: A young woman's efforts to save her family business when it suffers a setback and she must relinquish her corporate job to do so.

Family Crimes (Drama, Starz, 2018). *Producer:* Jerry Bruckheimer, Jonathan Littman, Kristie Anne Reed. *Creator-Writer:* David Ayer.
Story: When the FBI begins investigating her family, which has ties to the Mexican mob, a young Latina woman infiltrates the criminal underworld in an attempt to save her family from both the U.S. government and the mob.

The Family Gene (Drama, Fox, 2017). *Producer:* Jim Parsons, Todd Spiewak. *Creator-Writer:* Greg Spottiswood.
Story: A look at the work of Gwen Langer, a doctor who encompasses new medical procedures with advances in genetic research to help her patients.

Family History (Drama, ABC, 2018). *Producer:* David Hoberman, Todd Lieberman, Laurie Zaks. *Creator-Writer:* Deborah Schoeneman.
Story: The basic premise was to follow a young female tech reporter working out of San Francisco. ABC's rather skimpy press release also states that she uncovers a family secret (but

doesn't reveal what it is) while investigating a DNA-testing web site.

Family Style (Comedy, ABC, 2016).
Producer: Amy Poehler, Brooke Posch. *Creator-Writer:* Claudia Lonow, Scott King.
Story: Gay-themed proposal about two men from different cultures who meet in a Miami restaurant and begin a relationship.

Fantasy Island (Drama, ABC, 2015).
Producer: Josh Berman, Jennifer Klein. *Creator-Writer:* Sheldon Turner.
Story: A reworking of the 1978 ABC series of the same title here about a young woman who operates a San Francisco-based company that offers its clients a chance to live their fantasies for a steep price.

Fascinoma (Drama, CBS, 2015).
Producer: Sarah Timberman, Carl Beverly. *Creator-Writer:* Steve Maeda.
Story: A scientist and head of the FBI Scientific Response Unit, attempts to solve cases that are beyond the capabilities of ordinary law enforcement officers.

Fast Forward (Crime Drama, CBS, 2013).
Producer: Jamie Tarses, Andreas Kamm, Katharina Schenk. *Creator-Writer:* Wendy Battles.
Story: A young female detective teams with her mother and a recently divorced medical examiner to solve crimes.

Fat Chance (Comedy, TBS, 2011).
Producer: Conan O'Brien, David Kissinger, Jeff Ross. *Creator-Writer:* Jay Lacopo.
Story: The relationship between two male friends, one handsome, the other overweight and what happens when they encounter situations that test their friendship.

Fat Rob (Comedy, NBC, 2011).
Producer: Jimmy Fallon, Amy Ozols. *Creator-Writer:* Jeremy Bronson.
Story: A famous rap star attempts to balance his lucrative career with the responsibilities of becoming a good husband and father.

Faust (Anthology, NBC, 2014).
Producer: Roma Downey, Mark Burnett. *Creator:* Roberto Aquirre-Sacasa.
Story: Dramas based on people who make a deal with the Devil to achieve success then face the consequences when a mysterious stranger (assumed to be the Devil) returns to collect on the bargain they made.

The Favorite (Comedy, ABC, 2016).
Producer: Aaron Kaplan. *Creator-Writer:* Laura Krafft.
Story: At a plea from her younger siblings for help in caring for their aging parents, a woman temporarily resigns from her job and returns home only to find it becoming a full time situation when her parents favor her as their care taker.

The FBI (Crime Drama, Fox, 2008).
Producer: Brian Grazer, David Nevins. *Creator-Writer:* Chap Taylor.
Story: Stories based on the FBI's Critical Incidents Response Group, the division that investigates cases ranging from murder and kidnapping to hostage rescue and domestic terrorism.

Felony Review (Drama, CW, 2010).
Producer: Robert DeNiro, Jane Rosenthal. *Creator-Writer:* Julie Martin.
Story: A group of young Assistant District Attorneys are followed as they begin prosecuting cases.

Felony Twins (Crime Drama, ABC, 2014).
Producer: Stephanie Savage, Josh Schwartz.
Creator-Writer: David Hemingson.
Story: A lawyer enlists the help of two eccentric twin sisters who have an obsession with solving crimes as his associates—but all the time attempting to keep them secret from his superiors.

Fifth Wheel (Comedy, NBC, 2014).
Producer: Mark Gordon, Andrea Shay. *Creator-Writer:* Elena Crevello.
Story: A young woman, the only single member of her group of married friends, seeks a way to fit in until she finds that man of her dreams.

Fifty/Fifty (Comedy, NBC, 2005).
Producer: Gina Matthews, Grant Scharbo, Todd Garner. *Creator-Writer:* Ian Gurvitz.
Story: How four men deal with the various issues in their lives, including fatherhood, divorce and dating.

Fight Like a Girl (Drama, ABC, 2020).
Producer: Aaron Kaplan, Dana Honor. *Creator-Writer:* Kathryn Price, Nichole Millard.
Story: A profile of two young female attorneys as each incorporates her own unique style to defend clients.

Finders Keepers (Drama, USA, 2012).
Producer: Aaron Kaplan. *Creator-Writer:* Philip Levens.
Story: Jack Monroe, a former FBI agent turned private investigator, uses his knowledge as a missing person's specialist to find people reported as missing by becoming a part of the lives of the people who knew the subject.

First Lady (Drama, CW, 2014).
Producer: Jennifer Garner, Tariq Jalil. *Creator-Writer:* Jenni Ross.
Story: An adaptation of the Chilean series *Primera Dama* that chronicles the rags-to-riches journey of an illegal immigrant as she marries a man who would become the President of the United States and her battle to keep the dark secrets of her past from destroying her position as the First Lady.

First Responders (Drama, NBC, 2016).
Producer: Vin Diesel, Samantha Vincent, Brad Peyton. *Creator-Writer:* Jesse Stern.
Story: The work of first responders, members of a Search and Rescue Operation who are also young veterans just returning from military service overseas.

First Timers (Comedy, ABC, 2013).
Producer: Stephanie Savage, Josh Schwartz, Len Goldstein. *Creator-Writer:* Elizabeth Berger.
Story: Explores the prospect of male and female business partners attempting to work together without the hassles of one sex being capable of handling situations better than the other.

Five Finger Discount (Comedy, Fox, 2004).
Producer: David E. Kelly, Kert Ehrin.
Story: A ten-year-old girl being raised by a family of petty thieves tries her best to not only reform them, but not follow in their footsteps.

Five Head (Comedy, ABC, 2012).
Producer-Creator: Tyra Banks, Kenya Barris.
Story: Flashback proposal that explores the life of Tyra Banks, a future super model and TV host (of *America's Next Top Model*) as a teenager living with her family and attending high school.

Fives (Comedy, Fox, 2013).
Producer: Aaron Kaplan. *Creator-Writer:* Shawn Wines.

Story: How a group of people, considered fives (on a scale from one to ten) cope with the stress of everyday life living in Los Angeles.

Fix-It Men (Drama, TNT, 2014).
Producer: Mark Gordon, Nick Pepper. *Creator-Writer:* John Glenn, Joe Carnahan.
Story: A group of agents, known as Fix-It Men, travel back in time to change troublesome events before they effect the future.

Fix Me (Comedy, NBC, 2006).
Producer: Darryl Frank, Justin Falvey. *Creator-Writer:* Steven Spielberg, Larry Wilmore.
Story: A young woman who is an expert at helping others in her profession as a pediatrician finds that when it comes to helping herself, she is anything but successful.

The Fixer (Drama, ABC, 2007).
Producer: Brian Grazer, Daniel Rosenberg, David Nevins. *Creator-Writer:* Russell Gewirtz.
Story: A female public relations executive attempts to discretely solve (fix) the problems of the elite of New York City.

Flava Jones (Crime Drama, UPN, 2002).
Producer: Ron Howard, Brian Grazer. *Creator-Writer:* Steve Antin, Joe Voci.
Story: Take on the Pam Grier *Foxy Brown* theatrical films here about an African-American police officer (Flava Jones) who quits the force to become a private detective in Miami.

Fleet Street (Drama, Starz, 2013).
Producer: Piers Morgan, Justin Berfield, Jason Felts. *Creator-Writer:* Danny Brocklehurst.
Story: An American tabloid reporter's experiences stationed in England during the 1970s.

Fleishman Is in Trouble (Drama, FX, 2019).
Producer: Sarah Timberman, Carl Beverly, Susannah Grant. *Creator-Writer:* Taffy Brodesser-Akner.
Story: The changes that occur in the life of Toby Fleishman, age 41 and rather short, following his divorce from a controlling, social climbing wife (a talent agent).

Flesh & Blood (Drama, Lifetime, 2012).
Producer: Ben Silverman, Teri Weinberg. *Creator-Writer:* Nina Coleman.
Story: A young woman raised "on the wrong side of the tracks" struggles to navigate a new lifestyle when she pretends to be someone she is not and cons her way into a wealthy and powerful New York family.

Flight Risk (Drama, NBC, 2016).
Producer: John Wells. *Creator-Writer:* Krista Vernoff.
Story: A brilliant young lawyer (Maddie Silva) framed for a murder she did not commit, seeks help to clear her name from an unlikely source—a felon she is currently prosecuting.

The Flintstones (Cartoon, Fox, 2011).
Producer: Seth MacFarlane, Dan Palladino, Kara Vallow.
Story: A reboot of the ABC series (1960-1966) that explores the lives of two stone-age cave families (Fred and Wilma Flintstone and Barney and Betty Rubble) living in the prehistoric town of Bedrock.

The Flock (Drama, UPN, 2002).
Producer: Aaron Spelling, E. Duke Vincent. *Creator-Writer:* Terri Hughes, Ron Milbaur.
Story: A group of deceased teenagers are returned to earth as angels to help people in trouble.

Flukey Luke (Comedy, Syndication, 1954). *Producer-Creator:* Hal Seegar. *Story:* A modern-day cowboy (Flukey Luke) moves to the city with his Indian companion, Two Feathers, and his horse, Pronto, to become a private detective. According to press material, "The cast will consist of midgets wearing masks." An actual animated series was produced in 1965 as a segment of *The Milton the Monster Show*.

Flying Hospital (Drama, CBS, 2003). *Producer:* Ridley Scott, Tony Scott, Caroline Zelder. *Story:* An independent medical team incorporates air transport to help people in desperate need of assistance anywhere in the world.

Fobbit (Comedy, Showtime, 2015). *Producer:* Sarah Timberman, Carl Beverly. *Creator-Writer:* Scott Buck. *Story:* An adaptation of the book by David Abrams about the mishaps that befall members of a public affairs office during the Iraq War.

Follow Your Heart (Comedy, ABC, 2014). *Producer:* Aaron Kaplan. *Creator-Writer:* Nastaran Dibai. *Story:* Feeling that she will never again find the love she had with her late husband, a single mother finds she is mistaken when a bachelor moves into her apartment building and she is instantly drawn to him, unaware that he received her husband's heart in a transplant.

Foobar (Drama, ABC, 2008). *Producer:* Neil H. Moritz. *Creator-Writer:* Alice Wu. *Story:* Incidents in the lives of a group of workers at a software company who push the boundaries of technology.

Food & Familia (Comedy, ABC, 2018). *Producer:* Will Smith, James Lassiter. *Creator-Writer:* Peter Murrieta. *Story:* Following the passing of the family matriarch, her son, Danny, who has just been released from prison, and her granddaughter, Michelle, who is bitter over the fact that her father abandoned her, inherit her restaurant—and find they must work together to save the family business.

For Pete's Sake (Comedy, NBC, 2006). *Producer:* Ashton Kutcher, Karey Burke, Jason Goldberg. *Creator-Writer:* Eric Gilliland. *Story:* Five people killed through job-related accidents are, for various reasons, rejected for entry into Heaven. To help them, celestial forces return them to life—to be continually reborn until they do what is right to enter through the Pearly Gates.

Forrest's Treasure (Drama, Fox, 2018). *Producer:* McG, Mary Viola, Eric Robinson, Jeremy Bell. *Creator-Writer:* Elwood Reid. *Story:* A family's efforts to recapture the wonders of their pasts when they abandon the big city and return to their small town roots.

The 40-Year-Old Rookie (Drama, CBS, 2015). *Producer:* Eric Tennenbaum, Kim Tannenbaum. *Creator-Writer:* Brian Burns. *Story:* After serving as a criminal defense attorney for 20 years but dissatisfied with how criminals beat the system, a father joins the police force as a rookie cop to see that justice is served.

The Fosters (Comedy, NBC, 2012). *Producer:* Al Roker, Tracie Brennan. *Creator-Writer:* Gary Anthony Williams, Scott Ward. *Story:* Events in the life of single father who cares for a number of foster children.

Found (Drama, ABC, 2019).
Producer: Greg Berlanti, Sarah Schechter.
Creator: Nkechi Okoro Carroll.
Story: A look at how authorities find people who are reported missing, often with the help of the general public when alerts are issued.

Fountain of Youth (Reality, WB, 2006).
Producer: Ashton Kutcher, Jason Goldberg.
Story: Amazing Race–like proposal wherein eight college seniors team with eight senior citizens for a race around the U.S.

The Four Next Door (Comedy, NBC, 2006).
Producer: Eriq La Salle, Teri Lubaroff. *Creator-Writer:* Mark Legan.
Story: According to historical facts that have not yet occurred, the world is to end in ten years. Its destroyers, the Four Horsemen of the Apocalypse, miscalculate the time frame and arrive on earth ten years too soon. The proposal was to relate what happens as the Horsemen bide their time by attempting to live among humans before fulfilling their mission.

Four Play (Comedy, NBC, 2012).
Producer: Karey Burke, Flody Suarez, Todd Holland. *Creator-Writer:* Liz Vassey.
Story: After adopting a baby, a couple finds help in raising her from their two best friends.

The Fourth Estate (Drama, AMC, 2011).
Producer: J.J. Jamieson, Robert Cooper. *Creator-Writer:* Gideon Yago.
Story: Proposal about an investigative newspaper reporter who tackles stories that involve major scandals and how, through the power of the press, he manages to expose them.

Frauds (Comedy, Fox, 2014).
Producer: Jamie Tarses, David Caspe. *Creator-Writer:* Gil Ozeri.
Story: A family's efforts to survive the elaborate but failing cons they plan but can never seem to successfully execute.

Free Falling (Drama, ABC, 2004).
Producer: James D. Parriott, Michael Edelstein.
Creator-Writer: Daniel Voll.
Story: The relationship between a down-on-his-luck father and his 14-year-old-son who becomes his guiding light as he attempts to reconstruct his life.

Fubar (Drama, FX, 2003).
Producer: Gina Matthews, Eric Weiss. *Creator-Writer:* Grant Scharbo.
Story: Billed as "a reality look at military life" as seen through a group of recruits based near the U.S.-Mexico border.

Fugly (Comedy, Comedy Central, 2005).
Producer: Denis Leary, Jim Serpico.
Story: A man, now in his twenties, reflects on the traumas of his youth (seen in flashbacks) as an overweight and homely child.

Full Nelson (Drama, Fox, 2011).
Producer: Jerry Bruckheimer, Jonathan Littman, Kristie Anne Reed. *Creator-Writer:* Jeffrey Lieber.
Story: A woman's experiences as part of the music business during the 1980s.

Funhouse (Comedy, ABC, 2014).
Producer: David Hoberman, Todd Lieberman, Laurie Zaks. *Creator-Writer:* Fred Goss.
Story: A man's odd attempts to care for his aging father—by kidnapping him and his male attendant from a nursing home and securing them in his home.

Furious George (Comedy, CBS, 2003).
Producer: Jerry Bruckheimer, Jonathan Littman.
Story: A lawyer, frustrated by the fact that he cannot always see justice done in major cases, sets out to change the world by righting petty wrongs.

The Fuzz (Comedy, Comedy Central, 2010).
Producer: Tom Lassally, Dave Becky. *Creator-Writer:* Chris Ford, John Watts.
Story: In a future time when puppets co-exist with humans, there is also a police force that mixes puppets with humans. Such is the case for Herbie, the world's first puppet detective whose crime-solving abilities are tested when he is teamed with a human detective to stem the rising tide of puppet crimes.

G-Men (Drama, ABC, 1958).
Producer: William T. Orr. *Writer:* Mildred Gordon.
Story: An Adaptation of the 1935 feature film that depicts incidents in the lives of agents for the Department of Justice (called "G-Men"; later to be known as the F.B.I.)

The Game of Life (Comedy, TBS, 2009).
Producer-Creator-Writer: Kevin James, Jeff Sussman.
Story: Four men now in their thirties reconnect during a high school reunion to discover that for each, life didn't turn out as planned. But there is still time and their efforts to achieve those pre-set goals were to be depicted.

Geek Meets Girl (Reality, Syndication, 2011).
Producer: Ashton Kutcher, Jason Goldberg, Nick Santora.
Story: Dating proposal wherein a gorgeous girl has two dates with the same man to determine if he is the right guy for her: the first is as he actually is (a geek); the second after he has a makeover.

General Manager (Reality, HBO, 2001).
Producer: Ben Affleck, Matt Damon, Sean Bailey, Chris Moore.
Story: People with an interest in baseball compete in various coaching competitions to determine which contestant possesses the skills necessary to actually coach a professional baseball team.

Generation Ex (Comedy, ABC, 2012).
Producer: Mark Gordon, Andrea Shea. *Creator-Writer:* Moe Jelline.
Story: A look at people with children from first marriages who re-marry then must cope with the problems of blended families.

Generation Gap (Comedy, CBS, 2019).
Producer: Aaron Kaplan, Dana Honor. *Creator-Writer:* Dan Kopelman.
Story: A flashback proposal that relates the teenage years of a 16-year-old girl as told from her perspective and that of her father.

Generation Next (Drama, CBS, 2013).
Producer: Eric Tannenbaum, Kim Tannenbaum. *Creator-Writer:* Mark Steven Johnson.
Story: Set at the time of a virus outbreak that causes ordinary people to burst into fits of madness and the specialized team assigned to investigate and find the cure.

Generations (2006) (Comedy, CBS, 2006).
Producer: Darryl Frank, Justin Falvey. *Creator-Writer:* Cheryl Holliday.
Story: The relationship between an unlikely pair of roommates at a retirement community—a grandfather and his grandson.

Generations (2011) (Drama, TNT, 2011). *Producer:* Robert Redford, Bill Holdeman. *Creator-Writer:* John Sacret Young, Bill Holdeman. *Story:* The incidents that befall three generations of one family living in the same house.

Genes (Drama, CBS, 2015). *Producer-Creator:* Michael Crichton, Sherri Crichton, Rick Eid. *Story:* In an attempt to save the life of a dying patient, a doctor incorporates his DNA with that of an experiment he has been conducting on genes and injects it into her body. The process saves her life but both now must deal with the after effects—she has been transformed into a dangerous sociopath.

The Genie Chronicles (Anthology, TNT, 2008). *Producer:* Darryl Frank, Justin Falvey. *Story:* Proposal about what happens to people who come in contact with an ancient lamp that, when rubbed, produces a genie who will grant them one wish.

George Washington (Drama, NBC, 2012). *Producer:* Tom Fontana, Barry Levinson. *Creator-Writer:* David Seidler. *Story:* Period drama that explores the life of George Washington and the situations he faced as President of the United States.

G.I. (Anthology, Syndication, 1956). *Producer:* Harry Saltzman. *Story:* Dramatizations based on the experiences of combat infantrymen.

Gideon's Crew (Drama, NBC, 2019). *Producer:* David W. Zucker, Ridley Scott. *Creator-Writer:* Chap Taylor. *Story:* A specialized team of experts, handpicked by a billionaire, use social engineering to investigate cases ranging from murders to conspiracies.

Gifted (2007) (Reality, Fox, 2007). *Producer:* J.D. Roth, Marta Kauffman. *Creator-Writer:* Todd Nelson. *Story:* People who claim to possess psychic abilities are placed in various challenges to determine if their statements are true or false.

Gifted (2013) (Comedy, TV Land, 2013). *Producer:* Dave Bickel. *Creator-Writer:* David Janollari. *Story:* Parents of normal intelligence attempt to raise their teenage son who is diagnosed as intellectually gifted.

Girls in Film (Comedy, NBC, 2012). *Producer:* Jamie Tarses. *Creator-Writer:* Hilary Winston. *Story:* A look at three women, best friends, single and in their thirties, and how each approaches the dating scene.

Girls on a Bus (Drama, Netflix, 2020). *Producer:* Greg Berlanti, Sarah Schechter. *Story:* An adaptation of the book *Chasing Hillary* by Amy Chozick, about four female journalists as they cover the presidential candidates in the 2016 election.

Girls Without Boys (Comedy, ABC, 2013). *Producer:* Rashida Jones, Will McCormack, Caroline Williams. *Creator-Writer:* Sasha Spielberg, Emily Goldwyn. *Story:* Three intelligent but socially challenged young women attempt to break out of their rut and find dates based on advice from friends and family.

Glare (Science Fiction, HBO, 2016).
Producer: J.J. Abrams, Ben Stephenson. *Creator-Writer:* Javier Gullon.
Story: Explores the situations that could arise as humans' journey into space and attempt to colonize another planet.

Global Frequency (Drama, Fox, 2014).
Producer: Jerry Bruckheimer, Jonathan Littman, Kristie Anne Reed. *Creator-Writer:* Rockne S. O'Bannon.
Story: An adaptation of the Warren Ellis comic book about a mysterious organization that battles crime by recruiting ordinary people with extraordinary skills.

Golden Guys (Comedy, Fox, 2012).
Producer: Garry Marshall, Scott Marshall. *Creator-Writer:* Garry Marshall.
Story: A young man who became rich, abandoned his family then lost everything in a crooked scam finds that with no money and no place to live he must move back in with his family.

Good Christian Bitches (Drama, CW, 2019).
Producer: Aaron Kaplan, Dana Honor, Darren Star. *Creator-Writer:* Leila Cohan-Miccio.
Story: An adaptation of the book by Kim Gatlin that explores the clergy and members of The Flock, an Austin, Texas church where all have something to hide. The series G.C.B. *(Good Christian Bitches)* aired on ABC in 2012 with Kristin Chenoweth, Leslie Bibb and Jennifer Aspen as the stars.

Good Cop/Bad Cop (Crime Drama, Fox, 2016).
Producer: McG, Jennifer Klein, Mary Viola. *Creator-Writer:* Sheldon Turner.
Story: A mild-mannered San Francisco police detective receives help in solving crimes from a most unusual assistant—his imaginary partner, a rogue cop.

Good Girls (Comedy, CBS, 2009).
Producer: Ashton Kutcher, Karey Burke, Jason Goldberg. *Creator-Writer:* Ellen Kreamer, Shirley Bilsing-Graham.
Story: Two women attempt to reconstruct their lives after they realize the mistakes they made in the past are affecting their future happiness.

Good Guys/Bad Guys (Crime Drama, Fox, 1999).
Producer: Tom Fontana, Barry Levinson. *Creator-Writer:* Julie Martin.
Story: A female FBI agent teams with a former crime syndicate boss to solve complex crimes.

The Good Life (Comedy, Fox, 2011).
Producer: Peter Chernin, Katherine Pope, Brad Mendelsohn. *Creator-Writer:* Carlos Kotkin.
Story: A young man's efforts to cope with life's everyday problems.

The Good Shepherd (Drama, Showtime, 2012).
Producer: Robert DeNiro, Jane Rosenthal. *Creator-Writer:* Eric Roth.
Story: An adaptation of the feature film that explores the early years of the CIA.

The Gourmet Detective (Crime Drama, USA, 2009).
Producer: Randy Zisk, Steve Valentine.
Story: A brilliant detective with expensive tastes in food solves crimes associated with the culinary world.

Grace (Drama, ABC, 2016).
Producer: David Hoberman, Laurie Zaks, Todd Lieberman. *Creator-Writer:* Jonathan E. Stewart.
Story: A family's efforts to cope with the situations that arise when the father, a minister, reveals that he is gay.

Grandma Dearest (Comedy, ABC, 2014).
Producer: Jamie Tarses, Moses Port. *Creator-Writer:* Todd Linden.
Story: A young woman finds her life changing for the worst when her obnoxious, self-centered grandmother loses her fortune and with no place else to go moves in with her.

Granny Is My Wingman (Comedy, CBS, 2012).
Producer: Jerry Bruckheimer, Jonathan Littman, Kristie Anne Reed. *Creator-Writer:* Donald Todd, Kayli Stollak.
Story: Dating as seen through an unlikely pair: a 25 year-old man and his 76-year-old grandmother who are experimenting with on-line dating.

Grave Sight (Drama, CBS, 2011).
Producer: Ridley Scott, Tony Scott. *Creator-Writer:* Charlaine Harris.
Story: Harper Connelly is a young woman with an unusual ability to sense the final location of a person who has passed. She can also see their last moment and the proposal was to follow Harper as she seeks to bring closure to the living as well as the deceased souls who have unfinished business.

Graysmith (Crime Drama, TNT, 2010).
Producer: Tony Scott. *Creator-Writer:* Ridley Scott, Dan Gordon.
Story: The unconventional methods used by Robert Graysmith, cartoonist, writer and part-time detective to solve crimes.

The Graysons (Drama, WB, 2004).
Producer: McG, Peter Johnson. *Creator-Writer:* Brian Peterson, Kelly Souders.
Story: Events in the life of Dick Grayson before he aligned himself with Batman to become Robin, the Boy Wonder and battle criminals in Gotham City.

The Green Detective (Crime Drama, TNT, 2010).
Producer-Creator: Steven Bochco.
Story: A detective, who is also an environmentalist, tackles cases of fraud for insurance companies.

Grimjack (Drama, Amazon, 2019).
Producer: Anthony Russo, Joe Russo. *Creator-Writer:* Kevin Murphy.
Story: Cynosure, a pan dimensional city where all dimensions connect, is home to John Gaunt, "a sword-for-hire" known as Grimjack. He operates from Munden's Bar in a slum area called "The Pit" and his efforts to fulfill the conditions of his clients' wishes were to be related.

Grow Up (Comedy, Fox, 2019).
Producer: Aaron Kaplan, Dana Honor, Justin Halpern. *Creator-Writer:* Tommy Johnagin.
Story: Flashbacks were to be used to tell the story of the friendship between two men who became friends as children but never really matured as adults.

Guantanamo (Drama, Showtime, 2018).
Producer: Harvey Weinstein, Alexandra Milchan. *Creator-Writer:* Daniel Voll.
Story: A behind-the-scenes look at the inmates, guards and personnel at the U.S. prison Guantanamo.

Guardians (Comedy, NBC, 2010).
Producer: Karey Burke, Todd Holland. *Creator-Writer:* Carlos Jacott, Ajay Sahgal.
Story: Angels, posing as workers at Starbucks, attempt to perform good deeds by helping the troubled customers they serve.

Guinea Pigs (Drama, CBS, 2012).
Producer: Katherine Pope, Peter Chernin. *Creator-Writer:* Dahvi Waller.

Story: A team of doctors, based at a Philadelphia hospital, attempt to save lives through experimental treatments on human subjects.

The Gumm Sisters (Drama, Lifetime, 2005). *Producer:* Kathy Najimy, David Janollari. *Creator-Writer:* James Myhre.
Story: Events in the lives of three overweight sisters: a lawyer, a pastry chef and an actress. A similar idea appeared as the 1990s Fox series *Babes*.

Hacktivist (Drama, CW, 2017). *Producer:* Alyssa Milano, Ross Richie. *Creator-Writer:* Chris Ord.
Story: An adaptation of actress Alyssa Milano's comic book about Nat Grant and Ed Hickox, co-founders of a social networking company who are recruited by the CIA to bring about world-wide social change.

Half Full (Comedy, NBC, 2013). *Producer:* Jennifer Garner, Juliana Janes. *Creator-Writer:* Matthew Nicklaw.
Story: A newlywed couple about to move to Manhattan to start their new lives together encounter a setback when the wife learns she is pregnant (and for not disclosed reasons) must remain where she is to have her baby.

Hannibal (Cartoon, BET, 2007). *Producer:* Vin Diesel, Samantha Vincent.
Story: Exaggerated historical project that traces the life of Hannibal—from his birth to his training to become a warrior and king to his crossing the Alps with a herd of elephants to his ambition to defeat Rome.

Happily Ever After (Comedy, Showtime, 2013). *Producer-Creator:* Timothy Busfield, Jeff Daniels. *Story:* A young man with dreams of becoming a famous musician quits his job as a factory worker to pursue that ambition.

Harlem High (Drama, Freeform, 2019). *Producer:* Will Smith, Jada Pinkett Smith, Tommy Mottola. *Creator-Writer:* Sam Laybourne.
Story: Musical drama that focuses on a group of choir students at Harlem High School in Manhattan.

Harmony (Drama, ABC, 2017).
Producer: David Hoberman, Todd Lieberman. *Creator-Writer:* Bradley Bredeweg, Jacob Chase. *Story:* Incidents in the lives of people living in Harmony, a small town New York tourist attraction where they sing and dance to their emotions.

Harmony House (Comedy, NBC, 2013). *Producer:* Aaron Kaplan. *Creator-Writer:* Neil LaBute.
Story: Portrait of an unusual romance: A young male psychiatrist and the woman of his dreams—a patient he discovers at Harmony House, a psychiatric institution.

Hart to Hart (Crime Drama, NBC, 2015). *Producer:* Carol Mendelsohn, Julie Weitz. *Creator-Writer:* Christopher Fife.
Story: Although said to be a reboot of the 1979-1984 ABC series of the same title (which dealt with the crime-solving adventures of Jonathan Hart and his wife, Jennifer), it is far from it. Here Jonathan Hart is an attorney (not head of Hart Enterprises) and his partner is Dan Hartman, a private investigator who works with him to solve crimes.

Harvekarbo (Crime Drama, Fox, 2011). *Producer:* Brian Grazer, Francie Calfo. *Creator-Writer:* Joel Coen, Phil Johnston.

Story: Brian Harvekarbo, a Los Angeles private detective with a severe attitude problem, tackles cases that are a bit unusual—solving the "depraved doings" of Hollywood's elite celebrities.

Harvest (Drama, Spike TV, 2015).
Producer: Jerry Bruckheimer, Jonathan Littman, Kristie Anne Reed. *Creator-Writer:* Matt Morgan.
Story: To support his family, a father, working days as a cemetery caretaker and nights attending nursing school classes, joins with an unethical friend in a business that harvests black market human tissue and body parts.

Hawkshaw (Crime Drama, CW, 2010).
Producer: Samuel L. Jackson, Amanda Tracey. *Creator-Writer:* David Loughery.
Story: David Hawkshaw is a brilliant detective who solves complex crimes but is not sure how. He was adopted and not aware of his real identity but believes he is either a descendant of Sherlock Holmes or Holmes' creator, Sir Arthur Conan Doyle.

Headhunters (Drama, WE, 2013).
Producer: Tom Fontana, Barry Levinson. *Creator-Writer:* Susanna Styron.
Story: A look at a group of women and the choices they make in the situations that surround them.

Headquarters (Crime Drama, NBC, 1969).
Producer: Franklin Schaffner. *Writer:* Alvin Boretz.
Story: The cases tackled by the Headquarters Squad of the N.Y.P.D.

Heart Attack Grill (Comedy, ABC, 2012).
Producer: Courteney Cox, David Arquette. *Creator-Writer:* Rob Sheridan.

Story: A once overweight woman, now gorgeous and slim, attempts to adjust to a new set of circumstances (her looks) while working with her ex-husband in a diner that caters to people who love to eat.

Hearts & Clubs (Drama, ABC Family, 2014).
Producer: Christina Aguilera, Austin Winsberg, Matthew Rutler.
Story: Young people are profiled as they chase their dreams but battle the demons that could destroy their chances at success.

The Heavens (Drama, Amazon, 2019).
Producer: Anthony Russo, Joe Russo. *Creator-Writer:* Lev Grossman.
Story: A young woman's battle against evil as she incorporates a mysterious weapon, supposedly the remnant of a lost civilization that endows its possessor with amazing abilities.

Hellmart (Comedy, CW, 2016).
Producer: Eric Tannenbaum, Kim Tannenbaum. *Creator-Writer:* Ben Newmark, Dan Newmark.
Story: Souls not considered candidates for Heaven are regulated to Hellmart, a department store where workers must earn their wings by helping trouble store patrons overcome their problems.

Hello Again (Comedy, CBS, 2015).
Producer: Aaron Kaplan. *Creator-Writer:* Liz Feldman.
Story: The incidents that befall a happily married woman when the only other man she ever really loved moves into the house next door to her and her husband.

The Henchman (Comedy, Fox, 2013).
Producer: Aaron Kaplan, John Hamburg. *Creator-Writer:* Dan Kopelman.
Story: A middle-aged man struggles to deal with

single parenthood and a job he detests—being the henchman for the world's worst super villain.

Her Body and Other Parties (Anthology, FX, 2018).
Producer: Brian Grazer, Francie Calfo. *Creator-Writer:* Carmen Maria Machado, Gina Welch.
Story: Dramas based on the short story collection by Carmen Maria Machado that explores the fears and desires possessed by women.

Her Honor (Drama, CBS, 2016).
Producer: Judge Judith Sheindlin, Anne Kopelson, Arnold Kopelson. *Creator-Writer:* Judge Judith Sheindlin, Michael Chernuchin.
Story: Judith Sheindlin, better known as Judge Judy (and star of the TV series of the same name) provides the inspiration for a look at the life of a New York City Family Court judge who can handle the cases presented to her but has a difficult time maintaining control of her life outside the courtroom.

Here If You Need Me (Drama, CBS, 2013).
Producer: Carol Mendelsohn, Julie Weitz, Jeffrey Kramer. *Creator-Writer:* Neil Tolkin.
Story: After her husband is killed in the line of duty, a female state trooper finds help in apprehending law breakers through her husband's spiritual assistance.

Hero (Drama, Showtime, 2008).
Producer: Stan Lee, Gill Champion, Hunter Hill, Perry Moore. *Creator-Writer:* Stan Lee.
Story: Stan Lee's effort to introduce a gay super hero as seen through a budding hero who is struggling to not only keep his true identity a secret by hide his sexual orientation from his fellow super heroes.

Highway to Heaven (Drama, A&E, 2014).
Producer: Mark Wahlberg, Noreen Halpern, Stephen Levinson. *Creator-Writer:* John Wirth.
Story: A remake of the 1984-1989 NBC series of the same title about Jonathan Smith, an earthbound angel who helps people in trouble.

Hike (Crime Drama, TNT, 2011).
Producer-Creator: Forest Whittaker, Amanda Green.
Story: The cases handled by a female police detective who oversees the Home Invasion Kidnapping Enforcement Team in Phoenix, Arizona (termed "The kidnapping capital of the U.S.").

The History of Music (Drama, HBO, 2011).
Producer: Martin Scorsese, Mick Jagger, Victoria Pearman.
Story: The lives of two friends are chronicled over a forty year period as they navigate the world of music from the early days of Rhythm and Blues to the current trend of Hip Hop.

HIT (Crime Drama, TNT, 2012).
Producer: Jamie Foxx, Jamie King. *Creator-Writer:* Jamie Foxx, Robert Port.
Story: Two former high school friends and members of the football team are reunited when they become members of HIT (High Impact Team) of the Miami Police Department to use their athletic skills to battle crime.

Hit Man (Drama, FX, 2008).
Producer: Sarah Timberman, Carl Beverly. *Creator-Writer:* Michael Dinner.
Story: Incidents in the life of a seemingly normal suburban man who is secretly a hit man for hire.

Hit Men (Drama, Spike TV, 2013).
Producer: Gene Simmons, Leslie Greif. *Creator-Writer:* Chris Collins.
Story: Billed as "the untold story" of how the Mafia incorporates assassins to do their dirty work.

Hitch (Comedy, Fox, 2014).
Producer: Will Smith, Caleeb Pinkett, Deborah Kaplan. *Creator-Writer:* Ben Wexler, Harry Elfont.
Story: An adaptation of the feature film of the same title that humorously explores dating and sexual politics.

The Hitchhiker's Guide to the Galaxy (Comedy, ABC, 1982).
Producer: Don Taffner. *Creator-Writer:* Douglas Adams.
Story: Minutes before the Earth is destroyed by a Vogon ship to make way for a hyperspace bypass, Ford Prefect, an alien field researcher for *The Hitchhiker's Guide* rescues Arthur Dent, an earthling, from the impending doom. Arthur becomes Ford's assistant and the proposal, based on the British series of the same title (and the book by Carlton Cuse), was to chart their adventures as they become hitchhikers in space.

The Hobby (Drama, Showtime, 2004).
Producer: Neal H. Moritz, Dawn Olmstead, James Wong, Marty Adelstein.
Story: A look at the world of prostitution that focuses on the girls, the men who control them, and the high-end industry for which they work.

Hold Fast (Drama, CW, 2017).
Producer: Greg Berlanti, Sarah Schechter. *Creator-Writer:* Dana Stevens.
Story: After being injured during a battle, a Civil War Union soldier awakens from a coma to find himself in modern-day Charleston. Using two timelines (the 1860s and present day 2017) the project was to relate what happens as he attempts to navigate both worlds while attempting to hold onto memories of his past life, which are becoming increasingly hazy.

Hollows (Drama, CW, 2011).
Producer: Carol Mendelsohn, Julie Weitz. *Creator-Writer:* Jordan Hawley.
Story: Rachel Morgan, a demon bounty hunter, and her assistants, a vampire and a pixy, battle the supernatural beings (werewolves, vampires and witches) that inhabit an alternate universe in Cincinnati, Ohio. Based on the novels by Kim Harrison.

Holly Gale (Comedy, CBS, 2009).
Producer: Sarah Timberman, Carl Beverly. *Creator-Writer:* Tom Wolf, Barbara Wallace.
Story: A former cheerleading star returns to her small home town to become her former high school's cheerleading coach.

The Hollywood Story (Anthology, NBC, 1961).
Producer: David Wolper.
Story: A profile of Hollywood celebrities using film clips and reminisces of people associated with the chosen subject. A similar series called *Hollywood and the Stars* would appear in 1963 with Joseph Cotten as the host.

Home Economics (Comedy, Fox, 2018).
Producer: Eric Tannenbaum, Kim Tannenbaum. *Creator-Writer:* Michael Colton.
Story: Three adult siblings attempt to cope with life: one barely able to keep his head above water, one a middle class worker, and one rich and spoiled.

The Home Front (Comedy, ABC, 2015). *Producer:* Todd Holland. *Creator:* Colleen McGuinness.
Story: After serving his country for many years, a retired Green Beret finds that adjusting to civilian life in the suburbs a nightmare when he moves next door to his daughter and her children.

The Honeymooners (Comedy, CBS, 2016). *Producer:* Eric Tannenbaum, Kim Tannenbaum, Carl Beverly. *Creator-Writer:* Bob Kushell.
Story: A modern-day version of the classic 1955-1956 series of the same title about two best friends and neighbors living in the same apartment house. Here, however, one couple had been divorced but remarried four years later.

The Honorable & Mrs. (Drama, Fox, 2004). *Producer:* Shawn Levy, Sean Bailey, Amy Harris.
Story: A female ambassador to the United Nations teams with a male CIA agent to perform undercover assignments as a married couple.

Hood River (Comedy, Fox, 2018). *Producer:* Aaron Kaplan, Dana Honor. *Creator-Writer:* Travis Bowe.
Story: A look at the staff and clientele of a neighborhood bar in the town of Hood River.

Hoops (Drama, NBC, 2018). *Producer:* LeBron James, Elizabeth Banks, Max Handelman. *Creator-Writer:* Jennifer Cecil.
Story: A twist on high school and college athletic coaches wherein a former female star player with the WNBA becomes the first woman coach of a men's college basketball team.

Hopscotch (Crime Drama, ABC, 2010). *Producer:* Jerry Bruckheimer, Jonathan Littman, Kristie Anne Reed. *Creator-Writer:* Chris Levinson.
Story: Each case being investigated by homicide detectives is seen over several nonconsecutive days with each act (following a commercial break) representing a different day.

Horrorsror (Drama, Fox, 2015). *Producer:* Stephanie Savage, Charlie Kaufman, Gail Berman. *Creator-Writer:* Josh Schwartz.
Story: ORSK is the U.S. flagship store for a European furniture empire that uses it as a cover for their supernatural activities. It preys upon its customers by granting them their dreams or fantasies in unexpected and often insidious ways. Had the project sold, it would have explored the people whose lives are affected by shopping at ORSK.

Hospitality (Comedy, NBC, 2014). *Producer:* Sean Hayes, Todd Milliner. *Creator-Writer:* Chris Moynihan.
Story: A proposed live weekly series that was to focus on the hospitality staff of a busy Manhattan hotel.

Hotel Dix (Drama, USA, 2010). *Producer:* Tom Fontana, Adam Bernstein. *Creator-Writer:* Tom Fontana.
Story: A retired detective, accustomed to dealing with criminals in his antiquated ways, faces new challenges when he becomes a hotel house detective and must deal with a new breed of criminal.

Houdini (Crime Drama, ABC, 2013). *Producer:* David Hoberman, Laurie Zaks, Todd Lieberman. *Creator-Writer:* Jeff Addis.
Story: Period drama (set in early 1900s) that team illusionist Harry Houdini with a female detective to solve crimes for the L.A.P.D.

Hourman (Drama, CW, 2014).
Producer: Jennifer Gwartz, Dan Lin. *Creator-Writer:* Michael Caleo.
Story: An adaptation of the D.C. comic book about a pharmaceutical analyst who uses his ability to see events one hour into the future to solve crimes.

House Calls (2011) (Drama, ABC, 2011).
Producer: Jerry Bruckheimer, Jonathan Littman, Kristie Anne Reed. *Creator-Writer:* Sascha Penn.
Story: A doctor, feeling the need to help people away from a hospital setting, resigns and returns to his small town to do what doctors once did—make house calls.

House Calls (2012) (Drama, CW, 2012).
Producer: Jerry Bruckheimer, Jonathan Littman, Kristie Anne Reed. *Creator:* Sascha Penn.
Story: In an attempt to better serve the people of their community three young doctors begin a practice where they are on call 24 hours a day, 7 days a week.

House of Cards (Comedy, USA, 2011).
Producer: Gail Berman, Andy Weil, Gene Stein. *Creator-Writer:* Lloyd Braun.
Story: A college graduate's search for the girl of his dreams by taking various jobs until he finds her.

How the Other Half Hamptons (Drama, Freeform, 2020).
Producer: Aaron Kaplan, Dana Honor, Kelly Ripa, Mark Consuelos. *Creator-Writer:* Brian Buckner.
Story: Incidents in the lives of the people who vacation at the Hamptons, the luxurious Long Island, New York playground for the rich and famous.

How to Get Run Over By a Truck (Drama, CW, 2019).
Producer: Ellen DeGeneres, Jeff Kleeman. *Creator-Writer:* David Hein, Irene Sankoff.
Story: An adaptation of the book by Kate McKenna about her experiences after being hit by an 18-wheel truck and being brought to the best trauma center in New York—the prison hospital at Riker's Island.

How to Grow Up (Comedy, CBS, 2012).
Producer: Jeff Filgo, Jackie Filgo. *Creator-Writer:* Evan Susser.
Story: A lawyer, turning thirty and living a rather boring life, finds a box of VHS tapes he made when he was ten years old wherein he gave his future self advice on how to be an adult. As the lawyer watches the tapes, stories were to reflect how he incorporates that advice in his present situation.

How to Remodel a Man (Comedy, NBC, 2004).
Producer: David Schwimmer, Bruce Cameron.
Story: A newly divorced young man seeks relationship help from the women in his life.

How to Survive a Home Invasion (Comedy, ABC, 2011).
Producer: Mark Gordon, Andrea Say. *Creator-Writer:* David A. Katz.
Story: A middle-aged man's efforts to survive his own personal home invasion when he is pushed out of his comfort zone by his college-aged son and elderly mother when they move in with him.

Howl (Drama, Fox, 2010).
Producer: Darryl Frank, Justin Falvey. *Creator-Writer:* M.A. Fortin, Joshua Miller.
Story: Set in Alaska and billed as "an epic family saga" that details the warring rivalry between two werewolf clans.

Human Relations (Drama, Syfy, 2011).
Producer: Tom Lassally, Dave Krinsky. *Creator-Writer:* Scott Prendergast.
Story: An ad agency office worker plots to foil and alien invasion when he discovers that his employers are actually extraterrestrials who have taken human form and plan to destroy the earth.

Humanities (Drama, HBO, 2010).
Producer: Gavin Polone, Frank Spotnitz.
Story: Futuristic medical drama set at a time when major advances have been accomplished—but whose accomplishments also present new and more difficult challenges for doctors in treating patients.

Hungry (Drama, Fox, 2015).
Producer: Marti Noxon, Meryl Poster. *Creator-Writer:* Nina Coleman.
Story: A young chef school graduate's experiences when he acquires a thankless job—line chef to an obnoxious, demanding culinary celebrity.

The Hunt (Drama, A&E, 2007).
Producer: Sheldon Turner. *Creator-Writer:* Jennifer Klein.
Story: A former L.A.P.D. police officer who, after serving time in prison for his participation in a money scandal, resumes his role as a law enforcer but battling criminals outside the justice system.

Hurt People (Drama, Cinemax, 2012).
Producer: William Petersen, Cynthia Chvatal, Graham King. *Creator-Writer:* Peter MacManus.
Story: A young woman, intent on finding those responsible for killing her mother, begins her quest, unaware that she is being followed by her father, a hit man for the crime family responsible, who has been assigned to stop her.

Hustle (Drama, CW, 2011).
Producer: McG, Peter Johnson. *Creator-Writer:* Jeremy Miller, Dan Cohn.
Story: Five people in their mid-twenties become a modern day *Mod Squad* (ABC, 1968-1973) to help the FBI stop youth oriented crimes in Los Angeles.

Hyde (Drama, ABC, 2011).
Producer: Sheldon Turner, Jennifer Klein. *Writer:* Sheldon Turner.
Story: Adaptation of the Robert Louis Stevenson book, *Dr. Jekyll and Mr. Hyde*, here updated to the present where a man struggles to cope with a split personality—normal by day but a dangerous individual when he transforms into his other self at night.

The I Do Crew (Drama, CW, 2016).
Producer: Gina Matthews, Grant Scharbo. *Creator-Writer:* Erin Cardillo, Richard Keith.
Story: A look at the incidents that occurred before a destined-to-happen wedding as told through friends of the bride and groom.

I Got You Babies (Reality, TLC, 2015).
Producer: Drew Barrymore, Nancy Juvonen.
Story: A look at married couples who become first time parents.

I Guess I Do (Comedy, NBC, 2012).
Producer: Will Ferrell, Adam McKay. *Creator-Writer:* Kauryn Kahn.
Story: A psychology grad student marries a womanizing British celebrity trainer so she can stay in the U.S. while he uses her for his thesis on the modern male.

I Hate Los Angeles Dudes (Comedy, ABC, 2013).
Producer: Shonda Rhimes, Betsy Beers. *Creator-Writer:* Issa Rae.
Story: A young female journalist, new to Los Angeles and the only woman on a male based Internet talk show, struggles to understand and cope with the confusing rules of the West Coast dating scene.

I Hate the Internet (Drama, TNT, 2018).
Producer: Chelsea Handler, Katherine Pope, Michael Morris.
Story: An adaptation of the book by Jarett Kobek that explores a 40-year-old woman's experiences with the Internet as she seeks the answers to today's most perplexing questions.

I Love Faron Hitchman (Comedy, NBC, 2005).
Producer: Betty Thomas, Kelly Kulchak, J.B. Roberts. *Creator-Writer:* Carlos Jacott.
Story: Faron is a young man who, due to his irresponsible ways, has been cut off from his wealthy family's trust fund; Sally, a fun-loving girl, is the daughter of an over-bearing Italian-American family. Faron and Sally are also married and the proposal was to relate their efforts to survive a difficult marriage as they wed before they were ready (they are "55 percent in love with each other").

I Love Lakshmi (Comedy, NBC, 2015).
Producer-Creator-Writer: Jason Bateman, Muffy Bolding.
Story: Danny, an American, marries Lakshmi, an Indian woman, and must contend with her immigrant meddlesome parents—who came to the U.S. to pursue an American Dream that never included Danny.

I Love Your Ex (Comedy, ABC, 2014).
Producer: Will Gluck. *Creator:* Angela Kinsey, Audrey Wauchope, Darlene Hunt, Rachel Specter.
Story: The unusual life of a man caught in the middle of a best friend relationship between his wife and his ex-girlfriend.

I, P.I. (Crime Drama, ABC, 2010).
Producer: McG, Peter Johnson. *Creator-Writer:* Paul Scheuring.
Story: The cases of a private investigator whose knowledge about crime solving comes from his watching the TV detective series of the 1980s while growing up.

I Spike (Crime Drama, UPN, 2000).
Cast: Lisa Rinna, Daisy Fuentes.
Story: A battle against crime as seen through two female covert operatives who pose as professional volleyball players.

I Witness (Crime Drama, CBS, 2010).
Producer-Creator: Pam Veasey, Trey Callaway.
Story: Erin Bray, a college professor fascinated by crime solving, uses her psycho-physiological skills as an amateur detective to help the police solve baffling crimes.

I'll Cuddle When I'm Dead (Comedy, WB, 2005).
Producer: Jamie Tarses, Karey Burke. *Creator-Writer:* Stacy Traub.
Story: A young couple who married before they were ready attempt to make their marriage work.

I'm Not Myself These Days (Drama, Bravo, 2010).
Producer: Darren Star. *Creator-Writer:* Emily Branden.
Story: An adaptation of the novel of the same

name about a man (Josh) who, by day, is a loving family man and affluent power broker but by night works clubs as a drag queen.

ICE (2008) (Drama, CBS, 2008).
Producer: Eriq La Salle, Terri Lubaroff. *Writer:* Michael Steinberg.
Story: Agents with the Miami based Immigration and Customs Enforcement are followed as they tackle cases that involve dismantling global crime organizations.

Ice Cub Untitled Project (Crime Drama, Spike TV, 2005).
Producer: Ice Cube, Tony Krantz. *Creator-Writer:* Matthew Cirulnick.
Story: A 21-year-old career criminal, caught red-handed during a crime, becomes an undercover agent for the police department to expose the rackets that are destroying his city.

Iman & Andy (Comedy, ABC, 2013).
Producer: Whoopi Goldberg, Ben Silverman, Tom Leonardis. *Creator-Writer:* Angela Ruhinda.
Story: An interracial couple working as newspaper advice columnists dispenses advice based on the situations they encounter as they attempt to make their relationship work.

Imitation (Drama, NBC, 2014).
Producer: Jerry Bruckheimer, Jonathan Littman, Kristie Anne Reed, Leslie Morgenstein. *Creator-Writer:* Ian Sobel.
Story: An adaptation of the novel by Heather Hildebrand about Ven, a clone of a teenager named Raven Rogan, who, although she knows everything about the girl from which she was created, yearns to become a real person with her own personality and desires.

In Defense of Tom Parish (Drama, NBC, 2016).
Producer: Sean Hayes, Todd Milliner. *Creator-Writer:* Josh Posner, George Gallo.
Story: Tom Parish, a former art thief turned lawyer defends people who are falsely accused of crimes.

In Security (Comedy, ABC, 2014).
Producer: Aaron Kaplan, Sean Perrone. *Creator-Writer:* Annabel Oakes.
Story: Four women, working as private investigators tackle cases with ease as they just blend into society. The situation that develops when they are just themselves and find everything else hard to do was to be depicted.

In the Line of Fire (Drama, NBC, 2015).
Producer: Gail Katz, Julie Weitz. *Creator:* Carol Mendelsohn, Josh Berman.
Story: A Secret Service agent teams with a rogue CIA assassin to investigate threats made against the United States.

Infection (Drama, ABC, 2012).
Producer: Aaron Kaplan. *Creator-Writer:* Soo Hugh.
Story: Fictionalized account of what could happen if a deadly pandemic breaks out and the U.S. is divided in half with those infected confined to a border community to protect the rest of society.

Infidelity (Drama, Showtime, 2005).
Producer: Mark Gordon, Charles S. Dutton, Douglas Carter.
Story: Three strangers first seen by viewers in an elevator are tracked in individual stories as each drifts in an out of an extra-marital affair.

The Inn Crowd (Comedy, NBC, 2018). *Producer:* Jim Parsons, Todd Spiewak. *Creator-Writer:* David Holden.
Story: The situations that befall a gay couple when they open an inn in a small conservative town.

The Inside (Drama, FX, 2007). *Producer:* Jimmy Smits. *Creator-Writer:* Todd Robinson.
Story: A former Special Operatives agent faces new challenges when he agrees to become an undercover operative and infiltrate a dangerous drug cartel.

Inside Mary Baxter (Drama, NBC, 2009). *Producer:* Neil Meron, Craig Zadan.
Story: A look at life inside a women's prison as seen through the experiences of Mary Baxter, a young woman convicted of the murder of her abusive husband.

The Insiders (Drama, Fox, 2004). *Producer:* Leslie Morgenstein, Evan Katz.
Story: An adaptation of the book series by J. Menter about the incidents that befall five close friends who, as time passes, find themselves drifting apart and pursuing different interests.

The Interrogator (Crime Drama, ABC, 2004). *Producer:* Kelsey Grammer, Artie Mandelberg, Mark Israel. *Creator-Writer:* Steve Stark.
Story: An Atlanta-based psychiatrist uses his abilities as a human lie detector to help the police solve vicious crimes.

The Intruders (Comedy, Fox, 2009). *Producer:* McG, Peter Johnson. *Creator-Writer:* Danny Comden.
Story: A wealthy, divorced man with two children falls in love with "a white trash" single mother and creates problems for his family when he moves her and her family in with him.

The Invaders (Drama, ABC, 2015). *Producer:* Todd Lieberman, Laurie Zaks, David Hoberman. *Creator-Writer:* Ellen Fairey.
Story: A beachfront community provides the setting for a look at a group of residents and the dark secrets they keep hidden from "The Invaders" (outsiders who frequent their domain).

The Invincibles (Comedy, Fox, 2011). *Producer:* Tom Lassally, Jonathan Berry. *Creator-Writer:* Chris Sheridan.
Story: Four friends (three men and one woman) dump their mates, quit their jobs and choose to start over, hoping for a brighter future.

Invisible (2006) (Drama, NBC, 2006). *Producer:* Tom Lassally, Jonathan Berry. *Creator-Writer:* Chris Sheridan.
Story: A researcher for the Centers for Disease Control and Prevention seeks to find a cure for a mysterious illness that is threatening to infect the world's population.

Invisible (2008) (Drama, Fox 2008). *Producer:* Mc G., Peter Johnson. *Creator-Writer:* Ari Eisner.
Story: A criminal, coming in contact with a chemical compound during a heist, finds he can become invisible simply by willing it. Rather than continue his life of wrong doing, he chooses to use his ability to solve crimes.

Island Practice (Drama, CBS, 2012). *Producer:* Brain Grazer, Francie Calfo, Oly Obst. *Creator-Writer:* Amy Holden Jones.
Story: An adaptation of the book by Pam Belluck about a maverick doctor, operating on an island off the coast of Seattle, who uses controversial methods to treat his patients.

The IT Crowd (Comedy, NBC, 2014).
Producer: Thom Beers, Jeff Ingold, Bill Lawrence.
Story: A major corporation provides the setting for a look at three employees—two IT nerds confined to the basement who are clumsy at reacting with people; and their female manager, a woman who knows nothing about computers.

It Takes Two (Comedy, Fox, 2018).
Producer: Eric Tannenbaum, Kim Tannenbaum, Austin Winsberg. *Creator-Writer:* Jon Silberman.
Story: An adaptation of the book by Drew Scott that tells of him and his twin brother, Jonathan, and their efforts work together as owners of a real estate business.

It's a Date (Anthology, POP, 2017).
Producer: Sarah Jessica Parker, Alison Benson.
Creator-Writer: Laura Waters.
Story: Dramas that explore how men and women each pursue love in the modern-day world.

J. Edgar Hoover and the FBI (Anthology, CBS, 1957).
Creator: Don Whitehead (author of the book *The FBI Story*).
Story: Fictionalized accounts based on the real experiences of agents of the Federal Bureau of Investigation. At the time CBS had concerns that J. Edgar Hoover, head of the FBI, would not permit his name to be used in the title or even give his seal of approval. Had the project sold it would have likely been called *The FBI Story* with Mr. Hoover appearing briefly to explain that the fictionalized book, not the actual experiences of the FBI, are the subject of stories.

Jack Irish (Drama, Fox, 2014).
Producer: Katherine Pope, Peter Chernin. Anna Fricke. *Creator-Writer:* Seamus Kevin Fahey.
Story: Events in the life of Jack Irish, apprentice cabinet maker, debt collector and part-time lawyer as he struggles to readjust to life after the murder of his wife.

Jackie Guerra Untitled Project (Comedy, CBS, 2003).
Producer: Jackie Guerra, Freddy Soto.
Story: Incidents in the life of a socially conscious young woman and her hapless brother.

Jamie Kennedy Untitled Project (Reality, Comedy Central, 2004).
Producer: Jamie Kennedy, Charles Siskel.
Story: Hidden camera project wherein Jamie Kennedy approaches people on the street to get their reactions to issues that affect them in their daily lives.

Jax and Amber (Crime Drama, CBS, 2010).
Producer: Anthony Zuiker, Deren Sarafian.
Creator-Writer: Elizabeth Devine.
Story: Female detectives Jax and Amber use their unique ability to zero in on a criminal's actions to solve crimes.

Jekyll & Hyde (Drama, ABC, 2011).
Producer: Mark Gordon. *Creator-Writer:* Matt Lopez.
Story: A take on the Robert Lewis Stevenson novel *Dr. Jekyll and Mr. Hyde* here featuring a female criminal psychologist who befriends a brilliant scientist with an incredible secret—he has the ability to change from his mild-mannered self into a vicious alter ego.

Jenn-X (Drama, UPN, 2001).
Producer: Aaron Spelling, E. Duke Vincent.
Creator-Writer: Duncan Kennedy.
Story: A young woman, near death after an automobile accident, is given an experimental operation that not only saves her life, but

genetically enhances her. The proposal was to follow the girl (Jenn) as she struggles to adjust to life as the world's first cybernetic enhanced human.

Jennifer Garner Untitled Project (Comedy, NBC, 2012).
Producer: Jennifer Garner, Daniel Rappaport.
Creator-Writer: Ellen Rappaport.
Story: A nerdy, over-achieving girl in her twenties finds her life changing when she is befriended by two promiscuous party girls who want to make her like them.

Jennifer Lopez Untitled 2010 Project (Comedy, MTV, 2010).
Producer: Jennifer Lopez, Benny Medina, Simon Fields. *Creator-Writer:* Grace Parra.
Story: Unable to find a job due to the bad economy at the time, a recent New York University graduate finds she has no other choice but to return to her home in Texas where her mishaps living with her eccentric family were to be depicted.

Jennifer Lopez Untitled 2011 Project (Drama, Fox, 2011).
Producer: Jennifer Lopez, Simon Fields. *Creator-Writer:* Silvio Horta.
Story: Incidents in the lives of three close-knit Latina sisters.

Jennifer Lopez Untitled 2016 Project (Drama, CBS, 2016).
Producer: Jennifer Lopez, Elaine Goldsmith-Thomas. *Creator-Writer:* Michael Rauch.
Story: Twin brothers who are lawyers but polar opposites combine their talents to defend clients.

Jennifer Salt Untitled Project (Drama, NBC, 2010).
Producer: Karey Burke, Todd Holland. *Creator-Writer-Producer:* Jennifer Salt.
Story: A behind-the-scenes look at the preparations that make a successful restaurant as seen through the activities of a celebrity chef whose notoriety brings in the patrons.

The Jetsons (Comedy, ABC, 2017).
Producer: Robert Zemeckis, Jack Rapke. *Creator-Writer:* Gary Janetti.
Story: Live-action remake of the 1962 ABC animated series of the same title about the Jetsons, a futuristic family struggling to cope with the daily pressures of life.

Jigsaw (Drama, CBS, 2013).
Producer: Stephanie Savage, Len Goldstein, Josh Schwartz.
Story: Detectives with the Homicide Division of the San Francisco Police Department join with lawyers, the media and the Mayor's office to solve scandalous crimes.

Jim Parsons Untitled Project (Comedy, CBS, 2015).
Producer: Jim Parsons, Todd Spiewak. *Creator-Writer:* Alyssa Shelasky, Marisa Coughlan.
Story: A 40-year-old woman's experiences when she moves into a building where her eccentric neighbors begin acting like her supportive family.

Jimmy Kimmel Untitled Project (Comedy, ABC, 2014).
Producer: Carson Daly, Don Fogelman. *Creator-Producer-Writer:* Jimmy Kimmel.
Story: A once popular video d.j. attempts to adjust to a new life when he is fired, moves back in with his parents and degrades himself by taking a job as the host of a morning radio drive-time program.

Joe Duffy (Cartoon, Spike TV, 2002). *Producer-Writer:* Ed Weinberger.
Story: Incidents in the life of Joe Duffy, an outspoken, uncouth and somewhat racist character who works as a limo driver.

The Joe Squad (Cartoon, Comedy Central, 2010).
Producer: Marty Adelstein, Blake McCormick.
Story: The Joe Squad is an elite unit of super heroes who have banned together to save the world (even if it means destroying it first). Captain Falcon is the team's sex-obsessed leader; he is assisted by Auburn, a sexy redhead; Berserker, "the chiseled over-tanned" heavyweight; Butchley, a female Arnold Schwarzenegger–type; Brick House, the "insanely jaded" African-American Muslim; Dutch, the all–American "good guy" and Lone Wolf, a mute Ninja. Their enemies, who are as inept as they are, are Master Snake and his team, the Rattlers.

Joe 2.0 (Comedy, ABC, 2016).
Producer: Aaron Kaplan, Dana Honor. *Creator-Writer:* Courtney Lilly.
Story: The idea was to explore "what it means to be an African-American man" in today's world through a recently divorced high school teacher and his attempts to begin a new life without a wife by his side.

John Corey (Drama, ABC, 2016).
Producer: Mace Neufeld, John Davis, John Fox. *Creator-Writer:* Jason Richman.
Story: John Corey, a quick-witted and brash homicide detective with the N.Y.P.D. is followed as he deals his own brand of justice in the current social environment.

John Stamos Untitled Project (Drama, Amazon, 2017).
Producer: John Stamos, Neil Meron. *Creator-Writer:* Adam Stein, Craig Zadan.
Story: Tracks the rise to fame of an 18-year-old winner of a TV talent search when he is billed as "The Next Big Thing" and ventures forth into a world he has never known before.

Johnny Depp Untitled Project (Drama, Lifetime, 2011).
Producer: Johnny Depp, Graham King. *Creator-Writer:* Robert C. Cooper.
Story: Explores the life of William Wilkerson, the founder of *The Hollywood Reporter*, at a time when he was addicted to gambling and became indebted to the Mafia.

Johnny Dynamite (Drama, NBC, 2008).
Producer: Dick Wolf, D.J. Caruso, Peter Jankowski.
Story: An ex-cop's battle against Satan—who is living and buying souls in Las Vegas.

Johnny Galecki Untitled Project (Comedy, CBS, 2016).
Producer: Johnny Galecki. *Creator-Writer:* Scott King.
Story: A husband's efforts to exert some authority into his life when he invites his wife's twin sister to move in with them and he suddenly becomes the third wheel in his marriage.

J.S.I.D. (Drama, NBC, 2017).
Producer: Neal H. Moritz, Craig Borten. *Creator-Writer:* Adam Mazer.
Story: Agents for the J.S.I.D. (Justice System Integrity Division) of the U.S. government investigate cases involving corrupt politicians, judges, police officers and lawyers.

Juarez General (Drama, Fox, 2015).
Producer: Tom Fontana, Barry Levinson, Josh Davis. *Creator-Writer:* Tom Fontana.
Story: The situations that befall the doctors, nurses and patients of a hospital situated on the border town of Juarez, New Mexico, which is said to be "the deadliest city in the world and ground zero for drug wars."

Juggernaut (Drama, UPN, 2003).
Producer: Robert Halmi, Sr., Lindy DeKoven. *Creator-Writer:* Scott Nimerfro.
Story: A United Nations-assembled group of mercenaries battle the extraterrestrials that are suddenly invading Earth.

Jujitsu Rabbi & The Godless Blonde (Comedy, Fox, 2013).
Producer: Jamie Tarses. *Creator-Writer:* Lauren Blum, Rebecca Dana.
Story: A young woman's experiences moving from a small town to Brooklyn, New York, and becoming friends with Cosmo, a 30-year-old Russian rabbi who practices Jujitsu on the side.

Julie and the Phantoms (Comedy, Netflix, 2019).
Producer: Kenny Ortega, George Salinas. *Creator-Writer:* Dan Cross, David Hoge.
Story: A teenage girl's (Julie) love for music brings her in contact with the Phantoms, a trio of male ghosts who could never make it as a music group in life but now with Julie's help they hope to become the band they feel they were meant to be.

Jump Start (Comedy, Fox, 2014).
Producer: Aaron Kaplan, Bridget McMeel. *Creator-Writer:* Andrew Orenstein.
Story: An adaptation of the Robb Armstrong comic strip about a Philadelphia beat cop who finds patrolling the streets much easier than dealing with his dysfunctional family.

Jumper (Drama, CW, 2007).
Producer: Eric Tannenbaum, Kim Tannenbaum. *Creator-Writer:* Daniel Noah.
Story: A male FBI agent with the ability to "jump" (inhabit) the body of a future murder victim and his female partner attempt to find killers before they strike.

Jumpmen (Drama, CBS, 2017).
Producer: Ben Silverman. *Creator-Writer:* Craig Tuck, Grant Thompson.
Story: One woman's experiences as a member of an Air Force team of parachute jumpers who risk their lives to recover victims of disasters in remote and often dangerous areas.

Jurassic Park: Camp Cretaceous (Cartoon, Netflix, 2019).
Producer: Steven Spielberg, Scott Kreamer, Frank Marshall, Lane Lueras.
Story: Comedic take on the *Jurassic Park* movie franchise where an adventure camp has been established on the opposite side of Isla Nublar (the island dinosaur attraction) but where a group of campers must struggle for survival when dinosaurs invade their domain.

Justin & Abby & Oh Yea, Zack Too (Comedy, CBS, 2014).
Producer: Eric Tannenbaum, Kim Tannenbaum. *Creator-Writer:* Justin Noble.
Story: The incidents that befall two best friends, Justin and Abby, and Abby's boyfriend, Zack, who feels like a third wheel.

Justin Bieber Untitled Project (Comedy, ABC, 2012).
Producer: Justin Bieber, Scooter Braun. *Creator-*

Writer: Ben Nedivi, Matt Wolpert.
Story: Incidents drawn from singer Justin Bieber's life that detail a pop star's early teenage years growing up in a somewhat unorthodox family.

Kachinga (Comedy, HBO, 2005).
Producer: Mark Gordon. *Creator-Writer:* Chuck Sklar.
Story: The changes that occur in the lives of a Native American family living on a reservation when they open a casino and become filthy rich.

Kamelot (Drama, UPN, 2004).
Producer: Wes Craven, Marianne Maddalena. *Creator-Writer:* Terri Hughes, Ron Milbauer.
Story: Although spelled as Kamelot instead of Camelot, it is a reworking of the legend of King Arthur and His Knights of the Round Table that places Arthur in modern times as a hero in a futuristic Camelot-like society.

Kane (Comedy, Syndication, 2002).
Producer: Howard Stern, Ron Zimmerman.
Story: Incidents in the lives of a dysfunctional Southern family that is ruled by an equally dysfunctional but strong-willed father.

Kari Lizer Untitled 2012 Project (Comedy, CBS, 2012).
Producer-Creator: Kari Lizer.
Story: The awkward situations that develop when a young man meets the woman of his dreams only to learn that she is his cousin's fiancée.

Kari Lizer Untitled 2020 Project (Comedy, ABC, 2020).
Producer-Creator: Kari Lizer.
Story: A middle-aged mother, despondent over the empty life she lives since her children moved out, solves her problem by relocating and becoming their neighbor.

Kasher in the Rye (Comedy, Showtime, 2013).
Producer: Dave Becky, Josh Lieberman, Matt Tolmach. *Creator-Writer:* Moshe Kasher.
Story: A teenage boy's experiences, living in Oakland, California during the 1990s and being raised by a deaf mother.

Kasongo (Adventure, Syndication, 1958).
Producer: Sol Lesser. *Writer:* Eliza Schallert, Edwin Schallert.
Story: Explorer-photographers Miki and Peg Carter are followed as they explore Africa with the assist of "a giant Watusi warrior, a pygmy and a white hunter."

Keep It in the Family (Reality, CW, 2010).
Producer: Donald Trump, Andy Litinsky.
Story: A profile of a family run business with a particular focus on which family member will eventually run the empire.

Keep Swinging (Comedy, ABC, 2012).
Producer: Conan O'Brien, David Kissinger, Jeff Ross. *Creator-Writer:* Lew Schneider, Rick Marin.
Story: Role reversal of the movie and TV series *That's My Boy* (about athletic parents with an adverse-to-sports son). Here parents with zero interest in sports have to readjust their lives to accommodate their son—a teenager whose life revolves around sports.

Keenan Ivory Wayans Untitled Project (Comedy, ABC, 2013).
Producer: Katherine Pope, Peter Chernin. *Creator-Writer:* Keenan Ivory Wayans.
Story: The mishaps that befall a young man, called by ABC's press release, "The whitest guy in America," when he marries into a close-knit African-American family.

Kegs (Comedy, ABC, 2010).
Producer: Todd Lieberman, David Hoberman.
Creator-Writer: Mark Perez, Jason Filardi.
Story: The problems that befall a dysfunctional family who are also the owners of a beer distribution plant.

Kelly Ripa Untitled 2013 Project (Comedy, ABC, 2013).
Producer: Kelly Ripa, Mark Consuelos. *Creator-Writer:* Sri Rao.
Story: A single mother joins with her three best friends to become owners of a small design company.

Kelly Ripa Untitled 2016 Project (Comedy, ABC, 2016).
Producer: Kelly Ripa, Mark Consuelos. *Creator-Writer:* Andrew Leeds.
Story: A married couple's efforts to accept each of their three daughter's boyfriends—men they despise but reluctantly allow becoming a part of their lives.

Kelsey Grammer Untitled Project (Comedy, ABC, 2017).
Producer: Kelsey Grammer, Tom Russo. *Creator-Writer:* Robert Peacock.
Story: Seeing that a depressed job market is preventing him from finding work, an ex-Marine moves in with his widowed mother, an opinionated conservative who opposes everything he stands for.

The Keys (Crime Drama, Fox, 2012).
Producer: Katherine Pope, Peter Chernin. *Creator-Writer:* Gary Scott Thompson.
Story: The cases handled by two unorthodox Miami police detectives working the Florida Keys.

The Kill Book (Drama, Freeform, 2017).
Producer: Aaron Kaplan, Dana Honor, Jeff Rake.
Creator-Writer: Jeffrey Lippman.
Story: Following the death of her parents, murdered by hit men for unknown reasons, a young woman plots to kill them; she begins by becoming an apprentice to a hit man named Smith to learn from him how to seek out a target, kill and not be caught.

Kill Jill (Comedy, ABC, 2015).
Producer: Patricia Heaton, David Hunt. *Creator-Writer:* Laura Solon.
Story: A recent college graduate eager to leave her small town and make it on her own finds numerous mishaps when she acquires a job as an assistant to a high powered Los Angeles businesswoman.

Kill Switch (Drama, Syfy, 2008).
Producer: Howie Mandel, Mike Marks, Rick Kellard. *Creator:* Don Mancini.
Story: A woman, executed for killing the man who attacked her daughter, is prevented from entering Heaven by celestial forces until she can make up for taking a life—by entering the bodies of people who are about to be killed, then figuring out who the killer is and preventing the murder from happening.

Killer App (Drama, Fox, 2000).
Producer: Tom Fontana, Barry Levinson, Garry Trudeau. *Creator-Writer:* Tom Fontana.
Story: An upstart Internet company's battle to stay afloat and deal with a "tyrannical Microsoft-like nemesis."

Kin (Drama, Starz, 2019).
Producer: Reese Witherspoon, Lauren Neustadter, Chester Jones III. *Creator-Writer:* Davita Scarlett.

Story: The notion that "blood is thicker than water" is explored as seen through the experiences of three generations of women living in a small town.

King Arthur (Adventure, Syndication, 1952).
Producer: Leon Fromkiss.
Story: Dramas based on Sir Walter Scott's *King Arthur and the Knights of the Round Table*. Had the project sold it would have been filmed in color.

Kirbyland (Comedy, ABC, 2015).
Producer: Gail Berman, Magnus Martens.
Story: The problems that arise when a family declares their property as a sovereign nation to avoid paying taxes.

Kissing Outside the Lines (Comedy, NBC, 2012).
Producer: Diane Farr. *Creator-Writer:* Warren Hutcherson.
Story: An Italian girl and a Korean boy fall in love—then face the hostility of their parents who oppose their dating (and fearful of their eventual marriage).

Knife Fight (Drama, CBS, 2010).
Producer: Carl Beverly, Sarah Timberman. *Creator-Writer:* Michael Cuesta.
Story: In order to find greater satisfaction and put criminals behind bars, a female public defender switches sides and becomes a prosecutor.

Knock, Knock (Comedy, ABC, 2012).
Producer: Ben Stiller, Debbie Liebling. *Creator-Writer:* Kevin Napier.
Story: An actor, fearful that he is losing touch with reality, moves back home to New York and in with his parents in the hope that he can regain the stability he had before journeying to Hollywood.

Kung Fu (Drama, Fox, 2018).
Producer: Greg Berlanti, Albert Kim, Sarah Scheshter. *Creator-Writer:* Wendy Mericle.
Story: A sequel to the 1972 ABC series of the same title about Kwai Chang Caine, a Shaolin Priest of the 1870s who roams the American Frontier seeking an unknown brother. Here it is learned that descendants of Kwai Chang have established themselves in San Francisco and over the years begun a Kung Fu studio. When her father passes, a young Chinese-American woman inherits his studio and a mission: help the people of her Chinatown community who have nowhere else to turn.

Kyra (Drama, Syfy, 2004).
Producer: Vin Diesel, David Twohy.
Story: Kyra, a character in the feature film *The Chronicles of Riddick* (about Richard B. Riddick, a skilled assassin) is followed as she uses her skills with blades to battle injustice in a savage era.

Lady in the Mask (Drama, CW, 2017).
Producer: Darryl Frank, Justin Flavey. *Creator-Writer:* Thomas Brandon.
Story: A woman, awakening in a hospital after a car accident, learns that her memory was damaged and restored through a backup disk that was recorded two years ago. It is a future time where people backup their memories (like information stored on a computer) and her efforts to fill in the gap from her last download to what occurred before her accident were to be the focal point of the program.

Laid (Comedy, NBC, 2011).
Producer: Gail Berman, Gene Stein, Jeremy Fox. *Creator-Writer:* Ali Rushfield, Marieke Hardy.
Story: A promiscuous woman indulging in one night stands discovers that after each such affair,

her lovers are mysteriously killed. With the police unable to solve any of the murders, she begins a quest to discover who is responsible and why.

Lamp (Drama, Spike TV, 2013).
Producer: Tom Fontana, Barry Levinson. *Creator-Writer:* Tom Fontana.
Story: The Research and Acquisitions Department is a secretive unit of the U.S. government that is tasked with investigating religious and mythological texts to determine if they are really magical or just false beliefs. From this point on, the press release becomes very vague and states only that everything changes when the Aladdin's Lamp is found (which, according to mythology produced a genie that could grant its possessor any wish).

Lancaster (Crime Drama, CBS, 2011).
Producer: Sam Raimi, Joshua Donen. *Creator-Writer:* Andrew Lipsitz.
Story: A British inspector from New Scotland Yard joins the ranks of the L.A.P.D. to learn about American crime detection methods.

Lance 2.0 (Comedy, CBS, 2016).
Producer: Jim Parsons, Todd Spiewak. *Creator-Writer:* Alex McAulay.
Story: The situations that befall a young man when an accident changes his personality and causes him to lose his impulse control.

The Last Larry (Comedy, Comedy Central, 2007).
Producer: Dave Becky, Tom Lassally. *Creator-Writer:* Dana Gould.
Story: Post apocalyptic study of what happens when the few remaining survivors attempt to rebuild their lives.

The Last Spy (Drama, NBC, 2018).
Producer: Brian Grazer, Francie Calfo. *Creator-Writer:* David Guggenheim.
Story: When their covers are blown and the members of a CIA unit are attacked, the one surviving member (a woman) assembles a team of recruits to pick up where her prior team left off and bring the assassins to justice.

Late Bloomers (Comedy, Amazon, 2017).
Producer: Ben Stiller, Deborah Spera. *Creator:* Donal Lardner Ward.
Story: What emerges when a couple in their forties is selected to become the subject of an experimental drug that halts the aging process.

Late Bloomer's Revolution (Comedy, ABC, 2011).
Producer: Leslie Morganstein, Michelle Nader. *Creator-Writer:* Amy Cohen.
Story: A father's efforts to re-enter the dating scene at the same time as his teenage daughter after the passing of his wife and her mother.

Laurel Canyon (Drama, E!, 2013).
Producer: Stephanie Savage, Josh Schwartz, Len Goldstein. *Creator-Writer:* Karen Croner.
Story: Following the death of her father, a famous rock star, a young woman returns to her home in Laurel Canyon to again become part of the nest to look after her somewhat dysfunctional family.

Lean on Me (Drama, CW, 2018).
Producer: John Legend, LeBron James. *Creator-Writer:* Wendy Calhoun.
Story: Amarie Baldwin, a young African-American teacher, attempts to transform a failing Akron, Ohio high school when she is appointed its principal.

Leap (Drama, ABC, 2007).
Producer: Goldie Hawn. *Creator-Writer:* Marta Kaufman.
Story: An adaptation of the book by Sara Davidson that explores how people deal with the various stumbling blocks they encounter each day.

Left of Center (Comedy, Fox, 2015).
Producer: Gail Berman. *Creator-Writer:* Robert Horn.
Story: The incidents that befall a group of four backup singers who, while waiting for their big break, form an unconventional family where egos clash as each believes they have what it takes to become a star.

Legacy (Drama, CBS, 2011).
Producer: Darryl Frank, Justin Falvey, James Frey. *Creator-Writer:* Jonathan E. Steinberg.
Story: Matthew Jennings, a one term U.S. President, returns to his prior position as a lawyer with a new mission—accept only the cases that are important to him.

Legal Affairs (Drama, ABC, 2011).
Producer: Steven Bochco, Gary Felder, Jonathan Abrahams. *Creator-Writer:* Mary Beth Basile.
Story: Attorneys with a prestigious law firm are followed as they balance their personal issues with the high profile cases they acquire.

Legal Aid (Drama, CW, 2011).
Producer: Sarah Timberman, Carl Beverly. *Creator-Writer:* Jonathan Abrams.
Story: A young attorney, just acquiring a job with a prestigious law firm, finds her life changing when her father, a former lawyer turned actor, quits show business and joins the same firm.

Legal-Ish (Comedy, Comedy Central, 2016).
Producer: Melissa McCarthy, Dave Storrs, Ben Falcone. *Creator-Writer:* Steve Mallory.
Story: Based on the press release, it appears to be a difficult idea to sustain over time: A slacker becomes a jury member on the longest-running case at his local courthouse.

Legion (Drama, Syfy, 2003).
Producer: Whoopi Goldberg, Stephen Garrett.
Story: In an effort to save the life of his dying daughter, a man makes a deal with the Devil: He will search for people whose deeds make them candidates for Hell and persuade them to sell their souls to Satan.

Leisure Club (Comedy, NBC, 2012).
Producer: Neil H. Moritz, Vivian Cannon. *Creator-Writer:* Stephanie Weir.
Story: Although only in their late fifties and residing in a retirement community, a group of friends bored with the way they are living decide to do something about it and adapt the attitude and lifestyle they experienced and enjoyed as teenagers.

Leonardo DiCaprio Untitled Project (Drama, Showtime, 2015).
Producer: Leonardo DiCaprio, Jennifer Erwin, Jennifer Davisson. *Creator-Writer:* Brett Johnson.
Story: The uneasy relationship between an unstable Brooklyn Mafia boss and the man who is seeking to bring him down—a rogue FBI agent.

Let Bob Do It (Comedy, Nickelodeon, 2006).
Producer: Jason Alexander, Gay Rosenthal, Bob Perlow.
Story: A humorous behind-the-scenes look at the production of a reality show called *Let Bob Do It*.

Let's Stay Together (Comedy, ABC, 2016).
Producer: Ben Silverman. *Creator-Writer:* Amy B. Harris.
Story: An exploration of marriage and how three couples struggle to maintain their relationships without taking the final step—divorce.

The Life and Times of Vivienne Vyle (Comedy, ABC, 2012).
Producer: Chelsea Handler, Julie Gardner. *Creator-Writer:* Bill Martin.
Story: An adaptation of the British series that spoofs daytime talk shows as seen through the hectic life of Vivienne Vyle, the always demanding, always screaming neurotic host of *The Vivienne Vyle Show*.

The Life Changing Magic of Tidying Up (Comedy, NBC, 2015).
Producer: Gail Berman, Greg Malins. *Creator-Writer:* Erica Oyama.
Story: A young woman's efforts to redirect her life.

Life Is Murder (Drama, ABC, 2013).
Producer: Todd Lieberman, David Hoberman, Laurie Zaks. *Creator-Writer:* David Grae.
Story: A mother, who works as a criminal profiler, and her daughter, a detective with robbery and homicide, team to solve crimes.

Life Is Super (Comedy, ABC, 2007).
Producer: Anthony Russo, Joe Russo. *Creator-Writer:* Phil Johnston.
Story: Although single, a young woman had adopted five children, hoping to find one that is a prodigy. The proposal was to follow her efforts to care for five typical, mischievous kids while hoping that the next one she adopts will be the child she is seeking.

Lifeboat Clique (Drama, CW, 2018).
Producer: Jerry Bruckheimer, Jonathan Littman, Kristie Anne Reed. *Creator-Writer:* Katie Wech.
Story: A group of teenagers, swept away when a freak tsunami strikes Malibu Beach, California, face new challenges when they find themselves in a land where all they know is no longer the norm.

Little Ellen (Cartoon, HBO Max, 2019).
Producer: Ellen DeGeneres, Sam Register. *Creator-Writer:* Ellen DeGeneres.
Story: Life as seen through the eyes of Ellen DeGeneres as a seven-year-old girl living in New Orleans.

Live Talking Girls (Comedy, TV Land, 2012).
Producer: Linda Bloodworth-Thomason (also the writer), Tony Krantz, Reece Pearson.
Story: A spoof of female hosted talk shows (most notably, *The View*) that exposes the behind-the-scenes shenanigans of the female hosts of one such show (*Live Talking Girls*) as they prepare for their daily program.

Loco (Drama, CBS, 2012).
Producer: Sarah Timberman, Carl Beverly. *Creator:* Ayelet Waldman.
Story: Blended family proposal about four gifted children who come to live with a family of average children after their parents are killed in a car accident.

Los Hermanos (Comedy, Showtime, 2018).
Producer: Aaron Kaplan, Dana Honor. *Creator-Writer:* Hayes Davenport.
Story: Two brothers, living in Chula Vista, a California town near the U.S.-Mexican border, attempt to run a somewhat shady business to help pay for their mother's growing medical expenses.

Los Roldan (Drama, ABC, 2014).
Producer: Salma Hayek, Jose Tamez. *Creator-Writer:* Sarah Hooper, Veronica Becker.
Story: After saving the life of a woman, a working class young man finds a new position in life when she hires him to run her company and he faces the disapproval of her family, who object to her decision.

Losing Our Cool (Comedy, Fox, 2012).
Producer: Stephanie Savage, Josh Schwartz, Len Goldstein. *Creator-Writer:* Shauna Cross.
Story: A look at parenthood as seen through a group of adults who are forced to be friends "because their dumb ass kids play together."

Lost Boys and Technicolor Girls (Drama, Freeform, 2018).
Producer: Jennifer Gwartz, Jon Harmon Feldman. *Creator-Writer:* Jake Cobum.
Story: A group of close-knit friends, once members of a band and separated after going their separate ways, reunite after seven years to renew their friendship following the death of one of their group.

Lost Girls (Drama ABC, 2011).
Producer: Jerry Bruckheimer, Jonathan Littman, Kristie Anne Reed. *Writer:* Jennifer Baggett.
Story: Three women, discontent with their corporate jobs, leave the business world to seek inspiration, adventure and a meaning to life.

Lost in the 1980s (Drama, NBC, 2009).
Producer: Eric Tannenbaum, Kim Tannenbaum. *Creator-Writer:* Bob Brush.
Story: Life during the 1980s is recalled by a middle-aged man when he was a teenager and attending high school.

Lounge (Talk, Nickelodeon, 2014).
Producer: Whoopi Goldberg.
Story: Real life, everyday mothers express their views on life.

Love After Love (Drama, NBC, 2017).
Producer: Aaron Kaplan, Dan Honor. *Creator-Writer:* Lisa Cullen.
Story: A man and woman engaged in an extramarital affair are involved in a car accident that exposes the affair. The man is taken to the hospital and is in a coma but the woman is found dead of a gunshot wound. Was it a suicide attempt? Was it murder? As questions remain unanswered, the spouses of the man and woman join forces to help the police to discover what happened and why.

Love, American Style (Comedy, CBS, 2013).
Producer: Eric Tannenbaum, Kim Tannenbaum, Robyn Meisinger. *Creator-Writer:* Aaron Martin.
Story: Although the project carries the title of the 1969-1974 ABC series it drops the comic anthology aspect to focus on the trials and tribulations of four diverse married couples.

Love and Death (Crime Drama, ABC, 2010).
Producer: Betsy Beers, Shonda Rhimes. *Creator-Writer:* Mark Wilding.
Story: Amateur sleuths (here a married couple living in San Francisco) use their uncanny ability to unravel clues to help the police solve puzzling crimes.

Love Lindsay/Hate Hannah (Comedy, WB, 2005).
Producer: Eric Tannenbaum, Kim Tannenbaum. *Creator-Writer:* Andrew Kreisberg.
Story: George is married to Hannah. George also loves Lindsay, Hannah's younger sister. George's effort to cope with the situation he faces is the focal point of the proposal.

Luther (Crime Drama, Fox, 2014).
Producer: Peter Chernin, Katherine Pope, Julie Gardner. *Creator-Writer:* Neil Cross.
Story: An American version of the British TV series about John Luther, a homicide detective whose uses his extraordinary intellect to solve gruesome crimes.

Macho Steve (Comedy, Fox, 2006).
Producer: Neal H. Moritz, Vivian Cannon. *Creator-Writer:* Josh Lobis.
Story: A fantasized depiction of what life would be like if the world's last "manly man" was to take up residence in Los Angeles.

Maddox (Drama, NBC, 2012).
Producer: Aaron Kaplan, Rachel Kaplan, Lisa Zwerling. *Creator-Writer:* Moira McMahon.
Story: A family's experiences when they move into what they believe is an idyllic community but discover that it is anything but with dark forces present all around them.

Made in L.A. (Comedy, Freeform, 2016).
Producer: Mila Kunis, Stephanie Savage, Cami Curtis. *Creator-Writer:* Sascha Rothchild.
Story: Two female friends with completely different tastes in fashion, join forces to create their own fashion empire.

The Madonnas of Echo Park (Drama, HBO, 2012).
Producer: Aaron Kaplan, Kelly Marcel. *Creator-Writer:* Julia Cho.
Story: A look at the rich people of Los Angeles but seen through the eyes of the people who work for them—the immigrant cooks and maids and other servants who still hope to find the American dream.

Mafia Wives (Drama, NBC, 2007).
Producer: Gail Berman, Lloyd Baum. *Creator-Writer:* Lynda LaPlante.
Story: What could happen within the ranks of organized crime if the wives of Mafia bosses were to take over the organization.

Magicians (Drama, Fox, 2011).
Producer: Becky Clements, Shawn Levy. *Creator-Writer:* Ashley Miller.
Story: A group of young magicians who have access to a mystical kingdom use their abilities to help good defeat evil.

Magnum, P.I. (Drama, ABC, 2017).
Producer: Eva Longoria, Jennifer Court, Ben Spector. *Creator-Writer:* John Rogers.
Story: A sequel to the CBS series *Magnum, P.I.* (about Thomas Magnum, a private detective based in Hawaii) wherein Lilly "Tommy" Magnum, Thomas's daughter, moves to Hawaii to take over the reigns of her father's detective firm.

Maid in Manhattan (Drama, ABC, 2009).
Producer: Jennifer Lopez, Nina Lederman, Elaine Goldsmith. *Creator-Writer:* Chad Hodge.
Story: An adaptation of the feature film about a young Latina woman from the Bronx as she begins work as a maid in a Manhattan hotel.

Maison Close (Drama, HBO, 2013).
Producer: Mark Wahlberg, Stephen Levinson. *Creator-Writer:* Elizabeth Sarnoff.
Story: Three women, confined to a luxury brothel in Paris in 1871, attempt to free themselves from prostitution and make better lives for themselves.

Major (Drama, NBC, 2018).
Producer: Jennifer Lopez, Benny Medina. *Creator-Writer-Producer:* Todd Graff.

Story: The events that befall a group of dance students attending a prestigious but rigorously programmed arts university.

Make Divya Great Again (Drama, CW, 2017).
Producer: Eric Tannenbaum, Kim Tannenbaum, Alex Hertzberg. *Creator-Writer:* Devanshi Patel.
Story: A young Indian-American woman, stuck in an pre-arranged marriage she hates (but her traditional parents love) abruptly calls off her engagement, invents a perfect Indian boyfriend then finds herself involved in a situation where she must continue her pretense until she can actually find that man.

Malled (Comedy, CBS, 2011).
Producer: Eric Tannenbaum, Kim Tannenbaum. *Creator-Writer:* Bill Kunstler.
Story: A laid-off newspaper journalist attempts to make ends meet by becoming a salesman at a mall clothing store.

The Man Upstairs (Comedy, Fox, 2011).
Producer: Jennifer Gwartz. *Creator-Writer:* Jonathan Goldstein.
Story: After renting her first home, a young woman finds that she must share the residence with the elderly gentleman who owns it.

Man, Woman, Child (Comedy, NBC, 2018).
Producer: Sean Hayes, Todd Milliner, Sheila Ducksworth. *Creator-Writer:* Vanessa McCarthy.
Story: The situations that develop when a man in his thirties chooses to have a child through a surrogate mother and a romance develops between them.

Mariah Carey Untitled Project (Drama, Starz, 2017).
Producer: Mariah Carey, Brett Ratner, Teri Weinberg. *Creator-Writer:* Nina Coleman.

Story: Explores the life of singer Mariah Carey beginning in New York City in 1986 (when she was 16 years old) to her rise as music artist in the 1990s.

Marlowe (Crime Drama, CW, 2016).
Producer: Aaron Kaplan, Dana Honor. *Creator-Writer:* Devon Greggory.
Story: Philip Marlowe is a famous literary detective created by Raymond Chandler. The story behind Philip Marlowe was to be told through Chandler's inspiration for his character—Samuel Marlowe, a real life private detective of Jamaican descent and a World War I veteran.

The Marquis (Drama, ABC, 2016).
Producer: Greg Berlanti, Sarah Schechter. *Creator-Writer:* Jake Coburn.
Story: Serial proposal about the people who inhabit the Marquis, an exclusive building in Manhattan where residents are anything but upfront about their personal lives or what they do.

Martin Lawrence Untitled Project (Cartoon, Fox, 2009).
Producer: Martin Lawrence. *Creator-Writer:* Rodney Barnes.
Story: Incidents in the life of comedian Martin Lawrence as a 13-year-old boy living in Washington, D.C.

Martin Sheen Untitled Project (Comedy, NBC, 2005).
Producer: Martin Sheen, Ramon Estevez. *Writer:* Brian Bird.
Story: A straight man, living with a gay brother and his lover, attempt to care for his mother, a sickly, deeply Christian woman who has no idea one of her son's is gay.

Match (Drama, ABC, 2011).
Producer: Taye Diggs, Jennifer Bozell. *Creator-Writer:* Kiersten Van Horne.
Story: What happens behind the scenes as lawyers, doctors and adoption agency workers attempt to help people who are unable to have children prepare for the adoption process.

Mavericks (Drama, ABC, 2017).
Producer: David Hoberman, Todd Lieberman, Laurie Zaks. *Creator-Writer:* Gemma Burgess.
Story: Three young entrepreneurs are followed as they combine their resources and venture into the cut throat business world to create their own empire.

May It Please the Court (Anthology, A&E, 2002).
Producer: Gore Vidal, Sidney Lumet.
Story: Dramatic recreations of famous Supreme Court cases.

Maybe Angels (Drama, CBS, 2011).
Producer: Sarah Timberman, Carl Beverly, Mark Waters. *Creator-Writer:* Krista Vernoff.
Story: A recent widower and widow, both lawyers, find their lives changing when their former spouses return as angels to help them defend clients.

Maybe It's Me (Comedy, NBC, 2013).
Producer: Aaron Kaplan. *Creator-Writer:* Chris Chase.
Story: A single father of two children struggles to contend with the three women in his life—His ex-wife, his current girlfriend and his work wife.

Maybe You Should Talk to Someone (Drama, ABC, 2018).
Producer: Eva Longoria, Ben Spector. *Creator-Writer:* Maggie Friedman.
Story: A brilliant female therapist who can solve her patients' problems struggles to resolve her own issues which are threatening to destroy her life and those who are close to her.

McCabe (Crime Drama, Fox, 2005).
Producer: McG, Peter Johnson. *Creator-Writer:* John Glenn.
Story: When his wife is murdered and the police investigation fails to uncover any suspects, a school teacher resigns, joins the police force and, while attempting to solve his wife's murder, battles the criminals he encounters.

Me and My Needs (Comedy, NBC, 2013).
Producer: Ryan Seacrest, Gail Berman, Lloyd Braun. *Creator-Writer:* Cynthia Greenburg.
Story: The incidents that befall a television talk show producer as she navigates the "oddities and extremes" of dating in Manhattan.

Me and You (Comedy, NBC, 2018).
Producer: Fred Savage. *Creator-Writer:* Sarah Tapscott.
Story: The relationship between a forty-something man and a woman is explored when they decide to live together after having only one date.

Melanie (Drama, CBS, 2018).
Producer: Phil McGraw, Jay McGraw, Julia Eisenman. *Creator-Writer:* Scott Prendergast.
Story: A young defense attorney, equipped with the unique ability to charm judges and juries, resigns from her prestigious law firm to return home and work with her brother at his small but essential law firm.

Melissa McCarthy Untitled 2011 Project (Comedy, CBS, 2011).
Producer-Creator-Writer: Melissa McCarthy, Ben Falcone.

Story: A well-adjusted woman's efforts to cope with a mid-life crisis when she realizes that she is now in her forties.

Melissa McCarthy Untitled 2013 Project (Comedy, Fox, 2013).
Producer: Melissa McCarthy, Ben Falcone. *Creator-Writer:* Larry Dorf.
Story: The situations that befall two mismatched men when they become step-brothers upon their parents' marriage (sort of an adult version of the Nickelodeon series *Drake and Josh*).

Mercury 13 (Drama, Amazon, 2017).
Producer: Amy Pascal, Bradley Whitford, Liz Hannah. *Creator-Writer:* Martha Ackmann.
Story: An adaptation of the book by Martha Ackmann that profiles thirteen American women as they prepare to become astronauts.

Meridian Hills (Drama, CW, 2012).
Producer: Eric Tannenbaum, Kim Tannenbaum, Mila Kunis, Cami Curtis. *Creator-Writer:* Sydney Sidner.
Story: Believing that the laws that govern the land are for the most part unjust, a group of young women, all members of the Junior League, set out to change the system to benefit all Americans.

Miami Vice (Crime Drama, NBC, 2017).
Producer: Vin Diesel, Shana Waterman, Chris Morgan. *Creator-Writer:* Peter MacManus.
Story: A remake of the 1980s NBC series of the same title about the work of two undercover detectives with the Miami Metro-Dade Police Department.

Michael Bolton's Daughter Is Destroying My Life (Comedy, ABC, 2012).
Producer: Kelly Kulchak, Michael Bolton. *Creator-Writer:* Allison Miller.
Story: A young woman, working as the head of social media for singer-songwriter Michael Bolton, finds her job more than she bargained for when Bolton's "wild child daughter" takes a liking to her and she finds herself becoming her babysitter as well.

Midnight Club (Drama, TNT, 2005).
Producer-Writer: James Patterson.
Story: John Stefanovich, a wheelchair-bound New York detective, joins with a female journalist and a Harlem street cop to bring down the Midnight Club, an international society of crime lords that control the city.

Midnighters (Drama, NBC, 2010).
Producer: Leslie Morganstein. *Creator-Writer:* Chad Hodges.
Story: The unexplained happenings that occur in Bixby, a small Oklahoma town when, for one hour each night, time freezes for mortals and creatures of the dark roam free.

Mila 2.0 (Drama, ABC, 2012).
Producer: Betsy Beers, Shonda Rhimes. *Creator-Writer:* David DiGilio.
Story: When Mila (Mobile Intel Life-Like Android), an android created by a U.S. government scientist begins to develop human traits and is ordered destroyed, her creator kidnaps her and together seek to live a life free from the government agents assigned to find them.

MILF & Cookies (Comedy, CW, 2007).
Producer: Will Smith, Jada Pinkett Smith. *Creator-Writer:* Randi Mayem Singer.
Story: The activities of a group of middle-aged, divorced housewives as seen through the spying of a security guard at the large complex in which they live.

Mind Games (Drama, CBS, 2011).
Producer: Denis Leary, Jim Serpico. *Creator-Writer:* Roger Wolfson.
Story: A female psychologist who specializes in memory recovery and mind control teams with an unorthodox detective to solve crimes.

Miracle Man (Drama, ABC, 2008).
Producer: Todd Holland, Tina Minear.
Story: A television minister, exposed as a fake and disgraced, finds his life changing when God selects him to help people who are in need of spiritual guidance.

Misdemeanor Man (Drama, Fox, 2005).
Producer: John Mankiewicz, Daniel Pyne. *Creator-Writer:* Dylan Schaffer.
Story: A pubic defender (mostly of people facing misdemeanor charges) with a father suffering from Alzheimer's, finds relief from life's pressures by moonlighting as the lead singer in a Barry Manilow tribute band called Barry X and the Mandys.

Miss Philly (Drama, TNT, 2010).
Producer: Jamie Foxx, Marcus King. *Creator-Writer:* Barbara Hall.
Story: Philadelphia's first African-American police commissioner struggles to adjust to a position she finds more difficult than she expected.

Missing You (Reality, CBS, 2009).
Producer: Shaun Cassidy, James Bruce. *Creator-Writer:* Shaun Cassidy.
Story: Each week a team of investigators were to be profiled as they tackle a missing person's case.

Mr. and Mr. Nash (Drama, ABC, 2003).
Producer: Steve Martin, Stan Zimmerman, James Berg, Tom Werner, Marcy Carsey, Caryn Mandabach.
Story: A gay couple working as interior decorators uses their abilities as amateur sleuths to solve crimes when murder becomes a part of their business.

Mr. Erdman (Comedy, CBS, 2017).
Producer: Eric Tannenbaum, Kim Tannenbaum. *Creator-Writer:* Ryan Raddatz.
Story: A progressive family finds that befriending their neighbor, the lonely Mr. Erdman, a big mistake when he tries to impose his outspoken conservative views on them.

Mr. Untouchable (Drama, Showtime, 2007).
Producer: Forest Whitaker, Marc Levin. *Creator-Writer:* David Burke.
Story: Stories based on the real life of Leroy "Nicky" Barnes, a Harlem (New York) based drug dealer.

The Mix (Drama, ABC, 2012).
Producer: Betsy Beers, Shonda Rhimes. *Creator-Writer:* John Hoffman.
Story: The public and private lives of five women who host a morning television talk show.

Mixed Up (Comedy, HBO, 2006).
Producer: Halle Berry, Vincent Cirrincione. *Creator-Writer:* Angela Nissel.
Story: Three women face life on their own for the first time after graduating from college.

Mockingbird (Adventure, ABC Family, 2011).
Producer: Jeph Loeb.
Story: An adaptation of the Marvel comic book about Barbara "Bobbi" Morse, an agent for S.H.I.E.L.D. (Strategic Homeland Intervention, Enforcement and Logistics Division) better known as Mockingbird as she battles diabolical villains.

The Model (Comedy, ABC, 2006).
Producer: Darren Star. *Creator-Writer:* Darlene Hunt.
Story: A young woman, newly arrived in New York City, struggles to succeed as a model.

The Money Pit (Comedy, NBC, 2014).
Producer: Darryl Frank, Justin Falvey. *Creator-Writer:* Justin Spitzer.
Story: After purchasing what they believe will be their dream home, a young couple finds they have been swindled and have a house that needs extensive repairs. The proposal, based on the 1986 film, was to chart their mishaps in dealing with the situation they face (it also appears to have borrowed elements from the film *Mr. Blandings Builds His Dream House*).

Monstropolis (Drama, ABC, 2015).
Producer: Aaron Kaplan. *Creator-Writer:* Marcus Dunstan, Patrick Melton.
Story: As monsters become real and begin living side by side with humans in what was once New York City (now called Monstropolis) an unknown evil upsets the peaceful co-existence when it begins eliminating the monster population. With the police unable to find a culprit, a disgraced detective takes it upon himself to find the killer—or become one of his victims.

Moody Bitches (Comedy, HBO, 2013).
Producer: Oprah Winfrey. *Creator-Writer:* Diablo Cody.
Story: An adaptation of the book by Dr. Julie Holland that explores the various things that drive people crazy.

Morningside Heights (Comedy, NBC, 2005).
Producer: Eric McCormack, Michael Foreman. *Creator-Writer:* David Light.
Story: The incidents that befall a group of would-be priests, rabbis and monks who share the same dorm at a university college.

Mortified (Comedy, ABC, 2010).
Producer: Jamie Tarses, Julia Franz. *Creator:* Mark Rizzo.
Story: Flashback proposal in which characters share their childhood memories that, for the most part, would include their most embarrassing moments.

The Most Fun We Never Had (Drama, HBO, 2020).
Producer: Laura Dern, Amy Adams, Anya Epstein. *Creator:* Claire Lombardo.
Story: An adaptation of the novel by Claire Lombardo about four sisters, living in the shadow of their parent's perfect marriage, whose lives change when their unknown brothers, given up for adoption fifteen years earlier, become a part of their lives.

Mother Theresa (Comedy, ABC, 2011).
Producer: Jamie Tarses, Julia Franz. *Creator-Writer:* Teresa Strasser.
Story: A young couple finds their life changing when the wife's mother, a middle-aged woman who lives like a hippie, comes back into her life, moves in with them and volunteers to help care for their new-born baby.

Move (Drama, Fox, 2018).
Producer: Gail Berman, Mary J. Blige, Joe Earley. *Creator-Writer:* Silvio Horta.
Story: A choreographer's efforts to survive the cut throat world of music and dance by creating a unique tour for a famous singer.

Moving Pictures (Comedy, NBC, 2005).
Producer: Marcy Carsey, Tom Werner. *Writer:* David Israel, Jim O'Doherty.
Story: The antics of the staff of a film documentary company that supplies footage for TV programs.

M.R. (Drama, ABC, 1960).
Producer: John Florea. *Writer:* Charles Beaumont.
Story: A group of international lawyers help Americans abroad with their legal entanglements (the title means Mens Rea or criminal law).

Mrs. vs. Mr. (Drama, CBS, 2016).
Producer: David W. Zucker, Ridley Scott. *Creator-Writer:* Brett Mahoney.
Story: A wife, a defense attorney, and her husband, a prosecutor for the D.A.'s office, find themselves at odds in the courtroom when they are assigned to the same case.

The Munsters (Comedy, NBC, 2017).
Producer: Seth Meyers, Mike Shoemaker. *Creator-Writer:* Jill Kargman.
Story: A revised version of the CBS 1964-1966 series about a family who resemble movie monsters of the 1930s and 1940s and who believe they are normal and everyone else weird. The family (parents Herman and Lily; their son, Eddie; Lily's father, Count Dracula; and their normal looking niece, Marilyn) are transplanted from the original series setting of Mockingbird Heights to the more congested Brooklyn, New York.

Murder Room (2011) (Crime Drama, CBS, 2011).
Producer: Carol Mendelsohn, Julie Weitz. *Creator-Writer:* George Nolfi.
Story: A criminal profiler, a forensic artist and an FBI agent team to investigate crimes that are considered unsolvable.

Murder Room (2016) (Crime Drama, CBS, 2016).
Producer: Mark Gordon, Tatiana Kelly, Jim Young. *Creator:* Anna Fricke.
Story: The Vedic Society is an international organization where noted forensic experts devote their abilities to solve extremely complex cases. Had the idea sold, it would have followed a young society woman and her mother as they investigate crimes based on what has been theorized by the society.

Murder, Page 5 (Crime Drama, UPN, 2003).
Producer: Aaron Spelling, E. Duke Vincent, Denise Di Novi. *Creator-Writer:* Jeffrey Lieber.
Story: A New York newspaper columnist's efforts to go beyond reporting and solve the murders that make the news.

Murder Season (Crime Drama, ABC, 2011).
Producer: Laurie Zaks. *Creator-Writer:* Moira Kirland.
Story: A team of FBI agents, headed by a female criminal profiler, seek to apprehend the country's worst criminal offenders.

Musketeers 3.0 (Crime Drama, CW, 2011).
Producer: Barry Levinson, Tom Fontana. *Creator-Writer:* Tom Fontana.
Story: Three N.Y.P.D. homicide detectives (two men and one woman) use whatever tactics possible to bring criminals to justice.

Must Be Nice (Comedy, Fox, 2012).
Producer: Zooey Deschanel, Katherine Pope, Molly McAleer, Sophia Rossi. *Creator-Writer:* J.J. Philbin.
Story: The relationship between Melody, 27 years old and single who shuns responsibilities, and Dorothy, her stable, married 34-year-old sister.

Must Hire (Comedy, Fox, 2012).
Producer: Jamie Tarses, Julia Franz. *Creator-Writer:* Reed Agnew.
Story: A company executive hires his out-of-work father for an entry level position only to find that his father is anything but dedicated to working.

My Best Friend Is a Lesbo (Comedy, NBC, 2011).
Producer: Stephanie Savage, Josh Schwartz, Len Goldstein. *Creator-Writer:* Randi Barnes, Sascha Rothchild.
Story: Two friends sharing an apartment, a lesbian and a straight girl, help each other navigate life in Los Angeles.

My Ex-Life (Comedy, Fox, 2013).
Producer: Brian Grazer, Francie Calfo, Gregg Mettler. *Creator-Writer:* Joel Stein.
Story: A young man, recently divorced from a woman who did nothing but control his life, finds his life changing for the worse when he meets his ex-wife's new romantic interest, a man who thrives on being annoying.

My Other Life in Brooklyn (2004) (Comedy, NBC, 2004).
Producer: Kelsey Grammer, Steve Stark. *Creator-Writer:* D.J. Nash.
Story: An actor's experiences working on a Broadway production in Manhattan but living with two roommates in Brooklyn, New York.

My Other Life in Brooklyn (2017) (Comedy, CBS, 2017).
Producer: Aaron Kaplan, Dana Honor. *Creator-Writer:* D.J. Nash.
Story: Shortly after marrying, a young man acquires the job of a lifetime 200 miles from his home in Brooklyn, New York. Based on the press release, the project would relate the situations that arise with his wife remaining in Brooklyn (not explained why) while he commutes and lives with friends at work at his new job (flying home on weekends to be with her).

My Problem with Women (Drama, NBC, 2008).
Producer: Justin Timberlake, Chris Phillips, David Schiff.
Story: A bachelor's efforts to improve his romantic life by following the advice of a female therapist whose suggestions appear to cause more issues than solutions.

My World and Welcome to It (Comedy, CBS, 2008).
Producer: Eric Tannenbaum, Kim Tannenbaum, Barry Sonnenfeld. *Creator-Writer:* Jay Kogen.
Story: An adaptation of the stories by humorist James Thurber about a man who finds solace in the imaginary world he creates from Thurber's drawings. William Windom appeared in an NBC series in 1969.

The Mysteries of Oak Island (Mystery, Fox, 2010).
Producer-Creator: Tom Wheeler.
Story: A single mother and her two children inherit a centuries-old lighthouse off the coast of Nova Scotia—only to find themselves involved in the mystery of the Knights Templar treasure that is believed to be buried there. In 2014 The History Channel aired the series *The Curse of Oak Island* which presented an actual search for the supposed treasure that is said to be hidden on the Canadian island.

Mythos (Drama, USA, 2015).
Producer: Charlize Theron, Laverne McKinnon, Anna Halberg. *Creator-Writer:* Spenser Cohen.
Story: Nate Brigman's investigations for Mythos,

a mysterious organization that attempts to prove that myths are not fabricated tales but actual truths.

The Nanny Diaries (Drama, ABC, 2011).
Producer: Amy Sherman-Palladino. *Creator-Writer:* Emma McLaughlin, Nicola Kraus.
Story: The incidents that befall nannies who care for the children of wealthy Manhattan parents.

Nanny Land (Drama, ABC, 2011)
Producer: Jennifer Lopez, Simon Fields, Ann Blanchard. *Creator:* Alexa Junge.
Story: A profile of three Los Angeles families as seen through the eyes of their Latina nannies.

Nashville (Drama, TNT, 2006).
Producer: Darryl Frank, Justin Falvey. *Creator-Writer:* Les Bohem.
Story: A young singer-songwriter is followed as he pursues his dream of becoming a performer in Nashville.

Natchez Burning (Drama, Amazon, 2015).
Producer: Tobey Maguire. *Creator-Writer:* David Hudgins.
Story: An adaptation of the book by Greg Iles that follows a Southern attorney turned novelist.

Nature of Fire (Drama, CBS, 2010).
Producer: Ashton Kutcher, Karey Burke. *Creator-Writer:* Augusten Burroughs.
Story: A female arson investigator's experiences working with the crew of an all male fire company.

Near Dead (Crime Drama, CBS, 2012).
Producer: David W. Zucker, Ridley Scott. *Creator-Writer:* Glenn Gordon Caron.
Story: After surviving a near-fatal shooting, a homicide detective acquires the ability to envision how and who committed a murder after it has occurred. The detective is followed as he encompasses his ability to solve cold case homicides.

Neighbors of North Sycamore (Comedy, ABC, 2017).
Producer: Aaron Kaplan, Dana Honor. *Creator-Writer:* Ryan Raddatz.
Story: A young couple, moving into what they believe is their dream home in a dream neighborhood, discover that the block on which they live has no privacy and everything is exposed on the North Sycamore Street's "Secret Facebook Page."

The Nelsons (Drama, ABC, 2008).
Producer: Sarah Timberman, Carl Beverly, Barry Sonnenfeld. *Creator-Writer:* Dee Steinfeld, Peter Steinfeld.
Story: A live action version of the animated movie *The Incredibles* that focuses on a family as they use their super powers to battle evil.

Ness (Crime Drama, WGN, 2014).
Producer: Michael Dinner, John Davis. *Creator-Writer:* Dennis Lehane.
Story: Eliot Ness, head of The Untouchables, the prohibition-era team of incorruptible federal agents, was formed in 1930 to capture Chicago's mobsters, specifically Al Capone, who had a stronghold over the city. The project was to detail events in the life of Eliot Ness prior to heading The Untouchables as a "tough cop" in Cleveland, "The most dangerous city in America during the 1930s" (which contradicts The Untouchables founding and Ness's prior position as he was a federal agent with the Treasury Department beginning in 1926 and not a "tough cop" in the 1930s).

Never in My Wildest (Comedy, CBS, 2005). *Producer:* Darryl Frank, Howard Klein, Justin Falvey. *Creator-Writer:* Carol Leifer. *Story:* A man and a woman, each with their own set of standards, meet, fall in love and attempt to make their relationship work despite the impossible standards they have set for each other.

The Never List (Drama, CBS, 2013). *Producer:* Carl Beverly, Sarah Timberman. *Creator-Writer:* A.M. Holmes. *Story:* A New York City-based trauma surgeon struggles to unravel a mystery from her past: her kidnapping ten years earlier (along with three other girls) by whom and why.

The New McToms (Comedy, Fox, 2008). *Producer:* Salma Hayek, Jose Tamez. *Creator-Writer:* Boyce Bugliari, Jamie McLaughlin. *Story:* A woman's attempts to adjust to the fact that her three children are dating and will eventually marry spouses of different ethnic backgrounds.

New World (Drama, ABC, 2017). *Producer:* Jennifer Gwartz, John Harmon Feldman. *Creator-Writer:* Daniel Thomsen. *Story:* A struggle for survival as seen through the experiences of two families, marooned on a deserted island after a boating accident, as they seek a means of escape.

Nice Girls Don't Get the Corner Office (Comedy, Fox, 2011). *Producer:* Brian Grazer, David Nevins. *Creator-Writer:* Jennifer Robinson. *Story:* A bright young woman (Angela) who is competent at her job but too nice (easily taken advantage of) seeks to become more aggressive and advance her position within the company.

Nightfall (Crime Drama, Fox, 2017). *Producer:* Howard Gordon, Jennifer Klein. *Creator-Writer:* Sheldon Turner. *Story:* An N.Y.P.D. Anti Crime Unit's patrol of the streets during the hours of 10 p.m. to 6 a.m.

Nighty Night (Comedy, Showtime, 2006). *Producer:* Darren Star, Henry Normal, Steve Coogan. *Story:* A beauty salon owner's efforts to deal with numerous situations, especially her off-the-wall clients and her obsession with her neighbor, a married doctor.

911 Operators (Anthology, ABC, 2010). *Producer:* Courteney Cox, David Arquette. *Creator-Writer:* Michael Caleo. *Story:* Dramatizations based on calls placed to 911 operators.

Nine Lives (Drama, Syfy, 2010). *Producer:* Steven Spielberg, Darryl Frank, Justin Falvey. *Writer:* Leslie Bohem. *Story:* Strange proposal about an unknown force that gives grieving people the ability to reunite with their deceased loved ones but for its own sinister purposes—to bring forth an evil that could destroy mankind.

940 Saturdays (Comedy, ABC, 2016). *Producer:* Eva Longoria, Ben Spector. *Creator-Writer:* Jessica Goldstein. *Story:* The title refers to the time a child is born until the day they turn 18; the project focuses on the parents of three diverse families as they eagerly await that 940th Saturday and the day their children leave home.

1985 (Comedy, NBC, 2007). *Producer-Writer:* Amy Heckerling. *Story:* Sentimental female version of *The Wonder*

Years about a girl growing up in the 1980s—but narrated by that girl as an adult as she looks back on her childhood.

Ninth Street Woman (Drama, Amazon, 2019).
Producer-Creator-Writer: Amy Sherman-Palladino, Daniel Palladino.
Story: An adaptation of the novel by Mary Gabriel that chronicles the struggles of four women as they enter the political scene in Washington, D.C.

No Angels (Comedy, ABC, 2014).
Producer: Darryl Frank, Justin Falvey, Stacy Traub, Julie Anne Robinson. *Creator-Writer:* John Hoberg.
Story: The incidents that befall four female hospital nurses who not only work together but share the same home.

No One Son (Comedy, ABC, 2011).
Producer: Darryl Frank, Justin Falvey, Lisa Long. *Creator-Writer:* Cindy Caponera.
Story: Two families, one Italian-Irish and one Chinese, struggle to get along with one another when their eldest children marry and cultural difference divide them.

No Rest for the Wicked (Drama, ABC, 2012).
Producer: Mark Gordon, Josh Duhamel. *Creator-Writer:* Gretchen J. Berg, Aaron Harberts.
Story: Although billed as a drama and spoofing the behind-the-scenes action of a television soap opera, it reads more like a comedy as it explores "the antics of a cast and crew who are crazier than the plot lines they broadcast."

Nod (Mystery, Fox, 2014).
Producer: Peter Chernin, Katherine Pope. *Creator-Writer:* Jason Richman.
Story: A mystery is immediately established: people in various areas of the world are affected by a virus that prohibits sleeping. What happens to affected people while scientists struggle to figure out the cause was to be the focal point of the program.

Noir (Adventure, Starz, 2012).
Producer: Sam Raimi, Robert Tapert, Bill Hamm. *Creator-Writer:* Stephen Lightfoot.
Story: Live action adaptation of the Japanese anime series that tells the story of Mireille and Yumura, beautiful female assassins who seek to uncover the mysteries of their past (clues were to be given throughout the episodes). Mireille (French) and Yumura (Japanese) formed an alliance when working together under the code name Noir. Mireille was born into a crime family and it was her uncle who trained her to become an assassin. Yumura, suffering from amnesia, remembers only the word Noir and her ability to kill.

The Noise (Drama, CW, 2013).
Producer: Eric Tannenbaum, Kim Tannenbaum. *Creator-Writer:* Miles Feld.
Story: A young 1990s musician seeks stardom by creating a band with an unusual sound.

Not Ready (Comedy, Fox, 2017).
Producer: Fred Savage, Mandy Summers. *Creator-Writer:* Niki Schwartz-Wright.
Story: A woman's efforts to deal with a family who unlike her, have not yet grown up to become adults.

The Notorious Mollie Flowers (Comedy, ABC, 2012).
Producer: Ben Stiller, Debbie Liebling. *Creator-Writer:* Adam Resnick.
Story: Mollie Flowers, a sweet, kind and generous woman who finds time for everyone else but

herself, embarks on a new mission: focus on her life and her needs.

Nuclear Family (Comedy, ABC, 2014).
Producer: Karey Burke, Todd Holland. *Creator-Writer:* Alex Gregory.
Story: Incidents in the lives of Rick and Barbara Foley, a married couple with eight adopted children, some of whom have special needs.

Number One Fan (Comedy, Fox, 2011).
Producer: Katherine Pope, Peter Chernin. *Creator-Writer:* Matt Warburton.
Story: A young man, moving to Los Angeles and feeling he is finally free of his controlling parents, attempts to cope with the situations that arise when his parents leave their Midwestern home and become his down-the-street neighbors.

Oasis (Drama, CBS, 2013).
Producer: Jerry Bruckheimer, Jonathan Littman, Kristie Anne Reed. *Creator-Writer:* John Halvin.
Story: A look at a self-sustaining community and how it functions but also the dangers that go along with it.

Objects of Desire (Drama, CW, 2006).
Producer: Lauren Graham, Kathy Ebel. *Creator-Writer:* Holly Sorensen.
Story: A behind-the-scenes-look at the activities of a prestigious auction house.

The Obsolescents (Comedy, NBC, 2018).
Producer: Meg Ryan, Lorne Michaels, Andrew Singer. *Creator-Writer:* Andrew Gottlieb.
Story: While the title is not explained (on the series *All in the Family*, Archie Bunker would call adolescents "obsolescents") it is a depiction of life in a suburban New Jersey community with a false façade of peace and civility.

Oh, Mama! (Comedy, NBC, 2015).
Producer: Claudia Lonow, Peter Traugott. *Creator-Writer:* Claudia Lonow.
Story: An engaged couple (Daniel and Marjorie) face an unusual situation as they prepare for their wedding—their single mothers have begun a romantic relationship with each other.

The Okies of Bel Air (Cartoon, Fox, 2016).
Producer: Brian Grazer, Francie Calfo, Matt Silverstein. *Creator-Writer:* Sean O'Connor.
Story: When their son, a basketball prodigy working on the family catfish farm in Oklahoma is discovered and chosen in an NBA draft, his backwoods family follows him to Bel Air, California, where they attempt to fit into a world in which they simply do not belong.

Oliver Stone Untitled Project (Drama, FX, 2011).
Producer: Oliver Stone, Richard Branson. *Creator-Writer:* Adam Gibgot.
Story: A mysterious group of individuals known as "Dark Horses" are profiled as they create fake news stories to accomplish the goals of their powerful clients.

On the Edge (Drama, CW, 2006).
Producer: Penny Marshall. *Creator-Writer:* Michael Gleason, Alan Moskowitz.
Story: Female Jekyll/Hyde-like project about a young Assistant D.A., tormented by the unsolved murder of her parents, whose alter ego is bent on returning her to her former life of drugs and alcohol.

The One (Drama, Bravo, 2015).
Producer: Charlize Theron, Laverne McKinnon. *Creator-Writer:* Roger Wolfson.
Story: A look at the world of the super rich as seen through the experiences of the people who work for them.

Oprah Winfrey Untitled 2009 Project (Drama, HBO, 2009).
Producer: Oprah Winfrey, Kate Forte. *Creator-Writer:* Erin Cressida Wilson.
Story: Strange proposal about a seemingly normal woman with a perfect life and a perfect marriage who abandons her husband, children and home in Santa Monica, California, to live out her secret desires and fantasies in Los Angeles.

Oprah Winfrey Untitled 2012 Project (Drama, HBO, 2012).
Producer: Oprah Winfrey, Kate Forte. *Creator-Writer:* Thomas Bradshaw.
Story: Follows a wealthy academic who becomes the first African-American president of a prestigious liberal arts university.

The Order (Drama, TNT, 2011).
Producer: Darryl Frank, Justin Falvey. *Creator-Writer:* Joel Fields.
Story: The myths that surround objects are explored through the excavations of an archeologist professor working in Israel.

The Orderlies (Drama, UPN, 2003).
Producer: Ron Howard, Brian Grazer. *Creator-Writer:* Jonas Pate.
Story: Rogue lawyers defend people facing insurmountable odds against corporate America.

Otis the POTUS (Comedy, Fox, 2016).
Producer: Aaron Kaplan, Dana Honor. *Creator-Writer:* Richard Murphy.
Story: After his Doppelganger (one's other evil self) is elected President of the United States, Otis Chucker, the outcast member of a Cleveland family, devises a unique way to earn money—by becoming a presidential impersonator.

Out of Body (Drama, CBS, 2015).
Producer: Greg Berlanti, Todd Garner, Sarah Schechter, Jennifer Johnson.
Story: Shortly after his release from prison, a criminal mastermind inexplicably acquires the ability to leap into the bodies of people in danger. Unaware as to how it happened and with no way to stop it, he uses his ability to mysteriously help people in trouble.

Pages (Comedy, Fox, 2006).
Producer: Lorne Michaels, Simon Millar.
Story: A group of network pages are followed as they tend to guests at a New York based media company.

Paper (Drama, HBO, 2012).
Producer: Brad Pitt, Dede Gardner. *Creator-Writer:* Wells Tower.
Story: An ex-gangster and family man living in Buffalo, New York, attempts to turn his life around by becoming a professional debt collector.

Paradise (2006) (Drama, ABC, 2006).
Producer: Todd Lieberman, David Hoberman. *Creator-Writer:* Ted Humphrey.
Story: A behind-the-scenes look at the operations of the Internal Affairs Division of the Miami Police Department.

Paradise (2012) (Drama, NBC, 2012).
Producer: Greg Berlanti, Melissa Kellner. *Creator-Writer:* Seth Grahame-Smith.
Story: Life in a futuristic Las Vegas, now called Paradise, when it is turned into the world's largest maximum security prison.

Paranormal Housewives (Drama, Lifetime, 2012).
Producer: Julia Roberts, Elaine Goldsmith-Thomas, Robyn Meisinger. *Creator-Writer:* Katie Ford.

Story: A group of housewives fascinated by the occult join forces to investigate supernatural occurrences in their home state of California.

Parental Guidance (Comedy, ABC, 2007).
Producer: Ben Silverman. *Creator-Writer:* Marc Abrams, Michael Benson.
Story: A couple decides to raise their children as they were brought up 25 years ago while their kids have to deal with what they consider antiquated upbringing torture.

Parenting By Committee (Comedy, ABC, 2011).
Producer: Eva Longoria. *Creator-Writer:* Alyssa Embree, Jessica Koosed.
Story: A single woman, discovering she is going to have a baby, finds help with the pregnancy (and the eventual raising of her child) from her three best female friends.

Pariah (Drama, NBC, 2012).
Producer: Kelsey Grammer, Stella Stolper. *Creator-Writer:* Kevin Fox.
Story: A "rogue academic" attempts to institute alternate methods of law enforcement in the San Diego Police Department.

Paroled (Comedy, Fox, 2013).
Producer: Becky Clements, Marty Adelstein, Shawn Levy. *Creator-Writer:* Andrea Abbate.
Story: Two ex-cons, becoming friends in prison and released at the same time, decide to go straight by becoming roommates then seeking jobs and earning money the honest way.

Partners in Crime (Crime Drama, USA, 2010).
Producer: Denis Leary, Jim Serpico. *Creator-Writer:* Janine Sherman-Barrois.
Story: Husband and wife private detectives solve cases based more on the wife's intuition than on her abilities as a sleuth.

The Party (Mystery, ABC, 2015).
Producer-Creator: Stephanie Savage, Josh Schwartz.
Story: Had the project sold it would have followed a murder investigation (a corpse found in a pool at a lavish party) that takes place over the course 24 hours (but requires a full season to bring to a conclusion).

Party People (Comedy, NBC, 2011).
Producer: Ben Silverman. *Creator-Writer:* Dave Bickel.
Story: A group of unemployed young people pool their resources and begin a children's party entertainment business to earn money.

Past Imperfect (Drama, NBC, 2007).
Producer: Darryl Frank, Justin Falvey, Gardner Stern.
Story: Two lawyers (a white male and a black female) are mysteriously transported back in time to the 1950s to use their knowledge of the future to change the past by helping people falsely accused of crimes they did not commit.

Patriots (Drama, CBS, 2016).
Producer: David W. Zucker, Ridley Scott. *Creator-Writer:* Anna Fricke.
Story: An FBI agent and his estranged sister, a girl with ties to Islamic extremism, join forces to battle terrorism for the Boston Police Department.

Pecos (Drama, ABC, 2016).
Producer: Robert Redford, Bob Levy. *Creator-Writer:* Shawn Christensen.
Story: Seeking to make a name for himself, a novice journalist begins an investigation to prove that the richest and most powerful man in Texas is corrupt.

Pedro and Maria (Drama, ABC, 2013).
Producer: America Ferrera, Ben Silverman.
Story: Maria, the daughter of wealthy Puerto Rican real estate developers, and Pedro, a second generation Dominican who grew up on the mean streets of the Washington Heights district of New York City, attempt to make their relationship work despite their parents objections.

The People Under the Stairs (Drama, Syfy, 2015).
Producer: Wes Craven, Tracey Murray. *Creator-Writer:* Michael Reisz.
Story: A young woman's quest to uncover the mysteries surrounding the Robeson Family Manor and what are reputed to be centuries old horrors.

The Perez Family (Comedy, Fox, 2003).
Producer: Tom Werner, Marcy Carsey, Caryn Mandabach.
Story: Events in the lives of a Cuban-American family living in Miami as seen through the eyes of a 16-year-old boy.

Perfect 10 (Comedy, CBS, 2017).
Producer: Aaron Kaplan, Dana Honor. *Creator-Writer:* Matthew Zinman, Craig Gerard.
Story: A group of high school girls reunite ten years after graduating to recapture their past when they were inseparable and a part of each other's lives.

Peter Gunn (Crime Drama, TNT, 2013).
Producer: Steven Spielberg, Darryl Frank, Justin Falvey. *Creator-Writer:* Jeff Pinkner.
Story: A reboot of the 1958 NBC series of the same title (with Craig Stevens as Peter Gunn and created by Blake Edwards) about a sophisticated private detective who operates out of a waterfront nightclub (Mother's) and is not above the law when it comes to investigating cases.

Phenomenon (Drama, Syfy, 2007).
Producer: Kiefer Sutherland, Maggie Murphy.
Story: A team of paranormal experts, lead by a young female with heightened senses, investigates cases involving supernatural occurrences or anomalies of nature.

The Pickle Brothers (Comedy, ABC, 1967).
Producer-Creator-Writer: Gerald Gardner, Dee Caruso.
Story: Three mishap-prone brothers, billed as "The Uncalled for Three" attempt to break into show business.

Picture Paris (Comedy, EPIX, 2017).
Producer: Meg Ryan, Aaron Kaplan, Dana Honor. *Creator-Writer:* Brad Hall.
Story: When their last child moves out of their home, a suburban couple embarks on their dream to tour Paris. What they imagined it would be like is not what occurs and their effort to cope with what they encounter was to be depicted.

Planet Lucy (Comedy, ABC, 2009).
Producer: Jamie Tarses, Gabrielle Allen.
Story: A young, outgoing woman's experiences when she gives up her business career to become a stay-at-home mother.

Possessed (Drama, ABC, 2019).
Producer: Aaron Kaplan, Dana Honor. *Creator-Writer:* Carey Hayes, Chad Hayes.
Story: After nearly being killed in a hit-and-run accident, a young woman awakens from a coma to discover she is capable of communicating with the dead. Now, as a vessel for deceased spirits, she becomes their savior by avenging their deaths.

The Possession of Maggie Gill (Drama, NBC, 2014).
Producer: Darryl Frank, Justin Falvey, Adam Kane. *Creator-Writer:* John Glenn.
Story: Maggie Gill, the daughter of a middle-class Oregon family, finds her life changing when she becomes the vessel for the supernatural forces that inhabit their home.

The Post Graduate Project (Comedy, NBC, 2010).
Producer: Steve Carell, Thom Hinkle. *Creator-Writer:* Steve Carell.
Story: Life in a small town as seen through the eyes of a mail carrier whose post office is frequented by the town's most quirky characters.

Power (Drama, NBC, 2006).
Producer: Dick Wolf, Peter Jankowski.
Story: U.S. Federal agents and attorneys team to investigate the Hollywood power brokers who are involved in far deeper things than just producing movies.

The Power Playbook (Drama, Lifetime, 2016).
Producer: Queen Latifah, Meryl Poster, La La Anthony. *Creator-Writer:* Neena Beber.
Story: Fictionalized account of how a group of women use sports strategies to guide their personal and professional lives.

Pre-Madonna (Comedy, NBC, 2015).
Producer: Amy Poehler, Dave Becky. *Creator-Writer:* Nisha Ganatra.
Story: An awkward but pretty 14-year-old girl's experiences as she begins high school and a search to find her place in life.

Present Arms (Anthology, Syndication, 1951).
Producer: Robert L. Lippert.
Story: Dramas based on the official files of the U.S. Army.

Prey (Crime Drama, CBS, 2018).
Producer: Mark Harmon, Howard Braunstein. *Creator-Writer:* Ed Decter.
Story: Lucas Davenport, a Minneapolis Police Department homicide detective, teams with Sister Elle Krueger, his friend, a Catholic nun, psychology professor and profiler, to solve crimes.

Prince of Tides (Drama, ABC, 2010).
Producer: Eric Tannenbaum, Kim Tannenbaum, Craig Anderson. *Creator-Writer:* Bob Brush.
Story: An adaptation of the 1986 feature film (with Barbra Streisand and Nick Nolte) about the incidents that befall a family with an abusive father as seen through the eyes of one of his children, now grown and recalling the past (to be seen in flashbacks).

Private (Drama, CBS, 2009).
Producer: Brian Grazer, David Nevins. *Creator-Writer:* James Patterson, Jason Cahill.
Story: An ex-Marine finds himself reverting to his military skills when he assumes ownership of his late father's detective agency to help his clients.

Probe (Anthology, CBS, 1956).
Producer: Hal Roach, Jr.
Story: Dramas that detail the work of specialized medical professionals as they use pathology to help diagnose conditions that are unusual and may pose a health threat.

Prodigy (Drama, Fox, 2013).
Producer: Stephanie Savage, Josh Schwartz, Len Goldstein. *Creator-Writer:* Diablo Cody.
Story: A 16-year-old genius, sheltered from the outside world by her parents and home schooled, faces a drastic change in her life when she enrolls in high school to experience life as a normal teenage girl.

Project 13 (Drama, CW, 2017).
Producer: Elizabeth Banks, Max Handelman.
Creator-Writer: Daegan Fryklind.
Story: An adaptation of the D.C. comic book about Dr. Terrance Thirteen, a forensic scientist and believer in the paranormal, and his daughter, Traci Thirteen, a young girl with extrasensory abilities, who team to investigate the supernatural.

Pros and Cons (Drama, ABC, 2012).
Producer: Mark Gordon, Nichols Pepper.
Creator-Writer: Alexi Hawley.
Story: A young female FBI agent teams with her father, a master thief, to solve crimes wherein her father's expertise provides the help she needs to successfully conclude each assignment.

Pulling (Comedy, NBC, 2016).
Producer: Aaron Kaplan, Dana Honor. *Creator-Writer:* Sharon Horgan.
Story: An adaptation of the British series about a young woman who breaks off her engagement and attempts to reconstruct her life by moving in with her sister and her girlfriend.

Pump (Drama, Showtime, 2013).
Producer: Arnold Schwarzenegger, Eric Tannenbaum, Kim Tannenbaum.
Story: The genesis of the present-day physical fitness industry is seen in a flashback that shows its origins as beginning with a one room gym called Pump.

Punching Out (Comedy, CBS, 2013).
Producer: Katherine Pope, Peter Chernin.
Creator-Writer: Jonathan Goldstein, John Francis Daley.
Story: Three friends, working together in jobs they hate, quit and recreate their after school work experience as minimum wage earners in a shopping mall.

Pushing (Comedy, Fox, 2016).
Producer: Greg Berlanti, Sarah Schechter.
Creator-Writer: Marisa Coughlan.
Story: A former musician, turning 40, married and the mother of two children, has a mid-life awakening and decides to recapture the glory of her youth by becoming a rock band manager (and dragging her husband and kids along for the ride).

Quality Land (Comedy, HBO, 2019).
Producer: Michael Rotenberg. *Creator-Producer:* Mike Judge, Josh Lieb.
Story: A depiction of life in the near future where humanity is struggling to break away from a world where everything is done for you and you are no longer bound to a life where you had responsibilities.

Quantum and Woody (Comedy, TBS, 2018).
Producer-Creator: Anthony Russo, Joe Russo, Gabriel Ferrari.
Story: An adaptation of the Valiant Comics characters of Quantum and Woody, adoptive brothers who use their extraordinary powers to battle evil.

Queen (2012) (Drama, CBS, 2012).
Producer: Ilene Chaiken, Joel Silver. *Creator-Writer:* Ilene Chaiken.
Story: An Oakland Police Department detective teams with a pretty punk girl computer hacker to help him solve crimes.

Queen (2017) (Comedy, Hulu, 2017).
Producer: J.J. Abrams, Ben Stephenson, RuPaul Charles. *Creator-Writer:* Gary Lennon.
Story: Humorous (but fictionalized) account of drag queen RuPaul's rise to fame.

Queen of Shadows (Drama, Hulu, 2016).
Producer: Mark Gordon, Nick Pepper. *Creator-Writer:* Kira Snyder.
Story: An adaptation of the book *Throne of Glass* by Sarah J. Maas about Calaena Sardothien, a female assassin seeking a way to break away from her current situation and lead a normal life.

Queens of the Rodeo (Drama, Lifetime, 2009).
Producer: Neal H. Moritz, Vivian Cannon. *Creator-Writer:* Sara Goodman.
Story: Incidents in the lives of several women who follow the rodeo circuit.

Raffik (Crime Drama, Fox, 2007).
Producer: Darren Star. *Creator-Writer:* Anthony Horowitz.
Story: As part of a program to learn about law enforcement procedures in other countries, an Albanian police detective becomes a temporary member of the N.Y.P.D. where his experiences were to be depicted as he learns from his fellow officers but also teaches them techniques from his homeland.

The Raiding Party (Drama, Fox, 2011).
Producer: Darryl Frank, Justin Falvey. *Creator-Writer:* Nick Santora.
Story: Three brothers, bound to their domineering mother, attempt to carry on the family business after their father's passing—planning, executing and robbing banks.

The Rainmaker (Drama, CBS, 2011).
Producer: Carol Mendelsohn, Julie Weitz. *Creator-Writer:* Sharon Hoffman.
Story: A state prosecutor's efforts to maintain his job while at the same time raising his children following his wife's passing.

Raised By Wolves (Comedy, CBS, 2016).
Producer: Fred Savage, Matt Dearborn. *Creator-Writer:* Rachelle Rosett.
Story: A young man given custody of his seven-year-old daughter following his divorce finds help in raising her from his best friends.

Raising Helen (Comedy, ABC, 2004).
Producer: Garry Marshall, David Hoberman.
Story: A young Manhattan socialite must readjust her life when she becomes the guardian of her recently deceased sister's children.

Raising Men (Comedy, CBS, 2010).
Producer: Samuel L. Jackson, Amanda Tracey. *Creator-Writer:* Gregory Thompson, Aron Abrams.
Story: The relationship between a somewhat immature father and his three very masculine sons.

Raising Mom (Comedy, ABC, 2013).
Producer: Ben Silverman, Gail Mancuso, Sofia Bergara. *Creator-Writer:* Christine Zander.
Story: A middle-aged mother and her 21-year-old son, having practically raised each other, decide to strike out on their own and gain some independence from each other.

Random Acts (Comedy, AMC, 2014).
Producer: Karey Burke, Todd Holland, Kenton Allen. *Creator-Writer:* Andrea Abbate.
Story: Katie and Lisa appear to be ordinary young women dealing with family problems and relationship issues. They work, however, as contract killers and their effort to balance all they have to deal with was to be the focal point of the series.

Ranger (Crime Drama, CBS, 2018).
Producer: James Patterson, Bill Robinson. *Creator-Writer:* Jason Hall.

Story: An adaptation of the novel by James Patterson about the relationship between an overbearing father and his son, a former Texas Ranger turned homicide detective in South Florida.

Raw Materials (Comedy, ABC, 2007).
Producer: Will Smith, Jada Pinkett Smith, James Lassiter. *Creator-Writer:* Lowell Ganz.
Story: A look at the dating scene in today's world where it appears men and women are not hooking up together as they once did.

Read Bottom Up (Comedy, ABC, 2015).
Producer: Stephanie Savage, Josh Schwartz, Ben Karlin. *Creator-Writer:* Neel Shah, Sloane Crosley.
Story: A young Manhattan couple, Madeline and Elliott, are followed as they begin a relationship that is constantly being scrutinized by their parents.

Ready, Fire, Aim (Comedy, CBS, 2005).
Producer: Dick Wolf, Nena Rodrique. *Creator-Writer:* Les Firestein.
Story: A young man and woman, believing they have found a love at first sight, impulsively marry then face the issues of life together.

Reality Bites (Comedy, NBC, 2013).
Producer: Ben Stiller, Michael Shamberg, Stacey Sher. *Creator-Writer:* Helen Childress.
Story: A young female college graduate seeks to find her place in the 1990s recession-plagued world.

Rebel Law (Drama, CBS, 2016).
Producer: Lisa Kudrow, Dan Bucatinsky, Michael Rauch. *Creator-Writer:* Kit Williamson.
Story: An openly gay attorney attempts to begin a new life when he leaves his city practice to become a part of his family's small town Mississippi law practice.

The Rebel League (Comedy, Spike TV, 2010).
Producer: Denis Leary, Jim Serpico. *Creator-Writer:* Stephen Engel.
Story: A humorous look at the launch of a hockey league that is designed to rival the NHL (National Hockey League) and give fans what they crave—more brawls, attitude and scoring.

Recall (Drama, CBS, 2015).
Producer: Carl Beverly, Sarah Timberman. *Creator-Writer:* Mark Goffman.
Story: After scientists develop a way to travel back in time for 24 hours, a group of specialized CIA agents is formed to do what was once impossible: prevent crimes or events from happening.

Regulars (Comedy, USA, 2012).
Producer: Gail Berman, Lloyd Braun, Gene Stein. *Creator-Writer:* David Lampson.
Story: A suburban New Jersey bar provides the setting for a look at the staff and its slightly-off-the wall patrons (a retooling of the series *Cheers*).

Rehab (2009) (Comedy, Fox, 2009).
Producer: Katherine Pope, Peter Chernin. *Writer:* Sam Laybourne.
Story: When David Milkin learns that his former high school sweetheart, a famous rock star named Julie Lind is in rehab for drug abuse, he devises a scheme to rekindle the romance they once had: pretend to be an addict and join her in rehab.

Related (Comedy, ABC, 2013).
Producer: Laurie Zaks, Todd Lieberman, David Hoberman. *Creator-Writer:* Joe Syracuse.
Story: A husband and wife attempt to share their

house with his brother and her sister who have just married and moved in with them.

Remedy (Drama, Fox, 2018).
Producer: Sheldon Turner, Jennifer Klein. *Creator-Writer:* Katie Lovejoy.
Story: Remedy Shaw, a young doctor with a rare neurological condition that allows her to feel a patient's pain, uses her affliction to help people with difficult to diagnose and treat illnesses.

Republic (Drama, NBC, 2017).
Producer: Greg Berlanti, Sarah Schechter. *Creator-Writer:* Alex Berger.
Story: The political conflicts and tensions that arise from both sides of the isle as seen through a female Chief of Staff to a moderate Republican president.

The Residence (Drama, Netflix, 2018).
Producer: Betsy Beers, Shonda Rhimes. *Creator-Writer:* Kate Anderson Brower.
Story: An adaptation of the book by Kate Anderson Brower (which explains the story line): *The Residence: Inside the Private World of the White House*.

Resistance (2005) (Drama, ABC, 2005).
Producer: Ben Affleck, Sean Bailey. *Writer:* Ben Affleck.
Story: In a future time when terrorist attacks have caused the U.S. to split into two separate countries, a band of patriots battle to restore America to its original roots.

Resistance (2012) (Drama, CBS, 2012).
Producer: McG, Peter Johnson, *Creator-Writer:* Daniel Cerone.
Story: When she is fired for breaking the rules, a young female detective with the San Francisco Police Department is secretly hired by the Police Chief for a special assignment: pose as a vigilante to perform undercover assignments.

Rhapsody (Drama, Fox, 2003).
Producer: Shaun Cassidy, Elton John, Bernie Taupin.
Story: Music, mystery and murder mix to tell the story of a big business power struggle.

Rhodes to Recovery (Drama, CBS, 2011).
Producer: Eric Tannenbaum, Kim Tannenbaum. *Creator-Writer:* Ilene Chaiken.
Story: Medical proposal that focuses on a lesbian trauma surgeon (Nicole Rhodes) and her male colleague, a straight neurosurgeon.

Rice (Drama, ABC, 2020).
Producer: Todd Lieberman, Laurie Zaks, David Hoberman.
Story: Following her father's passing, a young woman (Melissa) inherits his restaurant and the title of head chef. With little experience as a chef, Melissa's struggles to keep the business afloat were to be depicted.

Rick (Comedy, NBC, 2011).
Producer: Jimmy Fallon, Gerard Bradford.
Story: A young man struggles to adjust to a new family situation when his mother remarries and he finds that he and his step father are the same age.

Ridin' Dirty (Comedy, FX, 2016).
Producer: Gail Berman, Joe Earley, Melanie Truhett. *Creator-Writer:* Allyn Rachel.
Story: Vicky Gursky is a jockey with a dream: To become the first woman in history to win the Triple Crown. Her efforts to achieve that dream were to be chronicled (despite her reputation as "The badest chick in the business").

The Rifleman (Western, CBS, 2012).
Producer: Arthur Gardner, Carol Mendelsohn, Julie Weitz, Stephen Gardner.
Story: A remake of the 1958-1963 ABC series of the same title (with Chuck Connors and Johnny Crawford) about Lucas McCain, an expert marksman with a rifle, as he and his young son, Mark, attempt to begin a new life in Northfork, New Mexico, after the death of his wife.

The Ripple Effect (Drama, Syfy, 2003).
Producer: Kelsey Grammer, Kenneth Johnson, Steve Stark.
Story: The small town of Pine Bluffs, Oregon, provides the setting for a look at what happens when its residents are caught in a time warp and relive the same day over and over with each day bringing about different results.

Rob Lowe Untitled Project (Crime Drama, Fox, 2014).
Producer-Creator: Rob Lowe, Alison Cross.
Story: Relates the cases of an anti crime unit of the L.A.P.D.

Robert DeNiro Untitled 2011 Project (Drama, CBS, 2012).
Producer: Robert DeNiro, Jane Rosenthal, Diane Nabatoff. *Creator-Writer:* Danny Strong.
Story: A father and daughter's defense of clients who believe they are above the law—notorious criminals.

Robert DeNiro Untitled 2012 Project (Drama, CBS, 2012).
Producer: Robert DeNiro, Jane Rosenthal. *Creator-Writer:* Diana Son.
Story: Following the death of her husband, a trauma surgeon at a Manhattan hospital becomes a stay-at-home mother when she relinquishes her position to take over her father-in-law's medical practice, which is located in a Brooklyn brownstone.

Robert DeNiro Untitled 2013 Project (Crime Drama, CBS, 2013).
Producer: Robert DeNiro, Jane Rosenthal. *Creator-Writer:* David Marshall Grant.
Story: A Counter Intelligence expert, returned to the U.S. following service in Afghanistan and rejoining his former police precinct, incorporates his military abilities to deal with gang violence.

The Robert Townsend Show (Comedy, TBS, 2008).
Producer-Writer-Star: Robert Townsend.
Story: A proposed late night series of skits by improvisational actors.

Romancing the Stone (Adventure, NBC, 2011).
Producer: Becky Clements, Marty Adelstein, Shawn Levy. *Creator-Writer:* Mark Friedman.
Story: A young woman, seeking her missing brother, joins with a rogue mercenary in his quest to find lost treasures as her only hope of achieving her goal. Based on the feature film of the same title.

Royal (Drama, Fox, 2013).
Producer: Katherine Pope, Peter Chernin. *Creator-Writer:* Joshua Safran.
Story: After being expelled from a royal family for having an illicit affair, a young woman begins a new life as an assistant and "baby sitter" to a drug-addicted, temperamental, suicidal fashion designer.

Rubber Guns (Crime Drama, CBS, 2015).
Producer: Ridley Scott, David W. Zucker. *Creator-Writer:* R. Scott Gemmill, T.J. Fixman.
Story: Four mentally unstable police officers, assigned to the Rubber Gun Squad of the

Miami Police Department, form their own team to solve crimes through their wits, not guns.

Rules for My Unborn Son (Comedy, Fox, 2010).
Producer: Darryl Frank, Justin Falvey. *Creator-Writer:* Dan Cohn, Jeremy Miller.
Story: A man, now 25 years old and raised by a family of eccentrics since he was adopted as an infant, struggles to cope with a world that he doesn't quite understand due to his strange upbringing.

Rush (Drama, TNT, 2011).
Producer: Jamie Tarses, Kevin Falls. *Creator-Writer:* Allan McDonald.
Story: Events that befall the doctors and nurses in an understaffed emergency room hospital.

Ryan Seacrest Untitled 2016 Project (Comedy, CBS, 2016).
Producer: Ryan Seacrest, Nina Wass. *Creator-Writer:* Lauren Gussis.
Story: An interracial couple's efforts to deal with the constant interference from their totally dissimilar parents who feel it is their duty to guide their lives.

Ryan Seacrest Untitled 2019 Project (Drama, Amazon, 2019).
Producer: Ryan Seacrest, Nina Wass. *Creator-Writer:* Lauren Gussis.
Story: A love story with a twist: a young man and a biological woman who begins to doubt her gender and believes she were meant to be a male.

Safe Harbor (Drama, Fox, 2018).
Producer: Jennifer Klein, McG, Mary Viola. *Creator-Producer-Writer:* Sheldon Turner.
Story: The work of the investigative branch of the U.S. Coast Guard as they patrol and protect the beaches of Miami Beach, Florida.

Safe House (Drama, ABC, 2011).
Producer: Sheldon Turner, Jennifer Klein. *Creator-Writer:* Chris Hollier.
Story: The investigations of a brash young CIA agent and the relationship he shares with his estranged mother—head of the CIA branch for which he works.

Saga (Drama, ABC, 2013).
Producer: Darryl Frank, Justin Falvey, Todd Cohen. *Creator-Writer:* Andrew Miller, Chris Black.
Story: A well-known author, just about to complete the final chapter in her fantasy saga book series, mysteriously vanishes and is thrust into what appears to be a real world of what she created. Unable to wait for authorities to investigate, a group of dedicated fans take action—and begin the search to find and rescue her.

St. Elmo's Fire (Drama, NBC, 2009).
Producer: Jamie Tarses, Topher Grace, Chris King. *Creator-Writer:* Dan Bucatinsky.
Story: An adaptation of the 1985 feature film about a group of Georgetown University graduates as they struggle with the responsibilities of adulthood.

Salma Hayek Untitled 2015 Project (Drama, ABC, 2015).
Producer: Salma Hayek, Jose Tamez, Michael McDonald. *Creator-Writer:* Diego Gutierrez.
Story: Soap opera-like proposal about a family who run a large Mexican conglomerate but who each conceal secrets that could destroy their family empire.

Salma Hayek Untitled 2018 Project (Comedy, Amazon, 2018).
Producer: Brian Grazer, Salma Hayek, Francie

Calfo. *Creator-Writer:* Pail Feig.
Story: An American ambassador's experiences when she is assigned to oversee the London office.

Salute (Testimonial, NBC, 1967).
Producer: Bob Finkel.
Story: Show business personalities were to be honored through live surprise performances by their contemporaries.

Samuel L. Jackson Untitled 2009 Project (Drama, CBS, 2009).
Producer: Samuel L. Jackson, Amanda Tracey.
Creator-Producer-Writer: Andrea Newman.
Story: An emergency room doctor's clash with his superiors as he incorporates often unconventional methods to treat patients.

Samuel L. Jackson Untitled 2010 Project (Comedy, CBS, 2009).
Producer: Samuel L. Jackson, Amanda Tracey.
Creator-Writer: Bob Kushell.
Story: When a U.S. Congressman passes away during the middle of his term, his wife inherits his seat and a truckload of problems when she finds she is totally incapable of handling the position.

Sand Men (Drama, NBC, 2011).
Producer: Karey Burke, Todd Holland. *Creator-Writer:* Craig Titley.
Story: Agents of a celestial unit called the Sleep and Nightmare Division enter people's dreams to help them confront their nightmares (which were to be seen in dream-like sequences).

Sandra Bullock Untitled Project (Drama, Amazon, 2019).
Producer: Sandra Bullock, John Legend, Akiva Goldsman. *Creator-Writer:* Marja-Lewis Ryan.

Story: A young woman, attending college in the Deep South during the 1980s, defies the expectations set for her to search for an identity of her own.

Santa Colita Blue (Crime Drama, ABC, 2004).
Producer: Francie Calfo, Michelle King. *Creator-Writer:* Robert King.
Story: Crime prevention in small communities as depicted through the activities of the Santa Colita, California, Police Department.

Sarah Jessica Parker Untitled Project (Comedy, HBO, 2006).
Producer: Sarah Jessica Parker. *Creator-Writer:* Amy Sacco.
Story: A New York nightclub owner's efforts to deal with both staff and clientele problems.

Sausage Fest (Comedy, NBC, 2009).
Producer: Gail Berman, Lloyd Braun. *Creator-Writer:* Josh Heald.
Story: Two best friends and how they deal with their intrusive fathers—one an easy-going widower; the other a three times divorced ladies' man.

Scales of Justice (Crime Drama, USA, 2012).
Producer: Denis Leary, Jim Serpico. *Creator-Writer:* Joe Sutton.
Story: An overweight former cop turned private detective solves crimes—with the help of his over eaters support group.

School of Fish (Comedy, Fox, 2013).
Producer: Katherine Pope, Peter Chernin. *Creator-Writer:* Kevin Biggins, Travis Bowe.
Story: The ups and downs of a rock group composed of friends who work at the Pike Place Fish Market in Seattle, Washington.

The Scroll (Anthology, Fox, 2017).
Producer: Queen Latifah, Holly Carter. *Creator-Writer:* Michael Elliot.
Story: Re-imagined stories from the Bible that were to be set in the present day and seen through a group of friends that are representative of the Bible's most recognizable characters.

Sean Hayes Untitled Project (Comedy, NBC, 2016).
Producer: Sean Hayes. *Creator-Writer:* Suzanne Martin, Todd Milliner.
Story: After a one night stand with a girl who is his complete opposite, a happy-go-lucky funeral parlor director finds his life changing when he becomes a part of her large, dysfunctional family.

Seattle Rescue (Drama, UPN, 2003).
Producer: Aaron Spelling, E. Duke Vincent. *Creator-Writer:* Jorge Zamacona.
Story: A group of extreme sports enthusiasts join forces to help people trapped in precarious situations.

Second Chances (Drama, Fox, 2011).
Producer: Katherine Pope, Peter Chernin. *Creator-Writer:* Gina Fattore.
Story: A female trauma surgeon, the only survivor of a car crash that killed her best friend, struggles to cope with the situation that occurred and why she was spared and for what reason.

Securing the City (Drama, CBS, 2009).
Producer: Robert DeNiro, Jane Rosenthal. *Creator-Writer:* Terry George.
Story: The operations of the Counter Terrorism and Counter Intelligence Division of the N.Y.P.D.

Sellevision (Comedy, NBC, 2011).
Producer: Karey Burke, Todd Holland. *Creator-Writer:* Bryan Singer.
Story: A spoof of the various home shopping networks as seen through the antics of four people who work for a fictional cable home shopping program.

Sensory (Drama, CBS, 2016).
Producer: David W. Zucker, Ridley Scott. *Creator-Writer:* David Zabel.
Story: A med student uses his unusual gift to help people: mirror-touch synesthesia (the ability to feel or mirror the emotional and physical sensations of his patients).

Separate Beds (Comedy, ABC, 2003).
Producer: Marty Adelstein, Dawn Olmstead. *Creator-Producer-Writer:* Neil Simon.
Story: Instead of divorcing, two couples who are also friends, resolve their issues by separating—with the women living together in one home and the husbands next door in the other.

Sequestered (Comedy, Fox, 2009).
Producer: Katherine Pope, Peter Chernin. *Creator-Writer:* Josh Helad.
Story: Incidents in the lives of a twelve member jury when they are sequestered during a long trial.

The Seranos (Drama, NBC, 2005).
Producer: Ben Silverman.
Story: Two former lovers, Diego Serano, a widower with three sons and a café owner; and Lucia, a divorced mother with two daughters, attempt to start a new life together when they reunite after a long absence.

The Seven Husbands of Evelyn Hugo (Drama, Freeform, 2020).
Producer: Jennifer Beals, Ilene Chaiken. *Creator-Writer:* Taylor Jenkins Reid.
Story: Flashback proposal about a young female journalist (Monique) as she takes on the assignment of a lifetime: write the story of Evelyn Hugo, a sex symbol of Hollywood's Golden Age (1950s and 1960s).

The Seven Wonders (Drama, ABC, 2011).
Producer: Mark Gordon. *Creator-Writer:* Michael Seitzman.
Story: A team of relic hunters seek an ancient and powerful relic whose completion can only be accomplished when its seven missing sections are placed together.

Several Children (Comedy, NBC, 2011).
Producer: Jamie Tarses, Barry Katz, Julia Franz. *Creator-Writer:* Dan Levy.
Story: A harried business woman attempts to not only care for her much younger husband and their children, but her husband's immature friends who have made their home their second home.

Shakespeare's Sisters (Drama, CW, 2014).
Producer: Eric Tannenbaum, Kim Tannenbaum, Mark Harmon. *Creator-Writer:* Scott Sullivan.
Story: Fantasized proposal about William Shakespeare's rise to prominence and his battle to save Queen Elizabeth from three witches seeking to dethrone her.

Shaun Cassidy Untitled Project (Drama, ABC, 2011).
Producer-Creator-Writer: Shaun Cassidy, Sheldon Turner. *Producer:* Jennifer Klein.
Story: A view of political strife in Washington, D.C. as seen through a male Vice President and his female Chief of Staff.

The Sheriff (Crime Drama, Spike TV, 2012).
Producer: Ben Silverman, Craig Armstrong.
Story: The battle against the drug cartels along the U.S.-Mexican border as depicted through the activities of the local community sheriff whose town is the center of criminal activity.

Shhh! Don't Tell Steve (Comedy, CBS, 2011).
Producer: Karey Burke, Ashton Kutcher, Jason Goldberg. *Creator-Writer:* Andrew Waller.
Story: Odd Couple parody about George, a seemingly decent young man who lives with an unemployed alcohol-addicted friend (Steve); the twist: George uses the Internet to "tweet" the antics of Steve.

Shining Vale (Drama, Starz, 2020).
Producer: Aaron Kaplan, Dana Honor. *Creator-Writer:* Sharon Horgan, Jeff Astrof.
Story: After relocating to a small town, a family finds their lives in jeopardy when the house into which they move appears to be haunted by malevolent spirits.

Shock Theater (Anthology, AMC, 2019).
Producer: Gail Berman, Joe Earley. *Creator-Writer:* Matt Lambert.
Story: A program of horror stories featuring different casts each week.

Shook Up (Drama, EPIX, 2019).
Producer: Sarah Timberman, Carl Beverly. *Creator-Writer:* Jennifer Schuur.
Story: A harsh depiction of life in New York City during the 1950s when the area known as Hell's Kitchen became the Mecca for street-ruled mob violence.

Significant Brother (Comedy, Fox, 2018).
Producer: Dave Becky, Jonathan Berry. *Creator-Writer:* Scott King.

Story: George and Emily are a newlywed couple facing difficult times. Bruce is George's estranged gay brother. When George suggests that Bruce move in with them to help solve their problems, he not only becomes their advisor but best friends with Emily.

Silicon Beach (Drama, Fox, 2017).
Producer: McG, Mary Viola. *Creator-Writer:* Brian Young.
Story: Maya Carter is a 26-year-old woman with the ability to change circumstances simply by concentrating. Alex Silva is an immoral billionaire who has befriended her for only one purpose: use her ability to change the world.

Silver Shields (Drama, Syfy, 2013).
Producer: Aaron Kaplan. *Creator-Writer:* Robert Hewitt Wolf.
Story: When his father, a member of the Point Royal Police Department, is killed by hired assassins for unknown reasons, his son joins the police department to not only solve his father's murder but deal with something sinister that may be connected to the crime—Point Royal is populated by magical creatures.

Sirens (Comedy, USA, 2012).
Producer: Denis Leary, Jim Serpico, Bob Fisher.
Story: An adaptation of the British series about incidents, both humorous and lightly dramatic, in the lives of a group of young paramedics.

Sister Land (Drama, ABC, 2013).
Producer: Stephanie Savage, Josh Schwartz, Len Goldstein. *Creator-Writer:* Rina Mimoun.
Story: Identical twin sisters, born with the ability to communicate with the dead, join forces to help restless spirits move on.

Six Months, Three Days (Drama, NBC, 2013).
Producer: Krysten Ritter, David Janollari, Lindsey Liberatore. *Creator-Writer:* Eric Garcia.
Story: Two San Francisco private detectives, each possessed with the ability to see the future, use their abilities to catch criminals before they act.

Sketch Off (Reality, TBS, 2005).
Producer: Whoopi Goldberg, Sue Fellow, Tom Leonardis.
Story: Talent search that travels across the U.S. to find the best improv sketch performers in comedy troupes.

Skin Deep (Drama, ABC, 2012).
Producer: Jennifer Klein. *Creator-Producer-Writer:* Sheldon Turner.
Story: Serial-like proposal about the intrigues that exist behind a family run beauty empire.

Skinny Dip (Drama, HBO, 2012).
Producer: Michael Keaton, Michael Oates Palmer. *Writer:* Carl Hiaasen. *Creator:* Garrett Lerner.
Story: A beautiful heiress, traveling with her husband on his yacht, is pushed overboard by him and left to drown. The girl survives and decides to remain "dead" to plot her revenge against him.

Skippy (Comedy, Syndication, 1958).
Producer: Jackie Cooper.
Story: An adaptation of the 1931 feature film that starred Jackie Cooper about the relationship between Skippy Skinner, a boy from a wealthy family, and Sooky, a poor boy who lives in the nearby poverty-stricken Shanty Town.

Sleeping Beauties (Drama, AMC, 2019).
Producer: Stephen King, Michael Sugar, Ashley Zalta. *Creator-Writer:* Stephen King, Owen King.

Story: An adaptation of the book by Stephen King and Owen King about life in a most unusual women's prison in a small Appalachian town. When inmates retire for the night, their bodies become shrouded in cocoon-like gauze that appears to take their consciousness to another world; however, if they are disturbed they awaken as feral, vicious killers.

Sleepy Hallow (Crime Drama, CW, 2012).
Producer: Gina Matthews, Aaron Berger, Carina Schulze. *Creator-Writer:* Grant Scharbo, Patrick MacManus.
Story: Ichabod Crane, an FBI agent assigned to the town of Sleepy Hollow (in Tarrytown, New York), finds that as he investigates crimes the characters and situations he encounters are connected to the tale of "The Legend of Sleepy Hollow" which tells of a headless horseman who searches the night seeking his lost head.

Small Town Love (Comedy, ABC, 2015).
Producer: Aaron Kaplan. *Creator-Writer:* Emily Halpern, Sarah Haskins.
Story: The situations that befall and mother and her daughter when each become pregnant at the same time by their slacker boyfriends.

Smoke (Drama, Fox, 2005).
Producer: Neal H. Moritz, Marty Adelstein, Dave Olmstead. *Writer:* Robert Peacock.
Story: Serialized project about the rich children of a North Carolina tobacco dynasty who head a campaign to revolutionize the cigarette packaging and selling market.

Social Circle (Drama, ABC, 2013).
Producer: Stephanie Savage, Joshua Schwartz. *Creator-Writer:* Joshua Safran.
Story: Several years after graduating from college, a group of friends reconnect to pick up where they left off only to discover they really did not know each other and the past is just that—the past.

Solve for X (Crime Drama, CBS, 2012).
Producer: Eric Tannenbaum, Kim Tannenbaum. *Creator-Writer:* Ilene Chaiken.
Story: A game developer working for a San Francisco gaming company is drafted by an anti-crime task force to program crimes and their possible solutions.

The Sorority Girl Who Saved Your Life (Drama, ABC, 2018).
Producer: Sarah Timberman, Carl Beverly, Ellen Pompeo.
Story: An adaptation of the book by Tracy Walder about her experiences as a student at the University of Southern California and a Delta Gamma sorority sister who is recruited as a spy by the CIA while using her school status as a cover.

The Source (Drama, CBS, 2017).
Producer: Phil McGraw, Jay McGraw. *Creator:* Amanda Green.
Story: An investigative reporter teams with an L.A.P.D. detective to solve crimes by her method of operating above the law to expose criminal activities through her newspaper.

Speak American (Comedy, Fox, 2013).
Producer: Ben Silverman, Sofia Vergara. *Creator-Writer:* Benjamin Brand.
Story: When his unconventional teaching methods forces a group of foreign students to question what it means to be an American, he forms them into an unlikely family to observe and experience life outside the classroom.

The Special (Crime Drama, USA, 2012).
Producer: Mark Gordon. *Creator-Writer:* Bill Wheeler.
Story: The cases of a dedicated L.A.P.D. detective who suffers from hypomania (a bipolar disorder wherein a person is prone to excessive energy and requires, in some cases, little sleep).

Spellbinder (Drama, MTV, 2012).
Producer: Vin Di Bona, Susan Levison. *Creator-Writer:* Erik Patterson, Jessica Scott.
Story: A teenage girl, possessed with the ability to see and hear ghosts, attempts to help restless spirits move on.

Spinsters (Comedy, NBC, 2012).
Producer: Mark Gordon, Andrea Shay. *Creator-Writer:* Jessica Goldstein, Chrissy Pietrosh.
Story: A young man's attempts to help three sisters, who consider themselves spinsters, discover there is life beyond the confines of their home and the seclusion they have chosen for themselves.

Spiral (Crime Drama, Showtime, 2015).
Producer: Jeremy Gold, Steve McPherson. *Creator-Producer-Writer:* Tom Fontana.
Story: An adaptation of the French series *Engrenages* that focuses on how a deputy prosecutor, a police captain and a judge combine their abilities to uphold the law.

Spirits (Drama, CW, 2011).
Producer: Anthony E. Zuiker. *Creator-Writer:* Jesse Alexander.
Story: Three beautiful young women team to solve mysteries supposedly associated with the supernatural.

Splitsville (Comedy, ABC, 2015).
Producer: Betsy Beers, Shonda Rhimes. *Creator-Writer:* Emily Halpern.
Story: A group of young divorcees, given custody of their children and living in an apartment complex that caters to single parents, join forces to help each other raise their children.

Splitting Adams (Drama, Fox, 2011).
Producer: Brian Grazer, David Hubbard. *Creator-Producer-Writer:* Francie Calfo.
Story: The cases of a young female prosecutor with a unique ability: see herself as the defendant in a trial she is prosecuting.

Splitting the Difference (Comedy, ABC, 2014).
Producer: Eva Longoria, Ben Spector. *Creator-Writer:* Kat Coiro.
Story: The relationship between a widowed 36-year-old mother and her estranged, 17-year-old daughter when they reunite and attempt to create a stable family.

Spoon Benders (Drama, Showtime, 2020).
Producer: Greg Berlanti, Sarah Schechter. *Creator-Writer:* Stephen Falk.
Story: A family of magicians possessing real powers and traveling in a road show called "The Amazing Telemachus Family" use their abilities to help authorities apprehend criminals.

Spy Girl (Drama, WB, 2005).
Producer: Sarah Timberman, Carl Beverly, Maggie Friedman. *Creator-Writer:* Amy Gray.
Story: A young Ivy League graduate, working in a boring job as an editor for a publishing house, quits her job to pursue her dream of becoming a private investigator.

Squad Goals (Comedy, CBS, 2015).
Producer: Ryan Seacrest, Nina Wass. *Creator-Writer:* Lindsey Rosin, Aaron Karo.
Story: Ten years after graduating from college, a group of friends reunite to better their lives when they find they have not changed.

The Squeeze (Comedy, CBS, 2018).
Producer: Aaron Kaplan, Dana Honor, Wendi Trilling. *Creator-Writer:* Dana Klein.
Story: A married couple's efforts to not only care for and raise their children, but care for their dependent parents.

The Stand-In (Drama, E!, 2013).
Producer: Ryan Seacrest, Nina Wass, Adam Sher. *Creator-Writer:* Craig Chester.
Story: A famous Hollywood actress (Melinda), disenchanted with the life she is leading, secretly places herself out of the spotlight to find the life she craves. Her family, desperate to hide the fact that Melinda has disappeared, find a girl who is her exact double and hire her to become Melinda. Unknown to the family, the girl is actually Melinda's evil doppelganger and what happens as the doppelganger slowly loses herself in the process of becoming someone else was to be depicted.

Star Crazy (Drama, CW, 2013).
Producer: George Lopez, Leslie Kolins Small. *Creator-Producer-Writer:* Mel Harris, Bob Brush.
Story: A young Latina singer is followed as she rises from poverty to fame.

Starsky & Hutch (Crime Drama, Amazon, 2018).
Producer: Neal H. Moritz. *Creator-Writer:* William Blinn.
Story: A remake of the 1970s ABC series about Dave Starsky and Ken "Hutch" Hutchinson, homicide detectives who like to do things their way even if it is above the law.

Statue of Liberty (Anthology, CBS, 1956).
Producer: Hollywood Television Service.
Story: Dramas based on Immigration Department records that tell of the people allowed entry into the U.S. and those found unsuitable and denied entry.

Statute of Limitations (Crime Drama, Spike TV, 2007).
Producer: Denis Leary, Jim Serpico.
Story: A specialized team of FBI agents race against time to apprehend felons who are on the verge of beating the statute of limitations for their crimes.

A Step Away (Comedy, NBC, 2017).
Producer: Jennifer Lopez, Benny Medina, Elaine Goldsmith-Thomas. *Creator-Writer:* David Holden.
Story: A group of young people considered misfits join a dance group in the hope of turning their lives around.

Step Dave (Comedy, NBC, 2017).
Producer: Sean Hayes, Todd Milliner. *Creator-Writer:* Emily Cutler.
Story: The relationship between two people with little in common but who love each other: a 24-year-old bar tender and a 36-year-old single working mother.

Stephen J. Cannell Untitled Project (Drama, USA, 2009).
Producer-Creator: Stephen J. Cannell, Scott Kaufer.
Story: An ex-con who is a master car mechanic is recruited by the FBI to work undercover and expose car theft rings.

Steven Bochco Untitled 2003 Project (Drama, NBC, 2003).
Producer-Writer: Steven Bochco.
Story: Follows a group of rookie cops in a suburban college town whose assignments are more bizarre than life threatening.

Steven Bochco Untitled 2005 Project (Crime Drama, WB, 2005).
Producer-Writer: Steven Bochco.
Story: Revolves around the cases of two homicide detectives with the L.A.P.D.

Steven Bochco Untitled 2006 Project (Drama, Fox, 2006).
Producer-Writer: Steven Bochco, Chris Gerolmo.
Story: High profile civil court cases are explored through the personal lives of the principals involved, including the lawyers, judges, plaintiffs and defendants.

Steven Spielberg Untitled 2006 Project (Drama, Fox, 2006).
Producer: Steven Spielberg, Darryl Frank, Justin Falvey.
Story: A look at the fashion industry as seen through the experiences of four people: a fashion designer, a photographer, a model and a makeup artist.

Steven Spielberg Untitled 2007 Project (Drama, Fox, 2007).
Producer: Steven Spielberg, Darryl Frank, Justin Falvey.
Story: World War II drama about two battlefield physicians capable of traveling though time who use future technology and medicine (2007 here) to treat wounded soldiers and help the war effort.

Sting (Drama, ABC, 2003).
Producer: Jerry Bruckheimer, Jonathan Littman.
Creator-Writer: Jeremy Littman.
Story: Specialized U.S. forces use sting operations to stop crises before they occur.

Stingray (Drama, CBS, 2016).
Producer: Sarah Timberman, Carl Beverly, Bill Robinson. *Creator-Writer:* David Marshall Grant.
Story: A group of highly skilled con artists team with an FBI unit to capture elusive criminals.

Strange Calls (Comedy, NBC, 2015).
Producer: Aaron Kaplan, Tracey Robertson. Nathan Mayfield. *Creator-Writer:* Blake McCormick.
Story: A young police officer and his friend, an elderly but peculiar night watchman, team to investigate cases that appear to be associated with the supernatural.

Strange Fiction (Drama, NBC, 2013).
Producer: Gina Matthews, Grant Scharbo, Jeff Okin. *Creator-Writer:* Andrew Cosby.
Story: A young book editor teams with a paranormal investigator to probe cases wherein spirits threaten the living.

Starting Up (Comedy, Fox, 2012).
Producer: Aaron Kaplan, Sean Perrone, Reuben Fleischer, John Phillips.
Story: A group of friends, dissatisfied with their boring office jobs, join forces to begin their own company. With no experience and numerous issues, their efforts to succeed were to be depicted.

State (Drama, WB, 2003).
Producer: Aaron Spelling. *Creator-Writer:* Justin Lin.
Story: Serial-like project that was to focus on college life as not only seen from the eyes of the students but the teachers as well.

Status Update (Comedy, ABC, 2011).
Producer: Mark Gordon, Andrea Shea.
Story: A young woman, having little luck in the dating department, changes her strategy and armed with advice from friends and various Internet sites, re-enters the dating scene only to find herself overwhelmed and often baffled by the men she meets.

Steps (Drama, CW, 2006).
Producer: Marta Kauffman.
Story: A family's efforts to operate a dance studio that is not only on the brink of closing but plagued by numerous family issues.

Strike Force (Crime Drama, CBS, 2016).
Producer: Jeffrey Kramer. *Creator-Writer:* Robert Port.
Story: Intelligence officers team with federal authorities to track down the country's most dangerous criminals.

Strong Girl (Drama, CW, 2018).
Producer: Ben Silverman, Ronda Rousey. *Creator-Writer:* Melissa Scrivner-Love.
Story: During an assignment in Afghanistan, a young female combat photographer (Rayna) is exposed to an unknown chemical that endows her with incredible strength. With her ability, she joins with her boyfriend, a Special Ops agent, to battle the enemies of the country.

Stuck (Comedy, Fox, 2013).
Producer: Rashida Jones, Will McCormack. *Creator-Writer:* Alexandra Rushfield.
Story: A look at two people stuck in a rut: a middle-aged mother who works as a bank teller and her daughter, a twenty-something girl who refuses to grow up.

Stuck in Reverse (Comedy, ABC, 2011).
Producer: Mark Gordon, Andrea Shay. *Creator-Producer-Writer:* Scott King.
Story: After suffering a near-death experience, a father attempts to reconnect with his estranged, now adult children in the hopes of forming a long neglected family.

The Studio (Drama, Showtime, 2015).
Producer: George Clooney, Grant Heslov, Michael Wimer. *Creator-Writer:* Peter Tolan.
Story: The business of making movies during the 1990s as seen through studio heads who are trying to overcome the conglomerates that are controlling their every move.

Stuff (Comedy, Freeform, 2016).
Producer: Aaron Kaplan. *Creator-Producer-Writer:* Darlene Hunt.
Story: The situations that befall a family of women who run a Kentucky consignment shop called "Been There Wore That."

Submarine (Anthology, NBC, 1955).
Producer: John Florea.
Story: Dramatizations based on the experiences of the men of the U.S. Navy with filming to be done at the San Diego Naval Base facilities. A series, called *Navy Log* would emerge in 1957.

Suckers (Drama, HBO, 2005).
Producer: Howard Klein. *Creator-Writer:* William Schmidt.

Story: A variation on the series *True Blood* wherein a mother attempts to raise her children—all of whom are vampires.

Sunny D (Comedy, Fox, 2018).
Producer: Eric Tannenbaum, Kim Tannenbaum.
Creator-Writer: Keenen Ivory Wayans, Saladin K. Papperson.
Story: A 30-year-old down-on-his luck man, considered a slacker by friends and family, attempts to restructure his life by moving out of his childhood bedroom, find an apartment and make something of himself.

Sunshine Scouts (Comedy, Netflix, 2019).
Producer: Betsy Beers, Shonda Rhimes. *Creator-Writer:* Jill Alexander.
Story: During a camp outing a group of teenage girls become unaffected when a mysterious force appears to have destroyed all life on earth. Their quest to discover what happened and find others who may have survived was to be depicted.

Super Sad True Love Story (Drama, Showtime, 2016).
Producer: Ben Stiller. *Creator-Writer:* Karl Gaidusek.
Story: Life in America is explored through a group of people and how they accept (or reject) contemporary values, trends, the political system, social networking and the obsession with youth.

Survival (Anthology, Syndication, 1957).
Producer: Stuart Reynolds, Tony Lazarino.
Story: Dramatizations based on the files of the North American Air Defense Command.

Suture Girl (Drama, Syfy, 2003).
Producer: Todd MacFarlane, Sheila Duckworth, Tracey E. Edmonds.
Story: While fleeing from a serial killer, Gretchen Culver runs into the street and is hit by a car. As she is being transported to the hospital, she is raped by the ambulance attendants who, to conceal their crime, take Gretchen to an underworld connection for disposal. The sadistic connection horribly disfigures Gretchen, slicing her with a knife then dumping her lifeless body on a desolate road. Gretchen is found by a mysterious Gypsy woman who stitches her wounds and endows her with special powers that heal her and make her appear normal again. Gretchen finds a home in the Gypsy community but uses her newly acquired gifts to battle evil in manner as was done to her: once she collars a murderer she tears them apart then stitches them back together—her branding as the mysterious vigilante Suture Girl. Based on the comic book character.

Swell (Comedy, ABC, 2003).
Producer: Ron Howard, Brian Grazer, David Nevins. *Creator-Writer:* Michael Chessler.
Story: A fashion designer was to be followed from her start in the business to her success as a fashion icon.

Swimming with Sharks (Drama, E!, 2016).
Producer: Kevin Spacey, Dana Brunetti. *Creator-Writer:* Kathleen Robertson.
Story: While the project carries the title of the 1994 feature film, it deviates somewhat from the premise to focus on a young woman, working as an assistant, as she tries to advance her position in a company filled with manipulators.

Switched (Comedy, NBC, 2010).
Producer: Karey Burke, Todd Holland. *Creator-Writer:* Paul Davies.
Story: Twin girls, separated at birth and raised by different families in neighboring towns, attempt to become sisters after an accidental meeting unites them.

Sword Fighting (Comedy, CW, 2012).
Producer: Neil Meron, Craig Zadan. *Creator-Writer:* Ben McMillan, Josh Greenbaum.
Story: Two men who are also best friends attempt to adjust to a new situation in their lives when their wives reveal they love each other.

Talent (Drama, NBC, 2015).
Producer: Shaun Cassidy, Josh Barry. *Creator-Writer:* Shaun Cassidy.
Story: A music prodigy turns vigilante to seek out and kill criminals in revenge for the murder of his fiancée.

Tales from Dickens (Anthology, Syndication, 1959).
Producer: Alan Towers.
Story: Self-contained dramas based on stories written by Charles Dickens. The program was to be filmed in England and two episodes had been planned: "Christmas at Dingley Hall" with James Donald as the star; and "The Runaways" starring Athene Seyler and Bobby Hewes.

Talk Nerdy to Me (Drama, CBS, 2015).
Producer: Jerry Bruckheimer, Jonathan Littman, Kristie Anne Reed. *Creator-Writer:* Morgan Murphy.
Story: Four women in their twenties, a doctor, two computer programmers and a musician are followed as they help each other navigate life.

The Tao of Martha (Comedy, Fox, 2012).
Producer: Brian Grazer, Francie Calfo. *Producer-Writer:* Martha Stewart.
Story: After being told she is a scatter-brained party girl, Julie McDonald makes an unusual pledge to improve herself—to become the next Martha Stewart and America's queen of home décor.

Tarrytown (Drama, ABC, 2010).
Producer: Todd Lieberman, David Hoberman. *Creator-Writer:* R. Lee Fleming.
Story: Siblings attempt to live together in a decrepit house they inherit from their father in an upscale Texas town.

Temps (Comedy, NBC, 2011).
Producer: Jennifer Gwartz, Rob Thomas. *Creator-Writer:* Rob Thomas, Dan Etheridge.
Story: A group of recent college graduates, unable to acquire jobs in their chosen fields, find themselves taking various odd jobs to make ends meet.

Ten Things You Don't Know About Women (Comedy, NBC, 2011).
Producer: Sean Hayes, Todd Milliner. *Creator-Writer-Producer:* Betsy Thomas.
Story: Events in the lives of three sisters—one who is single, one who is divorced and one who is happily married and how their lives interact with each other.

Ten Years (Comedy, NBC, 2011).
Producer: Courteney Cox, David Arquette. *Creator-Writer:* Howard J. Morris.
Story: A couple's relationship is charted over a ten year period—beginning with their separation and looking back on the events that led up to the point where the series would begin.

Tension (Anthology, Syndication, 1957).
Producer: Gene Feldman.
Story: Adaptations of stories that appeared in the Doubleday & Company book series *The Crime Club*.

The Terminal (Drama, CBS, 2020). *Producer:* Aaron Kaplan, Dana Honor, Tom Sullivan. *Creator-Writer:* Barbie Kligman. *Story:* Dana Macklin, the first female marine to earn the Medal of Honor, uses her experiences with the service to protect JFK International Airport in New York when she becomes its head of security.

The Terranauts (Drama, CW, 2016). *Producer:* Jim Parsons, Todd Spiewak. *Creator-Writer:* Zach Helm. *Story:* Eight scientists confined to a biosphere attempt to prove it is viable for sustaining life on a new planet to insure the survival of the human race.

Terrible People (Comedy, ABC, 2013). *Producer:* Betsy Thomas, Karey Burke, Todd Holland. *Creator-Writer:* Humphrey Ker. *Story:* A young man, whose life changed when his parents divorced and his father married a manipulative woman with two children, finds himself moving in with them to save his half-siblings from becoming just like their mother.

Texts from Last Night (Comedy, Fox, 2011). *Producer:* Adam Sandler, Doug Robinson. *Creator-Writer:* Steve Holland. *Story:* Stories based on Internet reader posts wherein people sent embarrassing messages to someone else in the middle of the night and most likely while intoxicated.

Thankless (Comedy, CBS, 2016). *Producer:* LeBron James, Maverick Carter. *Creator-Writer:* Craig Gerard, Matt Zinman. *Story:* The activities of a group of mismatched assistants hoping for bigger and better things while working at a Chicago sports agency.

Thanks a Million (Reality, Quibi, 2019). *Producer:* Jennifer Lopez. *Story:* Profiles the people helped by generous gifts of money from total strangers.

These Things Happen (Comedy, HBO, 2013). *Producer:* Oprah Winfrey. *Creator-Writer:* Richard Kramer. *Story:* Incidents in the lives of two couples—one straight and one gay who share a 15-year-old son (by the wife of the straight couple and the husband of the gay couple).

Thick as Thieves (Drama, Fox, 2011). *Producer:* Peter Chernin, Katherine Pope. *Creator-Writer:* Aaron Stockard. *Story:* Serial-like project about working class people in a Boston suburb.

Thin Air (Comedy, WB, 2003). *Producer:* Kelsey Grammer, Steve Stark. *Story:* A mother attempts to reconnect with her estranged son following her husband's passing.

Things They Left Behind (Drama, CBS, 2014). *Producer:* Greg Berlanti, Sarah Schechter. *Creator-Writer:* Seth Grahame-Smith. *Story:* An adaptation of the book by Stephen King about a pair of investigators who help spirits of the deceased complete unfinished business so they can move on.

Things You Should Already Know (Comedy, CBS, 2017). *Producer:* Will Ferrell, Adam McKay. *Creator-Writer:* Laura Moses, Will Ferrell. *Story:* A group of millennials decide to take charge of their lives, put down their cell phones and enjoy the world that surrounds them without the constant need for technology.

Think Tank (Comedy, Fox, 2007).
Producer: Neal H. Moritz, Vivian Cannon. *Creator-Writer:* Josh Stolberg, Bobby Florsheim.
Story: Four dysfunctional nerds are hired by an eccentric billionaire to solve the world's problems.

Third Platoon (Anthology, ABC, 1960).
Producer: Alan Ladd, Aaron Spelling.
Story: Dramas based on the actual experiences of the U.S. Army's Third Platoon stationed in the European Theater of War in 1944.

Thirty-Three and a Third (Comedy, NBC, 2012).
Producer: Aaron Kaplan. *Creator-Writer:* Kirk Butler.
Story: An aspiring thirty-three-year-old rock singer and single mother of a teenage girl struggles to reconstruct her life when her fiancé dumps her and she and her daughter move in with her mother and her gay, slacker brother.

Thirty-Year-Old Grandpa (Comedy, Fox, 2006).
Producer: Karey Burke, Ashton Kutcher, Jason Goldberg. *Creator-Writer:* Holly Hester.
Story: A thirty-year-old man marries an older woman then faces the prospect of becoming the step-father to her children—who are nearly his age.

This Place Is Awful (Comedy, ABC, 2011).
Producer: Ben Silverman, Sofia Vergara. *Creator-Writer:* Craig Doyle.
Story: A hard-working father and his frugal son attempt to run a family rooming house occupied by eccentric tenants.

A Thousand Days (Drama, Syfy, 2003).
Producer: Ben Silverman, Matt Holloway.
Story: An adaptation of the comic *Strike Force Moritori* about genetically engineered soldiers programmed to battle evil but who stop functioning after one thousand days.

The Thousandth Floor (Drama, ABC, 2015).
Producer: Greg Berlanti, Sarah Schechter, Leslie Morgenstein. *Creator-Writer:* Maggie Friedman.
Story: A one thousand floor Manhattan skyscraper in the year 2118 provides the setting for a look at its residents—from the lower working class to the super rich.

Threads (Drama, ABC, 2018).
Producer: Jennifer Gwartz, John Harmon Feldman. *Creator-Writer:* Lindsey Rosin.
Story: Jessica Lee, an up-and-coming fashion designer, is followed as she becomes involved in the power struggles and deceit that exist within the fashion industry.

3:52 (Science Fiction, Syfy, 2005).
Producer: John Tinker.
Story: On an unspecified day when the clock strikes 3:52 P.M., two billion people mysteriously vanish from the face of the earth. One American town, however, is not affected and the project was to relate how its citizens cope with the situation.

Three Card Monte (Drama, UPN, 2003).
Producer: Mel Gibson, Bruce Davey. *Creator-Writer:* Adi Hasak, Stuart Kelban.
Story: The adventures of a con man with a heart—targeting only those who deserve to be scammed.

Three Girls and a Bastard (Comedy, CW, 2007).
Producer: Darryl Frank, Justin Falvey. *Creator-Writer:* Alyssa Embree, Stacey Harmon, Jessica Koosed.
Story: A young woman, becoming pregnant but

abandoned by her boyfriend, finds help in raising her daughter by her two best girlfriends.

Three Pete (Comedy, Fox, 2011).
Producer: Shawn Levy, Marty Adelstein. *Creator-Writer:* Carter Covington.
Story: A father, a grandfather and a son who each share the same first name of Pete and little else as they all attempt to live together under the same roof.

Three Sisters (Comedy, CBS, 2010).
Producer: Ashton Kutcher, Karey Burke. *Creator-Writer:* Craig Doyle.
Story: Three alike and very close sisters marry three extremely opposite in nature men. How each attempt to cope with his or her partner's differing personality was to be depicted.

Three Thousand Hours (Drama, NBC, 2018).
Producer: Greg Berlanti, Sarah Schechter. *Creator-Writer:* Erin Cardillo.
Story: A group of students studying for their master's degree in psychology must spend 3,000 hours in the field with patients while balancing their personal and educational lives.

Tiger of Sonora (Drama, Syndication, 1958).
Producer: Russell Hayden.
Story: Incidents based on the life of Emilio Kosterlitsky, a Colonel with the Mexican Secret Service during the early 20th century.

Tightrope (Drama, Fox, 2011).
Producer: Katherine Pope, Peter Chernin. *Creator-Writer:* Jim Uhls.
Story: Law enforcement procedures as seen through the criminal informants used by skilled FBI agents.

Time (Drama, CBS, 2003).
Producer: Ridley Scott, Tony Scott.
Story: When archeologists uncover evidence that what is known about mankind's past did not actually occur as written, they begin a quest to discover what actually happened.

Tina Fey Untitled Project (Comedy, NBC, 2013).
Producer: Tina Fey, Robert Carlock. *Creator-Writer:* Colleen McGuinness.
Story: A young woman's mishaps when she reconnects with her estranged father and moves in with him.

Tiny Monsters (Cartoon, Fox, 2011).
Producer: Jack Black, Carolyn Bernstein, Ben Cooley. *Creator-Writer:* Ali Rushfield.
Story: A view of junior high school as seen through the Mean Girls, seventh graders who rule the student body.

Tips (Comedy-Drama, Spectrum, 2019).
Producer: Gabrielle Union, Neil H. Moritz.
Story: Dissatisfied with her job and suffering from the traumas of a recent breakup, a young woman turns her life around by becoming a pole dancer at a local bikini club.

Toast (Comedy, UPN, 2004).
Producer: Kelsey Grammer, Steve Stark. *Creator-Writer:* Nick La Rose.
Story: After their careers falter, a once famous celebrity couple seeks new ways to support themselves.

Tokyo Police (Crime Drama, Syndication, 1958).
Producer-Creator-Writer: Jack Webb.
Story: How Japanese police handle crime is depicted through two American police officers

when they are temporarily assigned to the Tokyo Police Department. Because Jack Webb created the program, it was first called *Tokyo Dragnet* (based on Jack's *Dragnet* series).

Tolliver's Trolley (Comedy, Syndication, 1960).
Producer: Phil Karlson. *Creator-Writer:* Steve Allen, Phil Karlson.
Story: The incidents that befall passengers who ride a street car running from Venice, California, to downtown Los Angeles.

Tomorrow/Today (Drama, NBC, 2005).
Producer: Justin Falvey, Darryl Frank, Bonnie Curtis. *Creator-Writer:* Mike Werb.
Story: Incidents in the lives of a television news station staff over a 20 year period (2010 to 2030).

Tongaloa (Adventure, CBS, 1962).
Producer: Al Gannaway.
Story: A young boy, the survivor of a plane crash in Africa that killed his parents, is found and raised by a noble tribe as Tongaloa, a mighty warrior. His efforts to protect his adopted homeland from evil were to be related.

Too Close to Home (Comedy, NBC, 2017).
Producer: Ellen DeGeneres, Jeff Kleeman. *Creator-Writer:* Nate Reger.
Story: The relationship between two sisters who came from humble beginnings—one who bettered herself and one who remained basically the same.

Torched (Comedy, Fox, 2014).
Producer: Johnny Depp, Norman Todd, Seth Cohen. *Creator-Writer:* Chris Romano.
Story: A family man with a rather questionable profession (breaking the law to earn money) strives to provide the best for his family, especially for his son, who is growing up in the same dead end environment as he did.

The Towers (Drama, Lifetime, 2008).
Producer: Donald Trump. *Creator-Writer:* Gay Walch.
Story: Incidents in the lives of people who reside at the actual Trump Towers building in Manhattan.

The Townspeople (Anthology, CBS, 1955).
Producer: Bretagne Windust.
Story: Weekly productions (comedy, drama, adventure) that were to feature a stock company of performers.

Toy Wars (Drama, Amazon, 2016).
Producer: Stephanie Savage, Seth Gordon. *Creator-Writer:* Josh Schwartz.
Story: A look at the actual battle for supremacy between toy companies Mattel, maker of the Barbie doll, and Hasbro, producers of such iconic toys as G.I. Joe, My Little Pony and The Transformers, during the 1980s and 1990s.

Trapped (Comedy, Starz, 2015).
Producer: Mila Kunis, Cami Curtis, Rob Zombie, Susan Curtis. *Creator-Writer:* Joey Slamon.
Story: A family's struggles to survive the night while being under attack by a mysterious cult seeking to kill them. The take-off on the movie *The Night of the Living Dead* was to cover the incidents that occur in one night over the course of a season.

Treasure (Drama, NBC, 2016).
Producer: Sean Hayes, Todd Milliner. *Creator-Writer:* Jim Kouf, David Greenwalt.
Story: After uncovering clues about a 40-year-old secret (involving murder and hidden money) in Washington, D.C., a group of recent college graduates begin a quest to discover what it is while avoiding mysterious individuals who are determined to stop them.

Tribe (Crime Drama, CW, 2005).
Producer: McG, Peter Johnson. *Writer:* R. Scott Gemmill.
Story: A group of misfit cops, branded rejects by their respective precincts, are united as a special unit of the L.A.P.D. to perform special undercover assignments.

Tribeca (Drama, NBC, 2019).
Producer: Greg Berlanti, Sarah Schechter. *Creator-Writer:* Jessica Queller.
Story: An adaptation of the South Korean series *Sky Castle* which here, set in New York City's Tribeca section, follows a group of people who live in the most expensive zip codes and who will do anything to ensure their children will succeed in life.

Trigger (Crime Drama, CW, 2011).
Producer: Denis Leary, Jim Serpico. *Creator-Writer:* Kyle Jarrowit.
Story: Proposal about four police officers who investigate cases as part of the Street Crimes Unit of the N.Y.P.D.

Trouble Finds Me (Crime Drama, ABC, 2017).
Producer: Greg Berlanti, Sarah Schechter. *Creator-Writer:* Brendan Gail.
Story: When Angela, a stuntwoman learns that the daughter (Gail) of the private detective who cleared her of a crime she didn't commit has inherited his agency, she joins with her to help bring criminals to justice.

The True Adventures of a Terrible Dater (Comedy, CBS, 2011).
Producer: Sheldon Turner, Jennifer Klein. *Creator-Writer:* Susan Brightbill.
Story: A single woman working as an architect in Chicago seeks the man of her dreams by navigating the local dating scene.

True Conviction (Drama, CBS, 2017).
Producer: Robert DeNiro, Seth Gordon, Jane Rosenthal. *Creator-Writer:* Angel Dean Lopez.
Story: Three ex-felons team to help people by investigating crimes to insure that the scales of justice are balanced.

True Lies (Drama, Fox, 2017).
Producer: James Cameron, McG, Jon Landau. *Creator-Writer:* Rene Echevarria.
Story: An adaptation of the 1994 feature film about a man leading a double life. His wife and daughter believe he is a computer salesman; he is actually a covert operative for Omega Sector, a U.S. Intelligence organization.

Trust (Drama, ABC, 2013).
Producer: Eva Longoria, Ben Spector, Gail Berman, Lloyd Braun. *Creator-Writer:* Katie Lovejoy.
Story: An adaptation of the Colombia telenovela *Pura Sangre* about David Montenegro, an attorney and the trustee of the estate of a wealthy family who becomes immersed in their corrupt lives.

Tuned (Comedy, NBC, 2014).
Producer: Ben Spector, Eva Longoria, Zachary Levi. *Creator-Writer:* Deborah Kaplan.
Story: Following a series of vivid hallucinations about becoming a musician, a young man begins a journey to make what he envisioned happen.

Twenty-Nine (Comedy, NBC, 2106).
Producer: John Davis, John Fox. *Creator-Writer:* Brian Gallivan.
Story: The relationship between a 75-year-old grandmother who better connects with her 29-year-old granddaughter than she does with her 55-year-old daughter.

Twig (Children, Syndication, 1956).
Producer: Don Fedderson, Bob Clampett. *Writer:* Bob Clampett.
Story: Puppet characters created by cartoonist Bob Clampett are incorporated to tell the story of a young boy and his friendship with the animals of the forest.

Two Badges (Crime Drama, CBS, 2011).
Producer: Carol Mendelsohn. *Creator-Writer:* Ted Humphrey.
Story: An adaptation of the book by Mona Ruiz about a tough, former female gang member who reforms by becoming a police officer but reverting to her gangland ways to solve crimes.

Two Dolls (Drama, Fox, 2019).
Producer: McG, Mary Viola, Corey Marsh. *Creator-Writer:* Katie Wech.
Story: A profile of two women and how they dominate the cutthroat world of the real estate business in Malibu, California.

Two for the Money and No Place to Go (Comedy, NBC, 1967).
Producer: Norman Felton. *Creator-Writer:* Dean Hargrove.
Story: Two down-on-their luck friends seek easy money through cons that rarely work as they had planned.

Two Men, Two Babies (Comedy, NBC, 2006).
Producer: Conan O'Brien, Jeff Ross, Sam Seder.
Story: Two fathers who are friends attempt to adjust to becoming house husbands when their wives become the breadwinners.

The Ultimate Getaway (Drama, Fox, 2014).
Producer: Sheldon Turner, Jennifer Klein, Seth Gordon. *Creator-Writer:* Kevin Costello.
Story: Members of a commercial airlines crew use their layover time for only one purpose: plan and execute robberies in the different cities they visit.

Under Exposed (Reality, Bravo, 2004).
Producer: Sean Hayes, Todd Milliner, R.J. Cutler.
Story: Two non-professional film makers are given the exact same script and challenged to produce a four-minute short-form film. The film maker who creates the best "movie" wins.

Under the Dome (Drama, Showtime, 2012).
Producer: Steven King, Darryl Frank, Justin Falvey, Brian K. Vaughn.
Story: A mysterious force from outer space surrounds a Maine town in an impenetrable force field, cutting its citizens off from the rest of the world. The project, based on the novel by Steven King, was to relate what happens to the people trapped inside the dome as they cope with their situation and seek not only a way out, but why they were selected as guinea pigs. The idea was restructured and made into the 2013 CBS series of the same title but set in Chester Mills, Maine.

Undercover Karaoke (Reality, TBS, 2011).
Producer: Will Ferrell, Adam McKay.
Story: Celebrities, disguised as everyday people, attend events but perform on stage as the celebrities they really are.

The Underlings (Drama, Fox, 2016).
Producer: Aaron Kaplan, Dana Honor. *Creator-Writer:* Leila Gerstein.
Story: A paralegal, working for a corporate law firm that thrives on greed and taking advantage of people, begins a crusade to right wrongs by seeing that "the little guy" gets equal justice.

The Understudy (Drama, Fox, 2002). *Producer:* David E. Kelley, Bill D'Elia. *Story:* A talented 21-year-old girl's experiences when she moves to New York City to pursue her dream of becoming a Broadway star.

Unearthly (Drama, CW, 2011). *Producer:* Carol Mendelsohn, Julie Weitz. *Creator-Writer:* Kevin Murphy. *Story:* A woman, believing she has received a mystical vision to become an angel, begins a mission to help people in trouble.

Unfamous (Drama, CW, 2014). *Producer:* Ellen DeGeneres, Jeff Kleeman. *Creator-Writer-Producer:* Lauren Graham. *Story:* Determined to become an actress, a young woman journeys to New York City to begin her quest; if, however, after three years she cannot achieve her goal, she will abandon her dream.

Unfinished Business (Drama, Syfy, 2009). *Producer:* Will Smith, James Lassister. *Creator-Writer:* Sally Robinson. *Story:* After being shot in the head while on duty, a police officer recovers with the ability to experience flashes of memories from the recently deceased; a gift he uses to help lost souls seek closure.

Unhitched (Drama, Fox, 2005). *Producer:* Sarah Timberman, Barry Sonnefeld, Carl Beverly. *Story:* Comical overtones are incorporated into the dramatic story of a dysfunctional husband and wife who are also divorce lawyers.

Unsub (Crime Drama, CBS, 2017). *Producer:* Carl Beverly, Sarah Timberman. *Creator-Writer:* Meg Gardner, Liz Friedman. *Story:* A female detective's relentless search to find an elusive serial killer, a man who struck while her father was a detective but was never captured and who has just now resumed his killing spree after a long absence.

Unthinkable (Crime Drama, CBS, 2017). *Producer:* Jerry Bruckheimer, Jonathan Littman, Kristie Anne Reed. *Creator-Writer:* David Slack. *Story:* A futurist (a person capable of perceiving danger) teams with an optimistic FBI agent to use her abilities to identify the situations only she can see to stop crimes before they happen.

Untouchable (Crime Drama, ABC, 2011). *Producer:* Mark Gordon, Rob Bowman. *Creator-Writer:* Chap Taylor. *Story:* A no-nonsense female FBI agent teams with a reckless, wealthy L.A.P.D. detective for undercover assignments to investigate organized crime.

U.P. Dispatch (Anthology, Syndication, 1955). *Producer:* Austin Television Associates. *Story:* Dramas based on the experiences of the newspapermen of the United Press.

U.S. Air Force (Anthology, Syndication, 1957). *Producer:* Desilu Productions. *Writer:* Frank Moss. *Story:* Produced with the cooperation of and dramas based on the files of the U.S. Air Force.

Valentines (Drama, Sundance, 2012). *Producer:* Robert Redford, Fred Berner. *Creator-Writer:* Olaf Olafsson. *Story:* Serial-like proposal that explores relationships between men and women and the hidden secrets that could destroy them.

Valley Girls (Comedy, ABC, 2017). *Producer:* Kelly Ripa, Mark Consuelos, Kristin

Newman. *Creator:* Heather Cabot. *Writer:* Samantha Walravens.
Story: Frustrated for not being recognized for their work skills or being paid salaries equal to their male co-workers, four women plot to work their way up the chain of command and take over their male dominated Silicone Valley company.

Valley of the Dolls (Drama, NBC, 2011).
Producer: Peter Chernin, Katherine Pope. *Creator-Writer:* Lee Daniels.
Story: An adaptation of the novel by Jacqueline Susann about three career women and their decline over a twenty-year period. The novel was also adapted into a 1967 movie with Patty Duke and Barbara Parkins and a 1981 TV pilot film with Catherine Hicks and Lisa Hartman.

Vanish (Drama, NBC, 2011).
Producer: Sam Raimi, Michael Dinner, Joshua Donen. *Creator-Writer:* Trevor Munson.
Story: Mark Meadows is a mysterious individual who helps people in trouble by placing them in seclusion until he can resolve the situation and make it safe for them to resume their normal lives.

Vanishing Act (Drama, CBS, 2011).
Producer: Carol Mendelsohn, Craig Sweeny, Julie Weitz. *Creator-Writer:* Natalie Chaidez.
Story: Jane Whitefield is a Native American and a member of the Wolf Clan of the Seneca Tribe. She has the ability to fool any pursuer, cover any trail and works as a private detective to help people by putting them in seclusion until it is safe for them to return to their normal lives.

Vatican City (Drama, Amazon, 2015).
Producer: David W. Zucker, Ridley Scott. *Creator-Writer:* Michelle King, Robert King.
Story: While interviewing Pope Clement in Rome, Italy, American journalist Madeline Summers learns that he has a plan to introduce women as priests but is blocked from doing so by the Catholic Church. In an effort to change the minds of his superiors, Pope Clement hires Madeline as the Papal spokesperson and her experiences in a position once only held by men were to be depicted.

The Vault (Drama, NBC, 2019).
Producer: Rachel Kaplan, Peter Traugott. *Creator-Writer:* Jesse Lasky.
Story: Following a cataclysmic event that appears to have destroyed much of the human race, survivors seek to find The Vault, a facility in the Arctic that holds the key to the future of the planet.

Vegas Baby (Comedy, Fox, 2007).
Producer: Darryl Frank, Justin Falvey. *Creator-Writer:* Steve Leff.
Story: The paths taken by three friends as they attempt to begin new lives in Las Vegas.

Vice (Crime Drama, CBS, 2013).
Producer: Stephanie Savage, Josh Schwartz, Len Goldstein. *Creator-Writer:* Michael Diliberti.
Story: Two young, somewhat inexperienced detectives with the Los Angeles Police Department Vice Squad investigate crimes involving the world of prostitution and the underage girls that are drawn into the vicious cycle.

Victory Lane (Drama, Fox, 2017).
Producer-Creator-Writer: Jennifer Klein, Sheldon Turner.
Story: Romantic tale of two accomplished race car drivers who fall in love but are rivals on the track.

Vigilant (Drama, Fox, 2012).
Producer: Howard Gordon, Hugh Fitzpatrick.
Creator-Writer: Max Landis.
Story: A 20-year-old woman, considered a social outcast, creates a vigilante persona to help her local police department solve crimes.

Virtual Virgin (Comedy, ABC, 2011).
Producer: Mark Gordon, Andrea Shay. *Creator-Writer:* Keith Merryman, David Newman.
Story: A young woman's experiences as she begins dating; armed with advice from friends and family as opposed to social media resources.

Voyages (Anthology, CBS, 2007).
Producer: Hugh Jackman, John Pamlero. *Creator-Writer:* Max Makowski.
Story: Love Boat–like proposal about brief incidents in the lives of the people who book passage on a luxury liner.

Wag the Dog (Comedy, HBO, 2017).
Producer: Robert DeNiro, Tom Fontana, Barry Levinson. *Creator-Writer:* Robert DeNero.
Story: An adaptation of the feature film about a Washington, D.C. publicist who goes to elaborate lengths to protect his clients from scandals.

Wake Up Call (Comedy, CBS, 2012).
Producer: Melissa McCarthy. *Creator-Writer:* Ben Falcone.
Story: Married friends face new challenges in life when each of their marriages slowly begins to fall apart.

Wanda Sykes Untitled Project (Comedy, ABC, 2017).
Producer: Wanda Sykes, Page Hurwitz. *Creator-Writer:* Tom Straw, Zainab Johnson.
Story: A beautiful Muslim model nearing her 30th birthday reflects on her life and the sometimes questionable choices she made.

Warriors (Drama, ABC, 2012).
Producer: Todd Lieberman, David Hoberman, Christopher Chulack.
Story: How military doctors and nurses use trail blazing medicine and procedures to treat wounded warriors returning from various battle zones.

Wasteland (Drama, NBC, 2014).
Producer: Gina Matthews, Bob Cooper. *Creator-Writer:* Mick Davis.
Story: A U.S. Marshal's seemingly impossible mission: track down and recapture escaped prisoners who possess supernatural powers.

The Watcher (Drama, NBC, 2015).
Producer: Aaron Kaplan. *Creator-Writer:* Alexander Cary.
Story: A young couple's efforts to solve a mystery when they move into a new home and suddenly become terrorized by a mysterious figure, sinister threats and anonymous phone calls and letters.

Waterloo (Comedy, Starz, 2009).
Producer: Jennifer Gwartz, Rob Thomas, Dan Etheridge.
Story: A comical look at a band's (Waterloo) rise to fame (and based on the experiences of rock star Rob Thomas).

We Are All Completely Fine (Drama, Syfy, 2015).
Producer: Wes Craven, Ben Smith, Sara Bottfeld. *Creator-Writer:* Wes Craven.
Story: After creating a support group for five horror movie actors, a psychologist must deal with a strange aftermath: controlling the evils he unleashes from their pasts.

We Are Here (Comedy, ABC, 2010).
Producer: Anthony Russo, Joe Russo. *Creator-Writer:* Hilary Watson.
Story: Four University of Texas graduates are profiled as they deal with adulthood in different ways.

We, the Jury (Comedy, Fox, 2006).
Producer: David E. Kelley, Marty Adelstein. *Creator-Writer:* Bryan Behar.
Story: The situations that befall a group of jurors that are sequestered in a motel during a high profile case.

Weekly World News (Comedy, Fox, 2010).
Producer: Darryl Frank, Justin Falvey. *Creator-Writer:* Michael Colton.
Story: The antics of the staff of *Weekly World News*, the supermarket tabloid that reports more on gossip than actual news-making events.

Weitz and Wong (Comedy, ABC, 2011).
Producer: Ellen DeGeneres. *Creator-Writer:* Lauren Corraro, Alex Herschlag.
Story: Henry Weitz, who is Jewish, and Mako Wong, who is Chinese, fall in love, marry and attempt to begin a new life together but face interference from their different extended families, some of whom oppose a mixed cultural marriage.

Welcome to America Town (Drama, HBO, 2008).
Producer: Tom Fontana, Barry Levinson, Kathleen Kennedy, Frank Marshall. *Creator-Writer:* Bradford Winters.
Story: Explores what could happen in a futuristic America when the economy declines and people must make new lives for themselves.

Wendy and Peter (2012) (Comedy, Fox, 2012).
Producer: Reese Witherspoon, Meghan Lyvers. *Creator-Writer-Producer:* Jill Soloway.
Story: The changes that occur in a single mother's life (Wendy) when she is hired as the den mother to a group of orphan boys cared for by an eccentric millionaire (Peter).

Wendy and Peter (2014) (Comedy, NBC, 2014).
Producer: Will McCormack, Marisa Coughlan, Rashida Jones.
Story: A young woman's (Wendy) search for her dream "manly man" but falling for a man who acts more like a child than adult (Peter).

Wes Craven Untitled Project (Drama, UPN, 2001).
Producer-Creator-Writer: Wes Craven, Marianne Maddalena, David Gerber, Kari Schaefer.
Story: A wealthy industrialist teams with a woman who is an expert on artificial intelligence to investigate supernatural occurrences.

Wet House (Crime Drama, CBS, 2019).
Producer: Aaron Kaplan, Dana Honor, Sasha Alexander. *Creator-Writer:* Barbie Kligman.
Story: After assaulting a fellow police officer during a minor altercation, Janice Williams is removed from active duty and placed in the station's Wet House for rehabilitation. Here she discovers her fellow officers are exceptional and forms them into a team to secretly battle crime.

Whiskey Tango Foxtrot (Comedy, HBO, 2015).
Producer: Brad Pitt. *Creator-Writer:* Zev Borow.
Story: A slightly off-center look at life as seen through three thirty-something young adults as they tackle various issues (like boredom, dating, working, and raising a family).

Whistleblower (Drama, CBS, 2017).
Producer: Jerry Bruckheimer, Jonathan Littman, Kristie Anne Reed. *Creator-Writer:* Christopher Sibler.
Story: After being exposed as a whistleblower and left with a damaged reputation, a man begins a company that protects whistleblowers but sees that those they have exposed are brought to justice.

White Eye (Drama, ABC, 2013).
Producer: Todd Lieberman, David Hoberman, Laurie Zaks. *Creator-Writer:* Stefan Jaworski.
Story: A strong-willed female and her paranoid male partner, agents for the NSA, incorporate state-of-the-art technology to monitor situations by accessing online cameras.

White House Confidential (Drama, NBC, 2012).
Producer: Neil Meron, Craig Zadan. *Creator-Writer:* Sri Rao.
Story: Incidents that occur at the White House as seen through the eyes of a young female doctor who is one of the President's personal physicians.

White Jeff (Comedy, Fox, 2015).
Producer-Writer-Creator: Dave Bickel.
Story: A CPA (Jeff) attempts to adjust to a new position when he becomes the only white person in a hip-hop clothing company owned by an eccentric rapper.

Whodunit (Anthology, NBC, 1960).
Producer: Dominick Dunne. *Writer:* Thelma Schnee.
Story: Mystery yarns in which all the clues are given to the viewer to allow him to play detective and identify the killer before he is exposed on camera.

The Whole Nine Yards (Comedy, CBS, 2016).
Producer: Eric Tannenbaum, Kim Tannenbaum, Jack Donaldson.
Story: A pro football player's experiences when he moves into a gated community followed by his overbearing parents who also become part of his household.

The Whole Truth (Drama, NBC, 2005).
Producer: Dick Wolf, Jonathan Greene, Neal Baer.
Story: The investigations of a female TV news reporter as she goes beyond the studio to acquire stories.

WHOT-FM (Comedy, UPN, 2004).
Producer: Queen Latifah, Yvette Lee Bowser. *Creator-Writer:* Buddy Sheffield.
Story: Julie Marks, a Caucasian woman who knows nothing about hip-hop music, attempts to save WHOT, an FM radio station on the brink of shutting down.

Wicked Good (Drama, ABC, 2011).
Producer: Todd Liberman, David Hoberman. *Creator-Writer:* Jason Richman.
Story: When Orange County, New Jersey, becomes threatened by the supernatural, a secretive society of witches and warlocks become its protectors by using their abilities to defeat evil.

Wife of Crime (Comedy, CBS, 2014).
Producer: Neal H. Moritz, Vivian Cannon. *Creator-Writer:* Kevin Sussman.
Story: A young man's efforts to adjust to a new life when he marries an Italian girl, moves in with her family then discovers she is part of a crime syndicate.

Wifey (Drama, VH-1, 2007).
Producer: Queen Latifah, Byron Phillips, Dedra Tate. *Creator-Writer:* Michael Elliot.
Story: Soon after inheriting her late husband's record company, a woman discovers that her family's wealth came from the corrupt operation of the company. Her effort to run the company as an honest business was to be the focal point of the series.

Wildwood (Drama, Fox, 2011).
Producer: Betsy Beers, Shonda Rhimes. *Creator-Writer:* Diane Ruggiero.
Story: Follows an underage teenage girl who poses as an adult to work at a bar on the New Jersey shore in 1985.

The Will (Drama, ABC, 2015).
Producer: Darryl Frank, Justin Falvey. *Creator-Writer:* K.J. Steinberg.
Story: In order to inherit a vast fortune from their late, eccentric father, members of his family must not only adhere to the strict conditions of the will but solve a bizarre riddle that will lead them to the treasure.

Will Ferrell Untitled Project (Comedy, NBC, 2011).
Producer: Will Ferrell, Adam McKay. *Creator-Writer:* Andrew Gurland.
Story: The unusual friendship between three people: A man, his ex-girlfriend and her husband, his childhood friend.

Will McCormack Untitled Project (Anthology, ABC, 2014).
Producer: Will McCormack, Rashida Jones.
Story: The Pioneer Square Bookstore in Seattle, Washington, provides the backdrop for a look a group of people dealing with issues of love and romance.

Will Smith Untitled Project (Comedy, ABC, 2006).
Producer: Will Smith, Jada Pinkett Smith, James Lassiter. *Creator-Writer:* Betsy Borns.
Story: A married couple, a Jewish girl from a liberal lower middle class family, and an upper class African-American man, attempt to deal with their meddling mothers-in-law who have moved in with them to help them raise their twin granddaughters.

Wing Men (Comedy, CW, 2004).
Producer: Will Smith, Jada Pinkett Smith, James Lassiter.
Story: Billed as "A male buddy-buddy comedy" wherein four friends help each other navigate life in the early 2000s.

Winners (Comedy, NBC, 2017).
Producer: Patricia Heaton, David Hunt. *Creator-Writer:* Ryan Koh.
Story: A look at how teenagers, enrolled in a residential life-coaching facility, prepare to adjust to adult life.

Wiseguy (Drama, NBC, 2011).
Producer: Katherine Pope, Peter Chernin. *Creator-Writer:* Alexander Cary.
Story: A revival of the 1990s CBS series (created by Stephen J. Cannell and Frank Lupo) about a disgraced cop who, to avoid serving time in prison, makes a deal with federal authorities to perform undercover assignments that involve criminal activities.

Witchblade (Drama, NBC, 2017).
Producer: Carol Mendelsohn, Julie Weitz, Marc Silvestri, Rick Jacobs. *Creator-Writer:* Brian Young.
Story: An adaptation of the comic book (and prior 2001 TV series) about Sara Pezzini, a police

detective (here with the San Francisco Police Department) who becomes a protector when a mysterious bracelet called the Witchblade attaches itself to her and grants her amazing abilities to battle evil.

Wolf (Drama, ABC, 2018).
Producer: Aaron Kaplan, Dana Honor. *Creator-Writer:* Michael Peterson.
Story: Dr. Charles Wolf, a veterinarian who believes murder is a primal, animalistic art, attempts to prove his theory when he is elected coroner of Boulder, Colorado, and puts his theories to the test while investigating homicides.

Women in Black (Drama, ABC, 2016).
Producer: Jamie Tarses, Dylan Clark, Scott Stuber. *Creator-Writer:* Amy B. Harris.
Story: A look at incidents in the lives of four widows at various stages in their lives as they navigate life, including dating and parenting.

Women's Murder Club (Crime Drama, USA, 2015).
Producer: James Patterson, Bill Robinson. *Creator-Writer-Producer:* Tony Krantz.
Story: Four women (a district attorney, homicide detective, reporter and coroner) combine their abilities to solve crimes.

Wonderland (Drama, NBC, 2013).
Producer: Anthony E. Zuiker, JoAnn Alfano. *Creator-Writer:* Whit Anderson.
Story: A fantasized update of Lewis Carroll's *Alice in Wonderland* that presents Alice as Wonderland's new Queen and introduces the character of Clara, a peasant girl who is seeking to dethrone Alice, who has become a wicked ruler.

The Woods (Drama, Syfy, 2013).
Producer: Darryl Frank, Justin Falvey. *Creator-Writer:* Liz Phang.
Story: After returning to her family home after a long absence, a woman attempts to solve a mystery that began years ago: uncover the presence of sinister beings that live in the woods surrounding her home and may be responsible for the mysterious disappearance of her younger sister.

The World of Bada (Adventure, CBS, 1967).
Producer: Leon Benson.
Story: A variation on the NBC series *Maya* that details the adventures of a young boy and his pet elephant in India.

The Wrecking Crew (Comedy, Fox, 2012).
Producer: Peter Chernin, Katherine Pope. *Creator-Writer:* Kay Cannon.
Story: A behind-the-scenes-look at a football themed sports show where the male anchors have been replaced by a single female lead.

Written in Stone (Comedy, ABC, 2002).
Producer: Mimi Rogers, Gavin Polone. *Creator-Writer:* David Seltzer.
Story: Life in prehistoric times as seen through the activities of three brothers who are members of a clan that live in a cave in the Pyrenees Mountains.

Wrongful Deaths (Drama, ABC, 2012).
Producer: Stephanie Savage, Josh Schwartz, Len Goldstein. *Creator-Writer:* Donald Todd.
Story: An insurance investigator teams with a private detective to investigate cases involving wrongful deaths.

Wunderland (Drama, CW, 2013).
Producer: McG, Peter Johnson. *Creator-Writer:* Chad Hodge.
Story: A contemporary version of Lewis Carroll's *Alice in Wonderland* that follows a young female detective when she stumbles upon another world under the surface of Los Angeles and becomes involved in the lives and mysteries of its people.

Xena: Warrior Princess (Adventure, NBC, 2017).
Producer: Robert Tapert, Sam Raimi. *Writer:* Javier Grillo-Marxyach.
Story: A revival of the 1995-2001 series of the same title that starred Lucy Lawless as Xena, a warrior princess based on Roman and Greek mythology who battled evil in a savage era.

Zeros (Drama, NBC, 2009).
Producer: Gail Berman, Lloyd Braun. *Creator-Writer:* Mark Neveldine, Brian Taylor.
Story: A crisis situation is established with the program exploring what happens in the last hour before it is resolved.

Zits (Comedy, CBS, 2011).
Producer: Jerry Bruckheimer, Jonathan Littman. *Creator-Writer:* Donald Todd.
Story: A sarcastic view of life as seen (and narrated) by a 16-year-old boy who is encountering all the problems of being a teen in high school.

Zombies vs. Vampires (Crime Drama, NBC, 2011).
Producer: McG, Peter Johnson. *Creator-Writer-Producer:* Austin Winsberg.
Story: A police officer, who is secretly a vampire, and his normal partner battle a new breed of criminals—rogue zombies.

Zone of Silence (Drama, NBC, 2015).
Producer: Eva Longoria, Ben Spector, Eric Winter. *Creator-Writer:* Rashad Raisani.
Story: An investigation by government agents into an invisible force that appears to be the key factor behind myths, legends and folklore and is currently confined to a zone in America's southwest.

CHAPTER 3
150 programs with intriguing story lines but on which no cast or credits were released.

Abaddon's Journal (CW, 2013). A woman, the assistant to an angel possessed of a book that records all who have made a deal with the devil, helps those who have sinned regain their souls.

Absolute Zero (Syfy, 2014). Miners on a remote Jupiter moon battle a deadly species planning to invade the Earth.

The Adventures of Buckaroo Banzai Across the 8th Dimension (Amazon, 2016). Buckaroo Banzai, a man of many talents joins with the Hong Kong Cavaliers to battle alien invaders from an 8th Dimension who are planning to take over the Earth.

The Adventures of Knickerbock Teetertop (Amazon, 2015). Inspired by the fantastic adventures his grandfather experienced in his youth, Knickerbock Teetertop, a brilliant boy living in the mystical Wonderpine Mountains, joins with friends Holly and Otto to experience exciting adventures in magical places.

Aeon Flux (MTV, 2018). Aeon Flux, a ruthless assassin, teams with a group of rebels to save humanity from an oppressive regime.

After (Freeform, 2016). An adaptation of the book *A Wicked Thing* by Rhiannon Thomas that finds Aurora, the girl awakened from her 100 year sleeping spell by a kiss from Prince Charming, involved in a power struggle to rule her fairy tale kingdom.

Alice in Arabia (ABC Family, 2014). Alice, an American teenage girl kidnapped by her extended Saudi Arabian family after her parents' death and now a prisoner in her grandfather's royal compound, seeks to adjust to a new life while secretly plotting to escape and find her way back home.

Alice Isn't Dead (USA, 2018). The dangerous road traveled by Keisha, a young female truck driver on a desperate quest to find her lover, Alice, who mysteriously disappeared and is presumed dead.

Allegiance (ABC, 2013). A dedicated FBI agent, tasked with stopping high tech attacks on the U.S. government, takes on the biggest case of her career: stopping her mother, deemed the country's deadliest domestic terrorist.

Alma (Netflix, 2018). After surviving a bus crash that killed her fellow classmates and now suffering from amnesia, a teenage girl (Alma) begins a quest to uncover her past before her true identity becomes lost forever.

The Almighty Johnsons (Syfy, 2014). After living a normal life for twenty-one years, the Johnson family discovers they are reincarnated Norse gods and must now battle injustice in a manner befitting their past lives.

Amazon (CW, 2012). A look at the history of Princess Diana, alias Wonder Woman, with a depiction of her life on the mysterious Paradise Island before she became a super hero during World War II.

Amped (USA, 2015). In an attempt to find a cure for his inability to focus, a young man takes an experimental "smart pill." The pill endows him with super powers and, believing he was meant to be somebody, begins a quest to battle evil—with the project chronicling the humiliating side effects caused by the pill.

Annika Erotica (IFC, 2018). Claire Radowski is an Associate Junior Pastor of the Colorado Springs Community Church who writes erotic novels under the pen name Annika Erotica. Her effort to conceal her secret life while serving her parish was the focal point of the project.

Artificial Intelligence (TNT, 2016). A team of specialists attempt to capture an escaped android with superior artificial intelligence that is on a mission to see that androids become dominant over the human race.

The B Team (Fox, 2016). To battle injustice, a former Navy SEAL forms the Badass Task Force of Elite Assault Mercenaries and with former military friends do what is necessary to help people in trouble.

Bad Beta (IFC, 2017). A scientist attempts to care for and improve an android she created when it falls short of what she had promised (extreme artificial intelligence, not the dim wit that resulted).

The Beard (Showtime, 2007). In order to survive in his chosen field, a gay baseball player begins a life of deception by pretending to be straight then encounters numerous problems as he attempts to form relationships with women.

Birthright (Fox, 2016). A young man, born in South Korea and adopted as an infant by white, Midwestern evangelical parents, begins an awkward search to finds his biological parents and discover who he really is.

Bitch off the Ol' Block (NBC, 2013). A young single business woman finds her life changing when her biological daughter, "a smart-ass version of herself," with no money and no place to live, moves in with her and her roommates.

Bitches (Fox, 2008). Four beautiful young women are profiled—women who live and work in Manhattan and who are secretly werewolves.

Bob the Valkyrie (CW, 2015). From the beginning of time three women, known as the Valkyrie, have been chosen by fate to defend humanity from evil. The women risk their lives and at the end of their reign, a new group of women is chosen. Through a miscalculation, as a new group is being selected, fate accidentally chooses a chauvinistic man named Bob and his efforts to work with two women who despise him were to be depicted.

Body Cam Cop (CBS, 2018). Police officers on duty as seen through live streams of their body cam equipment as they investigate crimes.

Broken Home (NBC, 2006). The strained relationship between an alcohol-addicted ex-beauty pageant queen when she attempts to reconnect with her estranged son, a gay man living in New York City.

Busy Bodies (USA, 2010). A soccer mom and a gay stay-at-home father team to solve mysteries in their suburban community.

Capturing Crazy (CBS, 2012). A look at a family's outrageous antics as captured on film by a young woman who believes her family is crazy and capturing them on video is the only way to prove it.

CCAT: Career Criminal Apprehension Team (CBS, 2004). Law enforcement officers track career criminals in an effort to stop them before they strike again.

Central Division (A&E, 2009). A profile of the only two female captains in the L.A.P.D. as they run the Central Division, the most dangerous precinct in Los Angeles.

Chasing Skips (Fox, 2013). With no experience and no brains, two broke friends set themselves up as bounty hunters to tackle any assignment, including chasing skips (criminals who jump bail).

Cherries in the Snow (CW, 2007). Girl Cosmetics is a New York firm that offers various lipstick shades, from Jailbait to Mystic Jukebox to Born to Run. Sadie, a twenty-something young woman, is the company's chief designer, a girl who is also looking for her signature color, something to match Revlon's famous Cherries in the Snow and something that will be loved by generations of women. Sadie was to be followed as she not only attempts to create that dream lipstick, but her romantic relationships as well.

Chess (Showtime, 2011). A calculating Mafia wife joins with the FBI to help them take down criminals while plotting to also have them kill her husband so she can assume his role.

Chew (Showtime, 2011). A detective solves complex cases from the psychic impressions he acquires from eating foods that were a part of the crime scene.

China Doll (HBO, 2012). A California contractor and his Asian-American wife (a university professor) navigate a marriage whose families extend to two continents.

Chosen (ABC, 2012). A family attempts to cope with their 15-year-old daughter when she is revealed to be the reincarnated prophet of a mysterious South American religion.

City of Ghosts (CW, 2018). Cassidy, a young woman studying paranormal psychology in Scotland, seeks to discover why and how she has a mysterious connection to the supernatural that enables her to communicate with the dead.

City of Ghosts (Netflix, 2019). A young girl with a mysterious connection to the supernatural becomes the pawn of ghosts seeking to relive a moment from their pasts to conclude unfinished business then move on.

Cleopatra (NBC, 2013). Period drama focusing not only on the lives of Cleopatra, Mark Antony and Julius Caesar, but the world in which they live, a world ruled by sorcery, gods and mythical creatures.

The Command (TNT, 2011). Detectives with the Borough Command Unit of the N.Y.P.D. tackle dangerous cases that affect any of the five boroughs of the city.

The Correctors (Syfy, 2011). Agents for the Exceptions Bureau travel to parallel universes to prevent events from happening by inhabiting the bodies of their identical selves.

Crooked (Fox, 2015). Following the release of a number of dangerous criminals who were convicted by false information from a corrupt detective, a special unit of agents is assembled to do the impossible: make the city safe again by gathering new evidence to bring those criminals back to face justice.

Cyber (Fox, 2012). A female FBI agent teams with a reformed male computer hacker to solve cyber-based criminal activity.

Dark Shadows: Reincarnation (CW, 2019). An update of *Dark Shadows* (ABC, 1966-1971) that focuses on Elizabeth Collins Stoddard, a woman whose family has ties to the supernatural.

Darwin's Blade (ABC, 2002). An insurance investigator reconstructs fatal automobile accidents to determine if they were actually accidents or something more sinister.

Daylight Robbery (Fox, 2010). Four housewives, who are also friends, seek a unique way to acquire money: by plotting daring daytime robberies.

Dead Mann Walking (CBS, 2015). Daniel Mann, a police detective falsely convicted of murdering his wife and executed, is brought back to life through a miracle drug and, while searching for his wife's real killer, helps people in trouble as a private investigator.

Deadman (CW, 2012). An adaptation of the DC comic about the spirit of a murdered man who, to achieve his own closure, inhabits the bodies of living people in an effort to help them solve a crisis in their lives.

Demonologist (NBC, 2004). A married couple battle demons as professional bounty hunters while at the same time trying to live a normal family life.

Detective Lady (IFC, 2016). Annie Barnes, a resident of Sicily, a small American town, works as a detective and brilliantly solves crimes but is hampered by two things: her drinking and a partner who is her complete opposite.

The Devil Wears Prada (Fox, 2006). An adaptation of the feature film about Andrea Sachs, a young woman who works as the assistant to Miranda Priestly, the demanding editor-in-chief of *Runway*, a high fashion magazine.

Diva Clown Killer (FX, 2012). The relationship between a former 1980s rock star diva and her dysfunctional son—a child's party clown who doubles as an assassin for hire.

The Divide (Syfy, 2007). A reincarnated dead girl, her twin brother, a radio disc jockey, and a coroner team to solve bizarre crimes.

Dorothy Gale (NBC, 2008). *The Wizard of Oz* set in modern times where a young woman from Kansas (Dorothy Gale) must cope with life in Manhattan and deal with "a witch-like" boss and co-workers who mimic the Scarecrow, Cowardly Lion and Tin Man.

Dorothy Must Die (CW, 2013). A look at what might have happened in the book *The Wizard of Oz* if Dorothy Gale, the young girl swept away by a tornado to the Land of Oz, remained in Oz and perpetually young and became a heartless ruler who turned Oz into a fascist fairytale land.

The Edge (NBC, 2013). A young female detective teams with a Mexican shaman turned police officer who uses his unique abilities to help them solve complex crimes.

Elna (FX, 2017). Elna, a 27-year-old Mormon who questions her faith, leaves her congregation to experience a life she has never known before.

Embody (CBS, 2018). A young woman, blinded during an assignment for the CIA, is able to see again when she becomes the subject of an experiment that allows her to temporarily transfer her consciousness into another person's body and visually function as she did before.

The Exceptions (USA, 2011). A young woman, released from jail after being falsely convicted of a crime, uses her resources as the daughter of the Mayor of New York City to help people whose cases have fallen through the cracks.

Faerborne (Syfy, 2011). When he learns that he is a "changeling," a fairy left to be raised by humans, a Seattle businessman must begin a new life—battle the mythical creatures that live among the human race in disguise.

Farmhand (AMC, 2019). Futuristic tale of a farmer who appears to grow corn but has secretly created his own unique crop: replacement human organs.

Feral (CW, 2016). A young woman, emerging from the forest after years of living in isolation, must not only adjust to a world she doesn't know, but avoid persons unknown who are trying to silence her for what she knows and what drove her to lead a feral existence.

The Fifth Season (TNT, 2017). Three women, each with an ability to control one aspect of an earthquake, combine their powers to battle evil in a time when the Earth has become a barbaric-like world.

Find the Good (NBC, 2017). A newspaper obituary writer living in Alaska raises her children based on the columns she writes: to avoid the faults of the recently deceased.

Finley & June (CW, 2018). June, a neurotic children's book author, and Finley, a real fairy with rage issues, meet in a San Francisco restroom, become friends and agree to help each other deal with the issues they have.

Finn & Sawyer (ABC, 2012). Mark Twain's 19th century literary characters, Tom Sawyer and Huckleberry Finn, as young men in their twenties and earning a living as private detectives in the New Orleans steam punk era.

Five Ghosts (Syfy, 2014). Treasure hunter Fabian Gray uses his ability to harness five ghosts ("The Arc," "The Detective," "The Samurai," "The Vampire" and "The Wizard") to help him defeat evil and uncover valuable lost treasures.

Fly Girls (UPN, 2004). Two actresses, the stars of a Saturday morning TV show wherein they play earthlings endowed by aliens with super powers, find that the costumes they wear on the program are more than they appear. When off the set, the costumes endow the girls with real super powers—which they use to battle the forces of evil.

Georgia and Her Seven Associates (Fox, 2009). A young female lawyer (Georgia), fired from her stepmother's law firm, finds employment at a storefront legal office run by seven lawyers—each of whom has the personality of one of the Seven Dwarfs (from the fairy tale *Snow White*).

Ghost Projekt (Syfy, 2012). A female KGB agent teams with a male American weapons inspector to find and destroy an evil force that was accidentally released from a Siberian research facility.

Ghost World (ABC, 2010). A male victim of crime returns to earth as a ghost—to help a young female homicide detective solve crimes and hopefully find the clues he needs to solve his own murder.

Gnarly (Comedy Central, 2009). Two men in their thirties travel back in time to their high school years to correct the mistakes they made that make them losers with women.

Gold Bug (NBC, 2018). After her estranged mother's passing, a young Ph.D. student picks up where she left off: find a mysterious and still elusive treasure.

Gold Digger (CW, 2011). A beautiful young female treasure hunter risks her life battling unscrupulous characters to uncover artifacts for her clients.

Grave Sight (Syfy, 2012). Harper Connelly, a young woman struck by lightning as a teenager and acquiring the ability to sense the location and lost memories of the deceased uses her gift to solve crimes and help spirits move on.

Halo (USA, 2008). A less-than-upstanding individual wakes up one morning to find a halo over his head. After numerous unsuccessful attempts to remove it, he realizes that he has been chosen by celestial forces to help people redeem themselves.

Harrow County (Syfy, 2015). On the eve of her 18th birthday, Emmy, who lives in a wooded area reputed to be haunted, discovers she is the reincarnation of a 17th century witch who was burned at the stake on the very land on which she lives and on the day she was born. The project was to follow Emmy as she struggles to embrace what she is and how to use her powers for good.

Haunted (Fox, 2015). A demonologist teams with his girlfriend, a former military agent, to help people who are threatened by the supernatural.

Hazel Rhodes (A&E, 2010). A murder is established in a teaser before the actual episode begins. Hazel Rhodes, a brilliant Nashville homicide detective who "might wear her concert T-shirt a little too tight and her lipstick two shades too bright" claims that "No murderer is too clever for her" and her effort to find the culprit were to be depicted.

Hilary Jones (Showtime, 2008). Events in the dual life of Hillary Jones, who works daily as a Los Angeles police officer and weekends as a legal prostitute in Nevada.

I Am Charlotte Simmons (HBO, 2009). A bright teenage girl, raised in a poor rural community, experiences a whole new life when she earns a free scholarship to a prestigious college.

I Love the Things I Hate About You (ABC, 2006). A happily married couple attempt to cope with a new situation in their lives: everything they love about each other are also the things that drive them crazy.

In the Dark (Syfy, 2011). A team of mishap prone ghost hunters investigate paranormal activity hoping to find what the real experts can't—actual ghosts.

Inside (ABC, 2006). An undercover female detective with the L.A.P.D. uses her perfect instincts to solve crimes.

Jason and the Argonauts (NBC, 2009). Adaptation of the feature film (and Greek myth) about Jason, a fearless sailor, and his crew (the Argonauts) as they seek treasures in mysterious and forbidding lands.

Joyland (Freeform, 2018). An adaptation of the book by Stephen King about a young man named Devin and the unnatural situations he encounters when he takes a summer job at Joyland, a mysterious amusement park in North Carolina.

Julia's Tango (SoapNet, 2009). Serial-like story about a young woman (Julia) who, after visiting her hometown of Buenos Aries after a long absence, decides to stay and begin a new career as the owner of a bed and breakfast.

Kali (TNT, 2014). After being found unconscious on a train and with no memory of who she is or what happened to her, a young woman (Kali) receives an operation wherein a chip is implanted in her brain to restore normal human functions. The chip however, endows her with amazing abilities that she now uses to battle evil while seeking to uncover the mystery of her past.

Krawl (MTV, 2016). While accessing her social media account a young woman (Jane) notices that her site is showing her posts one day in advance. Not sure as to how this is possible, Jane uses her knowledge of the future to help people whose lives will be adversely affected in twenty-four hours.

Larry Godmother (ABC Family, 2007). A 21-year-old unemployed man finds a new lease on life when he discovers he is a fairy godmother and has been assigned to help people in trouble.

Last Hour (CBS, 2014). An FBI investigation into a dangerous case is winding down as the program begins. Using real time, a female agent assigned to the case is followed as she risks her life to solve the case in the last hour of the operation.

Lee's Kill List (IFC, 2017). Lee, a young woman working as a cleaning solution salesperson, devises a way to keep her job—kill all those that threaten her livelihood.

Letters to Beyonce (NBC, 2015). Lily Gardner, a depressed, middle-aged school teacher who sees little chance of changing her life, hears a song by Beyonce and believes she is the inspiration she needs to reclaim her life. The proposal was to follow Lily as she programs her life based on Beyonce's songs and lifestyle.

Letters to My Daughter's Future Therapist (CBS, 2014). A mother, concerned that her unpredictable daughter may one day require a therapist, writes a series of letters wherein she records her daughter's actions and how she attempted to deal with it. Had the project sold these letters would be read by the mother as her daughter is seen in a counseling session.

Lily Dale (CBS, 2012). A family attempts to run Lily Dale, a New York State bed and breakfast that has links to the supernatural.

Mean Moms (USA, 2012). A group of young women, considered the mean girls in high school, are profiled as they become the mean mothers at their children's school.

Meet the Haunteds (NBC, 2005). A white middle-class family's experiences when they move into a renovated house that is haunted by a 1970s black family. The idea was reworked as the Nickelodeon series *The Haunted Hathaways* in 2013.

Miracle Man (ABC, 2007). A televangelist exposed as being a fraud, finds his life changing when God chooses him to perform real miracles.

Missing American Woman (Fox, 2006). A young woman who has never worked a day in her life, seizes upon an opportunity to change her life when she is reported missing after a shipwreck and begins work on a remote island resort with a group of slackers.

Mob Girl (CBS, 2003). A woman, inheriting the rank of Mafia Godfather from her late father, attempts to assert her position and rule as ruthlessly as he did.

Modern Gothic (CBS, 2014). Abraham Van Helsing, the 19th century vampire hunter who sought to destroy Count Dracula, is transported to the present day where he investigates supernatural happenings that modern science cannot explain.

My Mom Is Hot (ABC, 2009). A man attempts to adjust to the fact that his mother, "a hottie," has re-entered the dating scene.

My Nuclear Family (NBC, 2011). Events in the lives of a not-so-typical American family: parents, their seven children and a pig, named Francis Bacon, who lives in the closet of the guest room.

Mysteries of 71st Street (CBS, 2000). An upscale Manhattan couple, who are also amateur sleuths and living on 71st Street in Manhattan, team to help the police solve baffling crimes.

Near Beth Experience (CW, 2017). Beth, the survivor of a near-death experience, suddenly finds she can hear the prayers of people in close proximity to her. With her new ability she sets out on a path to help answer those prayers.

The New Nabors (NBC, 2011). The situations that befall two families living in the same neighborhood: one that is human and one that is puppet.

Night Crawler (CBS, 2012). A young woman, the daughter of a murder victim with a genius at solving crimes, teams with a homicide detective to bring criminals to justice; the problem: she suffers from a genetic disorder that prevents her from going in the sunlight.

Night Falls (A&E, 2009). A police officer, surviving a near-fatal shooting, finds his brain functions altering, becoming a Jekyll-Hyde type of person. When the day ends, he becomes a mysterious figure who crusades for justice in ways that he cannot do as a regular cop.

Nightingale (UPN, 2003). A battle against evil as depicted through a woman who has the ability to summon supernatural forces at night to help her but once dawn breaks she has no memory of what previously occurred.

99 Stories (AMC, 2008). A group of people, touring a state-of-the-art 99-story building become trapped inside when the computer system malfunctions and they find themselves at the mercy of an advanced artificial intelligence brain that can think for itself. The proposal was to follow the prisoners as they seek a way to escape from a menacing force that seeks only to kill.

The Nutshell Studies of Unexplained Death (HBO, 2012). Crime drama set in the 1950s about a young housewife who uses her unique observational abilities to help police solve complex crimes.

Olivia Jones Is My Girlfriend (NBC, 2013). The relationship that develops when two lonely people meet: A girl who has never had a boyfriend and a girl who has never had any girlfriends.

One Kick (NBC, 2014). A woman, once abducted by a kidnapper as a child but freed by the police, is approached by a mysterious billionaire for a most unusual job: hunt down predators and rescue kidnap victims.

Otherworld (CBS, 2018). A young woman, possessed with the ability to communicate with spirits, joins with a motley group of ghost hunters to help people threatened by the supernatural.

The Painted Girls (CW, 2013). Explores the lives of three sisters studying ballet at an academy in Paris in the 1880s at a time when poverty, sex and drugs are destroying the city.

Paradise Salvage (Spike TV, 2006). A history professor and a cop, friends since childhood, relinquish their careers to buy a salvage company in Florida. They soon uncover an old captain's diary and map and begin a quest to find a supposed treasure indicated by the map.

Rambo: New Blood (Fox, 2015). A continuation of the Sylvester Stallone series of *Rambo* films (about a tough ex-Vietnam Green Beret) that focus on the relationship between John Rambo and his son, John Rambo, Jr., an ex-Navy SEAL.

Randall and Hopkirk (Deceased) (Syfy, 2010). Remake of the 1969 British series of the same title (but aired in the U.S. as *My Partner the Ghost*) about Jeff Randall and Marty Hopkirk, private detectives who are a bit different: Marty, killed while investigating a case, has returned as a ghost to help Jeff and watch over his widow, Jean (who cannot see him).

Ravens Parish (Fox, 2010). A father returns to the home of his birth in rural Mississippi to unearth a legendary treasure that is supposedly buried in a mysterious cavern beneath a swamp.

The Real Amanda Strauss (Fox, 2009). Raised by a family of con artists, Amanda Strauss, now a prosecuting attorney for the district attorney, uses her knowledge of criminal activity to help bring felons to justice.

Reunited (NBC, 2017). A female genealogist uses her skills as a detective to track down long-lost loves and reunite estranged families.

Robyn (USA, 2010). When her father is exposed for bilking clients, a young woman (Robyn) realizes that all she has been given in life came from the ill-gotten money of other people. She decides to right the wrong by becoming a Robin Hood of sorts—ripping off the rich, but giving what she takes to the less fortunate.

Sex, Lies & Handwriting (ABC, 2014). Jennifer Lauren, a young woman who is both an artist and a handwriting expert, finds her life changing when she is asked by the police to use her skills to help them solve crimes by analyzing handwritten evidence found at murder scenes.

The Shop (TNT, 2014). The Shop is a mysterious organization that experiments with human genetics to create individuals for specific needs. Over time, however, their experiments have become horrific and dark creatures have been created (genetic mistakes). Charlie McGee, a girl created at the Shop as a child and now an adult, teams with Henry Talbot, a former Shop member, to destroy the Shop and track down the dark creatures that it has unleashed on society.

Sister Whipped (CBS, 2013). A young man's struggles to cope with life after being raised by his sisters who nurtured him like a woman.

Smoke Sex Magic (NBC, 2015). After inheriting their mother's restaurant, two sisters discover that she used black magic to enhance the flavor of food. However, not being as gifted as their mother, they attempt to carry on the tradition with results that are not always successful.

Spying in High Heels (USA, 2007). Maddie Springer is a fashion conscious private detective. She believes that her ability to discern shapes, colors and patterns (not to mention wearing high heels) are most helpful as she ventures forth to solve crimes.

Specter (Fox, 2011). Adaptation of the DC comic book about an ex-cop, killed in the line of duty, who is restored to the land of the living to track down criminals on behalf of the dead—and save the people who will become targets of those criminals.

Split Second (Lifetime, 2003). After making a spilt-second decision not to accept her boyfriend's marriage proposal, a young woman suddenly finds she can live in two worlds—one in which she is single and the one she could have had if she accepted the proposal.

Stephanie Spring (VH-1, 2007). How the friendship between two girls is affected when one joins a mysterious religious cult and the other tries to rescue her from what she fears is a dangerous situation with far reaching consequences.

The Strange Case of the Alchemist Daughter (CW, 2018). When two women, one of them the daughter of the scientist Dr. Henry Jekyll and the other the daughter of the evil Edward Hyde, discover they are half-sisters, they join forces to solve a series of gruesome murders that are plaguing Victorian England. Characters based on the novel *Dr. Jekyll and Mr. Hyde.*

Switch (Fox, 2018). The cases of an unusual unit of the FBI: Switch, which allows agents to go "undercover" inside the bodies of other human beings.

36-24-36 (Showtime, 2006). A strip club that requires their girls to measure at least 36-24-36 is the setting for a steamy, comical look at a young woman who, after a financial setback, rejoins her mother and grandmother—the owners of a strip club.

Tiny Ladies in Shiny Pants (ABC, 2005). A young single mother attempts to cope with life as she runs her small business, deals with obsessive parents and a sister who has come to terms with the fact that she is a lesbian.

Triangle (NBC, 2016). Wes Fallon and Marti Estevez, U.S. Naval Intelligence officers, investigate mysterious cases that involve the Bermuda Triangle.

Twilight Eyes (Starz, 2011). A man endowed with abilities far beyond normal humans sets out on a quest to destroy a new threat—extraterrestrials who have the ability to mimic humans.

The Unseen (A&E, 2013). Did something unnatural come into being at the time of the original 13 Colonies? A psychology professor and a police detective interested in the supernatural team to discover if that thesis is true when they begin investigating paranormal activity that is occurring in those thirteen states.

The Valiant (CW, 2017). Period drama about a captured Celtic princess forced into slavery under Julius Caesar and trained to become one of the first female Gladiators.

Vamp (ABC, 2014). A young ballerina, living in Manhattan with her mother, a former dancer with an unsavory past, slowly follows in her mother's footsteps when she begins dancing at Vamp, a decadent nightclub to escape the rigors of her ballet training.

Vampire in the Garden (Netflix, 2019). Musical drama about the unlikely friendship between two girls: one who is human and one who is a vampire.

Vampires (Netflix, 2018). As a young woman begins transforming into a vampire, her mother and her estranged siblings battle the supernatural to find a cure before she joins the world of the undead.

Vigilante Priest (Starz, 2011). An ex-cop turned priest takes a vow to not only to serve God but to rid the streets of his Los Angeles parish of crime—"one sinner at a time."

The Vine (TNT, 2012). Following the murder of her father, a lifestyle blogger takes it upon herself to solve crimes—with advice on how to do so from her many followers.

Wasteland (TNT, 2012). A U.S. Marshal's most unusual assignment: track down supernatural prisoners who escaped from a federal penitentiary.

Wish (HBO, 2015). People are given the opportunity to relive an important incident from their pasts simply by wishing.

Witch Doctor (Syfy, 2006). A quest to investigate medical issues linked to the supernatural as seen through the cases of David, a man who was cured of a fatal disease by a mysterious doctor with remarkable healing powers, and Diane, a young female healer who has the ability to expel demons that possess humans.

Witch Hunter Robin (Syfy, 2004). Robin, a young female witch and a member of a rogue team of witch hunters, use their powers to battle the supernatural, especially rogue witches that abuse their abilities.

Women in Space (HBO, 2014). A star ship, composed of a total female crew, begin an exploration to colonize another planet.

The Wonderful Women of Will's World (ABC, 2011). Will is a man with numerous problems, the most pressing of which are dealing with two ex-wives, a much younger current wife, and his three children.

Y 3 (A&E, 2007). Y 3 is police code for someone who impersonates a police officer. One such Y 3 is a thief who wears an N.Y.P.D. uniform to help solve crimes. The twist: he pretends to be a cop in the very precinct where he is being sought thus allowing him to continue his crusade against crime.

Zeroes (Syfy, 2011). The Zombie Extermination and Removal Operations Company, called Zeroes, has been established to keep the zombie population under control and within their own city zone. When the zombies go beyond their regulated area and fear begins to spread, the Zeroes go into action—fumbling their way to put down the rogue zombies.

Zombies and Cheerleaders (Disney Channel, 2012). There is a seemingly normal town with seemingly normal teenagers who attend a seemingly normal high school. But what seems normal isn't as the school also supports zombies attending and the proposal was to relate the efforts of Zed Necrodopolis and his zombie friends to become a part of the school's mainstream—and impress the gorgeous pom-pom wielding cheerleaders who want nothing to do with them. The idea was reworked into the 2018 Disney TV movie *Zombies*.

ACTORS INDEX

The index below refers to the programs on which actors were chosen. See also the Producer's Index for actor's producer-only credits.

Abdul, Paula 57
Ackerman, Leslie 20
Agar, John 40, 49
Aidman, Charles 32
Akins, Claude 8, 11, 32, 80
Alba, Jessica 29, 51
Albert, Eddie 15, 22, 47
Alda, Alan 2
Alexander, Jason 37
Alexander, Rod 18
Alley, Kirstie 42
Allyson, June 52
Alvarez, Izabella 62
Ameche, Don 20
Ames, Nancy 81
Amsterdam, Morey 21
Anderson, Steve 68
Andrews, Edward 47
Andrews, Tod 15
Angelini, Jude 35
Annable, Dave 56
Anthony, La La 36

Aprea, John 25
Arden, Eve 15, 24, 37
Arden, Tony 63
Arian, Yancey 78
Arkin, Adam 63
Arlen, Richard 62
Armendariz, Pedro 56, 66
Arnaz, Desi 19
Arnold, Tom 37, 55, 62
Arquette, Cliff 36
Arquette, David 16
Ashford, Aannaleigh 6
Atkins, Essence 72
Auer, Mischa 31
Averback, Hy 40
Azaria, Hank 54
Baccarin, Morena 51
Backus, Jim 24
Bacon, Kevin 49, 77
Baer, Buddy 68
Baines, Cindy 54
Baio, Scott 66

Baker, Stella 62
Baldwin, Alec 2
Baldwin, William 61, 80
Banderas, Antonio 32
Banks, Elizabeth 29
Barkin, Ellen 22
Barr, Roseanne 20
Barrymore, Drew 8, 21
Barrymore, John Drew 30
Barrymore, Jr., John 43
Bartok, Eva 26
Bassett, Angela 55, 77
Bateman, Jason 42, 80
Baxter, Dr. Frank 59
Baxter, Lex 56
Beaumont, Hugh 39
Beery, Jr., Noah 5, 44
Bel Geddes, Barbara 27
Belafonte, Harry 31
Bell, Tone 82
Bello, Maria 22, 29, 48, 62
Belushi, Jim 83
Bender, Landry 62
Bennett, Bruce 67
Bennett, Joan 82
Bergen, Polly 54
Berry, Halle 31, 44
Bettger, Lyle 3
Bialik, Mayim 12
Bilson, Rachel 28
Black, Michael Ian 51, 83
Black, Tom 79
Blair, Patricia 24
Bleeth, Yasmine 74
Boreanaz, David 18
Bowen, Julie 61
Boyd, Jimmy 1
Boyle, Lara Flynn 43
Bracken, Eddie 21
Bradbury, Ray 8
Bradley, Truman 60
Brady, Wayne 78
Brand, Jolene 60
Brand, Neville 66
Brandon, Michael 53
Brasselle, Keith 33, 47
Braxton, Toni 74
Breck, Peter 30, 83
Breeds, Rebecca 14
Brennan, Walter 28
Brent, George 39
Breuer, Jim 73
Brewster, Paget 82
Brian, David 20
Bridges, Lloyd 47
Britton, Barbara 51, 52
Bromfield, Louis 17
Brown, Jim 77
Bruce, Virginia 81
Brucker, April 5
Buchannon, Edgar 65
Burke, Delta 71
Burke, Nellie 31
Burns, Gene 27
Burns, Patricia 4
Burton, LeVar 38
Butler, Brett 10, 34, 48
Byner, John 54
Cabral, Angelique 82
Caplan, Lizzy 35
Carey, Jr., Harry 56
Carey, Macdonald 10, 50
Carlson, Richard 1, 82
Carson, Jack 8, 30, 32
Carson, Johnny 55
Carter, Nell 78
Case, Nelson 27
Cattrall, Kim 67
Caymares, Emma 52
Cedric the Entertainer 12, 13, 43, 74
Chalke, Sarah 65
Chamberlain, Richard 46, 57
Chapman, Shawn 71
Charisse, Cyd 53
Chase, Ilka 63
Chenoweth, Kristin 62

Chestnut, Morris 46
Cho, Margaret 51
Cigliuti, Natalie 27
Clark, Bobby 53, 72
Clarke, Lenny 44
Clooney, George 28
Cobb, Julie 55
Cobb, Lee J. 26
Coburn, Charles 15
Colbert, Claudette 6, 44
Colbert, Stephen 70
Coleman, Jack 25
Collins, Gary 50
Collins, Mo 6
Colton, Rita 44
Connick, Jr., Harry 18
Connolly, Kevin 35
Connors, Mike 75
Conrad, Robert 70
Conried, Hans 17
Considine, Bob 49
Consuelos, Mark 41, 59, 65, 81, 82
Convy, Bert 67
Conway, Pat 72
Cooker, Keith 54
Cooley, Dennis 66
Cooley, Spade 69
Cooper, Bradley 36
Corbett, John 64
Corby, Ellen 30
Corey, Wendell 14
Costello, Lou 5
Coughland, Marissa 17
Coulouris, George 29
Cox, Courteney 62
Cox, Laverne 69
Crawford, Broderick 34, 49
Crawford, Joan 3, 39
Crowley, Kathleen 42
Crute, Austin 52
Cuditz, Michael 14
Cugat, Xavier 5
Curtis, Jamie Lee 25, 60

Cusack, Joan 39
Dailey, Dan 38
Damon, Mark 11
Dang, Shannon 43
Danton, Ray 69
Danza, Tony 30
Darnell, Linda 72
Dauphin, Claude 31
Davis, Jim 34, 61
Davis, Geena 46
Davis, Kristin 42
Davis, Viola 78
Dawson, Rosario 54
Dean, Abner 63
DeCarlo, Yvonne 44, 73
DeFore, Don 10, 24, 34. 58
Demarest, William 50
Dempsey, Patrick 21
Dennehy, Brian 76
Denning, Richard 11, 37
Derek, John 55
DeRita, Joe 73
Deschanel Zooey 27, 36, 45, 60
Devicq, Paula 16
DeVito, Danny 18
Dexter, Tony 12
DiCaprio, Leonardo 19
Dick, Andy 4
Dick, Walter 78
Dickinson, Angie 4
Dietz, Howard 63
DiMaggio, Joe 39
Donald, Peter 74
Donlevy, Brian 1
D'Onofrio, Vincent 9
Douglas, Burt 27
Douglas, Illeana 13, 16
Douglas, Paul 47, 54
Downey, Roma 64
Drake, Alfred 73
Drew, Wendy 45
DuBois, Diane 64
Duchovny, David 82

Duff, Hilary 33
Duggan, Andrew 44
Duggan, Tom 42
Dullea, Keir 77
Duncan, Jimmy 2
Dunne, Irene 68
Dutton, Charles S. 57
Duvall, Robert 64
Dynely, Peter 74
Ebsen, Buddy 11
Edwards, Anthony 5
Edwards, Ronnie Claire 71
Eilbacher, Lisa 26
Eklund, Britt 29
Electra, Carmen 12
Elias, Alix 73
Elizondo, Hector 75
Elliott, Chris 13
Ely, Ron 32
Emerson, Faye 63
Emerson, Michael 54
Emery, Allan 10
English, Maria 59
Engvall, Bill 8
Estes, Rob 70
Estevez, Emilio 46
Etheridge, Melissa 49
Evans, Gene 27
Eve 23
Fahey, Jeff 57
Fairbanks, Jr., Douglas 26
Farr, Diane 19, 63
Farrell, Glenda 51
Farris, Anna 20
Fawcett, Farrah 24
Fawcett, William 66
Faxon, Nat 4
Feimster, Fortune 20
Felton, Verna 30
Ferrer, Miguel 43
Ferrera, America 17, 69
Field, Margaret 66
Fine, Larry 73

Fishburne, Lawrence 63
Flanagan, Maile 82
Flick, Ginger 68
Flynn, Errol 44
Flynn, Joe 7
Flynn, Neil 4
Foley, Scott 28
Foster, Preston 72
Fox, Vivica A. 17
Foxworthy, Jeff 38
Foxx, Jamie 37
Francis, Anne 14
Francis, Arlene 49, 78
Franciscus, James 6
Fraser, Sally 7
Frawley, William 50
Fuller, Penny 50
Gabor, Zsa Zsa 58
Garcia, JoAnna 39
Gardner, Reginald 11
Garner, Jennifer 80
Garrett, Brad 79
Garrison, Paul 47
Garvey, Cyndy 58
Gatson, Penny 70
Gazzara, Ben 16
Geller, Sarah Michelle 56
George, Sue 64
Gertz, Jamie 26
Gifford, Kathie Lee 21
Gilbert, Melissa 25
Gillespie, Gina 34
Glenn, Scott 19, 78
Gobel, George 80
Goddard, Paulette 20
Goggins, Walter 41
Goldberg, Whoopi 80
Gomez, Selena 63, 67
Good, Megan 26
Goodwin, Bill 36
Gordon, Gale 50
Gorham, Christopher 82
Grace, Topher 34

Graham, Lauren 41
Grammer, Camille 29
Granger, Stewart 65
Graves, Peter 43, 77
Gray, Colleen 76
Graziano, Rocky 15
Greer, Judy 36, 40, 56
Grier, David Allen 78
Griffin, Kathy 41
Griffith, Andy 20
Griffith, Melanie 72
Griffiths, Lucy 6
Grimes, Jack 70
Grizzard, George 55
Guttenberg, Steve 8
Gwynne, Fred 7
Hadley, Reed 33
Hagner, Meredith 6
Hale, Jr., Alan 71
Hale, Nancy 26
Hall, Jon 65, 75
Halliday, Hildegard 37
Halsey, Brett 35, 39, 76
Handler, Chelsea 7, 13
Hannigan, Alyson 3
Harper, Valerie 45
Harris, Mel 65
Harris, Tip "T.J." 6
Hart, Kevin 1
Hart, Melissa Joan 14
Hasselhoff, David 71
Hasso, Signe 14
Hawke, Ethan 9
Hayden, Sara 12
Hayward, Louis 59
Heche, Anne 36
Hefner, Hugh 32
Heigl, Katherine 75
Helberg, Simon 64
Henderson, Marcia 20
Hendrie, Phil 4
Henley, Perisa Fitz 75
Henrie, Sonja 69

Henry, Mike 71
Hewitt, Jennifer Love 38, 52
Hickman, Darryl 82
Hill, Arthur 22
Hines, Gregory 30
Hodges, Eddie 81
Hodiak, John 35
Holdridge, Cheryl 10, 40, 73, 82
Holly, Lauren 26
Holmes, Katie 41
Hopper, Dennis 19, 71
Horton, Edward Everett 27
Hough, Julianne 55
Hovis, Larry 70
Howard, Hope 79
Howard, Moe 73
Howell, Arlene 11
Huffman, Felicity 25, 34, 42
Hughley, D.L. 20, 69
Hunt, Bonnie 15
Hurst, Rick 70
Hutton, Robert 52
Jagger, Dean 50
Janiss, Vivi 60
Janney, Allison 2
Janssen, David 57
Jarmyn, Jill 7
Jason, Rick 48
Jenkins, Allen 32
Jergens, Diane 15
Jessel, George 28, 33
Jillian, Ann 58
Jobrani, Maz 16, 54
Johnson, Anjelah 2, 79
Johnson, Don 20
Johnson, Van 59
Jones, Brandon Scott 28
Jones, Carolyn 20, 73
Jones, Dean 31
Jones, Rashida 63
Jones, Shirley 21
Joyner, Mario 64
Kanakaredes, Melina 36

Karpovsky, Alex 42
Kaye, Sammy 65
Kaye, Stubby 30, 33
Keith, Robert 82
Kelly, Paul 35
Kenney, June 52
Kenney-Silver, Kerri 61
Kenyon, Doris 14
Kiley, Richard 36
Kilpatrick, Diarra 19
King, Alan 55
King, Dave 17
King, Dennis 34
Kirby, George 71
Kirkman, Jen 38
Kirkwood, Jack 7
Kline, Kevin 41
Knapp, Robert 67
Kopell, Bernie 76
Kraft, Lindsay 59
Kudrow, Lisa 46, 47, 61
Kunis, Mila 9, 34, 65, 68
La Salle, Eriq 75
Lake, Ricki 42
Lamarrr, Hedy 29
Lamour, Dorothy 11
Lampanelli, Lisa 8, 46
Landau, Martin 31
Landers, Judy 72
Landers, Kristy 72
Landers, Lindsay 72
Landes, Michael 3
Landon, Michael 71
Lane, Abbe 5
Lane, Rusty 45
Langan, Glenn 52
Lansing, Joi 6, 34, 65, 82
Larkin, John 48, 60
LaRoche, Mary 76
Larsen Darrel 53
Larson, Brie 10
Latifah, Queen 22
Laughton, Charles 9
Lauren, Hope 62
Laurents, John 2
Lee, Jason 77
Lee, Mac 47
Lee, Peggy 58
Lefevre, Rachelle 5
Leggero, Natasha 61
Leguizamo, John 40
Leifer, Carol 12, 56, 72, 78, 82
Levine, Sam 81
Liang, Olivia 43
Lindhome, Riki 71
Linn, Bambi 18
Liotta, Ray 16
Lizer, Kari 80
Logue, Donal 22
Lohan, Lindsay 45
Lombard, Louise 78
Lomond, Britt 26
London, Julie 71
Longoria, Eva 7, 17, 23, 56, 62, 67, 68, 71, 73, 77, 81
Lonow, Claudia 8, 22, 72
Lopez, Jennifer 38, 64
Lopez, Lynda 47
Lord, Jack 60, 65
Loring, Lynn 72
Lorre, Peter 9
Loughlin, Lori 73
Love, Faizon 14
Lovejoy, Frank 31, 35
Lovitz, Jon 40, 44
Lowe, Rob 64
Lowery, Robert 30
Loy, Myrna 32
Luna, Gabriel 48
Lundgren, Dolph 37, 63
Lynde, Paul 76
Lyonne, Natasha 53, 83
Ma, Tzi 43
Mabius, Eric 44
Mac, Bernie 7
Macchio, Ralph 61

MacDonald, Donald 53
MacDonald, Norm 44
MacRae, Gordon 54
MacRae, Sheila 54
Madison, Guy 38
Malia, Katie 3
Malone, Nancy 7
Manceri, Patricia 21
Mandell, Mo 50
Manheim, Camryn 11
Mara, Adele 52
Marie, Rose 40
Markey, Melinda 82
Marshall, Herbert 42
Marshall, Paula 58
Martin, Tony 53
Marx, Chico 19
Marx, Groucho 19
Marx, Harpo 19
Mason, Portland 59
Massey, Raymond 25
Mathis, Samantha 72
Matlin, Marlee 45, 51
Maxwell, Marilyn 60
May, Donald 21, 25
McCalman, Malcolm 68
McCarthy, Jenny 70
McCarthy, Lin 15
McCormack, Will 69
McCormick, Mary 57, 77
McDonald, Heather 52
McGrath, Derek 4
McGraw, Tim 64
McIver, Rosie 28
McLain, Duncan 9
McNally, Stephen 16
Meara, Anne 4, 76
Melchoir, Lauritz 29, 34
Merman, Ethel 12
Messing, Debra 19
Metcalf, Laurie 76
Meyer, Breckin 64
Meyers, Josh 24

Milano, Alyssa 3
Milland, Ray 3
Miller, Mark 25
Mitchell, Cameron 35, 75
Mitchell, Luke 62
Mohr, Gerald 33
Mohr, Jay 5
Mollen, Jenny 35
Mo'Nique 50
Moore, Candy 34
Moore, Mandy 50
Morgan, Debbi 44
Morisette, Alanis 79
Morris, Chester 69
Morris, Kathryn 67
Morrissey, David 21
Morrow, Rob 54
Morrow, Vic 48
Morse, Robert 80
Mowry, Tia 73
Muha, Santina 59
Mullally, Megan 76
Munn, Allison 71
Murphy, Charles 70
Musquiz, Carlos 66
Nash, Ogden 63
Neagle, Anna 4
Nelson, Barry 35
Nesbitt, John 70
Newhart, Bob 9
Newland, John 17, 36, 75
Newton, Becki 27
Nicholas, Barbara 82
Nicholas, Michelle 8
Nicol, Alex 15
Nolan, Jeanette 81
Norwood, Brandy 10
Nucci, Danny 42
Oberon, Merle 44
O'Brien, Pat 66
O'Connell, Jerry 38
O'Herlihy, Dan 58
O'Keefe, Dennis 50

O'Neal, Patrick 28, 44
O'Quinn, Terry 54
Orlando, Tony 74
Osmond, Donny 21
O'Sullivan, Maureen 64
Oswalt, Patton 36, 68, 82
Page, Ellen 70
Paige, Janis 26, 47
Paisley, Brad 25
Parker, Fess 75
Parr, Stephen 53
Parsons, Louella 46
Pastore, Vincent 29
Peeples, Nia 16
Penn, Kal 14
Pennell, Larry 7
Perlman, Heidi 32
Perry, Barbara 68
Persoff, Nehemiah 29
Peyton, Marlow 5
Pflug, Jo Ann 67
Phillips, Henry 60
Pickler, Kellie 41
Pierce, Robert 59
Pierce, Webb 79
Pitts, Zasu 7
Piven, Jeremy 37
Pleshette, Suzanne 6
Poehler, Amy 4, 83
Poitier, Sydney Tamila 72
Portman, Eric 20
Pratt, Deborah 73
Prescott, Allen 66
Price, Vincent 9, 26, 52, 77
Principal, Victoria 74
Purdom, Edmund 9
Quinn, Colin 64
Quinn, Ed 65
Raft, George 60
Ragon, Henriette 57
Rajo, Rustavio 73
Ramsey, David 72
Randall, Ron 60

Randall, Tony 22
Rathbone, Basil 13, 31
Reed, Don 53
Reed, Donna 43
Reed, Lydia 39
Reeves, Steve 68
Reid, Tara 6
Reymundo, Alex 33
Reynolds, Burt 11
Reynolds, Quentin 81
Rhames, Ving 8
Richie, Nicole 53
Rickles, Don 70
Ringwald, Molly 50
Ripa, Kelly 41, 59, 61, 81, 82
Ritcher, Andy 20
Ritter, Krysten 6, 12, 42
Ritter, Tex 32
Riva, Aria 35
Rivera, Erik 23
Rivers, Melissa 67
Robbins, Marty 79
Roberts, Emma 7
Roberts, John 22
Roberts, Julia 13, 71, 74
Roberts, Roy 26
Robertson, Cliff 61
Rodd, Marcia 73
Rodriquez, Paul 57
Rogers, Wayne 44
Rogers, Will 66
Romano, Ray 62
Romero, Cesar 48
Rudie, Evelyn 10, 14, 24, 26, 32, 34, 73
Rue, Sara 6, 59
Ruggles, Charlie 76
Ruick, Melville 21
Rush, Barbara 58
Russell, Connie 11
Russell, John 65
Russell, Nipsey 59
Ryan, Meg 49
Sabu 2, 42

Saget, Bob 9
Sami, Madeleine 70
Sanchez, Kiele 45
Sanders, George 24
Sarandon, Susan 30
Sasso, Will 80
Savage, Andrea 63
Schaal, Kristen 3, 42
Schallert, William 31
Schneider, John 21
Schwarzenegger, Arnold 56
Scott, Seann William 6
Seacrest, Ryan 82
Sedgwick, Kyra 43, 52, 83
Sennott, Rachel 52
Senor Wences 40
Seven, Johnny 77
Shackelford, Ted 79
Shannon, Molly 51
Sharp, Timm 56
Shawkat, Alia 70
Sheen, Charlie 13
Shelton, Marley 48
Shepherd, Sherri 67
Shlesinger, Iliza 26, 31
Shore, Roberta 1
Shull, Richard B. 66
Silverman, Sarah 4
Simpson, Jessica 38
Sinatra, Frank 9
Skulnik, Menasha 34
Smith, Alexis 47
Smith, Carl 79
Smith, Jada Pinkett 52
Smits, Jimmy 14
Snoop Dogg 69
Sokiloff, Maria 3
Sommers, Joanie 76
Sorbo, Kevin 49
Spacey, Kevin 17
Spade, David 18, 39
Spelling, Tori 75
Sterling, Jan 10, 40

Sterling, Robert 69
Stern, Howard 21
Stevens, Connie 15
Stevens, K.T. 72
Stevens, Mark 40
Stewart, French 7
Stewart, Kellee 7
Stockwell, Guy 35
Storm, Gale 20
Sturgess, Olive 71
Sullivan, Barry 66
Swenson, Karl 27
Talbot, Nita 31
Talbott, Gloria 3, 5, 40, 79
Tamblyn, Amber 3
Tapping, Amanda 67
Tatum, Channing 28
Taylor, Aisha 2
Taylor, Joan 27
Taylor, Regina 68
Thaxter, Phyllis 50
Thomas, Alex 71
Thomas, Dave 4
Thomas, Robin 26
Thompson, Tina 53
Thune, Nick 33
Tisdale, Ashley 5, 41, 76
Titus, Christopher 14
Todd, Richard 1
Tompkins, Paul F. 24
Tone, Franchot 81
Toomey, Regis 12
Trachtenberg, Michelle 49
Trammell, Sam 70
Traubel, Helen 60
Tremayne, Les 25
Tucci, Stanley 70
Tucker, Forrest 17, 59, 61
Tuerco, Paige 68
Tyler, Judy 63
Underwood, Carrie 76
Union, Gabrielle 79
Urie, Michael 27

Van Doren, Mamie 82
van Dreelen, John 69
Ventimiglia, Milo 63
Verdugo, Elena 8, 31
Vidal, Christina 78
Vidal, Lisa 78
Vidal, Tanya 78
Wahlberg, Donnie 14
Wallach, Eli 69
Walston, Ray 31
Ward, Sela 66
Washburn, Beverly 32, 34, 45, 73, 82
Washington, Kerry 55
Wayans, Damon 17, 18, 45
Wayans, Jr., Damon 32, 47
Wayans, Kim 78
Wayne, Patrick 80
Wayne, David 18
Weaver, Michael 29
Webb, Jack 25
Webb, Richard 11
Webber, Peggy 7, 10, 37
Webber, Robert 78
Weber, Steven 74
Wedgeworth, Anne 73
Weld, Tuesday 82
Weldman, Jerome 45
Welling, Tom 66
West, Brooks 15
Weston, Jack 75
White, Betty 81
White, Julie 81
White, Ron 21
Williams III, Clarence 76
Williams, Cara 27, 30
Williams, Cindy 53
Williams, Mae 47
Williams, Vanessa L. 77
Wills, Chill 18
Wilson, Lulu 77
Windom, William 27
Winninger, Charles 13, 72
Winokur, Marissa Jaret 48

Witherspoon, Reese 62, 74
Wyatt, Jane 5
Wyman, Jane 13
Wynter, Dana 79
Yasbeck, Amy 4
Yates, Cassie 20
York, Dick 29, 82
Young, Alan 60
Youngman, Henny 83
Zano, Nick 53
Zayid, Maysoon 11

PRODUCERS INDEX

Abrams, J.J. 54, 116, 129, 168
Ackerman, Harry 10, 15, 22, 53, 55, 58, 70, 71, 75
Adams, Amy 157
Adelstein, Marty 134, 143, 165, 172, 175, 178, 187, 194
Affleck, Ben 95, 171
Aguilera, Christina 132
Ainsworth, Helen 38
Akil, Mara Brock 10, 114
Alba, Jessica 29, 51
Alexander, Jason 37, 114
Alexander, Sasha 194
Alfano, JoAnn 197
Allen, Debbie 112
Allen, Gabrielle 114, 166
Allen, Kenton 100, 169
Amateau, Rod 58
Anthony, La La 36, 167
Anthony, Marc 38
Apatow, Judd 64
Appel, Eric 99
Armstrong, Craig 176
Armstrong, Scott 68, 90
Arnaz, Desi 5, 9, 26, 40, 82
Arnold, Tom 37, 55

Arquette, David 16, 62, 99, 108, 132, 161, 184
Austin, Bud 38
Baccarin, Morena 51
Bacon, Kevin 77
Baer, Neal 94, 195
Bahr, Fax 101
Bailey, Sean 135, 171
Baldwin, Alec 2
Banderas, Antonio 32
Banks, Elizabeth 28, 69, 135, 168
Banks, Tyra 123
Barker, Clive 105
Barnette, Alan 67
Barrett, James Lee 8
Barris, Kenya 123
Barry, Josh 87, 120, 184
Barry, Simon 37
Barrymore, Drew 8, 21, 105, 137
Bassett, Angela 77
Bateman, Jason 80, 138
Baum, Lloyd 152, 189, 198
Beals, Jennifer 116, 176
Becky, Dave 1, 4, 6, 20, 22, 53, 71, 89, 100, 127, 145, 148, 167, 176
Beers, Betsy 104, 138, 151, 155, 156, 171, 179,

183, 196
Beers, Thom 141
Bello, Maria 22, 62
Benson, Alison 141
Benson, Leon 197
Berg, James 156
Berger, Aaron 178
Berger, Andy 20
Bergman, Ted 79, 98
Berlanti, Greg 10, 43, 97, 100, 102, 109, 121, 126, 128, 134, 147, 153, 164, 168, 171, 179, 186, 187, 189
Berliner, Jane 49
Berman, Gail 104, 116, 136, 147, 149, 150, 152, 154, 157, 170, 171, 174, 176, 189, 198
Berman, Josh 107, 112, 122,
Berman, Melissa Kellner 97
Berman, Spencer 95
Berner, Fred 191
Bernstein, Adam 135
Bernstein, Carolyn 187
Berry, Halle 31, 44, 156
Berry, Jonathan 53, 115, 140, 176,
Beverly, Carl 21, 41, 78, 89, 95, 96, 102, 106, 113, 115, 122, 124, 125, 133, 134, 147, 149, 150, 154, 160, 161, 170, 176, 178, 179, 181, 191
Bialik, Mayim 12
Bickel, Dave 128, 195
Bieber, Justin 144
Billingsley, Peter 30, 90, 99
Bilson, George 65
Biolding, Muffy 138
Black, Chris 55
Black, Jack 95, 99, 187
Black, Todd 97
Blanchard, Ann 160
Blees, Robert 35, 69
Blevins, Lee R. 5
Blige, Mary J. 116, 157
Blinn, William 53
Bloodworth-Thomason, Linda 21, 150
Bloomberg, Stu 94
Bochco, Steven 105, 130, 149, 181

Bogart, Paul 80
Bonan, Gregory J. 63
Borten, Craig 143
Bottfeld, Sara 193
Bowen, Julie 61
Bowen, Marty 95, 115
Bowman, Rob 191
Bowser, Yvette Lee 195
Boyle, Lara Flynn 43
Bozell, Jennifer 154
Bradford, Gerald 171
Branson, Richard 163
Braun, Lloyd 154, 170, 174
Braun, Scooter 144
Braunstein, Howard 167
Brecher, Irving 8
Brennan, Tracie 125
Brillstein, Bernie 78
Briskin, Irving 11, 25, 26
Briskin, Mort 43
Brockovich, Erin 105
Brodax, Al 48
Brodkin, Herbert 55, 69
Broidy, William F. 12
Brosnan, Pierce 93, 110
Brown, Holly 93
Brown, Tasha 101
Bruckheimer, Jerry 5, 14, 19, 56, 76, 85, 88, 93, 94, 97, 98, 101, 103, 106, 108, 118, 121, 126, 127, 129, 130, 132, 135, 136, 139, 150, 151, 163, 181, 184, 191, 195, 198
Bruckner, Brad 55
Brunetti, Dana 17, 67, 183
Brush, Bob 97
Bucatinsky, Dan 45, 46, 170
Bullock, Sandra 174
Burgess, Mitchell 57
Burk, Bryan 54
Burke, Cecil 33
Burke, Karey 3, 90, 91, 95, 104, 111, 114, 115, 117, 121, 125, 126, 129, 130, 138, 142, 160, 163, 169, 174, 175, 176, 183, 185, 186, 187
Burke, Owen 72

Burnett, Mark 64, 92, 112, 113, 116, 122
Burns, George 24
Burns, Patricia 4
Burns, Scott 82
Burns, Seymour 33
Busfield, Timothy 131
Butler, Brett 10, 48
Buzzell, Eddie 60
Byron, Ed 25
Calfo, Francie 10, 18, 86, 92, 94, 107, 113, 115, 131, 133, 148, 159, 163, 173, 174, 184
Callaway, Trey 138
Cameron, James 189
Cannell, Stephen J. 180
Cannon, Vivian 92, 114, 149, 152, 169, 186, 195
Caplan, Lizzy 35
Carell, Steve 167
Carey, Marcey 156
Carey, Mariah 153
Carliner, Robert 108
Caro, Julia 47
Caron, Glenn Gordon 111
Carreras, Jennifer 77
Carrey, Jim 46
Carsey, Marcy 102, 158, 166
Carter, Holly 175
Carter, Lucas 87
Caruso, D.J. 143
Caruso, Dee 71, 166
Caspe, David 126
Cassidy, Shaun 117, 156, 171, 176, 184
Cates, Joseph 4
Cattrall, Kim 67
Cedric the Entertainer 43, 110
Chalken, Ilene 168, 176
Chappelle, Ernest 74
Charles, RuPaul 168
Chase, Stanley 21
Chenoweth, Kristin 62
Cher 103
Chernin, Peter 91, 101, 107, 121, 129, 130, 141, 145, 146, 152, 162, 163, 168, 170, 172, 174, 175, 185, 187, 192, 196, 197

Chestnut, Morris 46
Chevillat, Dick 15
Cho, Margaret 3
Clampett, Bob 190
Clark, John L. 45
Clements, Becky 50, 152, 165, 172
Clooney, George 115, 121, 182
Coe, Fred 27
Cohen, Seth 188
Colbert, Stephen 70
Cole, Sidney 68
Colodny, Lester 24
Connick, Jr., Harry 18
Conrad, Robert 70
Consuelos, Mark 41, 59, 61, 65, 81, 82, 136, 141, 146, 191
Cooper, Bob 94
Cooper, Bradley 36
Cooper, Jackie 177
Cooperman, Alvin 17, 31, 34
Coppola, Francis Ford 107
Cosby, Bill 8
Coughlin, Marisa 194
Cox, Barbara 100
Cox, Courteney 16, 62, 99, 108, 132, 161, 184
Cranston, Bryan 74
Craven Wes 145, 166, 193, 194
Crawford, Cindy 36
Crichton, Michael 128
Crichton, Sherri 128
Crittenden, Jennifer 29, 114
Croft, David 91
Crowe, Russell 22, 78
Crystal, Billy 121
Cuoco, Kaley 59
Curtis, Bonnie 188
Curtis, Cami 9, 33, 34, 65, 103, 152, 155, 188
Curtis, Jamie Lee 25, 60
Curtis, Susan 34, 65, 103
D'Onofrio, Vincent 9
Daly, Carson 142
Damon, Matt 95
Daniels, Suzanne 74, 96

Danza, Tony 30
Danziger, Eddie 2
Davey, Bruce 103, 186
David, Alan 59
David, Luther 54
Davis, John 16, 22, 90, 95, 143, 160, 189
Davis, Josh 144
Davis, Stephanie 94
Davis, Viola 78, 97
Davola, Joe 104
Dawson, Rosario 54
De Sica, Vittorio 5
Dearborn, Matt 169
DeGeneres, Ellen 40, 108, 117, 136, 150, 188, 191, 194
DeKoven, Linda 66
DeLaurentis, Robert 92
D'Elia, Bill 191
DeNiro, Robert 87, 122, 129, 172, 175, 189, 193
Depp, Johnny 143, 188
Dern, Laura 74, 157
Deschanel, Zooey 27, 45, 60, 74, 158
Devine, Jerry 16
DeVito, Danny 18, 56, 98
DeWitt, Jack 40
DiBona, Vin 94, 111, 115, 119, 179
DiCaprio, Leonardo 149
Dick, Walter 78
Diesel, Vin 107, 110, 123, 131, 147, 155
Diggs, Taye 94, 154
DiMassa, Ernie 74
Dinner, Michael 80, 106, 160, 192
Donovan, Dick 120
Dorfman, Sid 7
Douglas, Illana 13
Douglas, Paul 54
Downey, Roma 64, 112, 122
Drackovitch, Stephanie 80
Duckworth, Sheila 74, 96, 153, 183
Duff, Hilary 33
Duff, Howard 30
Duff, Susan 33
Duhamel, Josh 162

Dunkel, John 75
Dunne, Dominick 26, 195
Dutton, Charles S. 57, 139
Duvall, Robert 108
Earley, Joe 171, 176
Eastman, Carl 74
Ebel, Kathy 163
Edelman, Louis 25, 65
Edelstein, Michael 126
Edwards, Anthony 5
Edwards, Blake 9
Eells, Pamela 71
Eisenman, Julia 154
Eld, Rick 128
Elder, Caroline 125
Elliott, Chris 13
Ellis, Sid 47
Ellison, Megan 74
English, Diane 83
Engvall, Bill 8
Estevez, Ramon 153
Fairbanks, Jerry 59
Fairbanks, Jr., Douglas 5, 12, 26
Fairchild, Don 77
Fairman, Michael 98
Falcone, Ben 155
Fallon, Jimmy 93, 122, 171
Falls, Kevin 173
Falvey, Justin 12, 85, 86, 88, 93, 96, 101, 103, 106, 113, 116, 117, 118, 119, 120, 124, 128, 136, 147, 149, 157, 160, 161, 162, 164, 165, 167, 169, 173, 181, 186, 188, 190, 192, 194, 196, 197
Farentino, Debrah 110
Farr, Diane 19, 147
Farrell, Will 104
Faxon, Nat 41
Fedderson, Don 39, 190
Feldman, Edward 47
Feldman, Gene 184
Fellow, Sue 177
Felton, Norman 76, 190
Fenady, Andrew 47, 86

Fennelly, Vincent 40
Feresten, Spike 5, 80
Ferguson, Craig 109
Ferrell, Will 35, 63, 72, 137, 185, 190, 196
Ferrera, America 2, 17, 69, 88, 166
Ferrin, Frank 42
Fey, Tina 187
Fields, Simon 92, 116, 142
Filgo, Jackie 136
Filgo, Jeff 136
Fineman, Ross 45
Finkel, Bon 174
Fishburne, Lawrence 63
Fisher, Bob 177
Fisher, Lucy 95
Fitzpatrick, Hugh 193
Fleischer, Reuben 181
Florea, John 83, 120, 158, 182
Fogelman, Don 142
Fontana, Tom 32, 80, 99, 103, 128, 129, 135, 144, 146, 148, 158, 179, 193, 194
Forbes, Maya 57
Foreman, Michael 119, 157
Forte, Kate 164
Foster, Jodie 90, 99
Fox, Ben 31
Fox, John 22, 90, 142, 189
Foxworthy, Jeff 38
Foxx, Jamie 37, 96, 110, 133, 156
Foy, Jr., Eddie 34
Frank, Alan 74
Frank, Darryl 12, 85, 88, 93, 96, 106, 101, 103, 113, 117, 118, 119, 120, 124, 128, 136, 147, 149, 157, 160, 161, 162, 164, 165, 166, 169, 173, 181, 186, 188. 190, 192, 194, 197
Franklin, Jill 58
Franklin, John Jay 2
Franz, Julia 157, 159, 176
Fresco, Rob 90
Frey, James 149
Fricke, Anna 141
Fromkess, Leon 81, 147
Fryman, Patricia 76

Fuennntes, Lisa 138
Fuller, Simon 41
Gabor, Zsa Zsa 58
Galecki, Johnny 93
Gallo, Basil 17
Gallu, Sam 49, 67
Ganaway, Al 188
Gannaway, Albert C. 79
Gardner, Arthur 172
Gardner, Dede 164
Gardner, Gerald 166
Gardner, Julie 150, 152
Gardner, Stephen 172
Garner, Jennifer 80, 87, 102, 123, 131, 142
Garner, Todd 87, 164
Garrett, Brad 79
Garson, Willie 108
Gast, Harold 48
Gelbart, Larry 95, 115
Geller, Sarah Michelle 56
Gerard, Bernard 75
Gerber, David 5, 11, 194
Gersh, Bruce 119
Gibbons, Leeza 71
Gibson, Mel 103, 186
Gill, Jack 16
Girard, Bernard 37, 42, 44, 51, 66
Glazer, Ilana 100
Glenn, John 17, 119
Gluck, Will 87, 138
Gold, Eric 78
Gold, Jeremy 179
Gold, Josh 67
Goldberg, Jason 12, 91, 126, 127, 129, 176, 186
Goldberg, Jessica 62
Goldberg, Whoopi 80, 139, 149, 151, 177
Goldenberg, Jeff 40
Goldsmith-Thomas, Elaine 44, 64, 71, 113, 142, 152, 164, 180
Goldstein, Len 142, 148, 151, 159, 167, 177, 192, 197
Goldstein, Leonard 27
Gomez, Selena 63, 67

Goodman, Harry S. 81
Goodson, Mark 10, 30, 43
Gordon, Charles 111
Gordon, Howard 62, 107, 161, 193
Gordon, Mark 26, 55, 88, 106, 108, 111, 112, 114, 123, 124, 139, 141, 145, 158, 168, 169, 179, 182, 193
Gordon, Seth 94, 188, 189, 190
Gottlieb, Alex 29
Grace, Topher 34, 173
Graham, Lauren 163
Grammer, Kelsey 29, 97, 113, 119, 140, 146, 159, 165, 172, 185, 187
Grant, Susannah 124
Gray, Brad 55
Grazer, Ben 18, 24, 86, 92, 98, 64, 101, 103, 104, 113, 115, 122, 124, 131, 140, 148, 159, 161, 164, 167, 173, 179
Grazer, Brian 183, 184
Grean, Wendy 16
Green, Diana 34
Green, Robin 57
Greene, Jonathan 195
Greer, Judy 40
Greif, Leslie 134
Grey, Brad 49, 78
Griffin, Kathy 41
Gruber, Frank 60
Guerra, Jackie 141
Gurney, Robert 33
Gwartz, Jennifer 85, 94, 95, 99, 119, 136. 151, 153, 161, 184, 186, 193
Hacker, Peter 11
Hall, Jon 65
Halmi, Sr., Robert 144
Halpern, Justin 130
Halpern, Noreen 133
Hamburg, John 132
Hamilburg, Mitch 81
Hampton, Orville 3
Handelman, Max 29, 69, 135, 168
Handler, Chelsea 13, 20, 38, 52, 61, 77, 138, 150
Handley, Alan 38

Hanks, Tom 79, 88
Hannah, Liz 155
Hargitay, Mariska 88
Harmon, John 161, 186
Harmon, Mark 167
Harris, Amy 135
Harris, Mel 97
Hart, Kevin 1
Hart, Melissa Joan 14
Hart, Paula 14
Hawke, Ethan 9
Hawn, Goldie 149
Hayden, Russell 187
Hayek, Salma 94, 104, 151, 161, 173
Hayes, Sean 11, 22, 96, 100, 103, 120, 135, 139, 153, 175, 180, 184, 188, 190
Hayward, Chris 67
Heaton, Patricia 45, 146, 196
Heche, Anne 36
Heckerling, Amy 161
Hefner, Hugh 32
Heighl, Katherine 75
Heighl, Nancy 75
Helms, Ed 8, 79
Hertzog, Rupert 75
Heslov, Grant 115, 121
Hetzer, Jim 78
Hewitt, Jennifer Love 25, 38, 52, 90, 93, 111
Hicks, Regina 97
Hiken, Nat 57
Hines, Gregory 30
Hinkle, Thom 167
Hirsh, Caroline 102
Hoberman, David 98, 100, 103, 106. 112, 116, 118, 119, 121, 126, 131, 135, 140, 146, 154, 164, 169, 170, 171, 184, 193, 195
Hoberman, Todd 150
Hoblit, Gregory 110
Hodes, Jeff 41
Holdeman, Bill 128
Holland, Todd 61, 89, 90, 114, 117, 121, 126, 130, 135, 142, 156, 163, 169, 174, 175, 183, 185
Holloway, Matt 186

Holmes, Jill 105
Holmes, Katie 41
Honor, Dana 37, 93, 96, 105, 119, 121, 123, 129, 130, 135, 136, 142, 146, 150, 151, 153, 159, 160, 164, 166, 168, 176, 185, 190, 194, 197
Howard, Ron 64, 98, 101, 104, 107, 124, 164, 183
Hubbard, David 179
Hudgins, David 93
Huffman, Felicity 24, 34
Hughes, Finola 108
Hughley, D.L. 69
Humphrey, Ted 45
Hunt, David 146, 196
Hurd, Gale Anne 16, 54
Hurwitz, Page 193
Ice Cube 120, 139
Idelson, Bill 91
Ingold, Jeff 141
Irving, Charles S. 15, 31
Irwin, Carol 32
Isaac, Sandy 114
Jackman, Hugh 193
Jackson, Samuel L. 132, 169, 174
Jackson, Sarah 36
Jacobs, Katie 3
Jacobs, Michael 117
Jaffe, Henry 21
Jagger, Mick 133
Jalil, Tariq 81, 123
James, Chris 92
James, Ed 54
James, Kevin 127
James, LeBron 79, 100, 135, 148
Jamieson, J.J. 93, 94, 99, 126, 131
Jankowski, Peter 167
Janollari, David 131
Jessel, George 28, 33
Jewison, Norman 81
Joel, Billy 96
John, Elton 171
Johnson, Brad 41
Johnson, Don 20
Johnson, Dwayne 99

Johnson, Jennifer 164
Johnson, Kenneth 172
Johnson, Peter 189, 198
Johnson, Peter 88, 130, 137, 140, 154, 171
Jolie, Angelina 89
Jones, Rashida 30, 63, 69, 128, 182
Jordan, Becky 6
Judge, Alexa 92
Judge, Mike 168
Juvonen, Nancy 137
Kane, Henry 60
Kaplan Aaron 23, 34, 37, 41, 42, 43, 49, 59, 63, 70, 73, 85, 87, 91, 93, 96, 99, 105, 106, 109, 111, 112, 119, 121, 122, 123, 125, 129, 130, 131, 132, 135, 136, 139, 143, 144, 146, 150, 151, 152, 153, 154, 157, 160, 164, 166, 168, 176, 177, 178, 180, 181, 182, 186, 190, 193, 194, 197
Kaplan, Deborah 40, 134
Kaplan, Rachel 95, 152, 192
Karlin, Ben 81
Karlson, Phil 188
Katsky, Tracy 91
Katz, Alan 4
Katz, Arthur S. 33
Katz, Barry 176
Katz, Evan 140
Katz, Gail 139
Katzman, Sam 60, 69
Kaufman, Marta 97, 117, 128, 182
Keaton, Diane 113
Keaton, Michael 177
Kellard, Rick 146
Keller, Mary Page 115
Kelley, David E. 11, 123, 191, 194
Kellner, Melissa 164
Kelly, Tatiana 158
Kennedy, Kathleen 194
Kennedy, Jamie 141
Kern, James V. 58
Keys, Alicia 86
Kim, Albert 147
Kim, Daniel Dae 120

Kimbrough, Emily 37
King, Alan 7, 75
King, Graham 143
King, Jamie 110, 133
King, Kevin 120
King, Marcus 37, 96, 156
King, Marlene 116
King, Michelle 174
King, Stephen 177, 190
Kirshner, Don 66
Kissinger, David 89, 98, 108, 122, 145
Kleeman, Jeff 40, 136, 188, 191
Klein, Howard 19, 86, 96, 161, 182
Klein, Jennifer 86, 92, 100, 114, 116, 122, 129, 137, 161, 171, 173, 176, 177, 189, 190, 192
Klein, Joanna 91
Kramer, Jeffrey 33, 133, 182
Krantz, Tony 64, 115, 118, 139
Krasnow, Stuart 41
Kreamer, Scott 144
Kring, Tim 99
Krinsky Dave 137
Kudrow, Lisa 2, 45, 46, 47, 61, 114, 170
Kulchak, Kelly 138, 155
Kunis, Mila 9, 33, 34, 65, 103, 152, 155, 188
Kushner, Donald 58
Kutcher, Ashton 12, 91, 104, 111, 112, 115, 125, 126, 129, 160, 176, 186, 187
La Salle, Eriq 126, 139
Ladd, Alan 186
Lampanelli, Lisa 46
Landau, Jon 189
Landers, Judy 72
Landers, Lew 76
Lang, Jennings 3
LaPaglia, Anthony 94, 111
Larson, Brie 10
Lassallly, Tom 90, 115, 127, 137, 140, 148
Lassister, James 125, 191, 196
Latifah, Queen 22, 167, 175, 195, 196
Lawrence, Bill 141
Lawrence, Martin 153
Layton, Jerry 76

Lazar, Andrew 88
Leander, Jason 149
Lear, Norman 6, 32, 119
Leary, Dennis 90, 96, 102, 109, 112, 120, 126, 156, 165, 170, 174, 177, 180, 189
LeBlanc, Matt 19
Lederman, Nina 152
Lee, Spike 87
Lee, Stan 32, 133
Leeds, Andrew Harrison 96
Legend, John 115, 148, 174
Leguizamo, John 40
Leifer, Carol 51, 56, 78, 82
Lemons, Jayme 74
Leonard, Art 71
Leonard, Burt 77
Leonard. Herbert B. 113
Leonardi, Tom 80, 139
Lerner, Avi 120
Lesher, John 78
Lesser, Sol 145
Letterman, David 18
Levin, Jennifer 5, 116
Levin, Marc 156
Levine, Dan 87
Levinson, Barry 80, 99, 103, 128, 129, 132, 144, 146, 148, 158, 193, 194
Levinson, Stephen 35, 152, 179
Levison, Susan 119
Levy, Bob 165
Levy, Shawn 50, 87, 135, 152, 187
Levy, Stephen 51
Lewis, Al 24
Lewis, Richard 36, 68, 81
Lewis, Warren 45, 50, 73
Lieberman, Josh 145, 168
Lieberman, Robert 48
Lieberman, Todd 98, 103, 106, 112, 116, 120, 121, 126, 131, 135, 140, 146, 150, 154, 164, 170, 171, 184, 193, 195
Lieberman, Tony 118
Liebling, Debbie 15, 95, 147, 162
Liebman, Jon 61

Lin, Dan 136
Lindsay, Howard 78
Lippert, Robert L. 86, 145, 167
Litinsky, Andy 145
Litman, Jonathan 5, 7, 56, 76, 85, 82, 91, 93, 94, 97, 98, 101, 103, 106, 108, 118, 121, 126, 127, 130, 132, 135, 136, 139, 150, 151, 163, 181, 184, 191, 198
Lizer, Kari 43, 80, 145
LL Cool J 100
Lloyd, Jeremy 91
Lloyd, Ted 1, 13
Locke, Peter 58
Loeb, Jeph 48, 105, 111, 156
Logue, Donal 22
Lohan, Lindsay 45
Longoria, Eva 7, 17, 23, 56, 62, 67, 68, 71, 73, 77, 81, 88, 94, 96, 98, 99, 102, 118, 152, 154, 161, 165, 179, 189, 198
Lonow, Claudia 8, 72, 163
Lopez, George 78, 180
Lopez, Jennifer 38, 47, 64, 92, 100, 101, 109, 116, 116, 142, 152, 160, 180, 185
Lord, Phil 3
Lorre, Chuck 6, 76
Loveton, John W. 15, 66
Lowe, Rob 172
Lubaroff, Terri 139
Luber, Bernard 1
Lumet, Sidney 154
Lundgren, Dolph 37
Lupino, Ida 30
Lynch, Tommy 65
Lyonne, Natasha 53, 83
Mac, Bernie 7
MacDonald, Laurie 77
MacFarlane, Seth 124
MacFarlane, Todd 183
Maddalena, Marianne 145
Madonna 3
Maguire, Toby 160
Malins, Greg 150
Mancuso, Gail 169

Mandabach, Caryn 102, 114, 156, 166
Mandel, Howie 146
Mandelberg, Artie 140
Mandell, Mo 50
Mankiewica, John 156
Manulis, Martin 30
Marcus, Larry 36
Margolin, Arnold 50
Marks, Miek 146
Marshall, Frank 194
Marshall, Garry 91, 129, 169
Marshall, Penny 163
Marshall, Scott 129
Marshall, Tony 91
Martin, Bill 2
Martin, Peter 77
Martin, Quinn 54, 57
Martin, Steve 102, 156
Marx, Arthur 18
Mason, James 59
Mason, Pamela 59
Mathis, Judge Greg 117
Matlin, Marlee 45
Matthews, Gina 105, 112, 118, 123, 126, 137, 178, 181, 193
May, Christopher 114
Mazer, Adam 96
McAteer, Molly 45, 158
McCarthy, Melissa 149, 154, 155, 193
McCormack, Eric 98, 119, 157
McCormack, Will 63, 69, 128, 182, 194, 196
McCormick, Blake 143
McCrea, Joel 27, 31, 44, 43
McG 88, 92, 105, 107, 109, 110, 129, 125, 130, 137, 138, 140, 154, 171, 173, 177, 189, 190, 198
McGraw, Jay 154, 178
McGraw, Phil 154, 178
McKay, Adam 63, 104, 185, 190, 196
McKay, Will 137
McMartin, Susan 114
McMeel, Bridget 144

McPherson, Steve 179
Meadow, Herb 17, 47, 61
Medina, Benny 64, 101, 109, 142, 152, 180
Meehan, Shana-Goldberg 39
Meisinger, Robyn 91
Mendelsohn, Brad 111
Menselsohn, Carol 86, 102, 131, 133, 134, 158, 169, 172, 190, 191, 192, 196
Meron, Neil 10, 56, 101, 143, 184, 195
Messing, Debra 19
Meyers, Seth 24, 158
Michaels, Lorne 163, 164
Milano, Alyssa 3, 13
Milchan, Alexandra 130
Millar, Simon 164
Miller, Chris 3, 21, 105
Miller, Nancy 36
Miller, Paul 61, 86
Milliner, Todd 11, 22, 96, 100, 103, 119, 135, 139, 153, 180, 184, 188, 190
Mills, David 14
Minear, Tina 156
Miner, David 47
Miner, Steve 25
Miner, Worthington 10
Mirish, Walter 25, 27, 31, 44
Mohr, Gerald 33
Monash, Paul 57
Montague, Edward 22
Montoya, Scott 33
Moore, Mandy 50
Moranis, Rick 4
Morgan, Chris 155
Morgan, Peter 80
Morgan, Piers 124
Morganstein, Leslie 100, 107, 140, 148, 155, 186
Morheim, Lou 10, 58
Morisette, Alania 79
Moritz, Neal H. 92, 101, 114, 125, 134, 143, 149, 152, 169, 178, 180, 186, 187, 195
Morris, Howard J. 75
Morris, Kathryn 67
Morris, Michael 138
Morrow, Rob 54
Moses, Kim 114
Mottola, Tommy 131
Mowry, Tia 73
Mullally, Megan 76
Murphy, Maggie 166
Murray, Tracey 166
Nabatoff, Diane 172
Nader, Michelle 148
Nelson, Ralph 50
Neufeld, Mace 143
Neustadter, Lauren 146
Nevins, David 24, 100, 103, 107, 122, 161, 167, 183
Newhart, Bob 9
Newton, Becki 27
Nicoll, Don 68
Nijimy, Kathy 131
Norton, Charles 81
Noxon, Marti 104, 117, 137
O'Brien, Conan 89, 98, 108, 122, 145, 190
O'Malley, Mike 104
O'Neill, Evelyn 120
Obama, Barack 98
Olin, Ken 116, 120
Olmstead, Dan 175
Olmstead, Dawn 134
Oppenheimer, Deborah 19, 48
Orr, William T. 127
Ortega, Kenny 116, 144
Oswalt, Patton 36, 68, 82
Ozols, Amy 122
Paget, Louise 25
Paisley, Brad 25
Palladino, Daniel 103, 124, 162
Palmer, Maria 36
Paltrow, Gwyneth 28
Pamlero, John 193
Parent, Gail 73
Parker, James 50
Parker, Sarah Jessica 141, 174
Parouse, Dawn 113
Parriott, James D. 85, 126

Parsons, Jim 12, 98, 121, 140, 142, 148, 185
Parsons, Lindsay 11
Pascal, Amy 155
Pasetta, Marty 82
Patterson, James 27, 110, 155, 169, 197
Paulson, Tiffany 38
Pearl, Steven 36
Pearman, Victoria 133
Penette, Maria 58
Pepper, Nick 124, 169, 168
Perrone, Sean 139, 181
Petersen, William 137
Petrie, Jr., Daniel 10, 48
Peyron, Brad 123
Phillips, Byron 196
Phillips, John 181
Pitt, Brad 89, 164, 194
Piven, Jeremy 37
Platt, Marc E. 85
Poehler, Amy 4, 6, 22, 71, 83, 89, 100, 122, 167
Polin, Bart 5
Pollack, Sydney 61
Polone, Gavin 41, 48, 57, 71, 75, 137, 197
Pompeo, Ellen 178
Pope, Katherine 91, 101, 107, 121, 129, 130, 138, 141, 145, 146, 152, 158, 162, 163, 168, 170, 172, 174, 175, 185, 192, 196, 197
Port, Moses 130
Posch, Brooke 6, 122
Poster, Meryl 137
Pratt, Deborah 73
Price, Frank 80
Prince, Jonathan 6
Prinze, Jr., Freddie 97
Pyne, Daniel 156
Raimi, Sam 49, 148, 192, 198
Rake, Jeff 146
Rapf, Matthew 36
Rapf, Walter 78
Rapke, Jack 142
Rapp, Philip 19
Rappaport, Daniel 142
Ratner, Brett 153

Rauch, Michael 170
Reardon, Danielle 120
Redford, Robert 128, 165, 191
Reed, Kristie Anne 88, 103, 130, 132, 135, 139, 151, 163
Reed, Roland 26, 49, 72
Reeves, Keanu 107
Register, Sam 150
Reo, Don 9, 17, 18, 34, 44, 45
Reynolds, Gene 53
Reynolds, Stuart 183
Rhimes, Shonda 104, 138, 151, 156, 171, 179, 183, 196
Rhoades, Jessica 41, 76
Rich, John 8, 70
Rich, Ken 79
Richie, Ross 131
Rickabaugh, Kimber 86
Ringwald, Molly 50
Rinna, Lisa 138
Ripa, Kelly 41, 59, 61, 65, 81, 82, 136, 146, 191
Ritter, Krysten 6, 12, 42, 177
Rivers, Joan 67
Roach, Jr. Hal 12, 28, 39, 53, 70, 167
Robbins, Brian 104
Roberts, Emma 7
Roberts, Julia 13, 71, 74, 164
Roberts, Stanley 15, 50
Robertson, Tracey 181
Robinson, Bill 169, 197
Robinson, Doug 90, 185
Robinson, Hubbell 46, 79
Robinson, Julie Anne 162
Rogers, Al 54
Rogers, Mimi 197
Roker, Al 125
Romano, Ray 62
Romero, Ed 15
Rooney, Mickey 47
Rosenberg, Daniel 124
Rosenberg, Melissa 3, 86
Rosenthal, Everett 36
Rosenthal, Gay 38, 149

Rosenthal, Jane 189
Rosenthal, Jeff 79, 87, 122, 129, 172, 175
Ross, Jeff 98, 190
Ross, Michael 68
Rossi, Sophia 158
Ross-Leming, Eugenie 55
Roth, J.D. 128
Rothan, Bernard 25
Rothenberg, Michael 20, 38, 61, 68
Rouse, Russell 75
Rousey, Ronda 182
Roush, Leslie 31
Rudley, Herbert 63
Rue, Sara 59
Ruffalo, Mark 5
Russo, Anthony 90, 106, 117, 130, 132, 150, 168, 194
Russo, Joe 117, 130, 132, 150, 168, 194
Russo, Tom 146
Ryan, Meg 49, 163, 166
Sacks, David 7
Saget, Bob 9
Salinas, George 144
Salt, Jennifer 142
Saltzman, Harry 128
Sandler, Adam 11, 44, 90, 101, 185
Santora, Nick 127
Sarandon, Susan 30
Savage, Dave 63
Savage, Fred 154, 162, 168
Savage, Stephanie 27, 49, 92, 123, 135, 142, 148, 151, 152, 159, 165, 167, 170, 177, 178, 188, 192, 197
Savel, Dava 101
Sawyer, Alan 71
Say, Andrea 136
Schaal, Kristen 42
Schachter, Ted 83
Schaefer, Kari 194
Schafer, Jerry 44
Schaffner, Franklin 132
Scharbo, Grant 105, 112, 118, 123, 137, 181
Schechter, Sara 10, 43, 100, 109, 126, 128, 134, 147, 153, 164, 168, 179, 171, 185, 184, 187, 189
Schneider, John 16
Schubert, Bernard L. 15, 66
Schwab, Ben 7
Schwartz, Josh 49, 123, 142, 148, 151, 159, 165, 167, 170, 177, 178, 192, 197
Schwarzenegger, Arnold 56, 168
Schwimmer, David 3, 87, 136
Scorsese, Martin 15, 19, 133
Scott, Ridley 10, 91, 102, 109, 110, 113, 125, 128, 130, 158, 165, 172, 175, 187, 192
Scott, Tony 91, 109, 125, 130, 187
Seacrest, Ryan 46, 71, 81, 82, 115, 154, 173, 180
Sedgwick, Kyra 52, 83
Seegar, Hal 125
Serpico, Jim 64, 90, 96, 102, 112, 120, 126, 156, 165, 170, 174, 177, 180, 189
Serrano, Ana 78
Shamberg, Michael 170
Shannon, Molly 51
Sharpe, Don 35, 36, 39, 45, 73
Shawkat, Alia 70
Shay, Andrea 13, 14, 123, 179, 182, 193
Sheen, Charlie 13
Sheindlin, Judge Judith 133
Sher, Brian 97, 113
Sher, Stacey 170
Sherman-Palladino, Amy 16, 162
Shoemaker, Mike 158
Silver, Joel 57, 168
Silverman, Ben 38, 54, 62, 92, 96, 100, 124, 139, 144, 150, 165, 166, 169, 175, 176, 178, 182, 186
Silverman, Sarah 4, 60
Silvers, Phil 55
Silverstein, Matt 163
Silvestri, Marc 63
Simmons, Gene 103, 134
Simmons, Richard Alan 29
Simon, Al 40
Singer, Ray 15
Siodmak, Curt 1

Sisk, Robert 37
Siskel, Charles 141
Smith, Ben 193
Smith, Jada Pinkett 52, 87, 104, 131, 155, 170, 196
Smith, Judy 86
Smith, Will 87, 104, 125, 131, 134, 155, 170, 191, 196
Smits, Jimmy 140
Snoop Dogg 69
Soloway, Jill 36
Solt, Andrew 27
Sonnefeld, Barry 191
Sorbo, Kevin 49
Sorkin, Arleen 102
Spacey, Kevin 17, 67, 183
Spade, David 18
Spector, Ben 23, 62, 68, 77, 88, 97, 98, 99, 102, 118, 152, 154, 161, 179, 189, 198
Speiwak, Todd 185
Spelling, Aaron 24, 26, 66, 74, 88, 124, 141, 158, 175, 182, 186
Spelling, Tori 75
Spera, Deborah 77, 88, 112, 148
Spielberg, Steven 144, 161, 166, 181
Spier, William 15, 19
Spicwak, Todd 98, 121, 140, 148
Spotnitz, Frank 137
Stack, Timothy 16
Stagg, Jerry 27, 56
Stallone, Sylvester 37, 120
Stamos, John 143
Star, Darren 94, 113, 138, 157, 161
Stark, Steve 119, 159, 172, 187
Stearn, Andrew 77
Stefano, Joseph 31
Stein, Gene 33, 34, 80, 90, 136, 147, 170
Stein, Jennifer 87
Stephenson, Ben 129, 168
Stern, Gardner 165
Stern, George 67
Stern, Howard 21, 145
Stern, Johanna 79
Stern, Jonathan 102

Stevens, Leslie 26
Stevens, Mark 45, 52, 60
Stewart, Jon 70
Stickney, Dorothy 78
Stiller, Ben 15, 83, 95, 97, 147, 148, 162, 170, 183
Stolper, Stella 165
Stone, Oliver 163
Suarez, Flody 126
Sugar, Michael 177
Sugarman, Burt 38
Sullivan, Tom 185
Summers, Mandy 162
Surnow, Joel 62
Sussman, Jeff 127
Sutherland, Kiefer 166
Sweeney, Bob 70
Sykes, Wanda 193
Taffner, Don 134
Tamblyn, Amber 3
Tamez, Jose 173
Tannenbaum, Eric 13, 18, 19, 21, 34, 35, 46, 54, 74, 85, 101, 106, 117, 121, 125, 132, 134, 135, 141, 144, 151, 153, 155, 156, 159, 162, 167, 168, 171, 176, 178 , 183, 195
Tannenbaum, Kim 13, 18, 19, 21, 34, 35, 46, 54, 74, 85, 101, 106, 117, 121, 125, 132, 134, 135, 141, 144, 151, 153, 155, 156, 159, 162, 167, 168, 171, 176, 178, 183 195
Tapert, Robert 162, 198
Tapping, Amanda 67
Tarses, Jamie 3, 25, 53, 88, 95, 101, 119, 122, 126, 128, 130, 138, 144, 157, 159, 166, 173, 176, 197
Tate, Dedra 196
Tatum, Channing 28, 53
Tatum, Chuck 104
Taub, Stacy 23
Taupin, Bernie 171
Teefey, Mandy 67
Telford, Frank 15
Tewksbury, Peter 76
Theron, Charlize 57, 105159, 163
Thomas, Betty 138, 185

Thomas, Danielle 93
Thomas, Dave 4
Thomas, Rob 94, 109, 184, 193
Thomason, Harry 21, 113
Thomason, Linda Bloodworth 113
Thompson, Chris 59
Thor, Larry 53
Timberlake, Justin 159
Timberman, Sarah 21, 41, 78, 89, 95, 96, 102, 106, 113, 115, 120, 122, 124, 125, 134, 147, 149, 150, 154, 160, 161, 170, 176, 178, 179, 181, 191
Tinker, John 8, 186
Tisch, Steve 13
Tisdale, Ashley 41, 76
Titus, Christopher 14
Todd, Jennifer 95
Todd, Norman 188
Todman, Bill 10, 30, 43
Tolan, Peter 19
Tors, Ivan 1
Towers, Alan 184
Towers, Harry Alan 16, 54
Townsend, Robert 172
Tracey, Amanda 132, 169, 174
Traub, Stacy 42, 78, 162
Traugott, Peter 78
Trendle, George W. 30
Trilling, Wendi 85
Trudeau, Garry 146
Truhett, Melanie 171
Trump, Donald 145, 188
Tucci, Stanley 70
Tucker, Rebecca 109
Tupper, James 36
Turner, Richard Allen 24
Turner, Sheldon 17, 28, 86, 92, 100, 114, 116, 137, 171, 173, 176, 189, 190, 192
Underwood, Carrie 76
Union, Gabrielle 79, 97, 187
Vadnay, Lasslo 58
Valentine, Steve 89, 129
Vaughn, Victoria 90

Vaughn, Vince 90
Veasey, Pam 138
Ventimglia, Milo 117
Ventura, Ray 57
Vergara, Sofia 178
Victor, David 7, 20
Vidal, Gore 154
Vila, Scott 61
Vincent, E. Duke 24, 88, 124, 141, 159, 175
Vincent, Samantha 123, 131
Viola, Mary 110, 125, 129, 173, 177, 190
Volk-Weiss, Brian 89, 101, 104
Wade, Warren 77
Wahlberg, Donnie 14, 117
Wahlberg, Mark 35, 133, 152
Walker, Bill 74
Ward, Barney 14
Ward, Sela 66
Washington, Denzel 97
Washington, Kerry 55
Wass, Gene 80
Wass, Nina 33, 34, 46, 67, 81, 115, 173, 180
Waterman, Shana 155
Waters, Mark 154
Wayans, Damon 9, 17, 18, 45, 78
Wayans, Jr., Damon 32, 47
Wayne, John 80
Webb, Jack 25, 187
Webb, Marc 62
Weber, Steven 74
Weil, Andy 136
Weinberg, Jason 20, 26
Weinberg, Matthew 113
Weinberg, Terri 69, 88, 124, 153
Weinberger, Ed 143
Weinstein, Harvey 130
Weintraub, Charles 71
Weitz, Carol 158
Weitz, Julie 24, 46, 86, 106, 131, 133, 134, 139, 169, 172, 191, 192, 196
Welch, Jack 79
Welch, Robert 50
Welling, Tom 66

Wells, John 90, 100, 124
Werner, Tom 52, 102, 156, 158, 166
West, Bernie 68
West, Ron 92
Weyman, Andrew D. 75
Whitaker, Forest 133, 156
White, Andrew 79
Whitford, Bradley 155
Wilcox, Herbert 4
Williams, Caroline 128
Williams, Vanessa L. 77
Wilmore, Larry 12, 97
Windust, Bretagne 188
Winfrey, Oprah 42, 157, 164, 185
Winsberg, Austin 132
Winslow, Don 102
Winter, Eric 198
Wisbar, Frank 82
Witherspoon, Reese 62, 74, 89, 111, 112, 120, 146, 194
Wohl, Jack 25
Wolf, Dick 29, 104, 143, 170, 167, 195
Wolf, Fred 39
    Wollack, Brad 20, 38, 61
Wolper, David L. 54, 134
Wong, James 134
Woodrow, Danielle 119
Wrather, Jack 27
Yen, Julie 39
Young, Jim 158
Young, Paul 40
Young, Robert 5
Yuspa, Cathy 62
Zadan, Craig 10, 62, 63, 101, 140, 184
Zadan, Neil 195
Zaks, Laurie 100, 112, 129, 135, 140, 158, 170, 171
Zalta, Ashley 177
Zemeckis, Robert 91, 106, 108, 112, 142
Zimmerman, Ron 145
Zimmerman, Shelley 104
Zimmerman, Stan 156
Zisk, Randy 129

Zombie, Rob 188
Zuiker, Anthony 99, 103, 110, 113, 118, 141, 179, 197
Zuiker, David W. 109, 110, 113, 128, 158, 160, 165, 172, 175, 192
Zwerling, Lisa 152